Ukraine and Russia

D'Anieri explores the dynamics within Ukraine, between Ukraine and Russia, and between Russia and the West, that emerged with the collapse of the Soviet Union and eventually led to war in 2014. Proceeding chronologically, this book shows how Ukraine's separation from Russia in 1991, at the time called a "civilized divorce," led to what many are now calling "a new Cold War." He argues the conflict has worsened because of three underlying factors – the security dilemma, the impact of democratization on geopolitics, and the incompatible goals of a post-Cold War Europe. Rather than a peaceful situation that was squandered, D'Anieri argues that these were deep-seated pre-existing disagreements that could not be bridged, with concerning implications for the resolution of the Ukraine conflict. The book also shows how this war fits into broader patterns of contemporary international conflict and should therefore appeal to researchers working on the Russia-Ukraine conflict, Russia's relations with the West, and conflict and geopolitics more generally.

PAUL D´ANIERI is a professor of political science and public policy at the University of California, Riverside. He is author of *Understanding Ukrainian Politics* (2007) and *Economic Interdependence in Ukrainian-Russian Relations* (1999), as well as a widely-used textbook on international politics. D'Anieri is Vice President of the American Association of Ukrainian Studies.

Ukraine and Russia

From Civilized Divorce to Uncivil War

Paul D'Anieri

University of California, Riverside

CAMBRIDGE
UNIVERSITY PRESS

CAMBRIDGE
UNIVERSITY PRESS

University Printing House, Cambridge CB2 8BS, United Kingdom

One Liberty Plaza, 20th Floor, New York, NY 10006, USA

477 Williamstown Road, Port Melbourne, VIC 3207, Australia

314–321, 3rd Floor, Plot 3, Splendor Forum, Jasola District Centre,
New Delhi – 110025, India

79 Anson Road, #06–04/06, Singapore 079906

Cambridge University Press is part of the University of Cambridge.

It furthers the University's mission by disseminating knowledge in the pursuit of
education, learning, and research at the highest international levels of excellence.

www.cambridge.org
Information on this title: www.cambridge.org/9781108486095
DOI: 10.1017/9781108657044

First published 2019

A catalogue record for this publication is available from the British Library.

ISBN 978-1-108-48609-5 Hardback
ISBN 978-1-108-71395-5 Paperback

To
Sharon and Derick Hebert
Shelley and Dave Mellentine
Lori and Tom Raffy

Contents

Maps

Tables

Acknowledgments

I could not have written this book without the support of generous institutions, colleagues, and friends.

In the fall of 2017, I was fortunate to hold the Eugene and Daymel Shklar Research Fellowship in Ukrainian Studies at Harvard University. I am grateful to the Harvard Ukrainian Research Institute and its director, Serhii Plokhy, for providing an ideal environment in which to develop the project. Oleh Kotsyuba and George Grabowicz encouraged me to concentrate my thoughts in an article for *Krytyka*.

Early versions of the overall argument were presented at seminars at Harvard University, Syracuse University, Kyiv Polytechnic Institute, George Washington University, and at the Forsvarets Forskningsinstitutt, Oslo. The discussions in these meetings were valuable as I refined my analysis. I thank Kristina Conroy, Audie Klotz, Pavlo Kutuev and Volodymyr Ishchenko, Peter Rollberg and Henry Hale, and Tor Bukkvoll for arranging these visits.

For many years, Taras Kuzio has been generous in sharing his views and helping me make contacts in Kyiv. Eugene Fishel, Serhiy Kudelia, Henry Hale, and Volodymyr Ischenko, as well as two anonymous reviewers, read drafts of the manuscript and provided insightful comments. Their detailed suggestions have helped me sharpen the argument in some places, to add nuance in others and to avoid some factual errors. Perhaps unwisely, I have not taken all of their advice, and I am solely to blame for the shortcomings that remain.

The University of California, Riverside, provided research funding as well as a release from administrative and teaching duties.

I am especially grateful to a great group of friends who supported me through a difficult time. Over many sets of tennis, countless meals, and adventures in Europe, they have brought me immeasurable joy and wisdom, and I dedicate this book to them. Grateful Eight, this is for you!

Above all, I have to recognize the inspiration I receive from my wife, Laura. She cannot have imagined when we met that twenty-five years later I would still be writing and talking about Ukraine and Russia. If she is tired of it, she hides it well. Her encouragement has sustained me at every stage of this project.

Map 0.1 Ukraine, showing areas occupied by Russia as of 2019

1   The Sources of Conflict over Ukraine

> But our idea is that the wolves should be fed and the sheep kept safe.
>
> Leo Tolstoy, *War and Peace*

On the night of February 27, 2014, armed men took control of the Parliament and Cabinet of Ministers buildings in Crimea and raised Russian flags. Early the next morning, more men in unmarked uniforms seized the airports in Sevastopol and Simferopol. A Russian naval vessel blockaded the harbor at Balaklava, near Sevastopol, where Ukrainian sea guard troops were stationed, and Russian helicopters moved from Russia to Crimea. Eighteen days later, after a hastily arranged plebiscite, Vladimir Putin signed the documents formally annexing Crimea to the Russian Federation.

Then, on April 7, pro-Russian forces seized government buildings in Donetsk, Kharkiv, and Luhansk in eastern Ukraine and called for referendums on the regions' independence. Ukrainian forces regained control of Kharkiv the next day, but efforts to retake the other two regions led to a war between Ukraine and Russia that raged until February 2015, and only partly subsided thereafter. By 2019, over ten thousand people had been killed.

What started as a "civilized divorce" in 1991 became one of the most dangerous crises in post-Cold War Europe, and the crisis then became chronic. Ukraine and Russia have a great deal of shared history, and Ukraine's independence in 1991 took place without bloodshed. Moreover, the East-West tensions that defined the Cold War had fallen away. Yet by early 2014, disagreement over Ukraine not only led to armed conflict between Russia and Ukraine, but brought Russia and the West to what many saw as a new Cold War.

How did this happen, and why? How did the deeply connected Ukraine and Russia come to war? And how did their relationship come to shape the West's conflict with Russia? How we answer these questions will determine in large part how actors on all sides approach the choices yet to come, including how to find peace in Ukraine, how to increase security in Europe, and how to rebuild relations between Russia, its neighbors, and the West. There is a great deal at stake in how we understand this conflict, but prevailing understandings are deeply at odds with one another: one school sees the conflict as being caused by Russian revanchism; another attributes it to Putin's need to bolster his autocratic rule; and another blames western expansionism and Ukrainian nationalism. The first two views point to a western strategy of confronting, or at least containing, Putin's Russia. The third points to accommodating Russia's security needs by acquiescing to its desire to control Ukraine.

This book will argue that neither of those strategies is likely to work, because the roots of the conflict are deeper than is commonly understood and therefore will resist a simple change in policy. The violent earthquake that took place in 2014 was the result of deep "tectonic" forces as well as short-term triggers. Conflict between Ukraine and Russia is based on profound normative disagreements and conflicts of interest, and therefore does not depend on mistakes by leaders on whom we can easily pin blame. These disagreements undermined relations even in the 1990s, when post-Cold War mutual trust was at its highest.

Therefore, simply waiting for Putin to depart the stage in Russia, or for a more accommodating policy from the European Union or the United States, will not bring reconciliation. A return to peace and security will require agreement on a new architecture for security in Europe. Such an architecture could not be negotiated even when the cold war ended and Russia was democratizing. With an autocratic Russia, deep East-West antagonism, and ongoing conflict in Ukraine, it will be even harder to find.

This book has two connected goals. The first is to explain how and why this conflict came about. The second is to provide an account of the relationship between Ukraine, Russia, Europe, and the United States from the end of the Cold War to the signing of the Minsk-2 agreement in 2015. The chronology is a goal in its own right, for no such overview of Ukraine-Russia relations exists, and it is also essential for understanding the conflict, since one of the primary contentions of this book is that the problems that exploded in 2014 emerged at the beginning of the post-Cold War period and became increasingly salient over time.

Competing Visions and Interests after the Cold War

To boil down the argument to its simplest version: The end of the Cold War set in motion two forces that were necessarily in tension: democratization in eastern Europe and Russia's insistence that it retain its "great power" status and its domination over its immediate neighborhood. Ukraine was the place where democracy and independence most challenged Russia's conception of its national interests. It was not inevitable that this conflict would lead to violence, but neither was it likely to resolve itself.[1]

While Russia was determined to remain a great power and a regional hegemon, Ukraine – and not just its nationalists – was committed to independence. Even those Ukrainian leaders who pursued close economic ties with Russia staunchly defended Ukraine's sovereignty. As long as Russia's definition of its great power status included controlling Ukraine, Russia's notion of its national security was incompatible with Ukraine's democracy and independence. That was true in 1991 and has not changed fundamentally since.

Two broader dynamics – one a traditional problem in international politics, the other new to the post-Cold War era – connected the Russia-Ukraine conflict to broader European affairs in ways that made both harder to deal with. First, the security dilemma, an enduring problem in international relations, meant that the steps that one side saw as necessary to protect its security were seen as threatening by others and spurred a cycle of action and reaction. Russia's "peacekeeping" in Moldova and Georgia was one example. The enlargement to the east of the North Atlantic Treaty Organization (NATO) was another.

Second, the spread of democracy fed the security dilemma, making states in the West feel more secure but undermining Russia's perceived national interest. Because they believed in the importance of democracy, and because they believed that democracy strengthened security, western leaders promoted the extension of democracy and the institutions that supported it. While Russia did not appear to oppose democracy itself, it felt threatened as new democracies sought to "rejoin" Europe by joining NATO and the European Union. The further this process went, the more resentful Russia became, and Ukraine was more important to Russia's perception of its interests, to its national identity, and to Putin's regime, than any other state. Fyodor Lukyanov wrote that "[I]n their [Russians'] view, Russia's subordinate position is the illegitimate result of a never-ending U.S. campaign to keep Russia down and prevent it from regaining its proper status."[2]

---

[1] On conflicts of interest between Russia and the West, see William C. Wohlforth and Vladislav Zubok, "An Abiding Antagonism: Realism, Idealism, and the Mirage of Western-Russian Partnership after the Cold War," *International Politics* 54, 4 (2017): 405–419.

[2] Fyodor Lukyanov, "Putin's Foreign Policy: The Quest to Restore Russia's Rightful Place," *Foreign Affairs* 95, 3 (May/June 2016): 30–37.

This merger of democracy and geopolitics was new, but it had an effect
that looked familiar. To the extent that Russia turned away from liberal
democracy while Europe embraced it, it was inevitable that there would
be some border between democratic and nondemocratic Europe. Would
it be Russia's border with Ukraine, Ukraine's border with Poland, or
somewhere else? Could a zone of neutrals provide a "buffer" between
Europe's democratic and nondemocratic regions? Perhaps, but no one
wanted to be in that zone, and the idea of it clashed with European
norms. A new division of Europe could be avoided only if Russia consolidated democracy and gave up its great power aspirations. The first of
these failed and the second was rejected. It has been Ukraine's bad luck
to have the conflict played out on its territory, as has so often been the
case throughout history.

Debating the Causes of the War

Since the outbreak of conflict, a great deal of literature has emerged on it,
which has three defining characteristics. First, much of it focuses on
assigning blame. Second, much of it focuses on events beginning in
2013, and examines earlier developments only selectively. Third, it tends
to focus either on the international or domestic sources of behavior,
rather than investigating how they interact.

While much of the work published in the West takes it for granted that
Russia is responsible for the conflict, a strident minority takes a position,
closer to that of the Russian government, that the West and Ukraine
forced Russia into a corner where it had no choice but to act.[3]

---

[3] The tendency to focus on blame is discussed in Paul D'Anieri, "Ukraine, Russia, and the
West: The Battle over Blame," *The Russian Review* 75 (July 2016): 498–503. For other
reviews of the literature, see Peter Rutland, "Geopolitics and the Roots of Putin's Foreign
Policy," *Russian History* 43, 3–4 (2016): 425–436 and Michael E. Aleprete, Jr.,
"Minimizing Loss: Explaining Russian Policy: Choices during the Ukrainian Crisis,"
Soviet and Post-Soviet Review 44 (2017): 53–75. Among those blaming the West and
Ukrainian nationalists are two very prominent scholars of Russian politics, Richard Sakwa
and Stephen Cohen, and two prominent scholars of international security, John
Mearsheimer and Stephen Walt, as well as the scholar of Russian foreign policy Andrei
Tsygankov. See Richard Sakwa, *Frontline Ukraine: Crisis in the Borderlands* (London:
I. B. Tauris, 2016); Katherine K. Vanden Heuvel and Stephen F. Cohen, "Cold War
against Russia – Without Debate," *The Nation*, May 19, 2014; John Mearsheimer, "Why
the Ukraine Crisis Is the West's Fault: The Liberal Delusions That Provoked Putin,"
Foreign Affairs 93, 5 (September/October 2014): 77–89; Stephen M. Walt, "What Would
a Realist World Have Looked Like," *ForeignPolicy.com*, January 8, 2016; and Andrei
Tsygankov, "Vladimir Putin's Last Stand: The Sources of Russia's Ukraine Policy,"
Post-Soviet Affairs 31, 4 (2015): 279–303. For those who put the blame on Russia, see
Andrew Wilson, *Ukraine Crisis: What It Means for the West* (New Haven, CT: Yale
University Press, 2014); Taras Kuzio, *Putin's War against Ukraine: Revolution,
Nationalism, and Crime* (Toronto: Chair of Ukrainian Studies, University of Toronto,

While assigning blame is irresistible, work that focuses on prosecuting one side or another tends to choose facts and assemble them selectively, in ways that are at best one-sided and at worst misleading. Even excellent scholars have resorted to simplistic renderings of blame: John Mearsheimer stated that "the Ukraine Crisis Is the West's Fault," while Andrew Wilson wrote that "the Russians went ape."[4]

Assigning blame leads us to attribute considerable freedom of choice to leaders, minimizing the constraints they faced. Even those works that are more balanced in assigning blame tend to stress the ability of leaders to shape events and to underestimate the international and domestic political constraints on their policy choices. Some authors criticize the West for what it did, others for not doing more,[5] the common assumption being that leaders had a great deal of latitude to choose. Examination of the debates at the time makes clear that leaders frequently did not see the situation that way themselves. Policy makers often feel tightly constrained. The explanation developed here focuses on exploring those constraints, which include the security dilemma, the impact of democratization, and domestic politics.

Second, much of the scholarship on the conflict has been incomplete temporally. Much of it has focused, quite reasonably, on the extraordinary events that transpired in Ukraine from November 2013 through spring 2014. Daniel Treisman zeroes in on Putin's decision to invade Crimea, identifying four schools of thought: "Putin the defender," responding to the potential for Ukraine to join NATO; "Putin the imperialist," seizing Crimea as part of a broader project to recreate the Soviet Union; "Putin the populist," using the annexation of Crimea to build public support in the face of economic decline; and "Putin the improviser," seizing a fantastic opportunity.[6] Exploring that decision is

---

2017); Charles Clover, *Black Wind, White Snow: The Rise of Russia's New Nationalism* (New Haven, CT: Yale University Press, 2016); and Michael McFaul, *From Cold War to Hot Peace: An American Ambassador in Putin's Russia* (New York: Houghton Mifflin Harcourt, 2018), especially chapter 23. For a work that assigns blame more evenly, see Samuel Charap and Timothy Colton, *Everyone Loses: The Ukraine Crisis and the Ruinous Contest for Post-Soviet Eurasia* (London: Routledge, 2017).

[4] Mearsheimer, "Why the Ukraine Crisis Is the West's Fault," 1; Wilson, *Ukraine Crisis*, vii.

[5] See Kathryn Stoner and Michael McFaul, "Who Lost Russia (This Time)? Vladimir Putin," *The Washington Quarterly* 38, 2 (2015): 167–187.

[6] Daniel Treisman, *The New Autocracy: Information, Politics, and Policy in Putin's Russia* (Washington, DC: Brookings Institution, 2018), chapter 11. Treisman finds problems with all four explanations, and ends up arguing that the primary goal was preventing the loss of the naval base at Sevastopol. He points out that while the military part of the operation seemed well-prepared and ran very smoothly, the political arrangements, including who would be in charge in Crimea and whether Crimea would seek autonomy or to join Russia, seemed chaotic and improvised.

crucial, but it does not explain how we got to that point, or why Putin then pursued a wider conflict in eastern Ukraine.

This conflict was not caused simply by the overthrow of the Yanukovych government any more than World War I was caused only by the assassination of Archduke Franz Ferdinand. In both cases, deep mutual fears that the status quo in eastern Europe might change irreversibly prompted leaders to be more risk acceptant than they normally would be (the crucial difference was that in 2014, unlike in 1914, the other European powers did not rush to join the war).

Because the long-term antecedents of the invasion are crucial to our overall understanding of the conflict, this book chronicles the evolution of Ukrainian-Russian relations since 1991, showing that while violence was never inevitable, conflict over Ukraine's status emerged prior to the breakup of the Soviet Union and never receded. Similarly, while the collapse of communism ended the Cold War, it did not create a shared understanding of Russia's role relative to the West in post-Cold War Europe. While it seemed reasonable to believe that these disagreements would be resolved over time, several forces identified in this book made that difficult.

Third, the complexity of the relationships involved has been neglected, because it is difficult to focus at the same time on internal affairs in Ukraine and Russia, on their relationship with each other, and their relationships with the West. However, doing so is essential, because by the time of the Orange Revolution in 2004, Ukraine's domestic battle between pluralism and authoritarianism was tightly connected both to its battle for greater autonomy from Russia and to Russia's burgeoning conflict with the West. This conflict was neither simply a domestic Ukrainian conflict that became internationalized nor a great power conflict fought over Ukraine.

Locating the Sources of International Conflict

Few of the existing works make use of the large literature on international conflict. Using that literature, we can reframe the question in terms of where we look for sources.[7] One set of works locates its explanation inside of the Russian government, in the nature of the Putin regime itself. A common argument is that Putin's need to bolster his autocracy was a

---

[7] This categorization follows loosely that of Gideon Rose, "Neoclassical Realism and Theories of Foreign Policy," *World Politics* 51 (October 1998): 144–172.

driving force in the decision to go to war. In this view, Putin has a great deal of agency.[8]

Two other schools of thought see Russia responding to external rather than internal factors. One of these sees Russia as seeking expansion, but for international rather than domestic reasons. Another sees Russia as reacting against western expansion. While these approaches put the blame on different actors, they both fit into the school known as "defensive realism," which posits that states can usually manage the challenges inherent in the anarchic international system, absent an aggressive "rogue state." The assumption that conflict depends on aggression leads these authors to identify one side or the other as taking actions to undermine the region's security.[9]

The school of "offensive realism" is viewed as more pessimistic, in that it sees the international system as bringing even nonaggressive states into conflict, as states that seek only security unintentionally cause security threats to others. In this view, one does not need to identify an aggressor to explain conflict. This book takes that perspective seriously. While Russia, Ukraine, and the West can all be criticized for the policies they chose, there were, I contend, dynamics in post-Cold War Europe that resisted resolution. Even if one concludes that Russia was at fault for the final decision to go to war, it is important to recognize that it perceived security challenges that caused considerable concern. One does not need to see Russia's desire to control Ukraine as a "legitimate interest," as some authors do, to acknowledge that Russia considered the incorporation of Ukraine into the European Union as a loss. Similarly, even if one considers NATO enlargement to have been a mistake, it was a response to a security problem that did not have another easy solution.

The focus on international and domestic sources need not be mutually exclusive. It seems likely that annexing Crimea advanced both international and domestic goals for Putin, and may have been especially attractive because it did. Therefore, this book seeks to analyze how international and domestic factors interacted. Among the key themes are the way that the state of democracy in Ukraine interacted with its international orientation, and the fact that while the Ukrainian state was always weak, and then nearly collapsed in 2014, the Russian state, after going through a period of dramatic weakness in the 1990s, was gradually

---

[8] Wilson, *Ukraine Crisis*, and Stoner and McFaul, "Who Lost Russia," share this perspective.

[9] Not all the authors who advance these arguments have always been identified with defensive realism. Mearsheimer's extensive scholarship generally falls into the school of "offensive" realism, but his argument that the misguided West provoked the war in Ukraine is consistent with "defensive" realism.

strengthened such that by 2014 it had rebuilt a powerful military and could deploy a highly effective "hybrid" war in Ukraine.

Overall, then, the approach here is consistent with the school of thought known as "neoclassical realism," which finds that the security dilemma conditions international politics, but that internal factors influence how states respond to it. This approach differs from prevailing interpretations by acknowledging that the various leaders saw themselves as being constrained by both international factors and domestic politics, such that they had less freedom of maneuver than many analyses have attributed to them. In other words, we should be more cautious in charging aggression or stupidity. In order to understand these constraints, we need to examine both the security dilemma that existed in Europe after the collapse of the Soviet Union and the domestic politics of the various countries involved, especially Ukraine. In particular, we need to understand the ways in which democratization became merged with geopolitics, repeatedly disrupting the status quo and putting a core value of the West at odds with Russia's sense of its security.

The Approach: Historical and Analytical

This book combines historical and social science approaches. The questions of what happened and why are tightly linked. Therefore, we combine a chronological narrative with a set of social science concepts that help reveal the dynamics and patterns that connect events over twenty-five years. The book is not, strictly speaking, a work of history, as it is not based primarily on archival sources. But considerable attention is given to describing what happened, and to looking at how the actors at the time explained what they were doing. Their views are gleaned from the statements they made at the time, as well as later accounts and interviews conducted in Ukraine.

The narrative account, which traces the gradual evolution of Ukraine-Russia and Russia-West relations since 1989, is structured by a set of analytical themes that identify the underlying dynamics of the conflict, and that show the connections between this case and broader patterns in world politics. This approach requires a theoretical eclecticism that brings multiple theories to bear on the problem rather than insisting on fitting the complexities of the case into a single perspective.[10]

---

[10] Rudra Sil and Peter J. Katzenstein, "Analytic Eclecticism in the Study of World Politics: Reconfiguring Problems and Mechanisms across Research Traditions," *Perspectives on Politics* 8, 2 (2010): 411–431.

Analytical Themes

The conflict that turned violent in 2014 was rooted in deep disagreements about what the post-Cold War world should look like. Those differences emerged with the end of the Cold War and have endured to this day, and constitute each side's perception of what the status quo was or should be. Actors were willing to take heightened risks when it appeared their conception of the status quo was under threat. Three dynamics explain why those conflicts of interest could not be mitigated despite the presumably benign environment after the end of the Cold War. First, the dynamics of the security dilemma, a common phenomenon in international politics, meant that actions that each state took to preserve its security created problems for others, and induced fears about the acting states' intentions. Second, the spread of democracy complicated matters dramatically. Because new democracies sought to join Europe's democratic international institutions, the European Union and NATO, democratization took on geopolitical consequences that the West saw as natural and benevolent and that Russia saw as threatening. With Ukraine's 2004 Orange Revolution the merger of democratization and geopolitics became nearly complete. Moreover, the progress – and the backsliding – of democratization in the region meant that the status quo was repeatedly disrupted, raising new fears and new conflicts. Third, regardless of the level of democracy in the various states, domestic politics again and again undermined cooperation and concessions. In the United States, in Russia, and in Ukraine there was almost always more to lose and less to gain in domestic politics from taking a conciliatory policy than from taking a harder line. Moreover, the fact that Russia rebuilt a strong state after 2000, while Ukraine's remained weak and divided, made it possible for Russia to pull off the operations in Crimea and eastern Ukraine while Ukraine struggled to respond.

In sum, while the end of the Cold War resolved some questions, it created several more, including the status of Russia and Ukraine in relation to each other and to Europe more generally. Traditional security challenges such as the security dilemma remained, and a new one – the merger of democratization with geopolitics – emerged. Oddly, the end of the Cold War did not make conciliatory policies popular with voters or elites in the United States, Ukraine, or Russia. Taken together, the recipe was corrosive: conflicts of interest were reinforced and where strong, skilled leadership might have reduced conflict, leaders repeatedly faced countervailing domestic pressures.

These dynamics have been largely ignored in accounts of relations between Russia and the West and the role of Ukraine, but if we take them seriously, we need to look much less hard for someone to blame for the fact that Russia's goals collided with those of Ukraine and the West. The actors were impelled to step on each other's toes whether they wanted to or not. This did not make war inevitable, but it did guarantee a certain amount of friction, and it meant that unusual leadership would be required to manage the conflicts of interest and hard feelings that resulted.

Competing Goals and Incompatible Perceptions of the Status Quo

As the Cold War ended in 1989–1991, leaders in Russia, Europe, and the United States perceived a dramatic reduction in tension and an increasing harmony of interests and values. But Russia and Ukraine held vastly different expectations about whether their relationship would be based on sovereign equality or on traditional Russian hegemony. Similarly, while the West believed that the end of the Cold War meant that Russia was becoming a "normal" European country, Russia strongly believed that it would retain its traditional role as a great power, with privileges like a sphere of influence and a veto over security arrangements.

The actors had very different understandings of what the status quo was, and therefore which changes were "legitimate" or "illegitimate," which were benign or harmful, and which were signs of bad faith or aggressive intent on the part of others. While most Russians welcomed the end of communism and the end of the Cold War, they did not accept the loss of Ukraine. In the 1990s, even one of the leading liberals in Russia, Boris Nemtsov, advocated regaining Sevastopol by having Russian firms buy assets there: "Historical justice should be restored through capitalist methods."[11] In Nemtsov's view, increasing Russian control of Crimea would be a *restoration*, not a new gain for Russia. In 2014, Alexei Navalny, similarly seen as a leading liberal, said "I don't see any difference at all between Russians and Ukrainians."[12]

Russia's inability to reconcile itself to the loss of Ukraine is unsurprising. To many Russians, Ukraine is part of Russia, without which Russia

---

[11] OMRI Daily Digest Part I, February 19, 1997, as cited in Paul D'Anieri, *Economic Interdependence in Ukrainian-Russian Relations* (Albany: State University of New York Press, 1999), p. 211.

[12] Anna Dolgov, "Navalny Wouldn't Return Crimea, Considers Immigration Bigger Issue than Ukraine," *Moscow Times*, October 16, 2014. See also Marlene Laruelle, "Alexei Navalny and Challenges in Reconciling 'Nationalism' and 'Liberalism'," *Post-Soviet Affairs* 30, 4 (2014): 276–297.

is incomplete. This belief is rooted in the hundreds of years in which much of Ukraine was part of the Russian Empire and Soviet Union, in the Russian foundation myth which sees the origins of today's Russia in medieval Kyiv, and in the important role played by people from Ukraine – Gogol, Trotsky, Bulgakov, and Brezhnev among many others – in Russian/Soviet culture and politics. The sense of something important being lost was profound.[13] Vladimir Putin invoked this history to justify the seizure of Crimea in 2014.[14] The geographer Gerard Toal applies the concept of "thick geopolitics" and Elizabeth Wood refers to "imagined geography" to show how Russia's perception of its geopolitical situation shaped Russian policy in its "near abroad."[15]

"Status quo bias," or "loss aversion," the study of which earned Daniel Kahneman a Nobel Prize, is a phenomenon widely studied in psychology and behavioral economics. As Kahneman and Amos Tversky put it succinctly, "losses loom larger than gains."[16] Actors are willing to take disproportionate risks to avoid a perceived loss. Applied to international relations, states will try very hard to preserve the status quo or to restore it when they perceive it has been disrupted for the worse. Henry Kissinger, relying on history rather than behavioral economics, similarly argued that whether great powers accepted the status quo was crucial to the maintenance of stability.[17] After 1991, Ukraine, Russia, and the West had different understandings of the new status quo. Therefore, each saw itself as defending the status quo, and saw others' efforts to overturn it as signs of malicious intent.

[13] See Peter J. Potichnyj, Marc Raeff, Jaroslaw Pelenski, and Gleb N. Zekulin., eds., *Ukraine and Russia in Their Historical Encounter* (Edmonton: Canadian Institute of Ukrainian Studies, 1982).

[14] Address by President of the Russian Federation, March 18, 2014, Kremlin website, http://en.kremlin.ru/events/president/news/20603

[15] Gerard Toal, *Near Abroad: Putin, the West, and the Contest over Ukraine and the Caucasus* (Oxford: Oxford University Press, 2017). Toal deliberately takes an "empathetic" approach to understanding Russia's perception of its role in the region. Elizabeth A. Wood, "Introduction," in Elizabeth A. Wood, William E. Pomeranz, E. Wayne Merry, and Maxim Trudolyubov, *Roots of Russia's War in Ukraine* (Washington, DC: Woodrow Wilson Center Press, 2016), pp. 3–6.

[16] Daniel S. Kahneman and Amos Tversky, "Prospect Theory: An Analysis of Decision under Risk," *Econometrica* 47, 2 (March 1979): 279. For a general discussion of the application of prospect theory to international politics, see Jack S. Levy, "Prospect Theory and International Relations: Theoretical Approaches and Analytical Problems," *Political Psychology* 13, 2 (1992): 283–310. See also Jonathan Mercer, "Prospect Theory and Political Science," *Annual Review of Political Science* 8 (2005): 1–21.

[17] Kissinger divided great powers into "status quo" powers, which were satisfied with the status quo and defended it, and revolutionary powers, which were dissatisfied with the status quo and sought to overturn it. See Henry A. Kissinger, *A World Restored: Metternich, Castlereagh and the Problems of Peace, 1812–22* (Boston: Houghton Mifflin, 1957).

While Ukraine and the West saw Russia trying to overturn the post-Cold War status quo, Russia saw the West trying to overturn it by expanding NATO eastward and by promoting "colored revolutions" against governments that Russia supported. In 2005, Andrei Zagorsky lamented that "Russia acts as a status quo power that is no longer able to prevent or resist the rise of change."[18] As Kahneman and Tversky stressed, this sense of having lost something is especially dangerous: "[A] person who has not made peace with his losses is likely to accept gambles that would be unacceptable to him otherwise."[19] As Kissinger argued, in a situation where the status quo is not mutually agreed upon, states see each other as acting in bad faith, as unreasonable, and as subverting the established order.[20] That increasingly characterized diplomacy over Ukraine.[21]

The Security Dilemma

The underlying dynamics of international politics were stubborn, and the measures that each state took to improve its security naturally looked threatening to others, even if they were not intended to be so. The result was a self-reinforcing cycle. With Russia making claims on Ukrainian territory, Ukraine insisted on quickly building up its own military, and considered keeping the nuclear weapons on its territory. This was seen as threatening not only by Russia, but by the United States as well. Similarly, central European states, seeking security, sought to join NATO, which Russia feared. Russia's own actions reinforced the belief that it might again become a threat to its neighbors, and so on. In a letter to voters before his first election as president in 2000, Vladimir Putin stated: "It is unreasonable to fear a strong Russia, but she must be reckoned with. To offend us would cost anyone dearly."[22] Many of Russia's neighbors, based on recent history, felt that there was a lot to fear from a strong Russia, and the statement that offending Russia "would cost anyone dearly" was likely read as a threat against which precautions would be advisable.

---

[18] Andrei Zagorski, "Russia and the Shared Neighborhood," in Dov Lynch, ed., *What Russia Sees*, Chaillot Paper No. 74, Institute for Security Studies, January 2005, p. 69.

[19] Kahneman and Tversky, "Prospect Theory," p. 287. Levy ("Prospect Theory and International Relations," p. 286) applies this point to international politics: "A state which perceives itself to be in a deteriorating situation might be willing to take excessively risky actions in order to maintain the status quo."

[20] Kissinger, *A World Restored*, p. 2.

[21] The theory of loss aversion is applied specifically to the conflicts in Crimea and eastern Ukraine by Aleprete, "Minimizing Loss."

[22] "Putin's Foreign Policy Riddle," *BBC News Online*, Tuesday, March 28, 2000.

To scholars of international politics, this vicious circle, known as the "security dilemma," is a recurring problem of international politics throughout history, and is hard or even impossible to escape.[23] In this view, even peaceful states, as they pursue security, unintentionally create threats to others. Some recognized that the end of the Cold War did not solve this problem. After the fall of the Berlin Wall, John Mearsheimer predicted that if the United States withdrew from Europe, security fears would prompt Germany to acquire nuclear weapons.[24] That prediction was one reason why the United States did not depart and why NATO did not disband, but many worried that it was unclear where NATO expansion would stop or how far it could go "before the West more or less permanently alienates Russia."[25] The essence of the security dilemma is that either pursuing new security measures or not doing so can leave one feeling vulnerable. In this perspective it is the situation, or the system, which is to blame, not the individual actors, who find themselves trapped in this dynamic.

Escaping the security dilemma would have required one side or the other – or both – to abandon its understanding of what was acceptable as the status quo after the Cold War. Either the West and Ukraine would have to give up on the idea that in the new Europe democracy was the norm and democratic institutions were free to grow, or Russia would have to give up on its claims over Ukraine. Along the way, both sides had the opportunity to make smaller concessions. Whether one places the blame for the eventual conflict on Russia, Ukraine, or the West depends largely on which of these one thinks should have revised its expectations, and by extension on whose vision for post-Cold War Europe was more just.

Democracy and Power Politics

The end of the Cold War represented a massive geopolitical shift driven by mostly peaceful democratic revolutions in eastern Europe. Leaders in the West learned that democratization – something that people in the West fervently believed in – also brought important security gains. However, democratization repeatedly undid the status quo, each time

---

[23] There is an enormous literature on the security dilemma, its consequences, and the potential to resolve it. For a good short treatment, see Robert Jervis, "Cooperation under the Security Dilemma," *World Politics* 30, 2 (January 1978): 167–214.

[24] John J. Mearsheimer, "Back to the Future: Instability in Europe after the Cold War," *International Security* 15, 1 (Summer 1990): 5–56.

[25] Robert J. Art, "Creating a Disaster: NATO's Open Door Policy," *Political Science Quarterly* 113, 3 (1998): 383.

with geopolitical consequences that Russia feared. Initially, new democracies sought to join NATO. Then "colored revolutions" overturned pro-Russian governments in Serbia, Georgia, and Ukraine. "The emergence of the European Union as an economic superpower harnessed to a NATO alliance and steadily marching eastward confronted the new Russia with a prospect that has in the past represented the ultimate security nightmare – a frontier with a unified European "empire."[26] Moreover, as Russia focused on the development of a strong state rather than liberal democracy, a new ideological divide opened between it and the West.[27] Democracy came to be seen in Russia as an anti-Russian weapon, with the ultimate target being the Putin government. When Russia pushed back against the democratic revolutions of its neighbors, it was seen as aggressively interfering in their affairs. As a result, the West seemed like a "revisionist power" to Russia even as Russia seemed revisionist to the West.

This notion that democracy promoted security was bolstered by academic research on the "democratic peace theory," which held that war between democracies was impossible, and therefore that the spread of democracy would create an expanding region in which war was no longer possible. The theory had received enormous academic attention from the 1980s onward among western academics. The North Atlantic community looked like the kind of zone of peace envisioned by Kant and others, and many hoped that democracy and its security benefits could spread quickly and unproblematically to the postcommunist states.[28]

One of the political virtues of democratization as a foreign policy is that it resolved the traditional tension between doing good and pursuing one's interests, a tension felt particularly strongly in the United States during the Cold War. Rather than supporting dictators who were on the West's side against communism, the democratic peace held out the hope that by promoting democracy, the West could do good and increase international security at the same time.

Democracy promotion appealed to realists as much as to liberals. For realists, the geopolitical impact of democratization in Europe was

---

[26] Alfred J. Rieber, "How Persistent Are Persistent Factors?" in Robert Legvold, ed., *Russian Foreign Policy in the Twenty-First Century and the Shadow of the Past* (New York: Columbia University Press, 2007), p. 212.

[27] Maxime Henri André Larivé and Roger E. Kanet, "The Return to Europe and the Rise of EU-Russian Ideological Differences," *Whitehead Journal of Diplomacy and International Relations* 14, 1 (Winter/Spring 2013): 125–138.

[28] For a summary and critique of this perspective, see Philip G. Roeder, "Peoples and States after 1989: The Political Costs of Incomplete National Revolutions," *Slavic Review* 58, 4 (Winter 1999): 854–882.

the creation of a set of free states that would prevent the reassertion of a Russian empire. The joint appeal of democratization and institutional expansion was captured in the phrase "geopolitical pluralism," which Zbigniew Brzezinski argued should be the West's goal in the former Soviet Union. The democratic peace moved from theory to practice in part because it overlapped so neatly with a policy designed to expand the West's influence and check Russian reassertion.[29]

Thus, the expansion of western institutions into eastern Europe did not occur because liberalism triumphed over realism or because democrats outvoted republicans, but because it was supported by both realists and liberals, and by both republicans and democrats.[30] Liberals sought to promote democracy and international institutions, while realists sought to keep Russia from reestablishing control over central Europe. Not only Clinton, Warren Christopher, and Strobe Talbott supported NATO enlargement, but also Zbigniew Brzezinski, Henry Kissinger, and Richard Nixon. The dissent was limited to a small number of critics, such as George Kennan, who feared the impact on Russia (Kennan had also opposed the original founding of NATO in 1949).

For Russia, however, the geopolitical implications of democratization were threatening, and the biggest threat was in Ukraine. Given the choice, the people of eastern Europe would choose the market, democracy, and western Europe. If Russia did not join them, it would be isolated. To the extent that democracy in Russia was questionable – and it was never *not* questionable – Russia's neighbors would face a threat and a choice. They would almost certainly align with the democratic West, not an autocratic Russia. That threatened Russia's conception of its security and its identity as a "great power." Moreover, the keystone of geopolitical pluralism was a strong independent Ukraine, something most Russians strongly opposed. Western leaders downplayed Russian objections to the geopolitical implications of democratization because, according to the democratic peace argument and given the end of the Cold War, such implications seemed irrelevant.

Russia explicitly rejected the notion of geopolitical pluralism in its neighborhood. Russia considered it both essential to its interests and the general good for it to dominate the post-Soviet region, including Ukraine. Some states in the region (especially Belarus and Kazakhstan)

---

[29] This aspect of US foreign policy is critiqued by Toal, *Near Abroad*, pp. 10–12 and 291–297.

[30] On the tendency of transnational liberalism to bolster US dominance, see John M. Owen IV, "Transnational Liberalism and U.S. Primacy," *International Security* 26, 3 (Winter 2001–2002): 117–152.

accepted the need for Russian leadership and even welcomed it. Others (Ukraine, Georgia, Azerbaijan) opposed Russia's claims to primacy. If these states were democratic, they were going to reject Russian control.

The United States and western European countries increasingly encouraged the overthrow of Europe's remaining authoritarian regimes. The ouster of Slobodan Milosevic in the "Bulldozer Revolution" in October 2000 showed what was possible: a popular revolution ejected an autocratic leader, solving an intractable security problem. For the EU, a less violent but equally important case was that of Slovakia, where the European Union made it clear that progress on EU membership would be slowed as long as the autocratic government of Vladimir Meciar remained in power. Slovak elites isolated Meciar and forced him from power in order to preserve the country's goal of European integration.[31]

Georgia's 2003 Rose Revolution and Ukraine's 2004 Orange Revolution contributed to the belief that there was a "recipe" that could be replicated elsewhere.[32] The initial success of the revolutions of the "Arab Spring" in 2011 appeared to further demonstrate the power of contagion to bring democracy to long-time autocracies and to eliminate major security problems (though of course, in the longer term, the effect of the Arab Spring was less positive). Russia saw this practice as illegitimate and dangerous. The revolution in Serbia replaced a government that Russia had supported with one much more friendly to the West. The Rose Revolution in Georgia was more complicated, but the new Saakashvili government was strongly pro-United States and anti-Russian. The Orange Revolution was more threatening still, both because Ukraine was much more important to Russia and because the Orange Revolution was seen by many as a potential model to oust Putin himself. Some in the West openly hoped for a colored revolution in Russia.

After the colored revolutions, democracy promotion in general and democratic revolution in particular were so intertwined with geopolitical competition that they could not be separated. For the West, democracy promotion became not just the pursuit of an ideal, but a powerful weapon in the contest for influence in an increasingly chaotic world. For Russia, democracy promotion appeared to be a new form of warfare, capturing territory by replacing its leaders via protests, rather than by invading with armies. Moreover, it was a weapon that increasingly

[31] See Kevin Deegan-Krause, "Slovakia's Second Transition," *Journal of Democracy* 14, 2 (2003): 65–79.
[32] It is notable that one of the leading analysts of the colored revolutions, Michael McFaul, was named US Ambassador to Russia in 2011, much to the annoyance of the Putin government.

appeared to be aimed at the Putin regime in Russia. This was the context when protests forced Viktor Yanukovych from power in early 2014.

Domestic Constraints and State Strength

While international factors played an important role in fostering conflict, the spark was provided by Ukraine's internal politics. It is hard to see how the situation could have ended in military conflict in 2014 if not for the actions of the Yanukovych government. After being fairly elected president in 2010, Viktor Yanukovych sought to fundamentally reorder politics in the country in ways that many of its citizens and elites would not accept. These efforts, and the perception that the window to preserve democracy in Ukraine was closing quickly, turned a protest over integration policy into an effort to eject Yanukovych from power. More generally, international factors interacted with internal forces within Russia, Ukraine, and other key states in ways that undermined cooperation, and this has been underemphasized in most analyses of the conflict.

Throughout its independence period, Ukraine maintained three types of balance internally. The first was between the regions of the country. Ukraine's regional diversity was a challenge for leaders, but made it much more difficult for anyone to consolidate autocratic power, as happened in most of the post-Soviet region. Second was the foreign policy balance between Russia and the West. As long as Ukraine could credibly claim to be building ties with both the West and Russia, advocates of both policies could feel at least minimally satisfied. Third, and most important, was the pluralism that existed among the country's oligarchic groups or "clans." That pluralism did not make Ukraine democratic, but it kept it from becoming fully autocratic,[33] and the oligarchs defended that pluralism whenever anyone sought to establish political-economic dominance in the country. That explains why powerful oligarchs supported both the Orange Revolution of 2004 and the Euromaidan of 2013–2014.

After winning a close election in 2010, Yanukovych sought to permanently eliminate competition for power. Having taken control of the country's constitutional court, he was able to get it to invalidate the crucial "pact" limiting presidential power that had resolved the crisis during the Orange Revolution. He then used other illegal means to forge a majority in the parliament. All this pointed to autocracy. Perhaps more damaging, however, were his efforts to overturn the regional and

---

[33] See Lucan Way, *Pluralism by Default: Weak Autocrats and the Rise of Competitive Politics* (Baltimore, MD: Johns Hopkins University Press, 2015), especially chapter 3.

oligarchic balances in the country, gathering power in a narrowing circle of oligarchs that came to be called the "family." Seizing an increasing share of the country's economy shrank the coalition of oligarchs that had a stake in his survival, and increased the number who would benefit from his departure. This created the same dynamic that had provoked the Orange Revolution, fostering the transition of protests about the European Union into an effort to overthrow his government.

Two elements in Russian domestic politics are also crucial to the story: the erosion of democracy and the widespread belief that Russia should retain some sort of control over Ukraine. The erosion of democracy in Russia decreased the West's confidence that it could count on Russia as a partner. More important, an increasingly autocratic Russian government perceived an existential threat from the kind of democratic protest movement that emerged in Ukraine in 2004 and again in 2014.

The consensus in Russia that Ukraine was "really" part of Russia meant that there was always benefit to Russian politicians in making claims on Ukraine and risk in openly accepting its independence. In the 1990s, pressure from the "red-brown coalition" of leftists and nationalists forced Boris Yeltsin to take harder positions on various positions than he otherwise might have. Much later, it seems unlikely that Putin would have ordered the annexation of Crimea if it had not been massively popular. This raises a point that has been underappreciated: as much as analysts have focused on the erosion of democracy in Russia as a source of conflict, a more democratic Russia may not have had a more benign attitude toward Ukraine.

The importance of domestic politics goes beyond Russia and Ukraine. For example, early in the post-Soviet period the United States and the West considered whether to support Russian reform with a new version of the Marshall Plan or with something less robust. In retrospect, there has been much criticism of the meager aid provided, based on the plausible but unconfirmable premise that significant aid would have changed the subsequent course of events in Russia. Why was the chance not taken? In large part because it was unsustainable politically in the United States. The United States was in recession in 1991–1992, and US leaders hoped to divert a "peace dividend" from foreign policy to domestic spending. Worse still for foreign aid, the key year was 1992, a presidential and congressional election year. With Democrats hammering President George H. W. Bush for his handling of the economy, he felt that he could not push harder for a larger aid package to Russia, and it is almost certain that such a proposal would have stalled in the US Congress. When Bill Clinton entered the White House in 1993, and Russian reform was already on the ropes, he felt equally constrained from helping

Russia. Clinton was focused on a domestic spending package to help the United States out of recession, and was told that he could not get both that and a large aid package for Russia through Congress.

Domestic politics helps answer the questions that keep coming up concerning why the governments involved did not take steps that we believe might have led to better outcomes, reminding us that while we lay blame at various countries' or leaders' feet, those leaders themselves felt that their options were tightly constrained. The United States did not initiate a new Marshall Plan because it was in a recession and an election year. Russia did not simply let Ukraine go its own way because most Russians felt Ukraine was an intrinsic part of Russia. Ukraine did not reduce its economic dependence on Russia because remedying it would have required unpopular reforms and because that economic dependence was the source of so much revenue for corrupt officials.

The contrast between the evolution of the Ukrainian and Russian states is particularly telling. Ukraine's independence in 1991 was enabled by the weakening and collapse of the Soviet state in Moscow. Beginning at that time, both Ukraine and Russia struggled to build new, post-Soviet states, though Russia at least had much of the Soviet apparatus to repurpose. Throughout the 1990s, both states struggled to establish their authority and to perform basic functions such as collecting taxes and enforcing the rule of law.[34] Both were deeply penetrated by powerful economic and political figures known as oligarchs. After 2000, however, their paths diverged. Ukraine continued to have a state that was weak, corrupt, and penetrated by oligarchs, and yet somehow remained pluralistic and, to a large extent, democratic. In Russia, Vladimir Putin built a "vertikal" of power, brought the press under control, and curbed the independence of the oligarchs, all at the expense of democracy. He increased the internal coherence of the state and the state's control over societal actors. While Russia invested in rebuilding a strong military with operational readiness, Ukraine shrank the enormous military it had inherited from the Soviet Union but struggled to reform it into a viable fighting force. While it is common to observe that Russia was weakened in the 1990s and became much stronger by 2010, it is crucial to recognize that much of that weakness and strength was a function of the unity and

---

[34] For analyses of state strength in Russia, see Andrei P. Tsygankov, *The Strong State in Russia: Development and Crisis* (New York: Oxford University Press, 2014); Stephen E. Hanson, "The Uncertain Future of Russia's Weak State Authoritarianism," *East European Politics and Societies* 21, 1 (2007): 67–81; Peter H. Solomon, Jr., "Vladimir Putin's Quest for a Strong State," *International Journal on World Peace* 22, 2 (June 2005): 3–12; and Thomas E. Graham, "The Sources of Russian Conduct," *The National Interest*, August 24, 2016.

power of the state internally, and hence its ability or inability to bring Russia's enormous power resources effectively to bear internationally. The correlation between Russia's domestic state strength and its assertiveness internationally is notable. In other words, while the desire to exert itself in its neighborhood was more or less constant after 1991, Russia's internal capacity to assert itself varied, rising after 2000.

Proximate Causes

These factors – incompatible goals for the region and understandings of the status quo, exacerbated by the security dilemma, the merger of democratization with geopolitics, and the constraints of domestic politics – constitute the broad underlying sources of the conflict. The proximate and contingent factors need to be stressed as well, for despite those underlying sources of tension, violent conflict was never inevitable. Without events in 2013–2014 that were unpredictable and easily could have gone differently, Russia might never have seized Crimea and intervened in the Donbas.

To identify just a few of the contingencies: Had Viktor Yanukovych signed the EU Association Agreement, the Euromaidan protests would never have occurred (though Russia might still have responded to such a setback). Had the few protesters who initially showed up on the Maidan been ignored rather than beaten and arrested, the protests probably would not have grown. Had Yanukovych's government not passed a set of repressive "dictatorship" laws on January 16, the focus might have remained on the Association Agreement or on constitutional reform, not on ejecting Yanukovych from power. Had an agreement to resolve the crisis been reached before mass violence, rather than after, it likely would have stuck. Had Russia, the United States, and Europe maintained their support for that agreement after it had been rejected by protesters, it still might have stuck. Had more security forces loyal to the interim government been present in Donetsk and Luhansk, as they were in Kharkiv, the initial separatist militants there might have been ejected from the buildings before they became entrenched. And of course, had the Russian leadership chosen not to seize Crimea and intervene in eastern Ukraine, war would have been avoided. In sum, despite the underlying sources of conflict, which had become increasingly prominent, war was not inevitable until the point it began.

Overview of the Book

As Chapter 2 shows, the end of the Cold War left two problems for Russia, Ukraine, and the West. First, Russia did not accept Ukraine's independence. Second, there was no agreed security architecture for Europe to replace the division that had persisted from 1945 to 1991. Initially, the two problems were almost entirely separate, joined only in the general Russian insistence that it was and would continue to be a "great power."

From the moment of the Soviet collapse in August 1991, Russia sought to retain or recreate some kind of "center" to oversee military and economic policies. Ukraine resisted, and between 1991 and 1994 Russia and Ukraine skirmished over the role of the Commonwealth of Independent States (CIS), the status of the Black Sea Fleet and its base in Sevastopol, and the disposition of the nuclear weapons on Ukrainian territory. The United States and Russia jointly pressured Ukraine to surrender any claim to nuclear weapons, which Ukraine finally agreed to do in January 1994. Meanwhile, Ukraine's economy was in freefall, due in part to the decline that had begun under the Soviets, in part to the collapse of the unified Soviet economy, and in part to Ukrainian leaders' resistance to reform.

United States-Russia relations were at their best in this period, but even so, problems emerged almost immediately. In Moscow, conservatives regrouped to resist economic reform and Russia's nascent partnership with the West. The Bush and Clinton administrations sought to support Boris Yeltsin, but were wary of the growing influence of conservatives who saw the events of 1991 as a disaster. The violent dissolution of the Russian parliament in 1993 and the victory of new conservative parties in the subsequent parliamentary elections heightened the perceived threat from a reassertive Russia.

Chapter 3 documents an important repositioning of Ukraine, Russia, and the United States from 1994 to 1999. Ukraine's signing of the 1994 Trilateral agreement surrendering its nuclear weapons removed the primary obstacle to US support at the same time that Russian conservatives made hedging the West's bets on Russia seem prudent. Leonid Kuchma, elected President of Ukraine in mid-1994, was from eastern Ukraine and supported trade with Russia, diffusing separatist sentiment in Crimea. But he was as adamant as his predecessor that Ukraine would not compromise its sovereignty. Instead, he led Ukraine into extensive participation in NATO's Partnership for Peace. Already, Ukraine had come to be seen as a part of the West's strategic relationship with Russia. Despite ongoing tension, the high point of Ukraine-Russia relations came with the signing of a "Friendship Treaty" in 1997, in which Russia recognized Ukraine's borders, Ukraine agreed to lease Russia the naval base at Sevastopol in Crimea, and the Black Sea Fleet was finally divided. Ominously, many Russian politicians strongly opposed the treaty.

Despite the best efforts of Bill Clinton and Boris Yeltsin, United States-Russian relations continued to fray. The United States provided rhetorical support and campaign advisors (and supported a new IMF loan) to help Boris Yeltsin win reelection in 1996, but that support, and the connected "loans for shares" scheme, was a source of later Russian resentment. In 1998, the spread of the Asian financial crisis to Russia caused havoc, further convincing Russians that western advice was undermining their economy.

Meanwhile, the war in Yugoslavia had a deeply corrosive impact on Russia's relations with the West. Clinton committed himself to supporting NATO enlargement in 1994, and the war in Yugoslavia helped ensure that it actually happened, first by making it clear that the end of the Cold War was not going to eliminate security problems in Europe, second by undermining the notion that Russia could be counted on to help solve these problems, and third by showing that only NATO, with its military command and without a Russian veto, could address the biggest threats to peace. For both domestic and international reasons, Boris Yeltsin felt he had to support Serbia, both in 1994–1995 and again in 1999, with the effect that the West had to choose between honoring Russia's wishes and keeping its promise never again to stand by during a genocide in Europe.

Chapter 4 begins with the momentous year 1999. In March, NATO officially admitted three new members, and two weeks later the alliance began bombing Serbia. In November, Leonid Kuchma was reelected President of Ukraine, accelerating a trend toward autocracy that ended in the 2004 Orange Revolution. And on the final day of the year, Boris Yeltsin resigned, installing Vladimir Putin as acting president and putting him in position to win the permanent job a few months later. After the terrorist attacks in September 2001, Russia and the United States found common cause in combating terrorism, but by 2003 Russia opposed the Bush administration's defining foreign policy, the war to oust Saddam Hussein in Iraq.

Kuchma's efforts to consolidate power and eliminate competition initially looked likely to succeed, but the murder of the journalist Georgiy Gongadze, and recordings implicating Kuchma in that and other misdeeds, spurred opposition. The West kept him at arm's length, and he responded by seeking closer ties with Russia, where Vladimir Putin was more successfully eliminating political competition.

In the 2004 Ukraine presidential election, Russia saw the opportunity to finally get a leader in Kyiv who would support integration with Russia. Putin supported Yanukovych personally and with the resources of the Russian government and media. The protests and subsequent agreement to rerun the election turned a Russian victory into a stinging defeat. This episode, more than any other, merged Ukrainian-Russian relations into Russia's relations with the West.

Chapter 5 examines the period following the Orange Revolution, under President Viktor Yushchenko. The Orange Revolution promised domestic reform and integration with Europe, but neither occurred, and corruption continued unabated. The "orange coalition" dissolved into bitter conflict, undermining reform. Viktor Yushchenko despised his former ally Yuliya Tymoshenko so intensely that he supported Viktor Yanukovych – who had tried to steal the 2004 election – to become prime minister in 2006 and to become president in 2010.

NATO's 2008 Bucharest summit put Ukraine at the center of growing tension between Russia and the West. The United States supported giving Ukraine a "Membership Action Plan" to join NATO. Germany and France, striving not to alienate Russia, blocked the proposal. While the compromise statement that Ukraine would someday join the alliance was seen as a weak consolation prize in the West, it has since been viewed by Russia and by some analysts as a threat to Russia's interests that provoked (and to some justified) the subsequent invasion of Georgia and the 2014 invasion of Ukraine.

With NATO membership for Ukraine deferred indefinitely, the European Union-Ukraine relationship became, for the first time, the main focus of the West's interaction with Ukraine. The "Eastern Partnership" program started the European Union and Ukraine down the path toward an Association Agreement. Russia countered with a series of integration proposals of its own.

Chapter 6 analyzes the period of Viktor Yanukovych's presidency in Ukraine, beginning with his election in 2010. Yanukovych appeared to have remade himself as a legitimate pragmatic politician, but upon his election he immediately began taking dramatic steps to consolidate political power, amass economic assets, and gain the support of Russia. The political consolidation convinced the democratic opposition that he would not allow another free election, scheduled for 2015. The economic consolidation threatened many of Ukraine's oligarchs. While in retrospect the stage was set for the Euromaidan, few anticipated a new round of protests.

At the same time, rancor between Russia and the West intensified. The Obama "reset" policy yielded few results, and a new source of acrimony emerged in 2011, when another NATO-supported intervention ousted another autocrat, Libya's Muammar Gaddafi. The Arab Spring further demonstrated the power of popular revolutions to depose authoritarian regimes, angering and worrying Putin. While Putin's 2008 "castling" with

Dmitry Medvedev had demonstrated Putin's control over Russian elite politics, protests in 2011 and 2012 pointed to his potential vulnerability. Democratization and geopolitics had become almost completely fused.

By late 2013 Ukraine, Russia, and the West had gotten themselves into a contest in which a compromise was increasingly difficult to find. Incompatible integration proposals from Russia and the European Union created a zero-sum game between Russia and the West, and forced Ukrainians to make a binary choice that many of them did not want to make. What most Ukrainians supported, close economic ties with both Russia and the European Union, was increasingly impossible. Nor was it feasible to be a member of neither bloc, as isolation would have further undermined Ukraine's economy. At the last hour, in November 2013, Yanukovych announced that Ukraine would not sign the Association Agreement with the EU.

Chapter 7 examines the aftermath of that decision. Yanukovych's hesitation need not have led to his downfall or to an invasion. But his government repeatedly took steps that enraged protesters without foiling them. In February 2014, the shooting of protesters led to the evaporation of Yanukovych's support, and he fled the country. Within a week, "little green men" began the seizure of Crimea, and within a month the annexation was complete. Meanwhile, seizures of government buildings occurred in cities throughout eastern Ukraine. Many were quickly reversed, but in Donetsk and Luhansk support from Russians combined with the near absence of the Ukrainian state made it possible for separatist forces to gain a foothold.

Europe's reaction to the seizure of Crimea and intervention in the Donbas was initially muted, as most elites prioritized Russia over Ukraine, and many sympathized with Russia's claims on Crimea. Another unanticipated event, the downing of Malaysian Airlines Flight 17, changed opinion dramatically. The killing of innocents and Putin's transparently disingenuous response decimated support for Russia. That put European governments on the same page as the United States in enacting sanctions. Putin's actions were now being widely compared to those of Hitler in the run-up to World War II.

When the Ukrainian armed forces threatened to encircle Russian-backed rebels in Donetsk Oblast in the summer of 2014, Russia intervened with regular army forces. The ensuing rout forced Ukraine to accept a ceasefire agreement on Russian terms. The first Minsk agreement committed Ukraine to measures which it did not want to take, such as increasing regional autonomy. Following the seizure of the Donetsk airport by Russian-backed forces in February 2015, a second Minsk agreement acknowledged the revised lines of control. Since that time, ceasefire violations have been routine, and casualties have steadily mounted.

Chapter 8 returns to the question of explanation. The discussion asks how things might have been different. Any explanation of the war, and any assignment of blame, assumes that if particular decisions had been made differently, or some events had occurred differently, a different outcome would have resulted. Here we try to assess some of the decisions that might have had such an impact, as well as some of the events or forces that seem to have been beyond anyone's control. The hardest question of constraint and blame comes with Putin's decision to annex Crimea. It appears that the plan executed in March 2014 had been laid well in advance. Was Putin tightly constrained, as some analysts have argued? What other options were available? Leaders' assertions that they had no choice can often be a tactic to deflect blame elsewhere. Other contingencies range from enormous decisions to small ones. One of the biggest is the impact of NATO expansion. Did that decision really drive the conflict? To the extent it did, was it an obviously unwise decision, or did it help avert other looming dangers?[35]

One important conclusion is that the strategy of awaiting the departure of Putin is unlikely to succeed. Russia's insistence on being a great power and regional hegemon, as well as its claims over Ukraine, predate Putin's rise to power, and are widely shared across the Russian elite and populace. The implication is that democracy will not lead Russia to abandon these aspirations. Indeed, only Boris Yeltsin's personal power held this agenda back in the 1990s. More broadly, the belief, derived from the democratic peace theory, that a democratic Russia will necessarily reach an accommodation with the West, runs squarely into Russia's great power aspirations. The merger of democracy with geopolitics both reduces the likelihood that Russia will become a democracy and that a democratic Russia would voluntarily agree to restrain its power to reassure its neighbors, as Germany has done.

Summary

This account stresses that the war that began in 2014 was the product of both long-term forces in the post-Cold War environment and short-term decisions made by Ukrainian, Russian, and western leaders in 2013–2014. The chances for violent conflict between Russia and

---

[35] On these questions, see Kimberly Marten, "Reconsidering NATO Expansion: A Counterfactual Analysis of Russia and the West in the 1990s," *European Journal of International Security* 3, 2 (November 2017): 135–161.

Ukraine increased incrementally between 1989 and 2014, and it is necessary to trace this process to understand how, by 2014, it was possible the Russia would decide that invading its neighbor was its best policy.

The environment that emerged after the collapse of the Soviet Union was so much more benign than that of the Cold War that it was easy to believe that the conflicts that remained – such as the status of Ukraine – would resolve themselves over time. But three broad factors – the inability to reconcile the various actors' perceptions of the status quo and resulting security needs, the clash between the spread of western democratic institutions with Russia's views of its "sphere of interest," and the domestic costs of adopting conciliatory policies – combined to ensure that Ukraine's status was not resolved. Paradoxically, it was the likelihood that its status would be definitively resolved either in favor of the West or Russia that made both sides more risk acceptant in 2013 to 2014.

War did not have to happen, but by 2014 competition and mistrust were deeply ingrained in both the Ukraine-Russia and West-Russia relationships, and those two conflicts had become tightly connected. Those underlying conflicts were inherent in the post-Cold War system, and to see why, we need to go back to the stunning events that ended the Cold War in 1989–1991. That is where we begin in Chapter 2.

2   New World Order? 1989–1993

Introduction

On July 6, 1989, Mikhail Gorbachev spoke to the Council of Europe in Strasbourg of "Europe as a Common Home." One line in that speech grabbed headlines around the world: "Any interference in internal affairs, any attempts to limit the sovereignty of states – whether of friends and allies or anybody else – are inadmissible."[1] That sentence was interpreted, and apparently was meant, as a revocation of the Brezhnev Doctrine, which had been enunciated in 1968 to justify the Soviet invasion of Czechoslovakia, and held that the Soviet Union had the right to intervene in socialist countries when "forces that are hostile to socialism try to turn the development of some socialist country towards capitalism."[2] Gorbachev's apparent "permission" to push for reform and for greater independence encouraged movements already underway in the region. By October, peaceful protests were occurring regularly in cities in East Germany, where a KGB officer named Vladimir Putin witnessed them in Dresden.[3] In November, the Berlin Wall, the most tangible symbol of the Cold War division of Europe, was opened, symbolically ending the Cold War.

Gorbachev's speech provides a useful beginning point for understanding the sources of the Russia-Ukraine conflict. Not only did it hasten the

---

[1] James A. Markham, "Gorbachev Spurns the Use of Force in Eastern Europe," *New York Times*, July 7, 1989. The full text of Gorbachev's speech is at https://chnm.gmu.edu/1989/archive/files/gorbachev-speech-7-6-89_e3ccb87237.pdf.

[2] The relevant excerpt from Brezhnev's speech is translated at the "Modern History Sourcebook: The Brezhnev Doctrine, 1968," https://sourcebooks.fordham.edu/mod/1968brezhnev.asp. The original was in *Pravda*, September 25, 1968.

[3] Putin described the episode in his biographical interview, Vladimir Putin with Nataliya Gevorkyan, Natalya Timakova, and Andrei Kolesnikov, *First Person: An Astonishingly Frank Self-Portrait by Russia's President Vladimir Putin*, trans. Catherine A. Fitzpatrick (New York: PublicAffairs, 2000). Many have argued that the episode was formative for Putin, and helps explain the intensity of his opposition to protests such as those in Kyiv in 2004 and 2014. See for example Fiona Hill and Clifford Gaddy, "How the 1980s Explains Vladimir Putin," *The Atlantic*, February 14, 2013.

demise of the Soviet Bloc, it raised the question of the independence of the Soviet Republics, several of which had longstanding independence movements. Ever since that time, the question of Russia's role and rights in its region have been a source of contention, as Russia's claims have conflicted with those of Ukraine, the Baltic states, and the West. The principle that force would not be used was tested almost from the very beginning, when Soviet Special Purpose Police Unit (OMON) forces attacked the Latvian Interior Ministry in January 1991.

Gorbachev's "common European home" proposed an alternative to the "Europe whole and free" suggested by US President George H. W. Bush a few months earlier in Mainz, Germany. While Gorbachev imagined a Europe in which socialist and capitalist states got along peacefully and productively, Bush envisioned a Europe where liberal democracy and the market would unite the continent. "The path of freedom leads to a larger home, a home where West meets East, a democratic home, the commonwealth of free nations."[4] While Gorbachev's notion of Europe was inherently pluralist, Bush's vision stressed adherence to a single set of values. Thus, even as the Cold War was ending, a profound disagreement emerged about the principles that should underpin politics in Europe.[5]

By December 1993, nationalist and communist parties were ascendant in Russia's parliament. Already the parliament had passed a resolution stating that the port of Sevastopol, traditionally home to Russia's Black Sea Fleet, but since 1991 Ukrainian territory, should be considered Russian territory. In Ukraine, leaders had gained legal independence from Russia, but could not figure out how to break the country's dependence on Russian energy. Nor was the Soviet Union the only country to collapse in 1991. In December, the disintegration of Yugoslavia began, igniting a conflict which would bedevil the continent and would later be cited by Vladimir Putin as a justification for annexing Crimea.

---

[4] "A Europe Whole and Free Remarks to the Citizens in Mainz," President George Bush, Rheingoldhalle, Mainz, Federal Republic of Germany, May 31, 1989. Though the Cold War was not yet over, Bush was certain who had won: "[I]n the West, we have succeeded because we've been faithful to our values and our vision. And on the other side of the rusting Iron Curtain, their vision failed."

[5] Richard Sakwa, writing in 2016, finds this tension between "greater Europe" and "wider Europe" continuing to define the region's politics. See "How the Eurasian Elite Envisages the Role of the EEU in Global Perspective," *East European Politics and Society* 17 (2016): 11–13. For a detailed study of the challenge of developing a post-Cold War institutional framework that included Russia, see William H. Hill, *No Place for Russia: European Security Institutions since 1989* (New York: Columbia University Press, 2018).

These episodes illustrate the argument that guides this chapter. Many, if not all, of the basic ingredients of the crisis that emerged in late 2013 and early 2014 were already present by 1993. These problems resisted solution because they were rooted in three highly challenging environments that overlapped each other. First, Ukraine and Russia disagreed fundamentally about what their relationship would be. Second, while the international scene that emerged after the collapse of the Soviet Union seemed benevolent, it raised intractable questions about Russia's role in the new Europe. Third, the domestic situations in Ukraine and Russia were chaotic, with economic dislocation and institutional confrontation impeding a smooth transition to democracy.

The Road to Ukrainian Independence

Nationalists across the Soviet Union took advantage of Gorbachev's political liberalization to press for independence. In March 1990, elections were held for the republic-level parliaments, and for the first time candidates who were not members of the Communist Party of the Soviet Union (CPSU) were allowed to run. In Ukraine, the newly formed Rukh Party, which grew out of the dissident-led People's Movement for Ukraine, won a quarter of the seats in the Verkhovna Rada. Leonid Kravchuk, a communist leader who sought to co-opt the nationalists, was elected speaker. On June 12, the Russian Congress of People's Deputies issued a "Declaration of State Sovereignty of the Russian Soviet Federative Socialist Republic." The act declared the supremacy of Russian legislation over that of the Soviet government, kicking off what became known as the "war of laws," and spurring similar declarations in other republics.

On July 16, Ukraine's Verkhovna Rada followed the trend, passing (by a vote of 335–4) the "Declaration of State Sovereignty of Ukraine," which declared Ukraine's sovereignty but not its independence from the Soviet Union, a contradiction that was confusing but also pragmatic. There was a strong impetus to establishing as much self-control as possible, but Ukraine was not ready to secede or to force a showdown with central authorities. Ukrainian nationalists made a tactical decision to ally with "national communists," such as Kravchuk, rather than to oppose the Communist Party entirely, which would have left the nationalists in a minority. Therefore, Ukraine moved toward independence not by ejecting the communist establishment but by allowing the establishment to co-opt the cause of independence.

The sovereignty declaration stated Ukraine's "intention" to become a "permanently neutral" state and to adhere to three nonnuclear principles: not to accept, produce, or acquire nuclear weapons.[6] These two provisions were to generate much controversy in the coming years. What was entailed by neutrality, or "non-bloc status" as it came to called, and whether the policy continued to be wise, were questions that dogged Ukraine's foreign policy until 2014, when neutrality was decisively abandoned.

Gorbachev scrambled to keep the Soviet Union from disintegrating. In March 1991 he held a referendum across the Soviet Union, asking voters: "Do you consider necessary the preservation of the Union of Soviet Socialist Republics as a renewed federation of equal sovereign republics in which the rights and freedom of an individual of any nation- ality will be fully guaranteed?" The contradiction between sovereign equality and preservation of the Soviet Union was ignored, foreshadow- ing Russia's later insistence that an independent Ukraine join a Russia- led union of some sort. Ukrainian lawmakers added a second question: "Do you agree that Ukraine should be part of a Union of Soviet sovereign states on the basis on the Declaration of State Sovereignty of Ukraine?" Both questions won significant assent in Ukraine (71 percent and 82 percent, respectively).

Gorbachev proposed a new treaty, which would devolve considerable autonomy to the republics, but maintain a united military, a common foreign policy, and a single currency. The Verkhovna Rada, now divided between nationalists, "national communists," and pro-union commun- ists, debated the treaty throughout the summer of 1991, proposing amendments but deferring decisive action. The nationalists, supported by many of the national communists, were set on pursuing full independ- ence, but were unready to move decisively, fearing a crackdown. This put Ukraine between the position of eight republics, including Russia, that were planning to sign the treaty and six that had already rejected the process.[7] In July, the Verkhovna Rada created the position of a popularly elected president, analogous to the position Yeltsin held in Russia, and scheduled the election for December.

While Ukrainian leaders felt that the proposed Union Treaty would provide too little autonomy, conservatives in Moscow feared that it provided too much. Opposition to Gorbachev's economic reforms was also mounting. In late July, a group of prominent political and cultural figures published a "Word to the People" calling on the reforms to be halted. Addressed to "Russians, Citizens of the USSR, Compatriots,"

---

[6] Deklaratsiya Suverenitet Ukrayiny, July 16, 1990, Verkhovna Rada website, https:// zakon.rada.gov.ua/laws/show/55-12.
[7] Bohdan Nahaylo, *The Ukrainian Resurgence* (London: Hurst, 1999), pp. 364–365.

the letter equated Russian nationalism with the preservation of the Soviet Union, and saw the moves toward independence and economic reforms as a sellout of the country to outside enemies.[8]

As George H. W. Bush flew to Moscow at the end of July 1991, Gorbachev was trying to hold together the Soviet Union, to reform its economy, and to gain the support of the West. Gorbachev warned Bush that Ukraine's independence might lead to a conflict similar to that unfolding in Yugoslavia – but with thousands of nuclear weapons involved. Bush and National Security Advisor Brent Scowcroft, trying to consolidate the gains made in arms control, in the dissolution of the Warsaw Pact, and in the UN Security Council on Iraq, hoped to bolster Gorbachev's position.

This was the context when Bush stopped in Kyiv on his way back to Washington. In a speech to the Rada, Bush sought to persuade Ukrainians to move forward within, rather than apart from, the Soviet Union: "Freedom is not the same as independence. Americans will not support those who seek independence in order to replace a far-off tyranny with a local despotism. They will not aid those who promote a suicidal nationalism based on ethnic hatred." Bush went on to endorse Gorbachev's proposed union treaty: "The nine-plus-one agreement holds forth the hope that Republics will combine greater autonomy with greater voluntary interaction – political, social, cultural, economic – rather than pursuing the hopeless course of isolation."[9] The speech would likely have been forgotten were it not for *New York Times* columnist William Safire, who dubbed it the "Chicken Kiev Speech," representing the opinion of many in the United States who supported Ukraine's independence either as an intrinsic good or as a way to further weaken the Soviet Union.

A few weeks later, the coup against Gorbachev overwhelmed all of these leaders' plans. When it became clear that the coup had failed, on August 24, the Rada declared Ukraine independent (by a vote of 346 to 1 with three abstentions[10]), extended the authority of speaker Kravchuk to act as head of state, and scheduled a referendum on independence, to be held along with the presidential election already scheduled for December 1. The question now was not whether the Soviet Union would be maintained, but whether something new could be forged from its fragments. On August 25 Yeltsin announced his support for signing the

[8] *Sovietskaya Rossiya*, July 23, 1991.
[9] George H. W. Bush, "Remarks to the Supreme Soviet of the Republic of the Ukraine in Kiev, Soviet Union August 1, 1991," www.presidency.ucsb.edu/documents/remarks-the-supreme-soviet-the-republic-the-ukraine-kiev-soviet-union.
[10] Nahaylo, *The Ukrainian Resurgence*, p. 391.

Union Treaty and stressed that the union should be a federation, not a looser confederation. Two days later he threatened to resign if the treaty were not signed, putting himself at odds with the Ukrainian leadership.[11]

Creating a State

The fall of 1991 was a time of extraordinary improvisation. In Ukraine, the agenda included setting up the institutions of a sovereign government, securing international recognition, holding the referendum and presidential election, negotiating terms of separation with the Soviet and Russian governments (and the other successor states), forming a Ukrainian military, and stemming economic collapse. The scope of the task is hard to imagine. Many of Ukraine's biggest industrial enterprises, for example, had almost no relationship with Kyiv, having been run by ministries in Moscow. Similarly, Ukraine did not inherit an army but rather a variety of disconnected military units with no Defense Ministry or General Staff to command or control them.[12]

The leadership charged with turning these various pieces of the larger Soviet entity into a state was completely unprepared. Despite the monumental scope of the task, the surprise with which independence arose, and the inexperience of those making the changes, the state did not collapse. And while the economy declined severely in the early post-Soviet years, Ukrainian leaders did succeed in building a separate state, weak as it was.

While Ukraine had to create a state almost from scratch, Russia had two competing states: a Soviet one which ran the whole country, and a Russian one which was "hardly more than an empty shell."[13] In the fall of 1991, this problem was resolved through the incremental takeover of Soviet institutions, including the military, by Yeltsin's Russian government. Yeltsin's efforts to take control of Soviet institutions had the unintended consequence of reaffirming to the other republics that any "central" organization would in fact be controlled by Russia. This redoubled their resistance to creating new central institutions. Some of

---

[11] Raymond L. Garthoff, *The Great Transition: American-Soviet Relations and the End of the Cold War* (Washington, DC: Brookings Institution, 1994), p. 479.

[12] James Sherr, "Security, Democracy, and 'Civil Democratic Control' of Armed Forces in Ukraine," in Jennifer D. P. Moroney, Taras Kuzio, and Mikhail Molchanov, *Ukrainian Foreign and Security Policy: Theoretical and Comparative Perspectives* (Westport, CT: Praeger, 2002), p. 94.

[13] Mikhail E. Bezrukov, "The Creation of a Russian Foreign Policy," in James E. Goodby and Benoit Morel, eds., *The Limited Partnership: Building a Russian-US Security Community* (New York: Oxford University Press, 1993), pp. 82–83.

the rhetoric from the Russian government inflamed opinion in Ukraine, as when Yeltsin's press secretary said that unless there were an agreement on a new union "the RSFSR [Russian Soviet Federative Socialist Republic] reserves the right to raise the question of reviewing its borders."[14] While the Soviet military leadership subjected itself to Russian control, the Ukrainian leadership declared its control of all forces and ownership of all material on Ukrainian territory.[15]

There were some signs that Ukraine would join a new "Union of Sovereign States."[16] In late November, however, as the signing of a new draft treaty was being prepared, Yeltsin objected to the deal, seeking more power for Russia vis-à-vis the "center." Further discussion was deferred until after Ukraine's referendum.

The United States, anticipating the outcome of the referendum, announced that it would quickly recognize Ukraine's independence, a move that some in the Bush administration felt undermined Gorbachev's efforts to keep the Union together and reduced US leverage over the nascent Ukrainian government.[17] Yeltsin expressed frustration at the US announcement, fearing that it would provoke Russian nationalists.[18]

On December 1, Ukraine held its referendum on independence and its presidential election. All six presidential candidates supported independence. Kravchuk, the acting president, former speaker of the Verkhovna Rada, and former ideology chief the Communist Party of Ukraine, won easily, with 61.6 percent of the vote to 23.3 percent for Rukh leader Vyacheslav Chornovil, with the remainder split among the other candidates or "against all."[19]

---

[14] "Zayavlenie press-sekretarya Presidenta RSFSR," *Rossiiskaya Gazeta*, August 27, 1991, p. 2.

[15] Garthoff (*The Great Transition*, p. 481) points out that the military threats made by General Varennikov, one of the coup plotters, to Kravchuk during the coup attempt, helped convince Kravchuk that he urgently needed to subordinate the military forces in Ukraine to Ukrainian control.

[16] Garthoff, *The Great Transition*, pp. 481–482.

[17] The Bush administration was divided over recognition. The debate was resolved largely by domestic factors: the defeat of Republican Dick Thornburgh in a special election for the US Senate in Pennsylvania, a state with a large East European population, was blamed in part on the administration's slow recognition of Baltic independence, and with a reelection battle looming in 1992, Bush sought to cover this flank. See Michael R. Beschloss and Strobe Talbott, *At the Highest Levels: The Inside Story of the End of the Cold War* (New York: Little Brown & Company, 1994), pp. 448–449; and Garthoff, *The Great Transition*, p. 494.

[18] Gartoff, *The Great Transition*, p. 495.

[19] On the 1991 presidential elections and referendum, see Sarah Birch, *Elections and Democratization in Ukraine* (New York: St. Martin's, 2000), chapter 5.

The referendum asked simply: "Do you support the Declaration of Independence of Ukraine?" the text of which was appended. The result was overwhelming: 92.3 percent voted in favor of independence. In every single region of Ukraine, *including* Crimea and the city of Sevastopol, a majority supported independence. However, in Crimea and Sevastopol, the majorities were much smaller than elsewhere: 54.2 and 57.1 percent, respectively. In both Donetsk and Luhansk oblasts, 83.9 percent voted for independence.

Belavezha: The Civilized Divorce

Immediately following the vote in Ukraine, Yeltsin, Kravchuk, and Belarusian president Stanislav Shushkevich met at a dacha in the Belavezha park in Belarus to hammer out a deal on the relationship among the successor states. With large majorities supporting independence and his presidency, Kravchuk came to Belarus empowered, while Yeltsin was still trying to finish off Gorbachev in Moscow. As Mikhail Bezrukov asserted, until the end of 1991 the foreign policy of the Russian Federation was driven primarily by Yeltsin's "rivalry with the 'Gorbachev team.'"[20] Both Gorbachev and Yeltsin (along with Belarus and the five Central Asian states) supported signing the revised Union Treaty. But Ukraine was now opposed.[21]

Yeltsin had two goals that were in tension. The first was to get rid of the Soviet Union, and with it Gorbachev. The second was to retain a "center," dominated by Russia, that would control nuclear weapons and provide economic coordination. He stated upon arriving in Minsk that "we must without fail work out a viewpoint that will prevent our three Slav states from splitting apart, no matter what happens."[22]

There were many motivations for seeking to preserve a single market, military, and currency. Pragmatically, dissolving the Soviet economy would create chaos, given the combination of deep integration and lingering central planning. Dissolving the Soviet military would also create enormous problems. St. Petersburg Mayor Anatoly Sobchak

---

[20] Bezrukov, "The Creation of a Russian Foreign Policy," p. 88.

[21] The Belavezha meeting and the process leading up to it are discussed in detail in Serhii Plokhy, *The Last Empire: The Final Days of the Soviet Union* (New York: Basic Books, 2014), chapter 15.

[22] "Yeltsin's Arrival Statement in Minsk," Radio Moscow, December 7, 1991, in Foreign Broadcast Information Service (FBIS), Soviet Union, December 9, 1991, p. 50, as quoted in Garthoff, *The Great Transition*, p. 483.

called the formation of a Ukrainian military "a time bomb under the future of all mankind."[23]

In direct opposition, Kravchuk felt that he could not really be in control of Ukraine if it was part of some kind of supranational state controlled from Moscow. Kravchuk had the upper hand tactically, and he drove a hard bargain. Without his approval, the Soviet Union could not be disbanded and Gorbachev sidelined. His price was to dissolve the Soviet Union without a new union to replace it.

The three leaders agreed to dissolve the 1922 Union Treaty (the legal basis for the formation of the Soviet Union from Russia, Ukraine, and Belarus), thus, in international legal terms, dissolving the Soviet Union.[24] This served Yeltsin's need to make Gorbachev irrelevant and Kravchuk's need to dissolve central structures. Having dissolved the Soviet Union, Yeltsin was eager to forge a new set of common structures to manage common problems. Kravchuk was resolutely opposed. They papered over this profound disagreement by creating the "Commonwealth of Independent States" (CIS). The Commonwealth looked like a confederation, and had many of the structures that the Russian leadership wanted, but at Ukraine's insistence, none of the commitments were legally binding.[25] In Ukraine, the CIS was seen not as a new organization, but as a way of managing complete separation. Dmytro Pavlychko, the head of the Rada's Foreign Affairs Committee, called it "a bridge for us over the chaos."[26]

The details of what happened at Belavezha show that from the very beginning there was a conflict of interest between Russia's desire to retain some central control over the region and Ukraine's opposition. Even Boris Yeltsin, who was far more democratically and western oriented than other Russian leaders, sought central control over the republics, especially Ukraine. And even Kravchuk, who was elected Ukraine's president running *against* a nationalist, and had his highest support in eastern Ukraine and Crimea, adamantly refused to compromise Ukraine's sovereignty.

---

[23] Nahaylo, *The Ukrainian Resurgence*, p. 441.

[24] The legality of these measures was not uncontested. In addition to the 1922 Union Treaty, there was another artifact of the Soviet era that gave Ukraine and Belarus a claim to sovereignty that the others lacked: both were original members of the United Nations. This originated in the horse-trading that accompanied the founding of the UN.

[25] As Garthoff (*The Great Transition*, p. 485) points out, there was another option: a new Union Treaty could have been signed by Russia, Belarus, and the Central Asian states. But including Ukraine was an essential goal for Yeltsin, and so he chose the "least common denominator" that would also include Ukraine.

[26] Quoted in Fred Hiatt, "Russia, Ukraine See Commonwealth Differently," *Washington Post*, December 13, 1991, p. A1.

The Commonwealth of Independent States (CIS)

The CIS was formally founded at a meeting in Almaty on December 21 with eleven members – the three Slavic states; the five Central Asian states; and Armenia, Azerbaijan, and Moldova. The leaders in Almaty sent a joint statement to Gorbachev informing him that the Soviet Union and his presidency were at an end.[27] Gorbachev finally admitted defeat and resigned his post on December 25, and on the following day the Soviet Union officially ceased to exist.

While Russia sought to maintain a single CIS military, Ukraine was determined to build its own military out of the Soviet forces on its territory. Despite being nearly broke, Ukraine managed to find the funding to take over paying for the forces on its territory. This issue overlapped with arguments over the Black Sea Fleet and over Russian or CIS peacekeeping forces being deployed in the region. At a meeting of CIS defense ministers in April 1992, eleven drafts were discussed considering common defense structures; Ukraine (along with Azerbaijan) refused to sign any of them. Similarly, in May, when six states gathered in Tashkent to sign a Collective Security Treaty similar to NATO's Article V, Kravchuk did not even attend, and Ukraine (along with Moldova, Belarus, and Azerbaijan) refused to sign.[28]

Sergei Rogov of Russia's Institute for the USA and Canada captured the dilemma that Russia faced in trying to maintain a unified military. On the one hand, he worried that if Russia was not more assertive, the armed forces would disintegrate. On the other, if Russia was more assertive, it might irk its partners. "Each sovereign state has a right to build its own military forces, and an independent Ukraine cannot be blamed for doing so. However, in trying to achieve immediate military independence, Ukraine failed to take the security interests of Russia into account."[29] He was, in essence, recognizing the Russian-Ukrainian security dilemma.

Problems of Economic Coordination and the Collapse of the Ruble Zone

The Soviet Union was more tightly integrated than the European Union, and was dissolved with no prior planning. Already in the spring of 1991,

---

[27] Garthoff, *The Great Transition*, p. 486.

[28] The six signatories were Russia, Armenia, Kazakhstan, Kyrgyzstan, Tajikistan, and Uzbekistan.

[29] Sergei Rogov, "A National Security Policy for Russia," in James E. Goodby and Benoit Morel, eds., *The Limited Partnership: Building a Russian-US Security Community* (Oxford: SIPRI/Oxford University Press, 1993), pp. 77–78.

the liberalization of grain prices had spurred an outflow of food from Ukraine to Russia, where prices were higher. Ukraine first introduced an export ban and then in July announced a plan for rationing grain via a coupon system. The plan limited the quantity of cigarettes (four packs), eggs (ten), meat (half a kilogram), and vodka (one bottle) that an individual could carry out of the republic.[30] This angered other republics (and fueled corruption) but did not solve any of the underlying problems involving agricultural production and markets.[31]

All the successor states were still using the Soviet ruble in early 1992. They dealt with growing debt problems among enterprises by issuing credit and creating new money. This naturally led to massive inflation. The IMF recommended forming a single central bank to manage monetary policy for the ruble, and Russia supported this, but there were three barriers. First, Ukraine was not willing to compromise its independence. Second, monetary policy would either be dominated by Russia, which was unacceptable to Ukraine, or it would not, which was unacceptable to Russia. Third, the states did not agree on monetary policy. Russia, pursuing structural adjustment ("shock therapy"), prioritized controlling inflation by limiting currency emissions, while Ukraine and others sought to avoid hard choices by printing more money.

Ukraine's continuing issuance of credit had the effect of exporting inflation to Russia. In January 1992, Ukraine established a parallel currency, the *karbovanets*, which quickly lost value. In October 1992, to insulate Russia from the inflation caused by Ukrainian monetary policy, the Russian Central Bank stopped making payments based on Ukrainian ruble loans. Ukraine responded by leaving the ruble zone and establishing a "non-cash" *karbovanets*. The ruble zone held together a bit longer, but Russia effectively forced the others out in mid-1993 by replacing existing Soviet ruble notes in Russia with new Russian ones.[32]

Ukraine and Russia now controlled their own monetary policies, but wildly fluctuating exchange rates created a drag on trade. Ukraine's highly expansionary monetary policy led to rapid inflation from 1992 to 1994. If one needed evidence against the gradual economic reform that

---

[30] Sergei Tsikora, "Protiv "Utechki' Urozhaya," *Izvestia*, July 17, 1991, p. 1; Sergei Tsikora, "Ukraina: vnov' torgovlya po kuponam," *Izvestia*, July 27, 1991, p. 2.

[31] The dissolution of the Soviet economy in 1991 is described vividly in Yegor Gaidar, *Collapse of an Empire: Lessons for Modern Russia*, trans. Antonina W. Bouis (Washington, DC: Brookings Institution, 2007), chapter 8.

[32] Ukraine's economic problems and policies are detailed in Anders Åslund, *How Ukraine Became a Market Economy and Democracy* (Washington, DC: Peterson Institute for International Economics, 2009), and Oleh Havyrlyshyn, *The Political Economy of Independent Ukraine: Slow Starts, False Starts, and a Last Chance?* (London: Palgrave MacMillan, 2017).

some advocated for Russia, Ukraine was producing plenty of it, as inflation spiraled up, GDP shrank, and poverty increased. In 1993, the *Economist* wrote: "Rarely can misguided policies and mismanagement have led so quickly to a country's collapse."[33]

This early episode illustrated an enduring pattern. Ukraine and Russia recognized the need for economic coordination, but completely disagreed on how to achieve it. Ukraine resisted the creation of central institutions, or insisted at a minimum that such institutions not be controlled by Russia. Russia sought central institutions, and because its economy was by far the largest, insisted that it control them.

The Black Sea Fleet, Sevastopol, and Crimea

Crimea has a complex history, different elements of which support different contentions about who should control it today.[34] The peninsula has been essential to control of the Black Sea, with commercial and military significance dating back to the ancient Greeks. Long controlled by the Crimean Khanate, it was seized by the Russian empire in 1783, and its lands were distributed to Russian nobles, beginning a process in which the Russian population of the peninsula grew. Germany occupied the territory during World War II, and Sevastopol was labeled a "Hero City" by the Soviets. After the war, Stalin deported much of the Crimean Tatar population for its alleged collaboration with Germany during the occupation. This led to people officially identified as Russians becoming a majority. In 1954, Soviet leader Nikita Khrushchev transferred the territory from Russia to Ukraine, ostensibly to mark the 300th anniversary of Russian-Ukrainian "reunification," but more likely to win support from Ukrainian leaders in the ongoing post-Stalin succession battle in Moscow.[35]

As complicated as it is, Crimea's history is typical of the region. Territories passed among multiple states and populations changed dramatically through war, famine, and repression. As Elizabeth Wood stresses, the "imagined geography" of Crimea is as important as the actual geography.[36] For a variety of reasons, the post-Soviet Russian elite

---

[33] "Warnings from Massandra," *The Economist*, September 11, 1993, p. 52.

[34] See Paul R. Magosci, *This Blessed Land: Crimea and the Crimean Tatars* (Toronto: University of Toronto Press, 2014).

[35] The 1954 decision is examined in depth by Mark Kramer, "Why Did Russia Give Away Crimea Sixty Years Ago," Cold War International History Project e-Dossier No. 47, March 19, 2014.

[36] Elizabeth A. Wood, "Introduction," in Elizabeth A. Wood, William E. Pomeranz, E. Wayne Merry, and Maxim Trudolyubov, *Roots of Russia's War in Ukraine* (Washington, DC: Woodrow Wilson Center Press, 2016), pp. 3–6.

put immense stress on the need to recover Crimea. As Fyodor Lukyanov wrote in 2016, "Russians had always viewed Crimea as the most humiliating loss of all the territories left outside of Russia after the disintegration of the Soviet Union."[37]

In Crimea, Ukraine faced two connected problems. One was Russia's claims on Crimea, Sevastopol, and the Black Sea Fleet. The second was an internal Crimean move (encouraged by some in Russia) toward separatism.[38] While Russia in principle accepted Ukraine's claim to military assets on its territory,[39] it had two reservations: nuclear weapons (discussed below) and the Black Sea Fleet. The agreement forming the CIS in December 1991 had stated that the fleet would be part of the CIS military, but since there was to be no CIS military, that solution would not work.

Even many Russian liberals who accepted Ukraine's independence believed that Crimea, Sevastopol, and the Black Sea Fleet were Russian. Sevastopol was viewed as having "all-Union status" as a military city, and as therefore belonging to the Soviet Union's successor state, Russia. Similarly, the Black Sea Fleet was viewed as inherently Russian, and legally as part of the central Soviet assets that should revert to Russia. From this perspective, the deal struck at Belavezha, in which Ukraine gained independence with no resolution of these questions, represented both a blunder by Yeltsin and a deception by Kravchuk. Thus, in January 1992, Mayor Anatoly Sobchak of St. Petersburg, generally seen as pro-western and moderate, stated that "the Black Sea fleet was created centuries ago, and even a Communist Party hack [Kravchuk] can't change all that in a day." Yeltsin agreed: "The Black Sea fleet was, is and will be Russia's. No one, not even Kravchuk will take it away from Russia."[40] The question of the fleet itself was less important than that of the ownership of the base in Sevastopol and, by extension, Ukraine's

---

[37] Fyodor Lukyanov, "Putin's Foreign Policy: The Quest to Restore Russia's Rightful Place," *Foreign Affairs* 95, 3 (May/June 2016): 35.

[38] See Taras Kuzio, *Ukraine-Crimea-Russia* (Stuttgart: ibidem-Verlag, 2007); and Gwendoly Sasse, *The Crimea Question: Identity, Transition, and Conflict* (Cambridge, MA: Harvard University Press, 2014).

[39] An alternative principle, which Ukraine sought to invoke regarding the Black Sea Fleet, was that the military assets of the Soviet Union were the collective property of *all* of the successors, such that Ukraine should have received a proportional share of the *entire* Soviet navy, not just the Black Sea Fleet. This would have led to a far greater payout than it eventually received. Roman Wolczuk, *Ukraine's Foreign and Security Policy 1991–2000* (London: RoutledgeCurzon, 2003), p. 36.

[40] Sobchak and Yeltsin were quoted in John Rettie and James Meek, "Battle for Soviet Navy," *The Guardian*, January 10, 1992, p. 1. On the role of Sevastopol in Russian historical thinking, see Serhii Plokhy, "The City of Glory: Sevastopol in Russian Historical Mythology," *Journal of Contemporary History* 35, 3 (July 2000): 369–383.

sovereignty over Crimea, a point stressed by Sobchak.[41] Even the pro-western foreign minister, Andrei Kozyrev, said "Sevastopol was Russia's naval base and it must remain as such."[42] Thus, the base from which the annexation of Crimea was launched in 2014 was already a source of acrimony in January 1992.

The battle intensified in May 1992, when the Russian Congress of People's Deputies passed a resolution rejecting the legality of the 1954 transfer of Crimea to Ukraine. Ukrainian Foreign Minister Zlenko warned his own parliament that adopting "inflammatory resolutions ... would be precisely what the most conservative circles in Russia's political spectrum are trying to incite us to do." Instead, Ukraine's parliament declared the Russian statement to have no "legal consequences" and resolved "to proceed from the premise that the question of the status and fate of Crimea as a constituent part of Ukraine cannot be the subject of negotiations between states."[43] The back and forth over the Fleet and its base carried on until the 1997 Friendship Treaty, and was a constant reminder to Ukraine of what Kravchuk called Russia's "imperial disease."[44]

In January 1992, an initial agreement was reached in which Ukraine would receive 30 percent of the fleet, but that deal did not address basing rights, and was never implemented.[45] On April 5, Kravchuk issued a decree "On Urgent Measures Necessary for the Creation of Military Forces of Ukraine," ordering a Ukrainian navy to be built from assets of the Black Sea Fleet. Yeltsin responded two days later with "On the Transfer of the Black Sea Fleet to the Russian Federation." The next day, Ukraine's Defense Minister Kostyantyn Morozov produced "On the Formation of the Ukrainian Navy." On April 9, Kravchuk and Yeltsin spoke by phone and agreed to stop the "war of decrees."[46]

A second attempt to resolve the dispute was made at a summit meeting in Dagomys in June 1992. The two sides agreed that the fleet would

---

[41] Sobchak advocated "to resolve the problem of Sevastopol and the fleet together with the problem of Crimea." Maksym Yusin, "Protivostoyanie Rossii i Ukrainy prinimaet opasnyi oborot," *Izvestiya*, January 9, 1992, p. 5.

[42] Interfax, December 7, 1993, quoted in Fiona Hill and Pamela Jewitt, "'Back in the USSR': Russia's Intervention in the Internal Affairs of the Former Soviet Republics and the Implications for United States Policy Toward Russia," John F. Kennedy School of Government, Harvard University, 1994, p. 85.

[43] Sergey Tsikora, "Prezident L. Kravchuk: Ukraina Prilagayet Usiliya dlya Snizheniya Politicheskogo Napryazheniya s Rossiyey," *Izvestiya*, June 3, 1992, p. 1.

[44] Roman Solchanyk, "Russia, Ukraine, and the Imperial Legacy," *Post-Soviet Affairs* 9, 4 (October–December 1993): 337–365; Maria Drohobycky, ed., *Crimea: Dynamics, Challenges, and Prospects* (Lanham, MD: Rowman & Littlefield, 1995).

[45] Wolczuk, *Ukraine's Foreign and Security Policy*, p. 29.   [46] Ibid., pp. 29, 183.

remain under CIS control until it could be split, and that the "strategic" portion of the fleet (which ambiguously referred to ships capable of carrying nuclear weapons) would remain with Russia.[47] While both Kravchuk and Yeltsin made upbeat statements, almost all of the difficult issues were deferred.

In August 1992, the two sides agreed to split the fleet fifty/fifty, but remained at an impasse over the question of shore-based infrastructure. The ships were less important than the question of who owned Crimea. At a summit in Moscow in June 1993, the fifty/fifty split was reaffirmed and the leasing of shore facilities to Russia was broached. The leasing option was a compromise in that it would allow the Russian military to remain while acknowledging Ukrainian ownership, and it would defer the hardest questions into the future.

Ukraine's bargaining position was rapidly being undermined by economic collapse, and in particular by its inability to pay for the energy it was receiving from Russia. In February 1993, Russia threatened to cut gas deliveries to Ukraine and made it clear that further concessionary gas sales were contingent upon Ukrainian concessions elsewhere. Ukrainian Prime Minister Leonid Kuchma, generally considered more pro-Russian than Kravchuk, said: "Russia is trying to bring about a full paralysis of the Ukrainian economy ... I cannot understand the Russian position. It is not motivated by economics. It can only be seen as some sort of pressure on Ukraine. But Russia must realize that to return to the former Soviet Union is neither technically nor politically possible."[48]

In September, Presidents Kravchuk and Yeltsin met at Masandra, in Crimea, to work on a range of issues, the most prominent of which were the status of Sevastopol and the Black Sea Fleet, the disposition of Ukraine's nuclear arsenal, and Ukraine's gas debt.[49] The week before the summit began, Russia cut gas shipments to Ukraine by 25 percent, citing Ukraine's unpaid bills. The Russian delegation then proposed canceling the debt in exchange for Ukraine ceding the Black Sea Fleet and the base in Sevastopol and surrendering its nuclear warheads. The alternatives, Ukraine was told, were to pay its energy debt or have its gas

---

[47] Christina Lapychak, "Russia and Ukraine Begin to Close Rifts," *Christian Science Monitor*, June 25, 1992.

[48] *Financial Times*, February 19, 1993, quoted in Fiona Hill and Pamela Jewett, "'Back in the USSR': Russia's Intervention in the Internal Affairs of the Former Soviet Republics and the Implications for United States Policy toward Russia," Strengthening Democratic Institutions Project, John F. Kennedy School of Government, Harvard University, January 1994, p. 75.

[49] The discussion of the Masandra summit is based on Paul D'Anieri, *Economic Interdependence in Russian Ukrainian Relations* (Albany: State University of New York Press, 1999), chapter 4.

supply cut.[50] Ukrainian diplomats complained of "economic diktat," and indeed their options were limited. Kravchuk complied, explaining: "We had to act on the basis of realism. Suppose we had slammed the door and left. The gas would have been turned off and there would have been nothing else left to do."[51] The parliament's speaker, Oleksandr Moroz, was equally realistic: "The danger is not having a Russian base on [our] territory, it is having bad relations with Russia."[52] The Ukrainian parliament, however, rejected this position. Even those who supported close relations with Russia objected to the coercion Russia had applied. Kravchuk was forced to backtrack from the agreement, claiming (untruthfully, it appeared) that the agreement had been discussed but not signed. In any event, he said, such an agreement required parliamentary ratification, which was clearly impossible.

The Masandra episode heightened the sense even among pro-Russian Ukrainian elites that Russia was a threat. The Rada and the Ukrainian government became much more assertive on both the Black Sea Fleet and on Ukraine's nuclear weapons. Both issues remained unresolved, as did the question of how Ukraine would pay for the energy it consumed. Ukraine endured shortages of gas through the winter of 1993–1994, requiring the closing of many industries and the shutoff of heating in many public buildings. The reduction of supplies, accompanied by threats of further cuts and demand for payment, became a recurring feature in Ukrainian-Russian relations.

The second problem in Crimea was that of secessionist movements, which emerged in 1992 and again in 1994 (see Chapter 3).[53] As Ukraine pressed for independence in 1990–1991, local Communist Party leaders in Crimea raised the specter of seceding and joining Russia. In January 1991, they held a referendum supporting the status of autonomous republic within the USSR. Kravchuk, at that time the Chair of the Ukrainian Supreme Soviet, supported Crimean autonomy, arguing later that the only alternative was that the Crimean leaders would successfully petition the USSR Supreme Soviet to reverse the 1954 transfer of Crimea to Ukraine. The Rada responded by granting Crimea autonomy within

[50] "Kravchuk News Conference, 6 September 1993," translated in FBIS-SOV-93-171, September 7, 1993, p. 72. Boris Yeltsin, interview on Russian Television Network, September 4, 1993, translated in FBIS-SOV-93-171, September 7, 1993, p. 7.
[51] Reuters, September 6, 1993, quoted in John Morrison, "Pereyaslav and After: The Russian-Ukrainian Relationship," *International Affairs* 69, 4 (October 1993): 695.
[52] Agence France Press, September 3, 1993, translated in FBIS-SOV-93-171, September 7, 1993, p. 61.
[53] Events in 1991–1992 are chronicled in detail in Kuzio, *Ukraine-Crimea-Russia*, pp. 122–128, on which this paragraph draws.

Ukraine. Once Ukraine became independent and the Soviet government ceased to exist, Crimea became an internal Ukrainian issue, at least in theory. The leadership in Crimea, which remained unchanged after independence, was dominated by communist hardliners. In May 1992 Crimea's parliament declared Crimean sovereignty. In response, some wanted the Ukrainian government to dissolve the Crimean parliament and charge its leaders with treason, but Kravchuk negotiated instead. The crisis was resolved, as the Verkhovna Rada passed a law broadening Crimea's autonomy and, in return, the Crimean parliament reversed its sovereignty declaration.[54] From then until early 1994, talk of secession quieted down.

The Emergence of Energy Politics

The Masandra summit brought to the fore the use of energy as a weapon. The "gas wars," which have had several iterations, are a good example of how the same issue is seen dramatically differently on different sides.[55] By providing Ukraine gas at below-market prices, Russia was hugely subsidizing the Ukrainian economy. If Ukraine and Russia were somehow linked together politically, this might make sense, but the more Ukraine insisted on its complete independence, the more Russian leaders wondered why they should be subsidizing it. To Ukraine, and to some observers, Russia's policies appeared designed to undermine Ukraine's independence.

While the threat of gas cuts prompted a search for alternate suppliers, no one else would supply energy on the concessionary terms that Russia provided, leaving aside the logistical problems involved in changing suppliers. Reform of the domestic energy sector, including moving to market prices, would have reduced consumption and brought the government more revenue to pay Russia, but there were two obstacles to doing so. First, a move to market prices would impoverish many

[54] Crimea's autonomy is discussed in detail in Gwendoly Sasse, "Constitution-Making 'from Above': Crimea's Regional Autonomy," in Teofil Kis and Irena Makaryk, eds., *Toward a New Ukraine II: Meeting the New Century* (Ottawa: University of Ottawa Press, 1999), pp. 83–102.

[55] The literature on energy politics in the region is immense. For overviews focused on Ukraine and Russia, see Margarita M. Balmaceda, *Politics of Energy Dependency: Ukraine, Belarus, and Lithuania between Domestic Oligarchs and Russian Pressure* (Toronto: University of Toronto Press, 2015); Margarita M. Balmaceda, *Energy Dependency, Politics and Corruption in the Former Soviet Union: Russia's Power, Oligarchs' Profits and Ukraine's Missing Energy Policy* (London: Routledge, 2008); R. Newnham, "Oil, Carrots, and Sticks: Russia's Energy Resources as a Foreign Policy Tool," *Journal of Eurasian Studies* 2, 2 (2011): 134–143; A. N. Stulberg, *Well-Oiled Diplomacy: Strategic Manipulation and Russia's Energy Statecraft in Eurasia* (Albany: State University of New York Press, 2007); and D'Anieri, *Economic Interdependence in Ukrainian-Russian Relations*, chapter 4.

individuals and firms. Second, it would remove a massive source of rents. It is an exaggeration, but not a huge one, to say that Ukrainian politics since independence has largely been about who would control the gas trade and reap the (corrupt) benefits that came with it. Market prices would have ended that gravy train.

Poland: The Dog that Didn't Bark

Ukraine's relations with Poland appeared to play a minor role in this period. This was a considerable success for moderates in both states, and presented a stark contrast to how Ukraine's relations with Russia developed. As with Russia, Ukraine had a fraught historical relationship and a potential territorial conflict with Poland. From the early modern period at least through World War II, Ukrainian nationalism was defined as much in antagonism to Poland as to Russia. The western part of Ukraine was part of the Austrian empire before World War I and then of Poland between the world wars. During World War II the Ukrainian Insurgent Army (UPA) massacred thousands of Poles in the Volhynia and Galicia regions, and after World War II Ukrainians living in Polish border regions were forcibly resettled elsewhere in Poland. In sum, there were ample grounds for resentment and ammunition for those who wanted to claim that borders should be redrawn.

However, Polish and Ukrainian leaders moved quickly toward reconciliation after 1991, signing a "Treaty of Good Neighborship, Friendly Relations and Cooperation" in May 1992 (Poland signed a similar agreement with Russia a few days later). In particular, Poland made clear that it would not make any claims on Ukrainian territory. Efforts were made to promote reconciliation, one important example of which was the renovation of a section of Lviv's Lichakiv Cemetery, neglected under the Soviets, where 3,000 Polish soldiers killed in the Polish-Ukrainian war of 1920 were buried.

Ukraine's Domestic Political Instability

Apart from the euphoria of independence, Ukraine was undergoing a wrenching transformation, characterized as a "quadruple" transition, as it sought to build a state (government), a nation (political community), a market economy, and democracy.[56] Like Russia, Ukraine was operating

---

[56] See Alexander Motyl, *Dilemmas of Independence: Ukraine after Totalitarianism* (New York: Council on Foreign Relations, 1993); and Taras Kuzio, "Transition in Post-Communist States: Triple or Quadruple," *Politics* 21, 3 (2001): 168–177.

under an amended version of a Soviet-era constitution and, like Russia, its parliament had not been reelected since the end of communism. Many deputies representing agriculture and industry opposed economic reform, but in contrast to Russia, there was no strong constituency in favor of it.

Economic attitudes among the Ukrainian elite broke down into three groups. The most nationalist group supported breaking economic ties with Russia regardless of the cost, because doing so was seen as essential to establishing independence. A second group supported separating Ukraine's economy from Russia and redirecting trade, but only to the extent and at a pace that would avoid extensive disruption. A third view saw trade with Russia as beneficial. This question, rather than market reforms, drove early debate in Ukraine, with the result that Ukraine, even more than Russia, became stuck between the plan and the market.[57]

In June 1993, 400,000 workers in the Donbas went on strike, supported by many local elites, threatening to halt work in steel mills. The government responded by promising wage increases that it could not afford. While many outside Ukraine saw the sources of economic collapse in economic mismanagement and a complete lack of reform, many of the protesters and elites in eastern Ukraine saw the problem in the fracturing of economic ties with Russia, and sought a rapid reintegration that was anathema to Kravchuk and to nationalists.

The strikes were ended by two concessions. First, Prime Minister Kuchma resigned, and strikers were appeased by his replacement with Yukhym Zviayahilsky, who had run a coal mine in Donbas and had supported the strikes. Second, early presidential and parliamentary elections were set for 1994. This 1993 strike episode is noteworthy in retrospect for two things. First, it included some of the same repertoire of protest tactics that were used in 2004 and 2013, in particular the construction of a tent encampment on Kyiv's Maidan Nezalezhnosti. Second, the resolution of the conflict involved a "pact" between opposing forces. This too was echoed in the deals that resolved the standoff in 2004 and that failed to do so in 2014.

Russia, too, began 1992 completely transformed. Its population was 51.4 percent of that of the Soviet Union; its territory 76 percent. The Communist Party of the Soviet Union, the dominant institution for decades, had been banned. The economy, in transition between plan and market, was shrinking. But not everything had been changed. Like Ukraine, Russia did not hold new "founding elections" for either president or parliament (the Congress of People's Deputies). And while it

---

[57] D'Anieri, *Economic Interdependence in Ukrainian-Russian Relations*, pp. 175–177.

renamed and reorganized the security organs, it did not dissolve them, purge them, or reform them. Already in February 1992, the *Times* of London published an article (the first of many) with the title "Weimar Russia," warning of the dire conditions in the country and the likelihood of a coup against Yeltsin.[58] A year later, Yeltsin advisor Andranik Migranyan stated that "Weimar Russia is no longer a metaphor."[59]

Western Aid: A Missed Opportunity?

The end of communism prompted talk of a new "Marshall Plan," in which massive western aid would support rapid and far-reaching economic reform in Russia. The investment bank Morgan Stanley estimated in January 1992 that reforming the post-Soviet economies collectively would require at least $76 billion per year for at least three years to transform sectors such as energy, infrastructure, agriculture, and food.[60] However, several factors conspired to undermine that hope. First was uncertainty over Yeltsin's staying power in Russia. While he had defeated the coup, many in Russia strongly opposed the "shock therapy" being advocated. In August of 1992, when the IMF committed $1 billion to help stabilize the ruble, the reform plan of Yegor Gaidar was already faltering, and conservatives in the Congress of People's Deputies were already seeking his ouster.[61] Second, there was a significant perception in the United States that with the end of the Cold War, the United States would be able to focus less of its attention overseas. American citizens and politicians hoped for a "peace dividend," through which money freed up from defense spending could be redirected to domestic spending to combat recession. Third, 1992 was a presidential election year. With the economy struggling, and Bush under attack by a Clinton campaign whose mantra was "it's the economy, stupid," it was impossible to muster the support needed to take a really bold and expensive policy.

In March 1992, former president Richard Nixon, who had promoted détente with the Soviet Union, produced a "secret" memo to US leaders,

---

[58] "Weimar Russia," *The Times* (London), February 8, 1992.

[59] Quoted in Mark Frankland, "Bruiser Yeltsin Starts to Rough Up the Enemy Within," *The Observer*, February 21, 1993, p. 16.

[60] David Roche, "The CIS Renewal Plan," Memorandum of Information from the Global Strategy Division, Morgan Stanley, January 27, 1992, cited in Paige Bryan Sullivan, *U.S.-Russia Relations: From Idealism to Realism* (Washington, DC: Center for Strategic and International Studies, 2002). Coincidentally, the $76 billion figure is roughly what the $13 billion committed to the Marshall Plan would have been worth in 1992 dollars.

[61] James M. Goldgeier and Michael McFaul, *Power and Purpose: U.S. Policy toward Russia after the Cold War* (Washington, DC: Brookings Institution Press, 2003), pp. 82–83.

the contents of which were soon leaked to journalists.[62] He warned that the consequences of failure would be that "war could break out in the former Soviet Union as the new despots use force to restore the 'historical borders' of Russia." Bush did not disagree. "Where we might have a difference, is we're living in a time of constrained resources. There isn't a lot of money around. We are spending too much as it already is. So to do the things I would really like to do, I don't have a blank check for all that."[63] In April, he proposed what became the Freedom Support Act, which largely repackaged existing commitments and presumed contributions by allies that had not yet been consulted. One important component of that proposal, a $6 billion stabilization fund, never materialized.[64] Moreover, the Freedom Support Act aid was divided among the fifteen successor states.

In late April, just after Bush announced the Freedom Support Act, Los Angeles exploded into riots, contributing powerfully to the belief that US leaders needed to focus aid efforts domestically, not at Russia. In the *New York Times*, Thomas Friedman wrote:

The Russian aid bill's limbo reflects the ambivalent moment in which American foreign policy finds itself after the cold war. One day officials and lawmakers say the United States is the world's only superpower, and therefore it must lead on issues, such as Russian aid or peacekeeping in Yugoslavia. The next day, though, the same officials and lawmakers say that domestic problems should take precedence, foreign initiatives are too expensive, and therefore Washington cannot afford to lead. In the wake of the Los Angeles riots in particular, the latter mood seems to be dominating.[65]

Nuclear Weapons and the Security Dilemma

Ukraine's 1990 declaration of sovereignty had stated the desire to become a nonnuclear weapons state, and the United States and European states insisted that this was a binding commitment. The 1986 Chernobyl disaster had made denuclearization a popular theme among Ukrainian nationalists, but independence shifted their focus to the problem of national security. Immediately after the coup attempt,

---

[62] Nixon's memo and the fallout are discussed in detail in Bernard Kalb, *The Nixon Memo: Political Respectability, Russia, and the Press* (Chicago, IL: University of Chicago Press, 1994).

[63] Thomas L. Friedman, "Bush Cites Limits on Aid to Russia," *New York Times*, March 11, 1992, p. A1.

[64] Goldgeier and McFaul, *Power and Purpose*, pp. 81–83.

[65] Thomas L. Friedman, "Bill to Aid Former Soviet Lands Is Stuck in Capitol Hill Quagmire," *New York Times*, June 5, 1992, p. A1.

Kravchuk related to reporters his meeting with General Varennikov, one of the putsch leaders, who had flown to Kyiv on August 19, and told Ukrainian leaders that if they did not comply with the "Committee for the State of Emergency" the army would invade. "I realized that I had no one to defend me, [and] sensed that armed people could walk in at any time and take me away."[66]

Within a month, Ukrainians were debating what to do with the nuclear weapons, and the discussion showed the logic of the security dilemma.[67] Voldymyr Filenko, deputy head of the "Narodna Rada" opposition group in the Ukrainian parliament, said: "Most MPs think we cannot just give weapons to Russia. It would upset the balance of power between Russia and Ukraine. We're afraid of Russia, if you like. We're fighting for independence from Russia. We cannot say there's a nuclear threat, but they did recently raise territorial claims." Ivan Plyushch, the deputy speaker of the parliament, asked: "'If we say 'Take them away,' where will they go? To Russia? Why should they?"[68] While the weapons were on Ukrainian territory, and could not be removed without its collaboration, launch control was held by the Russian military. Uncertainty over whether and how quickly Ukraine could gain operational control of the weapons added complexity to the issue.

Kravchuk vacillated. Within a few days in the fall of 1991, he first told the UN General Assembly Ukraine intended to join the NPT as a non-nuclear weapons state and then, after returning to Kyiv, told a press conference that "We are against the transfer of nuclear weapons from one republic to another. The status quo has to be maintained ... We cannot disregard our security interests."[69] It did not help when *Nezavisimaya Gazeta* reported that Yeltsin had discussed with his military advisors the possibility of a nuclear first strike on Ukraine.[70] Thus, in the fall of 1991, prior to the Ukrainian referendum on independence, prior to Kravchuk's election as president, and prior to the meeting that formed the Commonwealth of Independent States, Ukraine and Russia were in a

---

[66] *Robitchnya Hazeta*, September 4, 1991, quoted in Bohdan Nahaylo, "The Shaping of Ukrainian Attitudes towards Nuclear Arms," *RFE/RL Research Report* 2, 8 (February 19, 1993): 23.

[67] The debate from this period is discussed in detail in Nahaylo, "The Shaping of Ukrainian Attitudes," pp. 21–45, and Mariana Budjeryn, "The Power of the NPT: International Norms and Ukraine's Nuclear Disarmament," *The Non-Proliferation Review* 22, 2 (2015): 203–237.

[68] Filenko and Plyushch were quoted in Jonathan Steele, "Ukraine May Backtrack on Nuclear Arms," *The Guardian*, September 30, 1991.

[69] Nahaylo, "The Shaping of Ukrainian Attitudes," p. 27.

[70] Paul Quinn-Judge, "Yeltsin Ruled Out 'Preventive Nuclear Strike' against Ukraine on Technical Grounds: Daily," *Montreal Gazette*, October 25, 1991, p. A2.

security dilemma, with both sides' behavior seen as threatening by the other.

In March 1992, Kravchuk announced the halt of shipments of nuclear warheads to Russia, complaining that it was not clear they were being destroyed (by this time, half the warheads had already been transferred).[71] Nonetheless, from the time the debate emerged in the fall of 1991, to the eventual Trilateral Agreement in early 1994, few Ukrainians advocated that Ukraine should actually keep the weapons and become a nuclear power. Even acknowledging the perceived threats from Russia and Ukraine's right to control the weapons while they remained on Ukrainian territory, nearly the whole range of elite opinion recommended getting rid of them eventually. That left a lot of debate over how fast they should be removed, where the warheads should be taken, what their status should be in the meantime, and what kind of security guarantees and financial compensation Ukraine should receive. The United States was paying Russia through the Cooperative Threat Reduction program for the highly enriched uranium in the warheads (which was then converted into fuel for power generation).[72]

The United States was uninterested in those concerns, and was focused solely on getting Ukraine to surrender its nuclear weapons as fast as possible. Ukraine's hesitation put both the START-I and START-II treaties at risk.[73] The signing of the Lisbon Protocol, in May 1992, appeared to solve the problem. The Protocol added Belarus, Kazakhstan, and Ukraine as signatories to the START-I Treaty, and committed all of them to surrendering their nuclear weapons and joining the Nuclear Nonproliferation Treaty (NPT) as nonnuclear weapons states. At Lisbon, Kravchuk verbally committed to US Secretary of State James Baker that Ukraine would complete its disarmament within seven years.[74] Baker made it clear that US aid would depend on progress on denuclearization.

However, Kravchuk did not have the support of his parliament. In September 1992, Ukraine's prime minister, Vitold Fokin, was replaced by Leonid Kuchma, who had been director of the Yuzhmash

---

[71] Serge Schmemann, "Ukraine Halting A-Arms Shift to Russia," *New York Times*, March 13, 1992.

[72] Budjeryn, "The Power of the NPT." On Ukrainian policy toward nuclear weapons in this period, see Sherman W. Garnett, "The Sources and Conduct of Ukrainian Nuclear Policy," in George Quester, ed., *The Nuclear Challenge in Russia and the New States of Eurasia* (Armonk, NY: M. E. Sharpe, 1995).

[73] For a detailed account of Ukraine's denuclearization by one of the US diplomats deeply involved, see Steven Pifer, *The Trilateral Process: The United States, Ukraine, Russia and Nuclear Weapons* (Washington, DC, Brookings Institution, 2011).

[74] Goldgeier and McFaul, *Power and Purpose*, p. 168.

(Pivden'mash) factory in Dnipropetrovsk, where Soviet Inter-Continental Ballistic Missiles (ICBMs) had been built. Kuchma put Yuriy Kostenko, who was among those skeptical about disarmament, in charge of nuclear weapons policy, even as Defense Minister Kostyantyn Morozov stressed in December 1992 that "the declaration of Ukraine as a nuclear state has no realistic basis and does not correspond with the current economic potential and strategic interests of our state."[75] Kuchma was inclined to be pragmatic, focusing on the compensation:

We removed the tactical nuclear weapons and what happened? Russia got a contract to supply the United States with nuclear fuel. Where is at least a minimal program of aid similar to Russia's? Our people are not fools ... What does Ukraine get in return? I am for ratification, but if we go to parliament with nothing it will be a fiasco, both for me and for the president.[76]

Similarly, after Russian Defense Minister Pavel Grachev warned in early 1993 that Ukraine's possession of the weapons could lead to a "second Chernobyl," Ukraine's Foreign Ministry responded that "the artificially created clamor over the nuclear weapons on Ukrainian territory is an attempt to extend Russian jurisdiction over these weapons and to deprive Ukraine of its right to compensation for the weapons' components."[77]

On June 3 and 4, 1993, the Rada debated what to do with the weapons.[78] Foreign Minister Zlenko advocated ratifying the START-I treaty and the NPT, pointing out that the alternative was political and economic isolation that Ukraine could not withstand. Prime Minister Kuchma, however, proposed that while Ukraine should ratify START-I, it should retain the weapons that did not have to be surrendered under the treaty and should declare itself a "temporary nuclear power."[79] Kuchma received a standing ovation. At its most extreme, the pro-nuclear position was voiced by Ukrainian General Volodymyr Tolubko,

---

[75] "Buduyemo derzhavu–buduyemo armiyu," *Uryadovyi Kuryer*, December 4, 1992, p. 3.
[76] Quoted in Nahaylo, "The Shaping of Ukrainian Attitudes"; Fred Hiatt, "Russian Legislature Ratifies START Pact; Further Arms Cuts Seen Facing Tougher Road," *Washington Post*, November 5, 1992, p. A3.
[77] Andrey Kamorin, "Ukraina Obinyayet Rossiyu v 'Shantazhye i Zapugivanii'," *Izvestia*, April 2, 1993, p. 3.
[78] The debate in the Rada is excerpted at length in Yuriy Kostenko, *Istoria Yadernoho Rozzbroyennya Ukrainy* (Kyiv: Vydavnytstvo "Yaroslaviv Val," 2015), pp. 251–257. The account in this paragraph is also based on Pavel Felgengauer, "Nuclear Ukraine," *Sevodnya*, June 8, 1993, p. 5, translated in *The Current Digest of the Russian Press*, No. 23, Vol. 45, July 7, 1993, p. 14.
[79] Kuchma's speech is recorded in Kostenko, *Istoria Yadernoho Rozzbroyennya Ukrainy*, pp. 262–264.

whose voice carried weight because his uncle had been commander of the USSR's Strategic Rocket Forces: "Do you know what an idiot is? An idiot is someone who gives up his own nuclear weapons."[80]

Following the Russian parliament's resolution declaring ownership of Sevastopol in July 1993, Kravchuk stopped advocating that the Rada ratify START-I. Russia's coercion at the Masandra summit in September further convinced many Ukrainians that it should retain the weapons at least until it got some kind of security guarantees. Having seen the international community reluctant to acknowledge Ukraine's sovereignty or to give it equal status to Russia, Ukraine adopted a crude realism, insisting that until its sovereignty and equality were recognized, it would keep the weapons. Becoming a nuclear weapons state never had significant support in Kyiv, but frustration over Ukraine's treatment by Russia and the United States convinced many to seek to use the issue to demand greater respect. Kuchma complained: "On the map of world leaders, Ukraine does not even exist. They are indifferent whether Ukraine is independent or not."[81] Steven Pifer, who participated in the negotiations and later served as US Ambassador to Ukraine, wrote that "by focusing so heavily on nuclear weapons in the first two years of its relations with independent Ukraine, Washington failed to create confidence in Kyiv that there would be a robust Ukrainian-American relationship once the nuclear weapons issue was resolved."[82]

The American scholar John Mearsheimer was among the few in the United States who advocated that Ukraine keep its nuclear weapons. "The conventional wisdom about Ukraine's nuclear weapons is wrong. In fact, as soon as it declared independence, Ukraine should have been quietly encouraged to fashion its own nuclear deterrent. Even now, pressing Ukraine to become a nonnuclear state is a mistake."[83] Mearsheimer contended that nuclear weapons were the only way for Ukraine to defend itself against Russia, and that no other state was going to help it. "A war between Russia and Ukraine would be a disaster … The likely result of that war – Russia's reconquest of Ukraine – would injure prospects for peace throughout Europe. It would increase the danger of a Russian-German collision, and sharply intensify the security

---

[80] Tolubko is quoted in Vladimir Nadein, "Amerika-myt'em, Rossiya-katan'em: dva podkhoda k raketno-yadernoy Ukrainye," *Izvestia*, June 15, 1993, p. 4. His views on the issue were laid out in detail in "Turbota Pro Bezpeku Chy Nazad do Falanhy?" *Holos Ukrainy*, November 10, 1992, p. 6 and November 21, 1992, p. 7.

[81] *The Economist*, May 15, 1993.   [82] Pifer, *The Trilateral Process*, p. 3.

[83] John J. Mearsheimer, "The Case for a Ukrainian Nuclear Deterrent," *Foreign Affairs* 72, 3 (Summer 1993): 50.

competition across the continent."[84] Mearsheimer's view never took hold in the United States.

Ukraine was in a particularly tight security dilemma: it could seek to protect its security by pursuing nuclear status, but doing so would cause reactions from the United States and Russia that would themselves endanger Ukraine's security. A Ukrainian colonel also serving in the Rada highlighted the problem: "For today's Iraq, [the Americans] have thought up the term 'potentially aggressive country.' If they look for a comparable definition for us, then our international isolation will be guaranteed."[85] Kravchuk was equally blunt: "Those who have quarreled with Russia have lost."[86]

In the fall of 1993, the United States took over the lead role in negotiating with Ukraine, in part because the collapse of the Masandra deal convinced US leaders that the bilateral Russia-Ukraine format would not produce a deal.[87] Ukraine said it would only surrender the nuclear weapons if the United States guaranteed its security and provided compensation.[88] When the Rada ratified the START-I Treaty in November, it attached numerous conditions that essentially negated ratification, angering US leaders. Yuriy Kostenko pointed to Russia's intervention elsewhere, saying "If there were no nuclear weapons on our territory the Russians would have done what they did in Georgia and Azerbaijan. They cannot push us around like that." "We do not control these weapons but at the same time they protect us. This is the paradox."[89] Foreign Minister Anatoliy Zlenko insisted that the matter could be resolved if "Ukraine's negotiation partners ... draw the proper conclusions" regarding security guarantees and compensation.[90]

In the weeks after the Rada's vote, the deal that became the 1994 Trilateral Agreement between the United States, Russia, and Ukraine was hammered out, first in meetings between the United States and Russia in Moscow, and then in joint meetings in Kyiv. The agreement

---

[84] Ibid., pp. 52–53.
[85] Valeriy Izmalkov, "Yaderna Raketa – Ne Kam'yana Sokyra," *Holos Ukrainy*, December 22, 1992, p. 7.
[86] *RFE/RL Daily Report*, September 23, 1993.
[87] Steven Pifer, *The Eagle and the Trident: U.S.-Ukraine Relations in Turbulent Times* (Washington, DC: Brookings Institution Press, 2017), p. 53. Pifer provides a detailed analysis of the US approach to Ukraine's denuclearization.
[88] Anatoly Zlenko, "The Foreign Policy of Ukraine: Principles of Shaping and Problems of Implementing It," *International Affairs* (Moscow) (January 1994): 14–15.
[89] Andrew Higgins, "Ukrainians Learn to Love Their Bombs; Despite the Chernobyl Legacy, Kiev now Embraces Nuclear Warheads to Guarantee Its Future," *The Independent* (London), November 20, 1993, p. 12.
[90] Dmitrii Zhdannikov, "Anatolii Zlenko raz'yasnyaet prichiny popravok v dogovore SNV-1," *Segodnya*, November 23, 1993, p. 5.

detailed Ukraine's compensation for the nuclear materials being surrendered, which was expected to come to a billion dollars plus seven years' worth of fuel for Ukraine's nuclear reactors. The United States agreed to provide a "security guarantee" using language similar to that in the NPT, but nothing approaching NATO's Article V guarantee, which Ukraine sought. The agreement explicitly stated the equality of Ukraine, Russia, and the United States, and their "respect for the independence, sovereignty, and territorial integrity of each nation." While it was not possible to enforce such a statement, it was extremely important symbolically to Ukraine at the time, because of the perception that Russia and the United States were treating it as an inferior. An immediate injection of $100 million in aid for Ukraine and an arrangement that President Clinton would make a brief stopover in Kyiv on his way to Moscow in January 1994, where the three presidents would sign the agreement, sealed the deal.[91]

Russia, the "Near Abroad," and Ukraine

From the early post-Soviet days, Russia claimed a military role beyond its borders. An early case was in Moldova, on Ukraine's southwestern border. In many respects, the Moldova intervention foreshadowed Russian action in Georgia and later in Crimea and eastern Ukraine. Following Moldovan independence, pro-Russian separatists sought to establish a separate republic in Transnistria.[92] In July 1992, Yeltsin sent General Aleksandr Lebed from Moscow with orders to end the conflict, which he did by deploying an artillery bombardment that defeated the main Moldovan force. The result was the de facto independence of Transnistria and a "frozen" conflict. The Transnistria episode was the most violent of several that occurred very early in the post-Soviet period that led leaders in Ukraine and elsewhere to be skittish about Russian intentions. Russian air support for Abkhaz separatists in Georgia in 1993 raised further concerns. These interventions showed strong signs of fanning rather than quelling the conflicts, and in both cases the result was the de facto partition of states that resisted integration with Russia.

In February 1993, Yeltsin asserted that "the time has come for distinguished international organizations, including the UN, to grant Russia

---

[91] Details in this paragraph are based on Goldgeier and McFaul, *Power and Purpose*, pp. 169–170.

[92] On this conflict, see William H. Hill, *Russia, the Near Abroad, and the West: Lessons from the Moldova-Transnistria Conflict* (Baltimore, MD: Johns Hopkins University Press, 2012).

special powers as a guarantor of peace and stability in the former regions of the USSR."[93] While Yeltsin stressed that reintegration of the CIS countries would happen voluntarily, many of his advisors took a harder line. Sergei Stankevich said: "Henceforth, you will not be dealing now with the ruins of an empire but a Power. The Russian Power has a thousand-year history, legitimate interests and serious traditions of protecting these interests."[94]

More worrying for Ukraine, Russian leaders repeatedly raised the view that Russia's respect for Ukraine's territorial integrity was contingent upon Ukraine's membership in the CIS. The original treaty founding the CIS, which stated respect for each other's borders "in the framework of the commonwealth," implied this contingency. The chairman of the Congress of People's Deputies inter-republican committee said in February 1992 that "the 1990 agreement between the two states to respect each other's borders is no longer valid because it was signed when both were members of a third state, the Soviet Union."[95] In a comment widely circulated at the time, the *Financial Times* newspaper cited unnamed Russian diplomats as telling eastern European countries "not to bother building large embassies in Kiev because within 18 months they will be downgraded to consular sections."[96]

The potential for Russia to reassert itself was demonstrated by Foreign Minister Andrei Kozyrev at a meeting of the Conference on Security and Cooperation in Europe (CSCE) in Stockholm in December 1992. Kozyrev declared the former Soviet Union "a post-imperial space where Russia has to defend its interests by all available means, including military and economic ones." He then demanded an end to United Nations sanctions against Serbia and expressed Slavic solidarity with Serbian nationalists.[97] Kozyrev later returned to the podium to tell the audience that he had only been pretending, but he said: "The text that I read out before is a rather thorough compilation of the demands that are being made by what is by no means the most extreme opposition in Russia."[98]

---

[93] Quoted in Hill and Jewett, "Back in the USSR," p. 1.   [94] Quoted in ibid., p. 5.

[95] *Financial Times*, February 25, 1992, quoted in Hill, *Russia, the Near Abroad, and the West*, p. 69.

[96] Quoted in Chrystia Freeland, "Russia 'Trying to Isolate Ukraine': Campaign Suspected to Bring Kiev Back under Moscow's Hegemony," *Financial Times*, March 17, 1993, p. 2.

[97] *The Independent*, December 15, 1992.

[98] Maksim Yusin, "Shokovaya Terapiya Andreya Kozyreva," *Izvestiya*, December 15, 1992, p. 6. Yusin reported that Kozyrev stressed that he deliberately did not include the demands of the more strident nationalists, such as Baburin and Anpilov, because to do so would have reduced the plausibility of his performance, and that the speech came largely from a draft foreign policy prepared by a leader of the centrist bloc "Civic Union."

Krasnaya Zvezda reported that "Genuine indignation was evoked in the delegations of the CIS. There is even information that someone rushed off to prepare draft appeals to the NATO states for protection."[99] Secretary of State Lawrence Eagleburger said afterwards that Kozyrev's speech gave him "heart palpitations." "It brought home ... that, should reform fail in Russia, we could well be faced with what we heard from Mr. Kozyrev this morning but in a far more serious vein."[100] The same day, Yeltsin replaced Yegor Gaidar, his reformist acting prime minister, with the establishment figure Viktor Chernomyrdin. Speaking to reporters on his flight back to Moscow, Kozyrev made what turned out to be an accurate prediction: "Any attempt by Moscow to depart from the principles of peaceful association will inevitably lead to our isolation and to confrontation with our neighbors, including the republics of the former USSR. One must not even dream of any new unification or confederation."[101]

Clinton, Yeltsin, and Russian Democracy

The Clinton administration that came to power in January 1993 saw the promotion of democracy as the key to its foreign policy, and was determined to bolster Yeltsin against the emerging "red-brown" (communist-nationalist) coalition. However, a variety of constraints meant that Clinton's policy did not differ dramatically from Bush's. Like Bush, Clinton was focused on reviving a struggling American economy. Like Bush, Clinton found that hope for the success of reform in Russia rested heavily on a single individual, Boris Yeltsin. While Clinton invested considerable personal effort in bolstering Yeltsin, he was not able to provide a massive aid program, which polls showed that the US electorate did not support.[102] Soon, the widening cracks in the edifice of Russian reform raised skepticism within Clinton's team about the likely success of democracy in Russia. This fear, along with the Yugoslavia conflict, drove the search for contingency plans.

Clinton introduced a new package of support for Russia at the Vancouver summit in April 1993. He had explained his "Strategic Alliance with Russian Reform" a few days earlier in Annapolis.

---

[99] Alexandr Golts, "Seans 'Shokovoi Diplomatii' v Stokgolme," *Krasnaya Zvezda*, December 16, 1992.

[100] Norman Kempster, "Just Kidding, Russian Says, after Cold War Blast Stuns Europeans," *Los Angeles Times*, December 15, 1992.

[101] Quoted in Yusin, "Shokovaya Terapiya Andreya Kozyreva."

[102] Thomas L. Friedman, "Summit in Vancouver: Clinton Presents Billion to Yeltsin in US Aid Package," *New York Times*, April 4, 1993.

[U]ltimately, the history of Russia will be written by Russians and the future of Russia must be charted by Russians. But I would argue that we must – that we must – do what we can and we must act now. Not out of charity but because it is a wise investment – a wise investment building on what has already been done and looking to our own future. While our efforts will entail new costs, we can reap even larger dividends for our safety and our prosperity if we act now.[103]

Clinton's urgency was fed by the tenuousness of Yeltsin's position. Russian politics and Russian-United States relations were increasingly dominated in 1993 by Boris Yeltsin's struggle for survival against conservative politicians who had opposed Gorbachev's reforms and now opposed Yeltsin's as well. Yeltsin had narrowly averted a vote by the Congress of People's Deputies to impeach him, and there were fears that a coup might be attempted while he was at the Vancouver summit. Accordingly Yeltsin was "seen off by the country's military leadership in a signal that they would insure that no one would try to topple the Russian leader while he was gone."[104]

Clinton's proposed aid program was ambitious in scope, aiming at institutions across Russian government and society. The funding that resulted, however, was less ambitious. A total of $2.5 billion was allocated for fiscal year 1994, but it was one-time money, and was for the entire "Newly Independent States" (NIS). The sum for Russia was about $1.6 billion, roughly half of which was for transfers of US food. That was the high-water mark: in 1995, the total package for the NIS was under a billion dollars, $379 million of which went to Russia; and in 1996 US bilateral aid to Russia was $100 million.[105] Clinton might have wished to do more, but his top priority was to get a domestic economic stimulus package through Congress, and he was told that a larger aid package to Russia would compete with that.[106] Russian Vice President Rutskoy ridiculed the aid, saying that it came out to less than $11 for each Russian, "less than the price of a bottle of whiskey," and pointing out that the comparable figure for Israel was $700.[107] Ruslan Khasbulatov, speaker of the Congress of People's Deputies, criticized the United States for "rushing to support ill-considered steps by one of the sides in Russia," and stating that "If as a result, blood is shed, then some

---

[103] President Bill Clinton, "A Strategic Alliance with Russian Reform," April 1, 1993, in *US Department of State Dispatch*, Vol. 4, No. 14 (April 5, 1993). For a discussion, see Goldgeier and McFaul, *Power and Purpose*, pp. 90–92.

[104] Friedman, "Summit in Vancouver."

[105] Goldgeier and McFaul, *Power and Purpose*, pp. 94, 111.   [106] Ibid., p. 99.

[107] Juliet O'Neill, "U.S. Help Ridiculed as '3 Cans of Coke'," *Vancouver Sun*, April 7, 1993, p. A1. The $700 figure for Israel had been noted by Senator Patrick Leahy in the runup to the summit. See Jonathan Steele, "Russian View: Scepticism Grows on Western Aid," *The Guardian*, April 2, 1993, p. 10.

responsibility for this would lie with the West."[108] At the same time, both Belarusian and Ukrainian leaders urged that aid be distributed more evenly, pointing out that aid to Russia did not help them.[109]

While the substantive disagreements between the parliament and Yeltsin focused on economic issues and institutional prerogatives, the status of Ukraine was also at stake. On July 9, the Supreme Soviet passed a resolution "to confirm the Russian federal status of the city of Sevastopol in the administrative and territorial boundaries of the city district as of December 1991." The measure directed the Supreme Soviet's Constitution Committee to draw up appropriate amendments to recognize Sevastopol as a part of Russia.[110] Ukraine requested that the issue be taken up by the UN Security Council, but the Russian Foreign Ministry issued a statement stating: "The foreign policy of Russia is made by the president, whose position in relation to Sevastopol is well-known ... The Russian leadership did not assert any territorial pretensions on Ukraine."[111] Western leaders accepted the argument that since Yeltsin's government had disclaimed the resolution, there was no issue to deal with. It was clear, however, where the majority in the Russian parliament stood.

After a few more rounds of escalation, including Yeltsin trying to fire Vice President Rutskoy, who supported the conservatives, and the parliament rejecting this move, Yeltsin sought to resolve the impasse decisively. On September 21, in contravention of the constitution, Yeltsin announced the disbanding of the parliament and declared that a referendum on a new constitution would be held in December along with the election of the new lower house of parliament (the Duma) envisioned in that new constitution.

Russia came to the brink of civil war. Supporters of the parliament barricaded themselves inside the building – the same building where Yeltsin had made his triumphant stand against the coup in 1991. On October 4, the Russian military shelled the parliament and then cleared it of the opposition. In order to "save" democracy in Russia, Yeltsin had forcibly disbanded an elected parliament.

---

[108] Seamus Martin, "US to Aid Russian Soldiers: The US Is Likely to Grant 'Most Favoured Nation' Trade Status to Russia," *The Irish Times*, April 3, 1993, p. 8.

[109] Andrey Kamorin, "Ukraina i Belarus' prizyvayut k boleye proportsional'nomu raspredeleniyu zapadnoy pomoshchi," *Izvestiya*, April 21, 1993, pp. 1, 3.

[110] "Postanovlenie Verkhovnogo Soveta Rossiiskoi Federatsii O Statusie Goroda Sevastopolia," July 9, 1993.

[111] Maksym Yusin, "Ukraina tebuyet srochnogo sozyva Soveta Bezopasnosti OON po Sevastopolyu," *Izvestiya*, July 21, 1993, p. 1.

The United States and other western governments were in a quandary. They saw Yeltsin as the only hope for democracy and reform in Russia, but hesitated to endorse the violence and violation of the constitution needed to resolve the situation. Ultimately, however, they firmly supported Yeltsin, leading some in Russia to react bitterly against what they saw as the West's hypocrisy.[112] The October incident sharply underlined that while democracy was popular in Russia, market reforms and the loss of territory were not. If democracy prevailed, economic reform and acceptance of Russia's reduced role might not.

The constitution that Yeltsin's team drafted placed immense powers in the hands of the president at the expense of parliament, which had the immediate effect of disempowering the hardliners. Scholars came to call this model "superpresidential," and in terms of powers vis-à-vis other institutions, the Russian president is one of the most powerful in the world.[113] While the defeat of Russian conservatives and the concentration of power in the hands of the reformist president looked to many like the best possible outcome at the time, the 1993 constitution paved the way for the autocracy that was to follow.

The shock of October was not the last one in Russia for 1993. The parliamentary elections for the new Duma empowered the red-browns at the expense of reformers and "westernizers." The largest share of votes (23 percent) went to the Liberal Democratic Party of Vladimir Zhirinovsky, a populist nationalist who opposed economic reform and supported Russian expansion. Yeltsin's "Russia's Choice" party finished second, with 16 percent, but not far behind was the Communist Party with 12 percent. The pro-reform Yabloko party received just 8 percent. This was a further wakeup call to those outside of Russia that reform and democracy might not succeed there, and that a very different kind of leadership might come to power.

---

[112] See, for example, Vadim Belotserkovsky, "Zapad i Yeltsin: Itak, demokratiya ne dlya Rossii" ["The West and Yeltsin: So, Democracy Is Not for Russia"], *Nezavisimaya Gazeta*, September 28, 1993, p. 5.

[113] On "superpresidentialism" in Russia, see Timothy J. Colton, "Superpresidentialism and Russia's Backward State," *Post-Soviet Affairs* 11, 2 (1995): 144–148; M. Steven Fish, "The Executive Deception: Superpresidentialism and the Degradation of Russian Politics," in Valerie Sperling, ed., *Building the Russian State* (Boulder, CO: Westview Press, 2000); M. Steven Fish, *Democracy Derailed in Russia* (New York: Cambridge University Press, 2005), chapter 7; Zoltan Barany, "Superpresidentialism and the Military: The Russian Variant," *Presidential Studies Quarterly* 38, 1 (March 2008): 14–38; and Eugene Huskey, *Presidential Power in Russia* (Armonk, NY: M. E. Sharpe, 1999).

In the West, the uncertainty over what might happen in Russia led to three different reactions. One was to increase rhetorical support for Yeltsin and his reforms. For all Yeltsin's weaknesses, he appeared to be the best hope for political reform and for good relations between Russia and the West. A second policy, which contradicted the first, was to reduce financial support, since internal support for reform in Russia was flagging. A third, which fit with either of the first two, was to hedge the West's bets internationally. It was in this context – along with the wars in Yugoslavia and Chechnya – that the discussion of NATO expansion was fated to take place.

The Prehistory of NATO Expansion

The idea of expanding NATO membership emerged almost immediately following the collapse of the Berlin Wall, as did the idea of disbanding NATO altogether. By late 1990, all of Hungary's major parties had abandoned the idea of pursuing neutrality after leaving the Warsaw Pact, and had adopted the goal of NATO membership. NATO leaders were discouraging such thinking, but it was already causing concern in Moscow.[114] In early 1991, Czechoslovak president Vaclav Havel cited insecurity as the reason to expand western institutions: "It is in the West's own interest to seek the integration of Eastern and Central Europe into the family of European democracy because otherwise it risks creating a zone of hopelessness, instability and chaos, which would threaten Western Europe every bit as much as the Warsaw Pact tank divisions of old."[115] Looking back, William H. Hill wrote that "Fears concerning the security and stability of the former Warsaw Pact states were certainly not without justification, given their history between the two world wars."[116] Russia preferred and expected that a pan-European institution such as the Conference (later Organization) on Security and Cooperation in Europe (CSCE) would play this role, but that did not happen, largely because it lacked the consensus that was possible in NATO.[117]

The central question later was whether a commitment was made concerning NATO expansion at the time of discussions about German reunification in early 1990. From the historical record, which is still

---

[114] F. Lukyanov, "Vstupit li Vengriya v NATO? Novyi etap otnoshenii," *Izvestia*, November 26, 1990, p. 5.

[115] Quoted in *The Independent*, March 21, 1991, p. 11.

[116] William H. Hill, *No Place for Russia: European Security Institutions since 1989* (New York: Columbia University Press, 2018), p. 4.

[117] Ibid., p. 8.

emerging,[118] we can conclude four things about this early period. First, Soviet leaders strongly objected to a reunified Germany becoming a NATO member.[119] When Gorbachev finally acquiesced, it was not because he agreed, but because he could not stop it.[120]

Second, various verbal assurances were given to Soviet leaders, but they were focused on East Germany, and were vague. The Warsaw Pact still existed and Gorbachev imagined transforming it, not dissolving it, even suggesting that united Germany should be a member of both NATO and the Warsaw Pact.[121] When NATO Secretary General Manfred Woerner said in May 1990 that "The very fact that we are ready not to deploy NATO troops beyond the territory of the Federal Republic gives the Soviet Union firm security guarantees," he was clearly speaking about eastern Germany, but this phrase was later seen as a broad and binding commitment.[122]

Third, no written commitment was made about anything other than eastern Germany. The "Two plus Four" treaty signed in September 1990 contained timetables both for the reduction in size of the German military and for the withdrawal of Soviet forces from East Germany. Article 6 then states: "The right of the united Germany to belong to alliances, with all the rights and responsibilities arising therefrom, shall not be affected by the present Treaty."[123] A commentary in *Pravda* at the

---

[118] For detailed analyses, see Steven Pifer, "Did NATO Promise Not to Enlarge? Gorbachev Says 'No'," Brookings Institution, November 2014; and Mark Kramer, "The Myth of a No-NATO-Enlargement Pledge to Russia," *The Washington Quarterly*, April 2009, pp. 39–61, which delves into the archival record. An update to the archival record is provided by "NATO Expansion, What Gorbachev Heard," National Security Archive, December 12, 2017. Appended are thirty documents detailing discussions at the time.

[119] See the detailed discussion in Garthoff, *The Great Transition*, pp. 416–417. Garthoff quotes the instructions given to the Soviet delegation negotiating the issue: "Emphasize that for us the inclusion of a future Germany in NATO is unacceptable – politically and psychologically. We cannot agree to what would in that case inevitably be a destruction of the balance of power and stability in Europe."

[120] The decisive signal came at a summit in Washington, DC, May 31–June 3, 1990, in which Bush showed Gorbachev his prepared remarks for the press conference, which stated that he and Gorbachev were "in full agreement that the matter of alliance membership is ... a matter for the Germans to decide," and Gorbachev did not object (Garthoff, *The Great Transition*, p. 427).

[121] Kramer, "The Myth of a No-NATO-Enlargement Pledge to Russia," p. 42; "NATO Expansion: What Gorbachev Heard." Only after Gorbachev had acquiesced to reunified Germany remaining a NATO member did Hungarian leader Jozef Antall call for the dissolution of the Warsaw Pact on June 6, 1990 (*New York Times*, June 7, 1990).

[122] "The Atlantic Alliance and European Security in the 1990s," Address by Secretary General, Manfred Woerner to the Bremer Tabaks Collegium, May 17, 1990.

[123] *Treaty on the Final Settlement with Respect to Germany*, September 12, 1990.

time shows that it was understood clearly that Gorbachev had agreed to a unified Germany in NATO, and that there was an understanding that NATO forces would not be deployed to the former East Germany, but no mention is made of any commitment on further NATO expansion.[124]

A Russian commentator at the time speculated about NATO enlargement, and pointed to the security dilemma that might drive it:

Today, having begun the withdrawal of our troops, we are abandoning the idea of a "forward defense" of the USSR in Central Europe. But this will not lead to a loss of strategic depth in defending our state if NATO remains within its current borders, and if the East European states become truly independent, prosperous and sufficiently strong to keep from becoming a "corridor" for adventurists. On the other hand, weak states, as everyone knows, seek strong protectors. Will we not push them under NATO's wing?[125]

Fourth, Russian leaders, following the collapse of the Soviet Union, believed that in *spirit*, a commitment was made that NATO would not expand eastward. Some western analysts agreed.[126] Therefore, Russia felt later that the *spirit* of the agreement to allow German reunification was later violated. Mikhail Gorbachev spoke to these issues in a 2014 interview:

The topic of "NATO expansion" was not discussed at all, and it wasn't brought up in those years. ... Not a single Eastern European country raised the issue, not even after the Warsaw Pact ceased to exist in 1991. Western leaders didn't bring it up, either. Another issue we brought up was discussed: making sure that NATO's military structures would not advance and that additional armed forces from the alliance would not be deployed on the territory of the then-GDR after German reunification. Baker's statement, [that "NATO will not move one inch further east"] was made in that context ...

The agreement on a final settlement with Germany said that no new military structures would be created in the eastern part of the country; no additional troops would be deployed; no weapons of mass destruction would be placed there. It has been observed all these years ...

The decision for the U.S. and its allies to expand NATO into the east was decisively made in 1993. ... It was definitely a violation of the spirit of the statements and assurances made to us in 1990.[127]

---

[124] Y. Grigoryev, "SSSR-FRG: Posle Vstrechi v Verkha Realism and Trust," *Pravda*, July 19, 1990, p. 6.

[125] S. Rogov, "Na Zapadnom Frontye Bez Peremen," *Izvestia*, September 21, 1990, p. 4.

[126] This point is stressed in "NATO Expansion: What Gorbachev Heard," which quotes Robert Gates, CIA Director at the time, as later saying that "Gorbachev and others were led to believe that [expansion] wouldn't happen."

[127] "Mikhail Gorbachev: I Am against All Walls," *Russia beyond the Headlines*, October 16, 2014.

For our purposes, the point is that the question of NATO and its future was one of competing expectations and contradictory aspirations almost from the very moment that the Berlin Wall came down. Two factors helped create misunderstanding. First, the pace of change at the time was bewildering, making the assumptions underlying key discussions obsolete within weeks. Second, western leaders repeatedly committed to not doing anything to undermine Soviet security. But then and in the future there was fundamental disagreement about what harmed Soviet/Russian security.

Conclusion

Nearly all the issues that plagued relations among Russia, Ukraine, the United States, and Europe emerged by the end of 1993. Opposition to democracy, the market, and the surrender of the Soviet Union's international position helped spur the coup attempt in 1991, and continued to powerfully shape Russian politics. James Goldgeier and Michael McFaul wrote later that "[m]uch of the drama of economic and political reform in Russia was over before the Clinton administration assumed the reins of executive power in Washington."[128]

Similarly:

- The United States and Russia disagreed about Russia's role in the post-Soviet world.
- The institutional basis for Russian autocracy was laid in the disbanding of parliament and imposition of a new superpresidential constitution in 1993.
- In Ukraine as well, the constitution was a loose constraint on political competition, as politicians responded to street protests by scheduling early elections for 1994.
- Ukraine and Russia were already arguing over a range of issues, including the Black Sea Fleet, Sevastopol, and Crimea; the terms on which the two countries would trade; and the terms on which Ukraine would get energy from Russia.
- Hoping to avoid turmoil, Ukraine eschewed reform. The result was a sagging economy and a ground ripe for corruption and oligarchic capitalism to take hold.
- Ukraine's regional diversity was already manifest, both in the presidential election and in regional attitudes toward reform and to Russia.

---

[128] Goldgeier and McFaul, *Power and Purpose*, p. 88.

- It was already clear that there was both an impetus for NATO to take an expanded role and a strong aversion to this in Russia.
- Russia had already intervened militarily beyond its borders in Moldova, Georgia, and Tajikistan.

Three key points emerge from this overview of the emergence of Russian-Ukrainian relations. First, the major issues of the day were emerging simultaneously and influencing one another. While Kravchuk and Kuchma were negotiating with Russia and the West over nuclear weapons and other issues, they were beset by large protests at home and then planning for new elections. While the United States and Russia were trying to convince Ukraine to surrender its nuclear weapons, Russian revanchists were ascendant and making claims on Crimea. While Yeltsin was trying to keep reform afloat in 1992, the United States was in the midst of a recession and a presidential election. While the Clinton administration was putting an aid package together, Yeltsin was under assault from right- and left-wing forces and Clinton was trying to get a stimulus package through Congress. The result was that there was much "negative spillover" across the multiple issues.

Second, the overlap of these issues, and the negative spillover, exacerbated the security dilemma, resulting in negative feedback loops. For example, reform in Russia was having very mixed results. This undermined support for it, which had never been high to begin with, and this in turn undermined US (and broader international) willingness to commit substantial aid. Absence of larger financial support (and the vote of confidence that went with it) further undermined support for the reforms as well as their chances of succeeding. Moreover, all of these things contributed to undermining Yeltsin's popularity and the legitimacy of the political changes he was pursuing.

Another vicious cycle emerged between the United States and Ukraine, concerning denuclearization. The United States pressed Ukraine to denuclearize unconditionally. Ukraine sought to get something in return. This struck the United States as reneging, and it responded by withholding full acknowledgement of Ukraine's sovereignty, which in turn made Ukraine more hesitant to surrender the weapons. The knot was broken at the end of 1993, but in the meantime a great deal of mistrust was generated, and the United States withheld economic aid during a crucial period in which reform stagnated in Ukraine.

A similar negative feedback loop broke out between Ukraine and Russia: the more Ukraine asserted its sovereignty, the more Russia questioned it, and vice versa, making it much harder to solve a whole range of very practical problems such as trade and monetary policy, contributing to the breakdown of trade between the two countries and increasing the perception that they were injuring one another.

Third, competing understandings of the status quo had already emerged. Both the West and Ukraine regarded the territorial changes of 1991 as final. In Russia, some rejected them, while others hedged, proclaiming their acceptance of the new borders while insisting on Russia's "special role" in the region. In contrast, Russian leaders regarded NATO's borders as fixed after German reunification, while western leaders did not.

3   Hope and Hardship, 1994–1999

On January 12, 1994, US President Bill Clinton stopped in Kyiv on his way to Moscow, where he and Leonid Kravchuk would join Russian President Boris Yeltsin to sign the Trilateral Agreement on nuclear weapons. Clinton stated that "Our meeting this evening begins a new era in our relations" and announced that Ukraine had been invited to join NATO's Partnership for Peace (PfP).[1] Earlier that day, before leaving Prague, Clinton had discussed the "Partnership for Peace" at a press conference with the leaders of the Czech Republic, Hungary, Poland, and Slovakia:

While the Partnership is not NATO membership, neither is it a permanent holding room. It changes the entire NATO dialogue so that now the question is no longer whether NATO will take on new members but when and how. It leaves the door open to the best possible outcome for our region, democracy, markets, and security all across a broader Europe, while providing time and preparation to deal with a lesser outcome.[2]

Just as one of the vexing issues of the early post-Soviet era, Ukraine's nuclear weapons, was put to rest, another was launched. Clinton's "no longer whether ... but when" remark committed the United States to NATO expansion. Nor was Clinton wrong when he said that a new era was beginning in United States-Ukrainian relations. Ukraine had moved quickly from being a problem to being a project. The United States would now be involved in Ukraine's security. Ukraine was the first state to formally join the Partnership for Peace, on February 8, 1994.

The events of that day represent two opposite responses to the security dilemma. The decision to expand NATO represented the classic response envisioned by realist international relations theory. The West

---

[1] The President's News Conference with President Leonid Kravchuk of Ukraine in Kiev, January 12, 1994, www.presidency.ucsb.edu/ws/index.php?pid=49843.
[2] The President's News Conference with Visegrad Leaders in Prague, January 12, 1994, www.presidency.ucsb.edu/documents/the-presidents-news-conference-with-visegrad-leaders-prague.

and the recently freed states in central Europe sought to augment their security even though it would likely engender a negative response from Russia. Clinton's reference to a potential "lesser outcome" made it clear that NATO expansion was, in part, a hedge against what might happen in Russia.

Ukraine's denuclearization, in contrast, was a rare response to the security dilemma. Understanding that pursuing security through arms would make others feel less secure, and in turn might make it less secure, Ukraine spurned the weapons. In terms of realist theory, it is irrational for a state to deliberately reduce its military potential, especially when faced with an obvious security threat,[3] but Ukraine was in an unusual position. The nuclear weapons on its territory – ownership was disputed – were making it a target of Russian and US coercion, and its newly won independence was threatened more by isolation than attack.

At another press conference, in Moscow on January 14, Yeltsin made clear that he had a different vision for the Partnership for Peace.

> This concept is a very important step toward building a security system from Vancouver to Vladivostok that excludes the emergence of new demarcation lines or areas of unequal security. We believe that this idea may prove just one of the scenarios for building a new Europe. Just one of those will well impart very specific cooperation in this dimension of cooperation, including the military area. Of course, we will keep track of other collective security structures in Europe, including such time-tested institutions like the United Nations and the CSCE.[4]

Yeltsin repeated here the Russian understanding of Europe's future that Gorbachev had articulated in Strasbourg in 1989 – one undivided and guided largely by organizations – the UN and CSCE – in which Russia wielded a veto. The distinction between Russian and western visions had not changed much in the intervening five years; nor would it in the future.

The final question in that press conference asked Clinton whether Yeltsin supported the recent NATO commitment to using air strikes in Bosnia if the situation there did not improve. Clinton responded: "We've all had our differences over Bosnia, and everybody's got a different idea about it."[5] Yugoslavia was continuing to drive a wedge between the United States and Russia. Their differences became much more heated

---

[3] This case was made by John J. Mearsheimer, "The Case for a Ukrainian Nuclear Deterrent," *Foreign Affairs* 72, 3 (Summer 1993): 50–66.

[4] The President's News Conference with President Boris Yeltsin of Russia in Moscow, January 14, 1994, www.presidency.ucsb.edu/ws/index.php?pid=50021.

[5] Ibid.

a few weeks later when Serbian forces shelled a market in Sarajevo, killing sixty-eight people, heightening the international consensus that something must be done, and intensifying disagreement over what that something should be. By the end of 1999, the conflict over Kosovo would nearly bring NATO and Russian forces to blows at Pristina airport.

The period from 1994 until 1999 was one in which Russia, Ukraine, Europe, and the United States struggled to come to terms with the consequences of the events of 1989–1991. Economic decline continued both in Russia, where "shock therapy" was employed with limited enthusiasm and little success, and in Ukraine, where a "go slow" strategy worked even worse. The 1997–1998 global economic crisis pummeled both economies and extinguished any remaining zeal for reform. In relations between Ukraine and Russia, two contradictory trends emerged. One was represented by Ukraine's ongoing establishment of the institutions of an independent state and by Russia's apparent acceptance of that, symbolized by the signing of a Friendship Treaty between the two states in 1997. The other was the continuing battle over the very same questions, as Russia sought to reassert its influence in the post-Soviet region and to bring Ukraine into its orbit. In many respects, the contradiction mirrored the battle within Russia between Boris Yeltsin and a shrinking group of "westernizers," on one hand, and a large and increasingly resurgent array of conservatives, leftists, and nationalists, on the other. Ukraine began this period by electing a president committed to closer relations with Russia, but he turned toward the West.

These tensions between Ukraine and Russia were linked to increased tensions between Russia and the West. Disagreement over Yugoslavia, Chechnya, NATO expansion, and economic reform increased mistrust. Despite the good intentions of Clinton and Yeltsin, the competing goals of the two states could not be bridged, especially with the series of wedges that emerged to drive them apart, including the wars in Yugoslavia and Chechnya and the 1997–1998 global financial crisis.

By 1999, Ukraine was becoming more autocratic; financial crisis had gutted reform in Russia; and war in Yugoslavia had severely undermined the notion that the West and Russia could agree on a common approach to security. NATO enlargement both reflected that disagreement and exacerbated it. Several of the issues that became the focus of recriminations in 2014 – NATO expansion, the independence of Kosovo, the erosion of democracy in Russia, and the violation of Russian treaty commitments to Ukraine – have their origins in this period.

The challenges were recognized by a 1994 exchange in the journal *Foreign Affairs* between former National Security Advisor Zbigniew Brzezinski and Russian Foreign Minister Andrei Kozyrev. Brzezinski argued that "If not openly imperial, the current objectives of Russian policy are at the very least proto-imperial."[6] To counter this, he said, "the central goal of a realistic and long-term grand strategy should be *the consolidation of geopolitical pluralism within the former Soviet Union*."[7] Ukraine was to be the pivot in this strategy. "It cannot be stressed strongly enough that without Ukraine, Russia ceases to be an empire, but with Ukraine suborned and then subordinated, Russia automatically becomes an empire."[8] Brzezinski had crystallized an emerging consensus that maintaining Ukraine's independence from Russia was an important security goal.

Kozyrev published a spirited rebuttal in the next issue:

The only policy with any chance of success is one that recognizes the equal rights and mutual benefit of partnership for both Russia and the West, as well as the status and significance of Russia as a world power. Russian foreign policy inevitably has to be of an independent and assertive nature. If Russian democrats fail to achieve it, they will be swept away by a wave of aggressive nationalism, which is now exploiting the need for national and state self-assertion ... *Russia is predestined to be a great power.*[9]

The exchange highlights that by mid-1994 the United States and Russia had identified largely conflicting goals, and that Ukraine was pivotal in the disagreement. What Russia regarded as essential to its security was seen by Brzezinski and an increasing number of western elites as bad for Russia, bad for its neighbors, and bad for the United States.

Russia Debates Its Role

Kozyrev's response to Brzezinski reflected an ongoing debate in Russia about its identity and role in the world. Four schools of thought emerged: westernizers, Slavophiles, Eurasianists, and statists or "*derzhavniks*."[10]

---

[6] Zbigniew Brzezinski, "The Premature Partnership," *Foreign Affairs* 73 (March/April 1994): 76.

[7] Ibid., p. 79, emphasis in original.   [8] Ibid., p. 80.

[9] Andrei Kozyrev, "The Lagging Partnership," *Foreign Affairs* 73 (May/June 1994): 60, emphasis added.

[10] As Marlene Laruelle stresses, we should not overstate the coherence of these "schools" of thought or their direct influence on foreign policy. See Marlene Laruelle, "Russia as a 'Divided Nation,' from Compatriots to Crimea," *Problems of Post-Communism* 62 (2015): 63. The typology advanced here is compatible with a large literature on post-Soviet Russian foreign policy. For different but comparable typologies, see Andrei Tsygankov, "Rediscovering National Interests after the 'End of History': Fukuyama, Russian Intellectuals, and a Post-Cold War Order," *International Politics* 39 (December 2002): 423–446; and Stephen White, "Elite Opinion and Foreign Policy in Post-Communist

All four had roots in Russia's past. By 1996, the westernizers had largely been defeated, and opinion was divided among the others, who all supported Russia's great power aspirations and an assertive policy on Ukraine.

Westernizers saw Russia becoming a "normal country," by which they meant a liberal democracy and market economy on the European model. Westernizers formed the core of Boris Yeltsin's team in 1991–1992, but even then they were a small minority among the elite and public. "Slavophiles" conceived of Russia in ethnic, linguistic, and religious (Orthodox) terms. Emblematic of this group was the émigré Nobel prize-winning author Aleksandr Solzhenitsyn, who returned to Russia in 1992 and advocated construction of a truly *Russian* state. This view shunned empire, but considered much of Ukraine to be part of Russia, and insisted that the boundary between Ukraine and Russia be revised accordingly. Whereas the Slavophiles defined Russia narrowly in terms of Russian ethnicity and language, Eurasianists defined Russia expansively, as a multinational and multiethnic state. Like Slavophiles, Eurasianists tended to believe that Russia was fundamentally different and separate from Europe, and that this was to be celebrated. For both the Slavophiles and Eurasianists, reintegration of the Soviet space had a strong cultural dimension, and Ukraine was central to that dimension.[11]

Finally, there was a group known in the West as "statists," a translation of the Russian word *derzhavniki*." "Great power statist" would be a more accurate translation in this context.[12] *Derzhavniki* saw Russia as a great power and as a strong centralized state. Rather than the mysticism or imperialism that infused Eurasian and Slavophile arguments, they espoused a more traditional *realpolitik*. Russia, they said, should pursue

Russia," *Perspectives on European Politics and Society* 8, 2 (June 2007): 147–167. Ted Hopf uses a tripartite version ("liberals," "conservatives," and "centrists"), concluding that centrists, which correspond to my "statists," were ascendant by the end of 1992. See Ted Hopf, "Identity, Legitimacy, and the Use of Military Force: Russia's Great Power Identities and Military Intervention in Abkhazia," *Review of International Studies* 31 (2005): 225–243. For an analysis that goes up to 2016, see Mariya Y. Omelicheva and Lidiya Zubytska, "An Unending Quest for Russia's Place in the World: The Discursive Co-evolution of the Study and Practice of International Relations in Russia," *New Perspectives* 24, 1 (2016): 19–51.

[11] Michael E. Aleprete, Jr., "Minimizing Loss: Explaining Russian Policy: Choices during the Ukrainian Crisis," *Soviet and Post-Soviet Review* 44 (2017): 59.

[12] Brian D. Taylor, "The Code of Putinism," PONARS Eurasia Policy Memo No. 399, November 2015. "*[D]erzhavnost'* refers to the state of possessing – and being recognized by others to possess – clear status as a great power." Seva Gunitsky and Andrei P. Tsygankov, "The Wilsonian Bias in the Study of Russian Foreign Policy," *Problems of Post-Communism* 65, 6 (2018): 385. In his December 1999 speech, quoted below, Putin used the word *gosudarstvennichestvo* to denote a strong state and *derzhavnost'* when he discussed Russia as a great power.

Russian national interests, even when these conflicted with those of the West, which they were naturally bound to do. Yeltsin himself stressed this point: "We are fond of repeating that [Russia] is a great country. And that is indeed the case. So then, in our foreign-policy thinking let us always meet this high standard."[13]

While Slavophilism, Eurasianism, and statism were theoretically distinct, they were politically compatible, and leaders tended to borrow from all of them. Crimea was in the "sweet spot" of Russian nationalism because it appealed to both Slavophile and Eurasian conceptions of nationalism.[14] The consensus on Ukraine was expressed by Andranik Migranyan: Ukraine would have to rejoin Russia whether it wanted to or not:

Ukraine is a loose, artificial, heterogeneous enthnopolitical formation that has no real chance of forming its own statehood, and the deterioration of the social and economic situation will lead to a further split in this formation along ethnoregional lines and will confront the Ukrainian leadership with a dilemma: either enter into closer economic and military-political integration with Russia, directly or within the CIS framework, in order to preserve Ukraine's territorial integrity, or the consequence will be Ukraine's breakup into several parts and possible civil war among the various regions.[15]

By 1994, consensus had consolidated around a more assertive conception of Russia's role, merging elements of the Slavophile, Eurasianist, and *derzhavnik* perspectives. *Izvestiya* pointed to the "new language of Russia's political leaders, where even liberals speak with Zhirinovsky's accent."[16] The replacement of Andrei Kozyrev as foreign minister by the former intelligence chief Yevgeny Primakov in January 1996 institutionalized the change. A commentator said:

There were romantic illusions about the West and a desire to get a tighter grip on power by getting support from firstly the United States against domestic opponents, the "red-browns." In the ecstasy of convergence the factor of strength, the principle of self-reliance, and the concept of the national, state interest as the foundation of any serious diplomacy and of any statehood were

[13] "Strategicheskaia tsel' – sozdat' protsvetaiushchuiu stranu: Vystuplenie Prezidenta Rossii v Federal'nom Sobranii," *Rossiiskaya Gazeta*, February 25, 1994, quoted in Jim Headley, "Sarajevo, February 1994: The First Russia-NATO Crisis of the Post-Cold War Era," *Review of International Studies* 29, 2 (April 2003): 222.

[14] Henry E. Hale, "Russian Nationalism and the Logic of the Kremlin's Actions on Ukraine," *The Guardian*, August 29, 2014.

[15] Andranik Migranyan, "Russia and the Near Abroad: Setting a New Foreign Policy Course for the Russian Federation," *Nezavisimaya Gazeta*, January 12, 1994, pp. 1, 4; translated in *Current Digest of the Russian Press*, March 9, 1994, pp. 1–4.

[16] Vladimir Nadein, "SShA Opasayutsya Vozrozhdeniya Rossiiskogo Imperializma i Obeshchayut Pozabotit'sya ob Ukrainye," *Izvestiya*, February 8, 1994, p. 3.

initially forgotten. ... Now everyone agrees that Kozyrev's line in the first Russian years was too pro-American and too ideologized.[17]

Others pointed to the wary reaction in the United States to Primakov's appointment, and concluded: "This reaction confirms the correctness of the choice of the President."[18]

Speaking on December 30, 1999, just as he was about to become acting president, Putin articulated both the need for Russia to be a great power and for it to have a strong state domestically:

> Russia has been and will continue to be a great country. This is due to the inherent characteristics of its geopolitical, economic, cultural existence. They determined the mentality of the Russians and the policy of the state throughout the entire history of Russia ... Russia will not soon, if ever, become a second edition, of say, the USA or England, where liberal values have deep historical traditions. For us the state, its institutions and structures have always played a crucially important role in the life of the country and the people. A strong state for Russia is not an anomaly, or something that should be combated, but, on the contrary, the source and guarantor of order, the initiator and the main driving force of any changes.[19]

Ukraine's 1994 Elections

Following the signing of the Trilateral Agreement in January 1994, attention in Ukraine shifted to the presidential elections scheduled for June and July. Economic collapse had driven demands for early elections, and the question of economic relations with Russia was a central issue in the presidential campaign. Leonid Kravchuk, the incumbent, had emphasized establishing Ukraine's sovereignty and independence by separating the country militarily, economically, and politically from Moscow. Many, especially in eastern Ukraine, felt that this policy was responsible for the crash in the Ukrainian economy that followed independence.

Kravchuk's main competitor was Leonid Kuchma, former prime minister and former industrialist associated with the "Dnipropetrovsk clan," from which Leonid Brezhnev had emerged. Kuchma ran on a platform of strengthening economic ties with Russia, supported by a wide range of

---

[17] Stanislav Kondrashov, "Ukhod Vernogo Andreya: Pochemu i chto dal'she?" *Izvestiya*, January 10, 1996, p. 3.

[18] Vladimir Kuznechevsky and Aleksandr Krasulin, "Yevgenii Primakov Ne Ukhodit ot Ostrykh Voprosov," *Rossiiskaya Gazeta*, January 16, 1996, p. 7.

[19] Vladimir Putin, "Rossiya na Rubezhe Tysyacheletii," *Nesavisimaya Gazeta*, December 30, 1999.

economic elites, including Ukraine's powerful agriculture, machine-building, and metallurgy sectors. All of these had been deeply integrated into Soviet-wide networks, and continued to need them. Many saw the election as a referendum on Kravchuk's policy of assertively breaking ties with Russia.

Russian elites were clear about their preference for Kuchma: Andranik Migranyan argued that "if this election results in the replacement of the incumbent President, who in the public mind is identified with the west, with Rukh, with the national-patriots and the democrat-patriots, then an entire phase in the establishment of Ukrainian statehood will have ended."[20]

While Kravchuk had been the less nationalist of the two candidates in 1991, in 1994 he was the more nationalist of the two. Accordingly, he got most of the vote in western Ukraine, where he had been weakest in 1991, while Kuchma dominated the east and south. Kuchma defeated Kravchuk 52 to 45 percent in the second round. The election reaffirmed Ukraine's regional divisions and demonstrated the electoral power of eastern Ukraine, with its large population.

In the parliamentary elections, held in March, local authorities in two eastern oblasts, Donetsk and Luhansk, added three "consultative" questions to the ballot about increasing the status of the Russian language, adopting a federal structure, and becoming a full member of the CIS. All three received 80 percent or more support from voters.[21] Whether this regionalism equated to separatism was questionable.[22]

Kuchma's election, paradoxically, undermined nascent autonomy movements in Crimea and eastern Ukraine. Kuchma was from eastern Ukraine, spoke Russian, was supported by large majorities in the east and south, had campaigned on restoring trade ties, and was openly supported by Russia. His election diminished the sense of grievance in eastern and southern Ukraine. The growing power of eastern Ukraine gave eastern elites and voters incentive to support Ukrainian independence over reintegration with Russia.[23] Kuchma promptly reassured Ukrainians that

[20] Andranik Migranyan, "Ukraina Nakanune Presidentskykh Vyborov: Predstoyashchie vybory v Belorussii I na Ukraine kak vyzov dlya Rossii," *Nezavisimaya Gazeta*, June 22, 1994, pp. 1, 3.

[21] Taras Kuzio, *Ukrainian Security Policy*, Washington Papers #167 (Westport, CT: Praeger, 1995, p. 37.

[22] Taras Kuzio, *Ukraine-Crimea-Russia: Triangle of Conflict* (Stuttgart: ibidem-Verlag, 2007), pp. 40–57.

[23] This phenomenon is explored in more detail in Paul D'Anieri, "Ethnic Tensions and State Strategies: Understanding the Survival of the Ukrainian State," *Journal of Communist Studies and Transition Politics* 23, 1 (March 2007): 4–29. When those

"Ukraine's foreign policy will remain predictable and balanced, based on those fundamental documents that have been adopted in recent years."[24]

Kuchma's "Multivector" Foreign Policy

While he was determined to rebuild trade with Russia, Kuchma faced the same dilemma that Kravchuk had. Ukraine's dependence on Russia left it vulnerable to coercion. Diversification was essential, and new opportunities were shaping sectoral interests.[25] Agriculture remained largely focused on Russia, as world markets were heavily protected. But the machine-building sector began to see more potential for markets in the West. The metallurgy sector divided, according to competitiveness. Firms that could compete in the EU, which dwarfed Russia as a market, focused on gaining greater access. Those that could not compete in the European Union sought to maintain ties with Russia. Banks were particularly worried about being put out of business by Russian competitors with far more capital.[26] Demand for arms from the Soviet military collapsed while the global arms market opened up. In Kuchma's former business, missiles, Ukraine could compete in the growing global satellite launch market.

Kuchma adopted the notion of a "national bourgeoisie" that merited protection from foreign competition. This suited Ukraine's emerging oligarchs, and served as a brake on integration with Russia, which would have facilitated the purchase of Ukrainian firms by Russian capital.[27] Having denounced the West in 1993, saying that "[t]he west has made it its goal ... to ruin everything for us,"[28] he adopted what came to be called a "multivector" foreign policy, balancing the West and Russia both

---

eastern elites lost control of the Ukrainian government in 2004, some (including Yanukovych) toyed with separatism. The same thing happened again in 2014.

[24] Leonid Kuchma, "Ukrayina Vidkryta dlya Spivrobitnytstva" (speech to the representatives of the diplomatic corps), July 22, 1994, in Leonid Kuchma, *Kroky Stanovlennya Natsional'noyi Ekonomiky 1994–2004 Roky, Knyha Persha, Podolannya Kryzy Radykal'ni Ekonomichni Reformy 1994–1999* (Kyiv: Lybid', 2008), p. 49.

[25] Tor Bukkvoll, "Defining a Ukrainian Foreign Policy Identity: Business and Geopolitics in the Formulation of Ukrainian Foreign Policy 1994–1999," in Jennifer D. P. Moroney, Taras Kuzio, and Mikhail Molchanov, eds., *Ukrainian Foreign and Security Policy: Theoretical and Comparative Perspectives* (Westport, CT: Praeger, 2002); Rosaria Puglisi, "Clashing Agendas? Economic Interests, Elite Coalitions and Prospects for Co-operation between Russia and Ukraine," *Europe-Asia Studies* 55, 6 (2003): 827–845; and Hans van Zon, "Political Culture and Neo-Patrimonialism under Leonid Kuchma," *Problems of Post-Communism* 52, 5 (2005): 12–22.

[26] Puglisi, "Clashing Agendas?" p. 836.

[27] Ibid., pp. 834–837; see Taras Kuzio, "Neither East nor West, Ukraine's Security Policy under Kuchma," *Problems of Post-Communism* 52, 5 (September/October 2005): 60.

[28] Quoted in Bukkvoll, "Defining a Ukrainian Foreign Policy Identity," p. 131.

economically and geopolitically. The multivector strategy was a domestic as well as an international strategy. By integrating neither with the West nor with Russia, Kuchma and Ukraine's oligarchs retained maximum latitude internally to seek rents and consolidate their power.[29]

The balance of oligarchic forces changed further as the battle for control of energy rents increasingly dominated Ukraine's politics.[30] In 1996–1997, Prime Minister Pavlo Lazarenko consolidated control over the gas market in Ukraine and skimmed off hundreds of millions of dollars. While he was forced from power (and eventually served a prison sentence in the United States for money laundering), the new model stuck. Because gas was subsidized, the sectors that depended on it, notably metallurgy and petrochemicals, were competitive internationally. Therefore, reducing subsidies would injure powerful oligarchs, undermine employment in eastern Ukraine, and reduce export earnings.[31]

Ihor Bakai, Chair of the state gas company Naftohaz Ukrainy, said that all the Ukrainian oligarchs had made their fortunes through the distorted energy trade with Russia.[32] In return, the oligarchs were expected to kick large sums back to Kuchma's team and to support them politically. As a result, an increasingly wealthy and powerful group of Ukrainian oligarchs shared an interest in maintaining stable relations between Russia and Ukraine. Overall, oligarchic politics reinforced regional politics in Ukraine, providing support for both pro-European and pro-Russian policies, and making it impossible for either side to completely gain the upper hand.

Trade and the Commonwealth of Independent States

While Ukraine hoped to redirect its foreign policy toward the West, the general agreements it reached with NATO and the European Union did little to actually open up trade opportunities, leaving Ukraine heavily dependent on Russian energy and on the Russian market. As economic performance stagnated, therefore, Kuchma needed to secure concessionary terms from Russia. The essential problem of Ukraine's independence

---

[29] See Kuzio, "Neither East nor West."

[30] On the role of Ukraine's oligarchs in the gas trade and on the role of the energy trade in Ukraine-Russia relations, see Anders Åslund, *How Ukraine Became a Market Economy and Democracy* (Washington, DC: Peterson Institute for International Economics, 2009), especially chapter 4; and Margarita Balmaceda, *Energy Dependency, Politics and Corruption in the Former Soviet Union* (Abingdon, Oxon: Routledge, 2009; and Margarita Balmaceda, *The Politics of Energy Dependency: Ukraine, Belarus, and Lithuania between Domestic Oligarchs and Russian Pressure* (Toronto: University of Toronto Press, 2013).

[31] Balmaceda, *Energy Dependence, Politics and Corruption*, p. 34.

[32] Puglisi, "Clashing Agendas?" p. 840.

– that it was economically dependent on its primary security threat – had not been mitigated.

While Ukraine's goal was to gain preferential access to Russian markets and to receive subsidized energy without any strings attached, Russia sought to make such privileges contingent upon accepting Russian economic and political leadership in the region. In October 1994, Ukraine joined the CIS Interstate Commerce Committee, but only with a whole series of reservations. This tactic – appearing to approve an agreement while declaring a series of exceptions – was used frequently. In part this was simply a matter of trying to publicly smooth over ongoing disagreements, but it frustrated Ukraine's negotiating partners, especially Russia.[33]

Foreign Minister Zlenko stated: "we consider that Ukraine's main foreign policy spheres are bilateral state-to-state relations, growing participation in European regional cooperation, cooperation within the CIS, membership in the UN and other universal international organizations."[34] Putting bilateral cooperation and cooperation with European organizations before cooperation with the CIS was certainly meant to reflect priorities. He says that "[t]he process of furthering ties within the CIS will be accompanied by comprehensive cooperation with the European Union."[35] In neither case did Zlenko refer to "integration." Similarly, in discussing institutions to promote security, Zlenko mentioned the CSCE, NATO, the NACC (North Atlantic Cooperation Council), and the WEU (Western European Union) but not the CIS.

Kozyrev focused on gaining western support for Russian-led reintegration:

What is wrong with Russia announcing as its goal the gradual reintegration – primarily economic reintegration – of the post-Soviet space on a voluntary and equal basis? The situation is similar to that of the European Union, where the economic leadership of the larger states like France and Germany is recognized. In the C.I.S., however, even a large and economically developed state like Ukraine cannot manage without close ties to Russia. Is there an alternative? Is the West prepared, for example, to pay for the oil and gas delivered to Ukraine, Georgia and the C.I.S. states from Russia or to take on the payment to Russia of the billion-dollar Ukrainian debt? That is why Russia's special role and

---

[33] Roman Wolczuk, *Ukraine's Foreign and Security Policy 1991–2000* (London: RoutledgeCurzon, 2003), p. 66 calculates that of 786 documents signed by the CIS between 1992 and 1997, Ukraine signed only 558 (71 percent) and attached reservations to 81 of those. Of the 558 signed agreements, 65 required parliamentary ratification, and only 15 received it.

[34] Anatoly Zlenko, "The Foreign Policy of Ukraine: Principles of Shaping and Problems of Implementing It," *International Affairs* (Moscow) (January 1994): 12–18.

[35] Ibid., p. 17.

responsibility within the former Soviet Union must be borne in mind by its Western partners and given support.[36]

In September 1994, just before a summit meeting between Yeltsin and Clinton, Yevgeny Primakov, head of Russia's foreign intelligence service and later prime minister, released a report entitled "Russia-CIS: Is a Change in the West's Position Needed?" Primakov worried that "The conclusion is being drawn that the policy of the leading Western countries toward the CIS should be adjusted with the aim of preserving the status quo that was created after the breakup of the Union."[37] On the contrary, he said, "The process of integration is an undoubted fact, and if the negative attitude to it gets rooted in Western capitals, it could strongly cool relations between these capitals and Moscow."[38] He identified a stark choice: either the region would forge a single economy and military under Russian leadership or "[w]ith overt or covert support from outside, forces advocating 'isolated development' will gain the upper hand in Russia and the other Commonwealth countries."[39]

Primakov's report was widely discussed (and printed in its entirety in *Rossiiskaya Gazeta*, the government newspaper), and it highlights the view that there was no alternative to integration. Moreover, Primakov believed that if Russia and its neighbors did not reintegrate, it would be due to "overt or covert support from outside forces." He did not believe they could choose this path themselves, due to the objective forces he pointed to. And he already suspected the West of trying to harm Russia by dividing it from its near abroad.

Speaking at the UN a few days later, Yeltsin endorsed Primakov's position, saying that Russia's "economic and foreign policy priorities lie in the countries of the Commonwealth of Independent States ... Russia's ties with them are closer than traditional neighborhood relations; rather, this is a blood relationship." He went on to say that "The main peace-keeping burden in the territory of the former Soviet Union lies upon the Russian Federation" and that "the people of Russia will not understand if I don't say now [that] the independent states have to prove through their actions that guaranteeing the human rights of national minorities is

---

[36] Kozyrev, "The Lagging Partnership," p. 69.

[37] "Nuzhdaetsya Li v Korrectirovkye Pozitsiya Zapada?" *Rossiiskaya Gazeta*, September 22, 1994, p. 1.

[38] David Hearst, "Russia Directs Salvo at the West: Yeltsin's Intelligence Chief Gets Blunt about 'Double Standards'," *The Guardian*, September 22, 1994, p. 13.

[39] Primakov asserted that in contrast to the United States, which intervened without the approval of those states' governments, Russia participated in peacekeeping only at the invitation of the governments.

indeed the cornerstone of their foreign policy. And here neither selective approaches nor double standards are permissible."[40]

Yeltsin advisor Sergei Kortunov echoed Primakov's argument that only western interference impeded the natural tendency for Ukraine to reintegrate with Russia:

The direction of priority in Russia's policy in the CIS are relations with Ukraine. In perspective, our relations must acquire an allied character; moreover, there are essentially no serious obstacles – not economic, nor cultural or civilizational, not even military or political – for the development of such an alliance. The basic problem here is external: the attempts of the US and other large countries not to allow a reunion of Russia and Ukraine, which would lead to the formation of a powerful state in Eurasia, almost of the same scale as was the former USSR. On the other hand, without a strategic alliance with Ukraine, Russia will not become a genuinely great power which would in reality be appreciated, respected and addressed as a real power in the new system of international relations. The departure of Ukraine from Russia, the conversion of brotherly Ukraine into a good-neighborly state, and later, into simply a neighboring state would be a strategic loss for Russia, not compensated neither by the number of stations in Sevastopol, nor the contracts for joint deliveries.[41]

In March 1996, Russia, Belarus, Kazakhstan, and Kyrgyzstan signed a new deal "On Deepening Integration" that was presented as building something akin to the European Union.[42] Without Ukrainian membership, this and other similar initiatives withered. Kuchma resisted but also sought to reassure Russia that it would not quickly move toward the West. "As the largest of Europe's non-bloc countries, Ukraine understands that under current conditions, its hypothetical joining of existing military-political groups could damage the international security system," and that that "Ukraine's future does not necessarily have to be non-bloc."[43] When Ukraine declined to join, Russia lost interest, as a major point of all such proposals was to bring Ukraine back into the fold.

The discussions in this period brought up again the question of Ukraine's neutrality or "non-bloc" status, which had been mentioned as an intention in the 1990 sovereignty declaration, and which many took to be a commitment. For those who wanted to resist integration with Russia, non-bloc status offered the perfect argument as to why Ukraine

---

[40] John M. Goshko, "Yeltsin Claims Russian Sphere of Influence: Regional Peacekeeping Role Asserted," *Washington Post*, September 27, 1994, p. A10.

[41] Sergei Kortunov, "Russia in Search of Allies," *International Affairs* (Moscow) 42, 3 (1996): 148.

[42] Wolczuk, *Ukraine's Foreign and Security Policy*, p. 63.

[43] Tatyana Ivzhenko, "Solana Na Ukraine i v Pribaltike," *Nezavisimaya Gazeta*, April 17, 1996, p. 1.

could not join the various projects put forth through the CIS and other formats. For opponents of collaboration with NATO, it offered a similar obstacle. For those advocating closer relations with NATO, collaboration short of membership did not violate Ukraine's non-bloc status. Ukraine's non-bloc status, even if not official, represented a compromise between competing perspectives of the country's future.

Crimea

The internal situation in Crimea threatened to boil over in 1994. In January, Crimeans elected Yuriy Meshkov, a pro-Russia separatist, to the newly created position of president of the autonomous republic.[44] Meshkov appointed a Russian citizen as premier, ignoring a warning from Ukraine's parliament to abide by the Ukrainian constitution. He then sought to hold a referendum on Crimean secession, but when this was rejected as unconstitutional, he instead held a nonbinding "opinion poll" to coincide with the first round of Ukraine's parliamentary elections in March.[45] One of the questions was whether Crimea's relations with Ukraine should be governed by a bilateral treaty, such as that which had been devised between Tatarstan and Moscow; one was on dual citizenship; and one was on increased autonomy. All received more than 75 percent support.

The Ukrainian parliament, divided on so many other things, passed a resolution condemning the poll and enacted laws against several of the steps taken by Crimean leaders. Chairman Ivan Plyushch said that Ukraine "can no longer tolerate violations of the constitution by the Crimean authorities," and blamed "Chauvinistic politicians from … Russia, who inherited their traits from the former USSR."[46] While some counseled taking decisive action before Crimea could consolidate independence, others feared that pursuit of a military solution would foster what had happened in Georgia, namely de facto partition. Kravchuk, while insisting that the Crimean actions were unconstitutional, did nothing other than pointing out that Crimea would be in deep trouble economically if it were cut off from Ukraine. "Let's speak frankly. Crimea today is a region which is subsidized by Ukraine. We don't have

---

[44] This episode is discussed in detail in Kuzio, *Ukraine-Crimea-Russia*, pp. 129–140.

[45] Kuzio, *Ukrainian Security Policy*, p. 38.

[46] The quotations are from the AP, February 25, 1994 and *Holos Ukrainy*, March 1, 1994, both quoted in Kuzio, *Ukraine-Crimea-Russia*, p. 135.

to go into all the figures, there's energy, water, etc. As the Russian saying goes, don't try to wear clothes that don't fit."[47]

In the summer of 1994, the city council in Sevastopol voted to transfer the city to Russian jurisdiction. The new Kuchma administration rapidly denounced the move as contradicting Ukraine's constitution and having no legal authority. From this high point of tension, the situation diffused, for several reasons. First, there were deepening conflicts within Crimea, and Meshkov rapidly lost political support. The Soviet-era communist "party of power" in Crimea, led by former speaker Nikolai Bagrov, whom Meshkov had succeeded, fought back. That group envisioned more influence in an independent Ukraine. Already in May 1994, a delegation from the Crimean parliament, led by Sergei Tsekov, met with one from the Ukrainian parliament led by the communist deputy Boris Oleinik, with Tsekov declaring that "the Republic of Crimea does not intend to secede from Ukraine."[48]

Second, the election of Kuchma changed the situation there as it had in Donbas. Having just won nearly 90 percent of the vote in Crimea, Kuchma had considerable political capital, and the narrative of a nationalist government in Kyiv no longer made sense. To deal with competing resolutions between the Crimean parliament and Meshkov, Kuchma proposed a "cooling off" period and a "zero-option" under which all of the controversial resolutions would be repealed.[49] He also pointed out that resolutions concerning the jurisdiction over Crimea and the institution of the President of Crimea were unconstitutional: "I could sign a decree right now and rescind all Meshkov's resolutions."[50] In the spring of 1995, Kuchma signed a decree abolishing the Crimean presidency. There was little fuss about it and the question of separatism from within Crimea moved to the back burner, both on the peninsula and in Kyiv.

Russia could have poured oil on this fire, but did not. In February, after Meshkov's election, Prime Minister Chernomyrdin stated that "Ukraine need not fear that Russia's position will change."[51] In August, after the Sevastopol city council's actions, a Yeltsin spokesperson reaffirmed that the matter "must be guided by the principles of the

---

[47] Quoted in Kuzio, *Ukrainian Security Policy*, p. 39.

[48] Vladimir Gavrilenko and Anatolii Polyakov, "Sobytiya i Kommentarii: Led Vokrug Kryma, Pokhozhe, Tronulsya," *Krasnaya Zvezda*, May 26, 1994, p. 3.

[49] Nikolay Semenov, "Meshkov Stremitsyak 'Nulyevomu' Variantu, Parlament Kryma Eto ne Ustraivaet," *Izvestiya*, September 24, 1994, p. 2.

[50] Yanina Sokolovskaya, "... A Kiev Daet Krymskim Vlastyam 40 Dney na Razmyshleniya," *Izvestia*, September 24, 1994, p. 2.

[51] Reuters, February 19, 1994, quoted in Kuzio, *Ukrainian Security Policy*, p. 38.

integrity of the CIS states and the inviolability of the CIS countries' borders."[52] Kuchma praised Russia for "acting prudently and … making no statements, understanding that this an internal affair of Ukraine."[53] Russia's restraint in this instance shows that, despite its claims on the peninsula, Russia was not pulling all the levers at its disposal. Russia's reluctance to support Crimean secession, even though many Russian elites supported it, may have been motivated by the fact that Ukraine's denuclearization was incomplete, and could have been reversed if Crimea were to secede. Taras Kuzio speculates that, as well, Russia may have felt that it would have more leverage with Crimea inside Ukraine (as with Transnistria in Moldova and Abkhazia in Georgia), than with it outside.[54]

The Black Sea Fleet and the 1997 Friendship Treaty

Ukraine and Russia hoped to sign a Friendship Treaty that would solidify their bilateral relations, but could not do so until the status of the Black Sea Fleet was resolved. Ukraine made further concessions in 1995, accepting a smaller share of the fleet and agreeing that the port of Sevastopol would remain the primary base for the Russian Black Sea Fleet. Ukrainian critics contended that having a foreign base on Ukrainian soil violated the Ukrainian constitution and legitimized Russia's claims to Sevastopol and the presence of its troops there.[55]

In May 1995, Yeltsin advisor Dmitry Ryurikov expressed Yeltsin's frustration that with Russia having agreed to the restructuring of Ukraine's debt, Ukraine did not make expected concessions on Sevastopol and the Black Sea Fleet. Ryurikov said "Yeltsin suggested that the Ukrainian side draw conclusions, and if there is no movement toward accommodation, it appears that Russia will start reconsidering the agreements reached with Ukraine on economic and financial matters."[56] However, Russia was constrained from turning the economic screws on

---

[52] Dmitry Kuznets, "Russian Politicians Don't Intend to Take Sevastopol: An Official in the Russian President's Administration Supports Leonid Kuchma's Position," *Sevodnya*, August 25, 1994, p. 2, in *Current Digest of the Russian Press*, No. 34, Vol. 46, September 21, 1994, p. 22.

[53] Quoted by Viktor Yadukha and Konstantin Parishkura, "'Zero Option' Remains Up in the Air: Both Sides Assert They Are Ready for Talks," *Sevodnya*, September 14, 1994, p. 1, in *Current Digest of the Russian Press*, No. 37, Vol. 46, October 12, 1994, pp. 6–7.

[54] Kuzio, *Ukrainian Security Policy*, p. 38.

[55] Wolczuk, *Ukraine's Foreign and Security Policy*, pp. 30–31, 37.

[56] Georgy Bovt and Natalya Kalashnikova, "Russian-Ukrainian Talks: Agreements with Ukraine Might Be Reconsidered," *Kommersant-Daily*, April 20, 1995, p. 1, translated in *Current Digest of the Russian Press*, No. 16, Vol. 47, May 17, 1995, p. 24.

The Black Sea Fleet and the 1997 Friendship Treaty

Ukraine too tightly, because it was receiving assistance from international financial institutions, and they did not want to see Ukraine's economic situation deteriorate dramatically.[57] A planned trip by Yeltsin to Kyiv to sign a treaty in September 1995 was delayed because disagreement remained over the issue of basing rights.

Yeltsin was then scheduled to go to Ukraine in April 1996 to sign the Friendship and Cooperation Treaty, but he postponed the trip again over the basing rights issue. With the Russian presidential election approaching, and with Yeltsin under fire from revanchists, he had powerful domestic incentives to avoid making concessions. "By replacing Kozyrev with Primakov and tacking to the right, Yeltsin was largely successful in taking foreign policy off the agenda in the election. ... Primakov neutralized the national-patriotic trump cards of the opposition, because he himself used them together with Yeltsin, actively and forcefully defending Russian interests and independence."[58] Once Yeltsin was reelected in July, he had more latitude to negotiate, but hardliners resumed their campaign on Sevastopol, and on October 16 the Duma passed a measure (334–1) prohibiting the division of the fleet and denying Ukrainian sovereignty over Sevastopol. They followed it up on October 24 with a resolution stating that Sevastopol remained under Moscow's jurisdiction.[59] In December, the Federation Council overwhelmingly (110–14)[60] endorsed the Duma's resolution. Yegor Stroyev, the chairman of the Federation Council, said "Sevastopol is a town of Russian Glory. So they voted correctly."[61]

In October 1996, Aleksandr Lebed, who had led Russian forces in Moldova and had recently been appointed Secretary of Russia's National Security Council, published an open letter entitled "Sevastopol is a Russian City," stating that "The question must be raised of the existence of a territorial dispute between Russia and Ukraine, with consideration of Russia's right to Sevastopol from a historical perspective."[62] A 1997 poll showed 70 percent of Russians supporting the transfer of Sevastopol to Russia.[63] These votes were not legally binding, and Yeltsin distanced himself. But members of his "Our Home is Russia" faction in parliament and his appointees to the Federation Council voted for the resolutions on Sevastopol.[64] It was clear that even if the Russian government grudgingly

---

[57] Ibid., p. 24.
[58] Stanislav Kondrashov, "Diplomaticheskoe Evangelie ot Yevgeniya v Kanun Vtorogo Votsareniya Boryisa," *Izvestia*, August 9, 1996, p. 3.
[59] Wolczuk, *Ukraine's Foreign and Security Policy*, p. 31.
[60] Kuzio, *Ukraine-Crimea-Russia*, p. 76.   [61] Quoted in ibid., pp. 75–76.
[62] *Kommersant*, October 13, 1996, p. 3.   [63] Kuzio, *Ukraine-Crimea-Russia*, p. 110.
[64] Ibid., p. 112.

acknowledged Ukraine's sovereignty and borders, much of its elite and its democratically elected parliament did not.

Even at this time, the potential for Ukraine to join NATO, however distant, colored the negotiations. Some speculated that Russia might want to maintain a border disagreement with Ukraine, since NATO had announced it would not consider new members with outstanding territorial disputes. Others believed that Russia sought a commitment that Ukraine would not join NATO in return for a Black Sea Fleet deal. Others worried that Russia's position on Crimea was increasing Ukrainian interest in NATO membership.[65]

At the same time, Ukraine's domestic politics were easing the path to agreement. In June 1996, Kuchma rammed a new Ukrainian constitution through parliament. While a prohibition on foreign bases remained, a "transitional provision" stated: "The use of existing military bases on the territory of Ukraine for the temporary stationing of foreign military formations is possible on the terms of lease."[66] This paved the way for a lease deal to be finalized.

In the first half of 1997, a deal came together. If Ukraine felt pressure due to its energy dependence on Russia, Russia may have felt that a deal would slow Ukraine's move to increased cooperation with NATO. A Ukraine-NATO "Charter on a Distinctive Partnership" was due to be signed in July at the Madrid summit (at which NATO officially decided to offer membership to the Czech Republic, Hungary, and Poland). On May 27, the NATO-Russia Founding Act was signed, and the Black Sea Fleet deal and Friendship Treaty followed within a week.

The Black Sea Fleet was divided, part of Ukraine's share was transferred back to Russia to defray Ukraine's debt to Russia, and port facilities and a base in Sevastopol were leased to Russia through 2017. Most important for Ukraine, Article 2 of the Treaty stated: "In accord with provisions of the UN Charter and the obligations of the Final Act on Security and Cooperation in Europe, the High Contracting Parties shall respect each other's territorial integrity and reaffirm the inviolability of the borders existing between them."

The signing of the Friendship Treaty largely ended agitation within Crimea for closer political ties with Russia.[67] But it did not quell demands from officials in Moscow that Russia take control of Sevastopol. Part of the reason why separatism diminished in Crimea (and never

---

[65] See James Sherr, "Russia-Ukraine Rapprochement? The Black Sea Fleet Accords," *Survival* 39, 3 (Autumn 1997): 28.

[66] Ukrainian Constitution, Chapter XV, Paragraph 14.

[67] Kuzio, *Ukraine-Crimea-Russia*, p. 33.

really got going in the Donbas) is that Ukraine's most pro-Russian party, the Communist Party of Ukraine (CPU) strongly supported Ukraine's territorial integrity. Its goal was not to divide Ukraine, but to have all of Ukraine align more closely with Russia. The CPU's leader, Petro Symonenko, complained that "certain media are currently trying to portray the Communist Party of Ukraine as the enemy of the country's territorial integrity. I once again repeat that the Communists consider the Crimea and Sevastopol as inalienable parts of Ukraine."[68]

Bosnia Drives a Wedge

No issue did more to corrode relations between the West and Russia than the war in Yugoslavia. The conflict seemed perfectly designed to drive them apart, pitting Russia's concerns for a traditional ally and its own status with the West's determination not to stand aside while genocide took place in Europe. While the war in Yugoslavia and the argument over what to do about it did not directly affect Ukraine, it helped drive the resentment in Russia that formed the context of subsequent events.

There was disagreement both within the West and between the West and Russia over the wisdom of using force to stop the violence in Yugoslavia. Many believed that the use of external force would make things worse, not better.[69] But as ethnic cleansing continued, the West became less patient, and Russia increasingly appeared to be an obstacle to ending the violence. The West, viewing Serbia as the cause of much of the violence, sought to coerce Serbia to submit to international peace plans. A commentary in *Pravda* lamented: "And what if the Serbs, our traditional comrades-in-arms, call for help from their 'Russian brothers'? This has happened in other times ... How insulting to our country, how bitter for Russia, which still hasn't yet said a single pointed word that world would have heard."[70]

Tension between the United States and Russia over Yugoslavia heightened after Serbian forces shelled a marketplace in Sarajevo, on February 5, 1994, killing sixty-eight people. United Nations Secretary General Boutros Boutros-Ghali asked NATO to agree to launch airstrikes at the UN's request. Russia objected. *Izvestiya* quoted a high-ranking Foreign Ministry official as saying: "We do not accept Boutros-

---

[68] *Vseukrainskiye Vedomosti*, January 15, 1997, quoted in Kuzio, *Ukraine-Crimea-Russia*, p. 34.

[69] Mike Bowker, "The Wars in Yugoslavia: Russia and the International Community," *Europe-Asia Studies* 50, 7 (1998): 1245–1261.

[70] Evgeniy Fadeev, "Stervyatniki," *Pravda*, August 11, 1993, p. 7.

Ghali's argument and do not believe that the current events fall under the previous resolution of the Security Council. Consultation with the members of the Security Council is required ... Until the responsibility of the Serbs is proven, the international community should not take any steps."[71] *Krasnaya Zvezda*, asserting "the guilt of the Muslim authorities for the tragedy in the Sarajevo market," argued that "the persistence with which NATO insists on bombing only Serbian positions calls into question the objectivity of this organization in Yugoslav conflict resolution ... If there is to be an ultimatum, it should be presented to all three sides, not just the Serbs."[72] In the West, questioning responsibility of the Serb forces for the attack appeared disingenuous.

Yeltsin insisted that "[w]e will not allow this problem to be resolved without the participation of Russia."[73] In 1992, Russia had supported a UN Security Council resolution (757) imposing sanctions on Serbia, and in 1993 Russia had endorsed the use of force to protect the "safe havens" established in Bosnia, but by 1994 it was unwilling to support measures that would likely lead to action against Serbia. Sergei Lavrov told the Duma that Russia would veto any new proposal to authorize force.[74] NATO nonetheless issued a threat that any heavy weapons or offensive fighting within a 20 kilometer "exclusion zone" around Sarajevo would be subject to NATO airstrikes.

The Russian envoy to the region, Vitaly Churkin, brokered a deal under which Serbian forces would withdraw from positions around Sarajevo, and Russian troops would be placed there to ensure that Bosnian forces did not occupy the positions. The deal was welcomed by some in the West as a compromise that kept Russia and the West together, and was lauded in the Russian press as a victory for Russia and as a sign of its continuing relevance. The need for NATO airstrikes was temporarily averted, but Russia and the West reached very different conclusions. NATO and the United States learned that credible threats were needed to halt Serbian aggression. Russia learned that diplomacy,

[71] Maksim Iusin, "Posle tragedii v Saraevo NATO skloniaetsia k reshitel'nym deistviiam protiv serbov: Moskva prizyvaet k sderzhannosti," *Izvestiia*, February 8, 1994, pp. 1, 3.
[72] Sergei Sidorov, "Vzryv v Sarayevo: Provokatsiya Musul'manskikh Ekstremistov," *Krasnaya Zvezda*, February 10, 1994. In a later article, citing Slobodan Milosevic, the same author insisted on the need to analyze "which of the belligerents in Bosnia has extracted political benefits from the crime." Sergei Sidorov, "Iz Belgrada: Serby Prizyvayut Moskvu Dovesti do Kontsa Rassledovanie Vzryva v Sarayevo," *Krasnaya Zvezda*, February 16, 1994.
[73] Vasiliy Kononenko, "V Moskvye Meidzhoru Prishlos' Opravdyvat'sya za Neterpenie Zapada v Bosniiskom Konfliktye," *Izvestiia*, February 16, 1994, p. 3.
[74] Headley, "Sarajevo, February 1994," pp. 213–215.

rather than force, had resolved the problem, and that problems could not be solved without Russia.[75]

A new irritant emerged at the same time. On February 21, 1994, Aldrich Ames, a high-ranking CIA counterintelligence officer, was charged with spying for Russia. Some took it for granted that allies spied on one another; after all, the agents Ames betrayed were Russians spying for the United States. But to many, the case seemed to show that the end of the Cold War had not changed anything, and the fact that Russia was spying on the United States while the United States was providing it with aid was galling.

Senators from both parties requested a suspension in aid to Russia while the case was investigated, but the Clinton administration resisted.[76] The Russian reaction to the scandal did not help: When the United States requested that Russia voluntarily withdraw a senior intelligence service employee from Washington, Russia refused. When the United States then expelled him, a tit-for-tat expulsion further reminded people of the Cold War. United States Senate Minority Leader Bob Dole stated: "Congressional and public support for aid to Russia will not endure in this environment."[77] As Raymond Garthoff wrote, "That such uproar could occur showed the fragility of the new American-Russian relationship of partnership."[78]

When NATO attacked Serb ground positions in April 1994, citing a UN resolution authorizing the use of force to protect UN peacekeepers, Yeltsin was enraged. Not only was NATO seemingly escalating the conflict unilaterally, but it was putting him in an exceedingly difficult position domestically. Russia reacted similarly in August 1995 when NATO increased bombing of Serb positions in Bosnia. By helping the Bosnian-Croat federation gain the territory allotted to it under the plan agreed by the "Contact Group," this campaign helped pave the way to the November 1995 Dayton Peace Agreement. But Russia was again outraged, with the government newspaper saying that the Bosnian Serbs

[75] Ibid., p. 220; Kozyrev, "The Lagging Partnership," p. 66.

[76] Douglas Jehl, "A Question of Espionage: Clinton Cautious in Rebuking Russia," *New York Times*, February 24, 1994, p. B8; Daniel Williams, "U.S. Calls End to Spy Incident: Administration Shifts to 'Basics' on Russia," *Washington Post*, March 1, 1994, p. A12.

[77] "Clinton Warns Russia on Spying but Won't Freeze Aid," *St. Louis Post-Dispatch*, February 24, 1994, p. 1A.

[78] Raymond L. Garthoff, *The Great Transition: American-Soviet Relations and the End of the Cold War* (Washington, DC: Brookings Institution, 1994), p. 790.

were "in effect threatened with genocide"[79] and *Pravda* headlining "Today Serbia, Tomorrow Russia."[80]

Bosnia put Russia in a bind. It did not want to sacrifice its relationship with the West to support Serbia, but it saw the West's approach as further undermining both Russia's position in the new Europe and the rules of the game more broadly. The West saw a different dilemma. Many did not want to use force in Yugoslavia, especially over the objections of Russia and without clear Security Council authorization. But the promise "never again," adopted after the Holocaust, pulled powerfully at western consciences, and Russia's foiling of efforts to stop ethnic cleansing puzzled and angered many.

Had Russia accepted that genocide was taking place, and supported action in the Security Council, the principle of Security Council approval could have been maintained without the West feeling that it was acquiescing in genocide. It is unclear why Russia resisted the use of force so resolutely. One hypothesis is that the policy was driven by Serbia's status as a tsarist-era ally and by notions of Orthodox unity. A second interpretation is that Russia was fighting to reestablish the understanding that it had a veto power in postcommunist Europe. Vitaly Churkin, the Russian envoy on Yugoslavia, said in 1993 that "the question is about the need to confirm our role as a great state."[81] In this vein, Russian journalist Konstantin Eggert criticized what he viewed as the "one-sided pro-Serbian position taken by Moscow solely to spite Washington."[82] Another factor might have been a desire to reject the practice of secession, since Russia was still reeling from the breakup of the Soviet Union and was threatened with further separatism.

It is unclear how subsequent relations between NATO and Russia might have been different if NATO had not had to choose between overriding Russia's veto and letting ethnic cleansing continue in Yugoslavia.[83] Eggert asserted that Russia's policy prolonged the war but did not yield influence, and that another option had been open: "In 1993 ... some ministry experts advised Andrei Kozyrev and the Presidential

---

[79] *Rossiiskaya Gazeta*, September 14, 1995, quoted in Bowker, "The Wars in Yugoslavia," p. 1254.

[80] Nikolay Krivomazov, "Segodnya-Serbiya, Zavtra-Rossiya," *Pravda*, September 14, 1995.

[81] A. Pushkov, "Golos Rossii Dolzhen Zvuchat' Na Balkanakh" [interview with Churkin], *Moskovskie Novosti*, March 21, 1993, p. 15. Quoted in Headley, "Sarajevo, February 1994," p. 212.

[82] Konstantin Eggert, "'Derzhavnaya' Vneshnaya Politika Stoit Slishkom Dorogo," *Izvestia*, December 16, 1995, p. 3.

[83] Ibid.

circle: 'We need to gradually curtail active policy in the former Yugoslavia, since we have neither real allies nor major interests there.'"

The consequences of the conflict were far-reaching. As it turned out, Yugoslavia undermined the principal of the veto, rather than reinforcing it, and it strengthened NATO rather than weakening it. It showed that in any organization where Russia wielded a veto, dealing with a problem like Bosnia might be impossible. It also demonstrated the essential importance of NATO in post-Cold War security in Europe. Richard Holbrooke, the main US negotiator on Yugoslavia, became a main force within the Clinton administration in support of NATO expansion.[84] The overlap between the discussion of NATO expansion and the Bosnia conflict was deeply injurious to Russia's hopes for the post-Cold War security order in Europe.

Kuchma and the United States

Ukraine's ratification of the NPT as a nonnuclear weapons state, in November 1994, removed the final obstacle to US support for Ukraine, and in late November Kuchma made a state visit to Washington. In addition to receiving praise from US officials, Kuchma returned with $900 million in aid pledges, as well a commitment from the IMF to disburse $370 million of a $700 million loan package. This aid provided essential support to the ravaged Ukrainian economy, and along with Ukraine's participation in the Partnership for Peace it symbolized the new collaborative relationship between the United States and Ukraine.

A further step that was to have important repercussions in 2014 came in December 1994 at the Organization for Security and Cooperation in Europe (OSCE) summit in Budapest, when the United States and Britain, along with Russia, signed the Budapest Memorandum guaranteeing Ukraine's security and its borders. This was the final part of the deal struck at the beginning of the year for Ukraine to surrender its weapons. While it was recognized that the declaration would not compel anyone to do (or not do) anything, it was regarded as significantly reassuring Ukraine that Russia would not use force and that the United States and United Kingdom would respond if it did.

In May 1995, the deepening bilateral relationship between the United States and Ukraine was marked by President Clinton's visit to Kyiv. Clinton stated his support unambiguously: "The US strongly supports

---

[84] James M. Goldgeier, "NATO Expansion: Anatomy of a Decision," *The Washington Quarterly* 21 (Winter 1998): 86. See also James M. Goldgeier, *Not Whether but When: The US Decision to Enlarge NATO* (Washington, DC: Brookings Institution Press, 1999).

an independent, democratic, stable and prosperous Ukraine that is becoming more deeply integrated into Europe. We support it because this kind of Ukraine interests us as a key political and economic partner, and also as a real force for stabilization in Europe."[85]

In 1998, a conflict over selling nuclear energy systems to Iran was resolved in a way that, while little noticed, showed how much influence the United States had over Ukraine, even when it went head-to-head with Russia. At issue was a Russian agreement to help Iran build a nuclear power station at Bushehr. The Ukrainian firm Turbatom, in Kharkiv, had a subcontract to build turbines for the facility, and the United States pressured Ukraine to cancel the contract. Faced with the loss of revenue and Russian ire on one side, and potential aid and US ire on the other side, Ukraine acquiesced to the US demand. In return, the United States supported Ukraine's accession to the Missile Technology Control Regime, which would make it eligible to participate in the international space launch business. This was particularly attractive to Kuchma, who had run Ukraine's largest missile factory.[86]

Ukraine and NATO

The burgeoning US relationship with Ukraine was matched by increasing Ukrainian interaction with NATO. When NATO announced its Partnership for Peace, the reaction was mixed. Those who hoped for rapid accession, such as the Czech Republic, Hungary, and Poland, worried that the Partnership would be used to put them in a holding pattern, possibly permanently. Ukraine, however, had no chance of joining the alliance in the foreseeable future and feared that NATO expansion "would leave Ukraine in a grey zone between an enlarged NATO and Russia."[87] Thus, already in 1994, the dynamic existed in which Ukraine's fear of being on the wrong side of a new dividing line pushed it to seek NATO protection. Foreign Minister Zlenko stated:

---

[85] Clinton is quoted in Vladimir Skachko, "Kiev Nadeetsya Na Poddershku Vashingtona," *Nezavisimaya Gazeta*, May 12, 1995, p. 1.

[86] Vitaly Panov, "Amerikanskii Zhuravl' Protiv Iranskoi Sinitsy," *Rossiiskaya Gazeta*, March 11, 1998, p. 7.

[87] Ukrainian Ambassador to Belgium Volodymyr Vasylenko, quoted in the *Wall Street Journal*, January 7–8, 1994, quoted in Kuzio, *Ukrainian Security Policy*, p. 57. Steven Pifer reports that Deputy Minister of Foreign Affairs Borys Tarasiuk, in a visit to Washington in October 1994, stressed the fear that "Ukraine would be consigned to a no-man's land or a gray zone of insecurity." Steven Pifer, *The Eagle and the Trident: US-Ukraine Relations in Turbulent Times* (Washington, DC: Brookings Institution Press, 2017), p. 92.

I must underline that the problem is by no means "Ukrainian." This is evident from an active search for security guarantees by Poland, Czechia, the Baltic countries, other Central and East European states. The disintegration of the Warsaw bloc left a security vacuum in this part of the continent, and practically all the new independent states expressed a desire to cooperate and eventually to join NATO and the WEU in order to ensure their national security. For various reasons, however, NATO will hardly be able to extend its membership in the foreseeable future by placing new independent states under its umbrella. Thus a whole group of countries, Ukraine among them, is experiencing common difficulties.[88]

After the supposedly pro-Russian Kuchma replaced Kravchuk in July 1994, Ukraine's enthusiasm for the PfP strengthened. This fit with Kuchma's "multivector" foreign policy. A high degree of interdependence with Russia was a fact of life whether Ukrainian leaders liked it or not. That necessitated a counterweight. Not only would cooperation with NATO help offset Russian influence, but the threat of aligning with the West was viewed as a useful lever in getting Russia to ease its pressure.[89] Ukraine was therefore the PfP's most eager participant, seeking to join in as many joint exercises and other activities as possible. It stressed its commitment by contributing 400 troops to the Implementation Force (IFOR) that NATO deployed in Bosnia in December 1995.

In January 1995, Kuchma proposed a "Charter on a Distinctive Partnership between Ukraine and NATO." Foreign Minister Hennadiy Udovenko caused a stir in mid-1996 when he discussed the potential for Ukraine to become an "Associate Member" of NATO (a category that did not exist). Though Kuchma disavowed Udovenko's statement, it was noticed in Moscow, where Arkadiy Moshes, after dismissing the chances of Ukraine joining NATO in the foreseeable future, wrote: "At the same time, politicians in Kiev must be given to understand that Ukraine's declaring the goal of joining NATO will be viewed as a shift to an openly unfriendly policy toward Russia, with all the resulting consequences."[90] In March 1997, Udovenko went further, surprising NATO interlocutors at a meeting in Brussels by saying: "I hope that NATO will back Ukraine in its efforts to achieve its strategic goal of complete integration into European and Euro-Atlantic security structures, including NATO."[91] Later that year, he voiced concern that NATO enlargement would lead

---

[88] Zlenko, "The Foreign Policy of Ukraine," p. 16.

[89] Kuzio, *Ukraine-Crimea-Russia*, pp. 81–82.

[90] Arkadiy Moshes, "Zybkii neitralitet Ukrainy," *Moskovskiye Novosti*, No. 26, June 30–July 7, 1996, p. 10.

[91] Aleksandr Koretsky, "NATO Border Could Come Up to Belgorod: Kiev Wants into NATO despite Older Brother's Wishes," *Sevodnya*, March 22, 1997, pp. 1, 4, in *Current Digest of the Russian Press*, No. 12, Vol. 49, April 23, 1997, pp. 17–18.

to the deployment of nuclear weapons in Ukraine's western neighbors, and recommended the creation of a nuclear-weapons-free zone in central Europe, which NATO opposed due to the key role the nuclear "umbrella" would play in guaranteeing the new members' security. Ukrainian leaders further sought "article 5-like" security guarantees, which NATO also rejected.[92]

While working closely with NATO through PfP, Ukraine also sought to reinforce its connections with Poland, which was on track to join the alliance. Poland was to become an important advocate for Ukraine in both NATO and the European Union. In March 1994, the two states signed a document "On Principles of the Establishment of Polish-Ukrainian Partnership" that referred to the need to prevent hegemonic tendencies or spheres of influence from arising in the region, an obvious reference to shared fears of Russia.[93]

In May 1997 Polish President Aleksander Kwaśniewski visited Kyiv to sign a "Declaration on Agreement and Unity." Poland clearly recognized the danger of Ukraine being isolated between NATO and Russia, and sought to help.[94] A "senior Polish diplomat" was quoted in the *Wall Street Journal* as saying:

We would not like to become part of NATO if the price for that would be giving Ukraine back to Russia ... Basically, [the Ukrainians] say that bordering the Western system would be beneficial and would enhance their independence and security too – provided that NATO expansion would not be a deal with Russia that Poland gets in, but the dividing line is the Bug River and Ukraine is on the wrong side.[95]

Recognizing Ukraine's fear of falling in between NATO and Russia, NATO signed a "Charter on a Distinctive Partnership" with Ukraine at the July 1997 Madrid summit that offered membership to Poland, the Czech Republic, and Hungary.[96] The Charter signaled that Ukraine was considered to be an important partner, and that NATO was taking a stake in its future and its security. Rather than the firm security guarantee

---

[92] Pifer, *The Eagle and the Trident*, pp. 94–95.

[93] Mikhail Tretyakov, "So Stratigicheskim Sotrudnichestvom Pridetsya Podolzhdat'," *Pravda*, March 24, 1994, p. 3.

[94] Roman Wolczuk, "Polish-Ukrainian Relations: A Strategic Partnership Conditioned by Externalities," in David H. Dunn and Marcin Zaborowski, eds., *Poland: A New Power in Transatlantic Security* (London: Frank Cass, 2003), p. 146.

[95] Elizabeth Pond, "Poland and Ukraine Learn to Be Friends," *Wall Street Journal, Europe*, June 26, 1996, p. 8.

[96] The text of the Ukraine-NATO Charter can be viewed at www.nato.int/cps/en/natohq/official_texts_25457.htm. On the legacy of the Charter, see James Greene, "NATO-Ukraine Distinctive Partnership Turns Twenty: Lessons to Take Forward," *NATO Review*, April 2017.

Ukraine sought, the document referred back to the assurances concerning its territorial integrity made when Ukraine acceded to the NPT and contained in the Budapest Memorandum.

Russia did not formally object to the Charter. When the Russian and Ukrainian foreign ministers met in Kyiv in May 1998, and Borys Tarasiuk said "Our policy of integration into European and North Atlantic structures remains unchanged," Primakov commented simply: "They're not talking about Ukraine's accession to NATO; I suppose so."[97]

In practice, PfP led to less substantive change than its symbolic importance implied. NATO official James Greene later wrote:

> Ukraine's formal institutions have frequently proven a weak vessel for carrying forward the knowledge and know-how gained from work with the Alliance. Ukrainian units would train to PfP standards, but their core manuals would remain unchanged. A unit would be put together for deployment to an operation, only to have its members sent back to home units on their return. Officers would go for training abroad, only to find their new-found experience was valued more by civilian think tanks than the Armed Forces.[98]

The relationships between the United States and Ukraine were regarded as having helped keep the army from intervening during the Orange Revolution in 2004, but the absence of genuine military reform was to be exposed badly in 2014.

In February 1994, Vitaly Portnikov argued in *Nezavisimaya Gazeta* that it was understandable that the central European states would move from NATO's "waiting room" into the organization itself. But by putting Ukraine in the same waiting room, Portnikov argued, NATO was begging the question: if the Czech Republic and Poland could join, and perhaps even Russia, "Why not Ukraine?" But if Ukraine were offered membership,

> then Western politicians will have to listen to quite a few bitter words and reproaches from their Russian partners. So, on closer scrutiny, the "waiting-room effect" invented by US President Bill Clinton is an even more dangerous thing than immediate admission to the guest room. It would be interesting to know, how would they react in the West if Moscow joined the Partnership? Then what would come of all the crafty geopolitics of the American administration? And how will they explain in Washington why Prague was being kept in the

---

[97] Sergey Il'chenko, "Rossiya-NATO-Ukrayina: Kuchma Shantazhiruyet Moskvu," *Pravda-5*, May 30, 1998. Il'chenko opined that Kuchma was blackmailing the Russian leadership: that unless he received much more economic aid, Ukraine would join NATO and there would be "NATO tanks on the borders of Smolensk region."

[98] Greene, "NATO-Ukraine."

waiting room for a short time and Kiev for a little longer, while Moscow waits in the fresh air on the porch?[99]

While Russia did join the PfP, it was noticeably less eager than Ukraine, and it remained deeply concerned about NATO expansion.[100] Alexei Pushkov lamented what he viewed as the irony that NATO enlargement was occurring not because Russia was a threat, but because it was so *unthreatening*. He cited an anonymous western diplomat as saying that had Zhironovsky been president rather that Yeltsin, western policy would have been much more restrained.

The fact that Moscow agreed to these steps without the physical coercion that was applied to Germany and Japan in their time is fundamental. This gave us every reason to expect the West to meet us halfway. However, that movement proved to be very limited. After a brief honeymoon, ... the West's intentions began to die. First we learned that the West wanted to provide money but did not have it, so to speak ... Then we found out that it was in the US's interests to encourage centrifugal tendencies in the post-Soviet space (Zbigniew Brzezinski, with his characteristic elegance, called this line support for "geopolitical pluralism" in the former USSR). Finally, the West reached the conclusion that the countries of Eastern Europe should be admitted to NATO, just to be on the safe side, instead of pursuing some path of some abstract system of European security.[101]

In 1997, just before the Madrid summit invited the Czech Republic, Hungary, and Poland to join NATO, NATO and Russia signed the "NATO-Russia Founding Act," which was intended to reassure Russia that expansion would not harm its interests. Russia was further compensated by being invited to join the G-7 group of leading economies. While some in Russia were indeed reassured by these measures, and while Yeltsin sought to make the best of the situation, opinion in Russia was overwhelmingly negative.

Some western analysts opposed expansion for the same reasons Russia did, and some anticipated the problems it would cause for Ukraine. Once the process began, a new dividing line would be drawn in Europe, and those on the "wrong" side of it would push for inclusion. The process of eastward enlargement of NATO would eventually reach Ukraine, but "[t]aking in Ukraine without also inducting Russia is the quickest way to alienate Russia, because Russians across the political spectrum consider

---

[99] Vitaly Portnikov, "Partnerstvo Radi Ukrainy: Vpustyat li Kiev v evropeiskuyu gostinuyu?" *Nezavisimaya Gazeta*, February 12, 1994, p. 1.

[100] For a detailed analysis of Russia's perspective on NATO expansion, see J. L. Black, *Russia Faces NATO Expansion: Bearing Gifts or Bearing Arms* (Lanham, MD: Rowman & Littlefield, 2000).

[101] Alexei Pushkov, "Vneshnyaya Politika Rossii," *Nezavisimaya Gazeta*, November 16, 1995, pp. 1, 5.

Ukraine to be part of Russia."[102] Stephen Walt later argued that focusing on the Partnership for Peace, which "included many of the same benefits of NATO expansion ... but also included Russia," would have worked better.[103] What security problems might have arisen had NATO not enlarged, or whether any of these alternative strategies might have yielded better outcomes, is a matter of speculation, but there can be no doubt that the enlargement of NATO irritated Russia and made people wonder where, in relation to Ukraine, it might end.

Ukraine and the European Union

Kuchma's turn to the West included the European Union, which was less controversial within Ukraine and less threatening to Russia. In the summer of 1994, the European Union and Ukraine signed a "Partnership and Cooperation Agreement" (PCA). The timing of the signing of the PCA could not have been more important, for it coincided with a surge, especially in eastern Ukraine, in favor of joining the CIS Customs Union. The signing of the PCA, at least symbolically, showed that there was another alternative to reintegration with Russia. Ukraine's deputy foreign minister, Oleksandr Makarenko, made it clear that the EU, not the CIS, was where Ukraine intended to head: "The very fact that the agreement was signed in the form that it was and that we were able to do that answers the question: Where, in the final analysis, should Ukraine be moving – to the East, back to the past, or to the West, toward the future?"[104]

At a meeting with his foreign affairs team in July, Kuchma carefully distinguished between *integration* with western Europe and *cooperation* with the CIS:

Along with the strategic choice of adhering to the process of European integration, Ukraine's firm and consistent line is the line of maximum broadening and deepening of bilateral and multilateral forms of cooperation both within and outside the framework of the CIS while safeguarding the principles of mutual benefit and respect for each other's interests and abiding by the generally recognized norms of international law.[105]

---

[102] Robert J. Art, "Creating a Disaster: NATO's Open Door Policy," *Political Science Quarterly* 113, 3 (1998): 383–384. Art (pp. 399ff) recommended a new "concert of Europe" as an alternative to NATO expansion.
[103] Stephen M. Walt, "NATO Owes Putin a Big Thank-You," ForeignPolicy.com, September 4, 2014.
[104] Quoted in Roman Solchanyk, *Ukraine and Russia: The Post-Soviet Transition* (Lanham, MD: Rowman & Littlefield, 2001), p. 92.
[105] Quoted in ibid., pp. 92–93.

Over time, Kuchma strengthened this European rhetoric. Speaking in Helsinki in 1996, he deployed a civilizational argument:

One of the most important tasks on our agenda in the sphere of foreign policy is to overcome the artificial isolation of Ukraine from Europe, which for centuries deprived the Ukrainian people from, as our poet said, "the feeling of a single family," which is necessary today to all of us Europeans. The cradle of European culture is the European Christian civilization.[106]

This was a very different reading of history and culture than the Russian version, which saw Ukraine as fundamentally Russian.

The signing of the PCA was followed by the establishment of a range of bilateral EU-Ukraine bodies, including the EU-Ukraine Cooperation Council. In 1998 Ukraine adopted an official strategy on EU integration and created a National Agency for Development of European Integration. However, the PCA had to be ratified by EU member state parliaments, and this dragged on, demonstrating the lack of enthusiasm around the European Union for integration with Ukraine. To deal with that delay, the two sides reached an "Interim Agreement" in 1995 to move forward with those parts of the PCA which were not subject to ratification.

As with NATO, Ukraine feared being left on the outside of an enlarged European Union, and as with NATO, the main concern was with Poland. Poland was a vital trade partner as well as a source of remittances from Ukrainian workers there. Polish membership in the European Union would heighten trade barriers between Ukraine and Poland and redirect Poland's economy toward the EU, reducing Ukraine's access to the Polish market and inhibiting the cross-border shuttle trade on which many Ukrainians relied.

Even as Kuchma was seeking greater political support from Russia, and making limited economic concessions, Ukraine was trying to build an alliance of non-Russian states in the region. In 1997, the leaders of Georgia, Ukraine, Azerbaijan, and Moldova formed a group (known as GUAM; Uzbekistan joined in 1999) to find an energy transportation corridor from the Caspian basin to Europe, bypassing Russia. The original four participants also shared experience with separatist movements being supported by Russia. Azerbaijan and Uzbekistan were major energy producers but were hampered by Russian control of the pipelines that took their products to market. Georgia, Ukraine, and Moldova were

[106] Leonid Kuchma, "Ukrayina i Maibutnye Yevropy," February 8, 1996, reprinted in Leonid Kuchma, *Kroky Stanovlennya Natsional'noyi Ekonomiky 1994–2004 Roky, Knyha Persha, Podolannya Kryzy Radykal'ni Ekonomichni Reformy 1994–1999* (Kyiv: Lybid', 2008), p. 196.

consumers that sought to diversify their supply away from Russia to the other Caspian suppliers. Georgia and Ukraine were also transport corridors, and so potentially provided part of the solution for Azerbaijan and Uzbekistan. While the organization was more form than substance, the United States sought to reinvigorate it after 2001. Combined with the establishment of basing and overflight agreements to support the war in Afghanistan, Russia increasingly had the perception that the United States was supplanting its role in Central Asia.[107] Even if Russia supported the overthrow of the Taliban government in Afghanistan, it did not want to sanction a long-term US presence along its southern flank. There were insufficient interests to keep the group going, and it withered after 2001.

The appointment in 1998 of the strongly pro-European Borys Tarasiuk, who had previously been ambassador both to the Benelux countries and to NATO, as foreign minister was a further sign of Kuchma's commitment to the European vector in Ukrainian foreign policy. Tarasiuk stated that the "European idea has become Ukraine's national idea."[108] In June 1998, he approved "Ukraine's Strategy of Integration into the European Union."[109] That Tarasiuk, who was returned to the post of foreign minister by President Yushchenko after the Orange Revolution, was appointed to the same position by Kuchma, is some measure of how ardently pro-European Ukrainian policy was at this time.

Kuchma's turn to the West was strengthened by his 1999 reelection campaign. As Yeltsin had in 1996, Kuchma ran as the alternative to a return to communism. He positioned himself as the candidate of European integration, saying: "We should move further to the West and become full members of the European community."[110] Western Ukraine, which had voted heavily against Kuchma in 1994, now voted heavily for him. The campaign was notable for charges of manipulation based on tactics that Andrew Wilson called "virtual politics," which have since come to seem commonplace.[111]

Much of this emphasis on the EU, however, was insincere. European integration was as much about transformation of the government and legal system as about the agreements that were signed, and by this

[107] Lynch, *Misperceptions and Divergences*, pp. 10–11.
[108] Solchanyk, *Ukraine and Russia*, p. 94.   [109] Ibid., p. 93.
[110] Mikhail Melnik, "Kuchma Confident and Hopes to Win in First Round – Ukraine," *Itar-Tass Weekly News*, October 29, 1999.
[111] Andrew Wilson, *Virtual Politics: Faking Democracy in the Post-Soviet World* (New Haven, CT: Yale University Press, 2005).

measure (as with NATO) Ukraine made very little progress.[112] Ukraine's "strategy" of European integration obscured a deep contradiction in goals. While Kuchma and other Ukrainian leaders sought the geopolitical and national identity benefits of "integration" and the economic benefits of access to the EU market, they rejected what went with it – rule of law, economic reform, reduction of corruption, and strengthening of democracy. Ukraine continued to enact new nontariff barriers to trade, in direct contradiction of the PCA commitment to reduce them. Over time, Ukraine's credibility with EU technocrats diminished.

Like many other governments, Ukraine was torn between the desire to pursue integration and the intense domestic pressure to protect existing jobs. The situation was particularly frustrating for Ukraine because the sectors in which it was most competitive internationally – agriculture and steel – were those that were most subject to protectionism, such as the EU's Common Agriculture Policy and World Trade Organization (WTO) antidumping rules. While Ukraine received an IMF Standby Program in August 1997, the December tranche of that was not disbursed due to Ukraine's failure to meet IMF requirements.[113] Measured by aid, the relationship was also relatively modest. Roman Wolczuk estimates that total EU aid in the years 1996–1999 totaled ECU 538 million (or $608 million at 1997 exchange rates).[114]

In this sense, there was a parallel between Ukraine's policy toward EU integration and that toward CIS integration. In both cases, the Ukrainian leadership sought narrow economic and political benefits while resisting the two different kinds of political changes being demanded: internal reform (by the EU) and acceptance of Russian leadership (by Russia). While the European Union responded to Ukraine by losing interest and shifting its attention to other problems, Russia persisted in seeking ways to get Ukraine to change its position.

The 1998 economic crisis in Ukraine further undermined integration with the European Union. The Asian financial crisis that began in Thailand in mid-1997 spread to Russia and Ukraine in early 1998. Ukraine's economic output fell again, just as it seemed the economy might finally turn the corner on its post-Soviet contraction, and its ability to make loan payments was endangered. At least rhetorically, Kuchma

---

[112] See Paul J. Kubicek, "The European Union and Ukraine: Real Partners or Relationship of Convenience?" in Paul J. Kubicek, ed., *The European Union and Democratization* (London: Routledge, 2004), pp. 150–173.

[113] *Ukrainian Weekly*, December 27, 1998, No. 52, Vol. LXVI.

[114] Wolczuk, *Ukraine's Foreign and Security Policy*, p. 112.

recognized the danger that Ukraine's economy still posed to its independence:

First among these [priorities] is state strength and national security ... I hope that future generations will evaluate with understanding our mistakes and miscalculation, our difficulties and unresolved problems that we could not overcome. But they will never forgive us if we, in determining the plans for future economic development, undermine the fundamentals of the national security and sovereignty of the state, endangering Ukraine's independence.[115]

In practice, however, rent-seeking continued to block reform.

For Russia, the crisis had even worse consequences. Because Russia had reformed faster than Ukraine, it had more to lose. GDP had grown in 1997 for the first time since before the Soviet collapse and inflation had finally been brought under control. Foreign capital was flowing in. But the system was fragile, and the crisis in Asia spurred a withdrawal of capital from Russia. The ruble crashed in value, the state defaulted on domestic bond payments, and the macroeconomic stabilization policy was abandoned under pressure.[116] Much of the resentment generated by the collapse was directed at the West, which had advocated the financial policies that many held responsible for the mess.[117] Andrei Illarionov wrote afterwards that

The most serious ideological consequence of the crisis was a powerful shift in public opinion. The words "democracy," "reforms," and "liberal" and the concepts and the people associated with them have been discredited ... The Russian population at large has become much more receptive to vigorous government intervention in economic and social life, theories of a Western conspiracy against Russia, and the idea of a unique "Russian way" ... One can hardly avoid the painful conclusion that the repeated attempts to create a stable democratic society with an effective market economy in Russia have failed.[118]

Kosovo Deepens Russia's Conflict with the West

NATO's decision to bomb Serbia in March 1999 could not have come at a worse time, just a few weeks after the ceremony in which the Czech Republic, Hungary, and Poland officially became NATO members.

---

[115] "Zmishchnennya derzhavnosti ta Natsional'noyi Bezpeky – Osnova Ekonomichnoyi Stratehiyi," March 3, 1999, in Kuchma, *Kroky Stanovlennya*, p. 396.

[116] See Andrey Vavilov, *The Russian Public Debt and Financial Meltdowns* (London: Palgrave Macmillan, 2010), chapter 5.

[117] Whether the West was really to blame remains hotly debated. Some blame the West's advice, others blame the fact that it wasn't applied more fully, especially in fiscal policies.

[118] Andrei Illarionov, "The Roots of the Economic Crisis," *Journal of Democracy* 10 (Spring 1999): 68–69.

Conflict between Kosovar insurgents and the Yugoslavian government escalated in early 1999, leading to fears of further ethnic cleansing in the region. After Yugoslavia rejected a plan to introduce international peacekeepers to the territory, NATO leaders decided that force was needed to stop Yugoslavia from committing further violence in Kosovo. Speaking in May 1999, US President Clinton referred to "at least 100,000 missing; many young men led away in front of their families; over 500 cities, towns and villages torched." "With just seven months left in the 20th century, Kosovo is a crucial test. Can we strengthen a global community grounded in cooperation and tolerance, rooted in common humanity, or will repression and brutality, rooted in ethnic, racial and religious hatreds dominate the agenda for the new century and the new millennium?"[119]

In both Russia and Ukraine, elites were outraged by the attacks. The difference was that while in Russia the outrage reinforced anger toward NATO, in Ukraine it cut across the grain of a perception of an increasingly fruitful relationship. Ukrainian opposition to NATO bombing cut across the political spectrum for several reasons.[120] Most supported the principle that force could not be used without the approval of the UN Security Council, and most tended to agree that NATO was interfering with Yugoslavia's sovereignty. There were also worries about the precedent potentially set for Russia to intervene in the region. The leftist leadership of the parliament brought forth a motion calling for Ukraine to suspend cooperation with NATO due to the "aggressive" attacks on Yugoslavia, but received only 191 votes (of 226 required for passage).[121] Without endorsing NATO's action, Kuchma argued that Ukraine benefited from its relationship with NATO, and reassured NATO that Ukraine's "European choice" remained in place.

In Russia, there was outrage not only at NATO, but at the Russian government (and particularly Viktor Chernomyrdin) for persuading Milosevic to acquiesce to NATO's demands to end the bombing. *Sovietskaya Rossiya* published a long article by political party leaders Gennady Zyuganov (Communist), Nikolai Ryzhkov (Narodovlastie Party), and Nikolai Kharitonov (Agrarian Party), asserting that "The facts show that Mr. V. Chernomyrdin, the Russian President's special envoy for a settlement in Yugoslavia, has played a sinister role in compelling Yugoslavia to accept NATO's ultimatum." They complained that Chernomyrdin's

---

[119] Bill Clinton, "Transcript: Clinton Justifies U.S. Involvement in Kosovo," CNN, May 13, 1999.

[120] "Die Ukraine im Labilen Gleichgewicht; Einsicht folgt hysterischen Reaktionen auf Kosovo-Konflikt," *Neue Zuercher Zeitung*, May 5, 1999.

[121] "Ukraine's Parliament Fails to Approve Anti-NATO Measures," Associated Press, April 6, 1999.

involvement circumvented the influence of the Foreign and Defense ministries, which were charged with defending Russia's national interests. Viewing Yugoslavia as a "fraternal" country that had shown "heroic resistance," they went on to say:

> The events in Yugoslavia constitute the first attempt since World War II to redraw European borders by force. Russia's firm initial stance gave the world community hope that the aggression would be decisively rebuffed. The damage that the ultimatum imposed on Yugoslavia has done to Russia's international reputation is incalculable ... This shameful agreement is identical to the Munich compact that paved the way for the Second World War. Appeasement of the aggressor will undoubtedly spur it to launch other wars of conquest. There is no doubt that the next target of NATO aggression will be Russia.[122]

This rhetoric indicates the extent to which many leading Russians now felt that the United States and Russia were full-blown adversaries. They also stressed that the UN Security Council should play the "decisive" role in settling the conflict and governing peacekeepers in the region. This, they concluded, would protect Russia's national interests.

At the same time, however, the episode also demonstrated what happened when Russia and the West collaborated. While Russia was bitterly opposed to the bombing, it also played a major role in stopping it. After weeks of bombing, with Serbia holding out, and NATO planning for a ground invasion that no one wanted, Boris Yeltsin sent Viktor Chernomyrdin to Belgrade to persuade Milosevic to acquiesce to NATO's demands, warning that Russia would not support him if he did not. This move was the key to ending the military conflict.

The Kosovo episode is one of the bridges between the 1990s and the 2000s. While the conflict in Yugoslavia had bedeviled Russia's relations with the West since the early 1990s, by the time the bombing ceased in 1999, Russia had yet another prime minister, Vladimir Putin. In June, as the crisis was finally being resolved, Strobe Talbott met with Putin in Moscow, and reported US concern that Russian troops had been spotted moving toward Kosovo. Putin reassured him that no such movement would take place without prior consultation, and said he had not even heard of the general whom the United States had identified as leading the force. As Talbott flew back to Washington, the movement of Russian

---

[122] G. A. Zyuganov, N. I. Ryzhkov, and N. M. Kharitonov, "Usherb Neismernim Zayavlenie ob Ocherednom Predatl'stvye Interesov Mezhdunarodnoi Bezopasnosti," *Sovetskaya Rossiya*, June 10, 1999, p. 1.

troops into Kosovo was confirmed.[123] Thus, one of the first interactions of Putin as prime minister with the US government was seen as an act of deception. As for Kosovo, the West's later support for its full independence was again to outrage Russia, and was invoked by Putin in 2014 as a precedent for Russia's seizure of Crimea.

Looking back from 2016, one of Russia's leading spokespeople on foreign policy issues, Fyodor Lukyanov, wrote that

> From the Russian point of view, a critical turning point came when NATO intervened in the Kosovo war in 1999. Many Russians – even strong advocates of liberal reform – were appalled by NATO's bombing raids against Serbia, a European country with close ties to Moscow ... [I]t is not only NATO's expansion that has alarmed Russia, but its transformation ... [I]t is now a fighting group, which it was not during the cold war.[124]

The restarting of war in Chechnya further divided the West from Russia. Russia sought to reestablish control of the territory after militants based there had attacked Dagestan, among other acts of insurgency and terrorism within Russia. The level of violence that Russia used in prosecuting the war aroused severe criticism in the West, and that criticism was seen in Russia as hostile.

Conclusion

Relations among Ukraine, Russia, and the West evolved significantly between 1994 and 1999, but many core differences endured. In 1994, Ukraine began emerging from the isolation that the United States had imposed while Ukraine hesitated over its nuclear weapons. By the end, Ukraine was increasingly carving out for itself a role in the region. There were several gains in Ukraine-Russia-United States-Europe relations in the period, most importantly the signing of the Friendship Treaty. Moreover, none of the biggest dangers had come to pass. NATO expansion, while deeply opposed by Russia, had been achieved in the context of the NATO-Russia Founding Act and NATO-Ukraine Charter, which helped to reassure everyone.

At the same time, few of the dangers to Ukraine had been removed, and many of its internal problems were unresolved. While Russia had signed a treaty promising to respect Ukraine's independence, many of its actions and other statements called that commitment into question.

---

[123] The episode is related in Strobe Talbott, *The Russia Hand: A Memoir of Presidential Diplomacy* (New York: Random House 2002), p. 336.

[124] Fyodor Lukyanov, "Putin's Foreign Policy: The Quest to Restore Russia's Rightful Place," *Foreign Affairs* 95, 3 (May/June 2016): 32–33.

Leading politicians repeatedly made claims on Crimea, economic coercion went on, and Russian policy continued to assume that reintegration of the region under Russian hegemony was both necessary and
inevitable.

Moreover, Ukraine's domestic politics had evolved in ways that facilitated future Russian influence. The state remained weak and captured by
interest groups. Regional and institutional divisions undermined efforts
at building a strong working majority in the parliament. As a result,
Leonid Kuchma aggrandized executive power at the expense of parliament, such that Ukraine's politics began to resemble the superpresidentialism of Russia. The Ukrainian government was increasingly captured
by a swarm of competing oligarchic groups engaged in rent-seeking
opportunities, the most important of which was energy, which was
closely connected to Russia.

Relations between Russia and the West deteriorated, and while this
appeared to benefit Ukraine in the short term, it would eventually be
caught in the gap that was emerging. The sources of increasing tension
between Russia and the West were many: Yugoslavia, Chechnya, NATO
expansion, revanchism in Russia, economic crisis, energy politics, and
more. Underlying all of them was a basic contradiction between Russia's
vision of itself as a traditional great power and Europe's efforts to move
beyond traditional great power politics.

These problems tended to complicate one another, often at what
seemed the worst possible moment. As highlighted at the outset of the
chapter, 1994 began positively for the West, Russia, and Ukraine, as the
agreement on denuclearization was coupled with aid to Ukraine and
commitments to respect its borders. But that positive development came
just a month after Russia's 1993 parliamentary elections shook everyone's confidence in Russian reform and its commitment to friendly
relations with Ukraine and the West. Yet just as the denuclearization
deal was being signed, Clinton announced that NATO would expand.
Then the next month the Ames scandal sent the US Congress into a fury,
and Serbian shelling of the Sarajevo marketplace put Russia and NATO
on opposite side of the biggest conflict of the new post-Cold War era.

Much the same thing happened toward the end of the period: the
consummation of NATO expansion, in the works for five years, just as
the alliance was bombing Serbia, strengthened Russia's worst beliefs
about what NATO expansion meant. The brutal reescalation of the
war in Chechnya shortly thereafter confirmed the West's worst fears
about Russia.

In a book published in 1994, Raymond Garthoff, one of the great
scholars of United States-Soviet relations, wrote: "Russia must recognize

its international responsibilities and the appropriate constraints on pursuit of its interests. The United States, for its part, needs to be more understanding of Russian pursuit of its national interests."[125] By the time Garthoff wrote these reasonable lines, it was already becoming very difficult for either side to heed his advice. The security dilemma and incompatible understandings of the status quo interacted corrosively. Russians saw each US or NATO move as an offense requiring a response, while the United States and NATO saw each Russian move that complicated Yugoslavia or worried Ukraine, and each sign that conservatives were gaining ground in Russia, as a reason to hedge their bets.

By 1999 the increasingly erratic Boris Yeltsin was ceding power to the young, vigorous, and pragmatic Vladimir Putin. Bill Clinton would be leaving power in another year. Ukraine's Kuchma, freshly reelected, promised further stability. The 1990s had been a period of unthinkable transformation that would be remembered very differently in different places. For the West it was a time of triumph between the Cold War and the wars of the post-9/11 era. For Ukraine it was an era of national independence, painful but celebrated. For Russia it was an era of almost unmitigated disaster, as the fall of communism was overshadowed by the collapse of Russia's economy and its international position.

[125] Garthoff, *The Great Transition*, p. 792.

4   Autocracy and Revolution, 1999–2004

On November 30, 1999, Leonid Kuchma was inaugurated for his second term as Ukraine's president. Speaking in the Palace "Ukrayina," Kuchma laid out his program. He stated that Ukraine's independence was inviolable, and went on first to assert that Russia was Ukraine's most important partner, and then that Ukraine would seek to strengthen its relationships with NATO and the United States and to pursue EU membership.[1] In December, following a trip to the United States, Kuchma nominated Viktor Yushchenko to be Ukraine's prime minister. Yushchenko's selection was seen as having been influenced by a meeting Kuchma had with Vice President Al Gore, as well as by pressure from the IMF amid the need to restructure debts.[2] Yushchenko's appointment conveyed that Ukraine was serious about economic reform, about remaining democratic, and about its ties with the West.

Kuchma's "multivector" foreign policy was highly pragmatic. Ukraine could not turn its back on Russia, but did not trust it, and longed for closer relations with Europe. Yushchenko's economic reforms furthered the European "vector," but Kuchma's consolidation of power undermined it. This consolidation, epitomized by the murder of the journalist Georgiy Gongadze, put in motion the chain of events that led to the Orange Revolution in 2004. By the end of 2000, Ukraine's relationship with the West was deteriorating, and relations with Russia were improving.

The period from Kuchma's reelection as president in Ukraine and Putin's appointment as acting president in Russia to the Orange Revolution was a pivotal one in relations between Ukraine, Russia, and the

---

[1] Yanina Sokolovskaya, "Leonid Kuchma Delivers 'Coronation Speech' Intended to Please Everyone," *Izvestia*, December 1, 1999, p. 3, in *The Current Digest of the Russian Press*, No. 48, Vol. 51, December 29, 1999, p. 22.

[2] Gennady Sysoyev, "Premier Turns Ukraine to West," *Kommersant*, December 12, 1999, p. 3, in *Russian Press Digest*, December 23, 1999; Hans Van Zon, "Political Culture and Neo-Patrimonialism under Leonid Kuchma," *Problems of Post-Communism* 52, 5 (2005): 12–22.

West. Three important developments characterized this period. First, the connection between geopolitics and democratization came to the fore, in the impact of Kuchma's consolidation of power on relations with the West and Russia, and the similar impact of Putin's elimination of opposition on Russia's relations with the West, and then more definitively in the Orange Revolution. Second, the US war in Iraq steeled Russian determination to push back against US hegemony and confirmed the United States' focus on democracy promotion. Third, the Orange Revolution brought together two issues that had been linked only loosely: Ukraine's bid for independence from Russia and Russia's disagreement with the West. After 2004, there was no doubt that there was a competition between Russia and the West over Ukraine.

Kuchma's Consolidation and the Foreign Policy Effects

The 1999 election helped Leonid Kuchma to continue consolidating his power. Building from his ability to control access to rent-seeking opportunities, Kuchma increasingly used selective prosecution to punish potential challengers.[3] This included putting increasing pressure on independent media. In many respects, Kuchma was pursuing similar policies to those of Putin in Russia, signaling to oligarchs that they could keep their ill-gotten gains only if they supported him. For various reasons, not least of which was that his power was not rooted in the KGB, Kuchma eventually failed where Putin succeeded. Kuchma's political popularity plummeted, and his support shifted from western Ukraine back toward the east. Moreover, he struggled to control the oligarchs. The pro-presidential oligarchs became more powerful, and those from the Donbas, represented by the Party of Regions, became more influential.

The pressure on the independent media was symbolized by the murder of Gongadze. Gongadze was a journalist on a relatively obscure website, *Ukrayinska Pravda*, which relentlessly exposed the misdeeds of the government. He got under Kuchma's skin, and Kuchma told Minister of Internal Affairs Yuriy Kravchenko to "drive him out, throw [him] out. Give him to the Chechens."[4] In September 2000, Gongadze disappeared, and in November his decapitated body was found near Kyiv.

---

[3] See Keith Darden, "The Integrity of Corrupt States: Graft as an Informal State Institution," *Politics and Society* 36, 1 (March 2008): 35–60.

[4] This and several other incriminating excerpts regarding Gongadze are translated in RFE/RL, "Transcript: What Do Melnychenko's Tapes Say about Gongadze Case," March 3, 2005, www.rferl.org/a/1057789.html.

It was later determined that he had been murdered by a team of officers from the Interior Ministry. Exactly who ordered his murder and why remains debated, but his disappearance was viewed as an assault on the media, and the grisly remains of his body were seen as a particularly aggressive warning to others.

The Gongadze case also showed the ability of Kuchma's opponents among the elite to push back. On November 28, 2000, Oleksandr Moroz, leader of the Socialist Party of Ukraine and Speaker of the parliament, played excerpts of recordings in which Kuchma discussed his desire to get rid of Gongadze. The recordings had apparently been made by a member of Kuchma's security detail, Major Mykola Melnychenko. There has been widespread speculation about who might have been behind the recordings, but the truth remains unclear.

The revelations kicked off the "Ukraine without Kuchma" movement, which was in many respects a precursor to the Orange Revolution.[5] Moroz and Yuliya Tymoshenko joined forces in a "National Salvation Committee." A series of street protests was held, and in February 2001 Moroz predicted that by June "we will have enough support either for the president's impeachment, a referendum on no-confidence, or he will be simply forced to resign."[6] Instead, the opposition split and the security forces backed Kuchma. Ukraine's most popular politician, Viktor Yushchenko, remained loyal to Kuchma, co-signing with him a letter criticizing the National Salvation Committee. Yuliya Tymoshenko was arrested on smuggling charges (later dropped) that were widely seen as politically motivated. Kyiv Mayor Oleksandr Omelchenko scheduled a construction project on the Maidan, and when the opposition scheduled a large protest in April 2001, authorities obstructed transportation access to Kyiv, depressing turnout.[7]

With his popularity flagging, Kuchma had to search for allies. The 2002 parliamentary election made the Party of Regions the key to Kuchma's coalition. While Kuchma was increasingly powerful, he was unable to build either a commanding pro-presidential party like Putin's United Russia or to forge a reliable pro-presidential coalition out of other parties (as Putin had secured the cooperation of the LDP and the Communist Party). Instead, he relied heavily on the Party of Regions. Donetsk oblast was the only region in which Kuchma's party, Za Yedinu Ukrainu

---

[5] The two protests are compared in Paul D'Anieri, "Explaining the Success and Failure of Post-Communist Revolutions," *Communist and Post-Communist Studies* 39, 3 (2006): 331–350.

[6] Agence France Presse, February 27, 2001.

[7] D'Anieri, "Explaining the Success and Failure," p. 343.

(ZYU),[8] finished first in the proportional representation vote. More important, the Donbas provided many of the deputies elected in the single-member districts, where ZYU did much better (winning 86 of 225 seats). The election was in many respects a defeat for Kuchma, but by combining the members elected under his party and the Party of Regions with independents that he would threaten or bribe to join him, he still managed to control the parliament. Yet there was a shift in power from the Dnipropetrovsk clan led by Kuchma to the Donetsk clan led by Yanukovych, whom Kuchma named prime minister.

The rise of the Donetsk clan and its political arm, the Party of Regions, was among the most important developments during Kuchma's second term, reshaping the oligarchic balance of power in Ukraine and the political base of support for pro-Russian policies. In the 1990s, the Kyiv and Dnipropetrovsk clans were predominant, while Donetsk was still being contested. Donetsk was Ukraine's most populous region; its leading oligarch, Rinat Akhmetov, emerged as Ukraine's wealthiest man, and in the Party of Regions it built a party more adept than any other in the country at converting patronage into votes and party discipline. This combination made its rise irresistible. The rise of the Party of Regions helps explain why Yanukovych, rather than someone more polished, more popular, or more mainstream was chosen to be Kuchma's successor in the 2004 presidential elections.

The emergence of the Party of Regions also represented a major shift in the domestic coalition supporting better relations with Russia. In the 1990s, the pro-Russian contingent was led by the communist and socialist parties, which had significant support in parliament but never in the executive branch. The Party of Regions supported good relations with Russia based on oligarchic economic interests, rather than ideology or nostalgia. Kuchma's reliance on the Party of Regions and its oligarchs helped pro-Russian forces forge a powerful foothold in the executive branch.[9]

Equally important, the rise of the Party of Regions, and especially the transition from Yushchenko to Anatoliy Kinakh and then Yanukovych as prime minister completely changed the regional balance in Kuchma's government, leaving western Ukraine alienated. "The rise of the Donetsk clan upset the delicate balance between western and eastern Ukraine."[10]

---

[8] "Za Yedinu Ukrainu" means "For a United Ukraine" and echoes the title of the pro-government "United Russia" party in Russia. In Ukraine, many called the party by the nickname "Za Yedy," which in Russian means "for food," referring to the inducements that presumably motivated many of the party's voters.

[9] I am grateful to Serhiy Kudelia for this point.

[10] Van Zon, "Political Culture and Neo-Patrimonialism," p. 15.

As Kuchma's consolidation of power crested and then ebbed, so did his ability to control Ukraine's various oligarchic clans. Meanwhile, in Russia, Putin was much more successful in bringing oligarchs under state control. This contributed to a new asymmetry in Russia-Ukraine relations: Russia's state became stronger while Ukraine's remained weak. In Russia, Putin could resist pressure from firms, and could even make them serve his or the state's interest. In Ukraine, Kuchma was increasingly unable to do the same. This allowed an expanded mechanism for Russian influence. The Russian government controlled Russian firms, which bought or influenced Ukrainian firms, who increasingly captured the Ukrainian state. The IMF was insisting that Ukraine become more open to foreign investment, and a privatization program made more assets available.[11] At the same time, Ukrainian oligarchs had powerful incentives to prevent the kind of extensive integration that would allow Russian oligarchs and firms, backed by the power of the Russian state, to do to them what they had done to weaker actors in Ukraine.

Deteriorating Ties with the West

The question of democracy played an increasing role in Ukraine's latitude to choose its political alignments. Kuchma's efforts to control politics domestically undermined relations with the West, leaving him more dependent on Russia. In September 2000, Kuchma dismissed Borys Tarasiuk as foreign minister, in what was widely seen an adjustment away from the West and toward Russia.[12] Then Yushchenko left the government in April 2001. While Yushchenko was praised by reformers and respected abroad, Ukraine's leftists loathed him for his economic reforms, and during the denouement of the Ukraine without Kuchma movement, the Communist Party sponsored a no confidence vote that succeeded in ousting him as prime minister. Yushchenko's dismissal removed the Ukrainian leader in whom the West had the most confidence and pushed Yushchenko into opposition.

Despite these moves and despite increasing efforts to solidify ties with Russia, Kuchma continued to say that integrating with the West was a top priority. In February 2002, Kuchma established a schedule for Ukraine to meet EU accession requirements by 2011, and in May

[11] Rosaria Publisi, "Clashing Agendas? Economic Interests, Elite Coalitions and Prospects for Co-operation between Russia and Ukraine," *Europe-Asia Studies* 55, 6 (2003): 837.
[12] See James Sherr, "The Dismissal of Borys Tarasiuk," Occasional Brief 79, Conflict Studies Research Centre, October 6, 2000. Kuchma accused Tarasiuk of "miscalculations in implementing European integration" (quoted p. 2).

2002 the National Security and Defense Council discussed the need to "start practical implementation of the course to join NATO."[13]

The United States, and the West more broadly, were trying to walk a tightrope on Kuchma, supporting his efforts to maintain Ukraine's independence from Russia while rejecting his authoritarian inclinations. After meeting with Kuchma in Kyiv in June 2001, US Secretary of Defense Donald Rumsfeld reported that Kuchma had assured him that Ukraine would "continue on a path of western-style democracy" and would fully investigate Gongadze's murder.[14] Rumsfeld said:

We recognize that no book has been written as to exactly how a nation moves from communism to free political and free economic institutions ... What I do know is that relationships need to be nurtured and tended and strengthened and they are leaning very far forward to have a relationship with NATO, with the United States, and with their neighbors and other countries.[15]

The relationship with the United States worsened. In the fall of 2002, just as the United States was gearing up to attack Iraq, the State Department revealed that the Melnychenko recordings showed that Kuchma had approved selling *Kolchuga* air defense radar systems to Iraq. The Bush administration, tightly focused on Iraq, was outraged. State Department Spokesman Richard Boucher said: "This recording's authentication has led us to reexamine our policy towards Ukraine, in particular towards President Kuchma. We've initiated a temporary pause in new obligations of Freedom Support Act assistance that goes to the central government of Ukraine while we carry out this review ... we're having a pause in programs that are with the central government authorities."[16]

The timing of these developments could not have been worse for Kuchma's hope to gain a commitment that Ukraine might someday join NATO. He sought to atone by deploying, against domestic protest, a small but symbolically important force (1,650 troops) to support the US coalition in Iraq. Ukraine's goal of joining NATO continued to be stated in numerous documents and even parliamentary resolutions up until mid-2004.[17] Nonetheless, Kuchma's hopes that Ukraine would receive

---

[13] Olexiy Haran and Rostyslav Pavlenko, "The Paradoxes of Kuchma's Russian Policy," PONARS Policy Memo 291, September 2003, p. 1.

[14] Jim Mannion, "Rumsfeld Meets Kuchma, Cites Promises on Democracy, Dead Journalist," Agence France Presse, June 5, 2001.

[15] Ibid.

[16] Transcript of Press Briefing on Ukraine, Iraq and Kolchuga Radar, US State Department, September 25, 2002.

[17] Several examples are provided in Marten Malek, "The 'Western Vector' of the Foreign and Security Policy of Ukraine," *Journal of Slavic Military Studies* 22, 4 (2009): 520.

a "Membership Action Plan" were left unmet. Instead, Ukraine and NATO signed an "Action Plan" in November 2002, with the crucial word "membership" left out.[18] This required extensive reforms on Ukraine's part without any commitment to future membership. For Kuchma, this was a disappointment. For both Ukraine and the West, however, the commitment to deepening ties further was seen as important to countering Russian pressure on Ukraine, and in December 2003 NATO defense ministers praised Ukraine's progress on military reform.[19]

Kuchma's relations with the West fractured further as his efforts to consolidate power progressed. Finally, in July 2004, Kuchma suddenly dropped the goal of joining NATO (and the EU), from Ukraine's new military doctrine, which had been adopted only the previous month. Former Foreign Minister Borys Tarasiuk speculated that the move was prompted by Kuchma's annoyance that NATO Secretary General Jaap de Hoop Scheffer had criticized Kuchma on democracy and free elections.[20] This was implied by the title of Kuchma's decree, "On further development of relations with NATO with account for results of the Ukraine-NATO summit on June 29, 2004."[21] The Russian Foreign Ministry released a statement in support of the revised doctrine.[22] In September, Kuchma acquiesced in the dismissal of Defense Minister Yevhen Marchuk, the last remaining advocate of NATO membership in his cabinet.

Kuchma continued to claim to want strong ties with the EU, complaining that leaving Ukraine outside of the West would lead to instability. He used a visit by Pope John Paul II in June 2001 both to bolster his reputation in general and to stress Ukraine's ambition to increase ties with the EU. "We would not like Ukraine to be a bridge between Europe and Russia – I personally do not like this idea because bridges get trampled upon."[23] A week after becoming head of the CIS Council of Presidents, Kuchma created a "State Council on European and

[18] James Greene, "NATO-Ukraine Distinctive Partnership Turns Twenty: Lessons to Take Forward," *NATO Review*, April 7, 2017.

[19] Bertil Nygren, *The Rebuilding of Greater Russia: Putin's Foreign Policy Toward the CIS* (Abingdon, Oxon: Routledge, 2008), p. 55.

[20] Anna Melnichuk, "Ukrainian Official: NATO, EU Give no Timetable for Ukraine's Accession, Prompting Changes in Defense Doctrine," Associated Press, July 27, 2004.

[21] "Leonid Kuchma Amends Ukraine's Military Doctrine on Accession to NATO, EU," *RIA Novosti*, July 26, 2004.

[22] Melnichuk, "Ukrainian Official."

[23] "Roundup: Ukraine's Kuchma Sends Firm Offer of 'Partnership' with Europe," Deutsche Presse-Agentur, June 28, 2001.

Euro-Atlantic Integration," and led it himself.[24] The problem for Kuchma was that while his desire for closer ties with Europe was probably genuine, his desire to sideline opposition domestically was incompatible with that goal. In 2003, the parliament passed a "Law on Fundamentals of National Security in Ukraine," supported by the Party of Regions and Yanukovych, which made joining NATO and the European Union a priority.[25] However, there was no avoiding the fact that relations with the West were ebbing due to Kuchma's increasing authoritarianism.

Kuchma's Turn toward Russia

As the West distanced itself from Kuchma, Kuchma turned to Moscow. From 2000 to 2002, Kuchma met with Putin eighteen times.[26] In December 2000, Kuchma went to Moscow, in what was widely seen as an attempt to gain support from Russia as the West pulled back. "Whether or not Leonid Kuchma secures Moscow's support will determine if he will cope with the acute internal political crisis back home."[27] In February 2001, at a meeting with Putin in Dnipropetrovsk, Kuchma agreed to new ties with Russia, including linking the two countries' power grids and cooperation in military production.[28] Of the turmoil in Ukraine, Putin had said before leaving Moscow: "What is happening is a political struggle. There is nothing extraordinary about it. I think this is a feature of a normal democratic society."[29] The events that caused the West to limit support for Kuchma did not faze Putin.

While Ukraine continued to seek to cooperate with Russia but not integrate with it, Putin was renewing Russia's focus on Ukraine. From the time Putin came to power, he emphasized the primacy of the "near abroad," and as his confidence in forging a close relationship with the European Union faded, he put increased emphasis on integrating the post-Soviet space. Speaking to Russia's ambassadors in 2004, he stressed the importance of "supporting, by all means, the integration processes evolving in different trans-regional associations."[30] Kuchma's problems with the West facilitated that emphasis.

---

[24] Haran and Pavlenko, "The Paradoxes of Kuchma's Russian Policy," p. 4.
[25] Olexiy Haran and Maria Zolkina, "Ukraine's Long Road to European Integration," PONARS Eurasia Policy Memo No. 311, February 2014, p. 2.
[26] Puglisi, "Clashing Agendas?" p. 840.
[27] *Vremya Novostei*, quoted in *Russian Press Digest*, December 22, 2000.
[28] Ariel Cohen, "Analysis: Ukraine Scandals," *UPI*, February 23, 2001.
[29] Craig Nelson, "Kuchma's Guest Fails to Notice the Stench," *Sydney Morning Herald*, February 17, 2001, p. 18.
[30] Quoted in Andrei Zagorski, "Russia and the Shared Neighborhood," in Dov Lynch, ed., *What Russia Sees*, Chaillot Paper No. 74 (Paris: Institute for Security Studies, 2005) p. 68.

In May 2001, Putin appointed Viktor Chernomyrdin ambassador to Kyiv. Given Chernomyrdin's status in Russia as a former prime minister and favorite of the *derzhavniki*, his appointment was seen as a sign that relations with Ukraine would be a high priority for Putin. The warming of relations was institutionalized when Putin declared 2002 the "Year of Ukraine in Russia," and Kuchma declared 2003 the "Year of Russia in Ukraine." Putin then offered to make Kuchma the head of the Council of CIS leaders and, despite the fact that Ukraine continued to reject full membership in the CIS, Kuchma assumed this position in early 2003.[31]

Putin said: "We would like to restore what was lost with the Soviet Union's disintegration ... We must steer toward integration ... concerted action is the only way to survive in conditions of [global] competition."[32] To this end, Russia advanced two successive integration projects, the Eurasian Economic Community (EurAsEC) and the Common Economic Space (CES).[33] The EurAsEC was modeled on the European Union and was intended to remedy the shortcomings of the Commonwealth of Independent States. It was designed to be a supranational organization, with a set of decision-making bodies mirroring those of the EU, including a judicial entity and a parliament. Its permanent executive, to be known as the Integration Committee, had voting rules that would allow Russia to effectively control it. These institutions would overcome the ability of single countries (including Ukraine) to block integration in the CIS.

Russia deployed familiar tactics to get Ukraine to join the EurAsEc. The organization did not include energy cooperation, which allowed Russia to continue using energy to entice or coerce Ukraine into joining. But while leaving energy out of the EurAsEc maintained Russian leverage, it also eliminated Ukraine's main incentive to join. With Chernomyrdin, who had run Gazprom, based in Kyiv as ambassador, Russia sought to appeal directly to Ukrainian business interests to support the deal. In March 2002, Kuchma signaled his intention to join the organization, but backed off after parliament objected, and by December 2002 he rejected full membership.[34] While the EurAsEc continued to exist, Ukraine never went beyond "observer status" in it. In February 2003, Russia proposed a less stringent alternative, the

[31] Haran and Pavlenko, "The Paradoxes of Kuchma's Russian Policy," p. 4.
[32] Fred Weir, "Putin Woos Ukraine with a Russian Common Market," *Christian Science Monitor*, November 18, 2004, p. 7.
[33] These projects are described in detail in Rilke Dragneva-Lewers and Kataryna Wolczuk, *Ukraine between the EU and Russia: The Integration Challenge* (London: Palgrave MacMillan, 2015), pp. 20–23, on which this discussion draws.
[34] Haran and Pavlenko, "The Paradoxes of Kuchma's Russian Policy," p. 4.

Common Economic Space (CES), initially to include Russia, Ukraine, Belarus, and Kazakhstan.

Kuchma surprised many by agreeing to join the Common Economic Space, with the organization officially being founded in September 2003.[35] Kuchma's decision appears to have been motivated by domestic concerns as much as international needs. After the Gongadze scandal, the Ukraine without Kuchma movement, and the 2002 parliamentary elections, his domestic status was at a nadir, and he increasingly relied on support in eastern Ukraine, where integration with Russia was popular. "Most of the oligarchs who wanted an independent Ukraine and good relations with the West saw this move as contrary to their interests."[36] Kuchma's signing the agreement fitted with his long-term practice of signing integration deals (not only with Russia but also with NATO and the EU) but seeking the benefits without fulfilling the commitments. Accordingly, Ukraine's participation in the CES was more symbolic than real. Kuchma and Prime Minister Yanukovych were particularly focused on energy prices, with Deputy Prime Minister Nikolai Azarov telling the Rada that "If there is no single price on energy, there will not be a common economic space."[37]

For much of this period, the Black Sea Fleet and Crimea largely receded as issues. While Russian politicians, most notably Moscow Mayor Yuri Luzhkov, continued to pledge involvement in Sevastopol, state-to-state acrimony diminished. This was largely a result of the Friendship Treaty and Black Sea Fleet agreements of 1997. In July 2001, Kuchma and Putin jointly reviewed a procession of warships at Sevastopol, in what was called "an historic moment of amity."[38] In 2003, Russia announced plans to build a base at Novorossiisk, leading to speculation that it accepted the need to move the Black Sea Fleet from Sevastopol, which Russian leaders denied.[39] Having agreed to honor the existing state border, the two sides needed to actually demarcate it, leading to many squabbles.[40]

---

[35] Dragneva-Lewers and Wolczuk, *Ukraine between the EU and Russia*, p. 22. Hans Van Zon ("Political Culture and Neo-Patrimonialism," p. 13) reports that, in keeping with the consolidation of power in the presidential administration, the decision to sign the agreement was reached in secret, without the participation of the Cabinet of Ministers, with Yanukovych then compelled to sign it.

[36] Van Zon, "Political Culture and Neo-Patrimonialism," p. 15.

[37] Quoted in Dragneva-Lewers and Wolczuk, *Ukraine between the EU and Russia*, p. 23.

[38] "Putin and Kuchma Review Black Sea Fleet together in Sevastopol," Deutsche Presse-Agentur, July 29, 2001.

[39] *RIA Novosti*, August 12, 2003.

[40] On the demarcation issue, see Taras Kuzio, *Ukraine-Crimea-Russia* (Stuttgart: ibidem-Verlag, 2007), pp. 85–93.

Just as things seemed to be going better with Ukraine, Russia inexplicably poisoned the relationship by starting a border squabble in the Kerch Strait, the strip of water separating the Crimean peninsula from Russia's Krasnodar region. In October 2003, a week after an EU-Ukraine summit in Yalta, Russia began building a dam from Russia toward an island (Tuzla) in the middle of the strait. Russia appeared to be unilaterally claiming the island, which had been regarded as part of Crimea.[41] Kuchma cut short a Latin American trip to return to Ukraine and visit Tuzla, saying "The closer the causeway gets to our coast, the closer we move towards the West."[42] While the crisis was quelled by an agreement to stop construction and negotiate the border through the Kerch Strait, the crisis renewed Ukraine's fears of Russian aggression and further undermined the likelihood that Kuchma would implement the CES agreement in a way that Russia had hoped.

The EU, Ukraine, and Russia

Relations between the European Union, Russia and Ukraine in this period showed the dynamics of the security dilemma in the area of economic integration. The EU's planned 2004 expansion was going to add ten new members, of which four had been part of the Warsaw Pact and three others had been part of the Soviet Union. This process, which had progressed incrementally since 1990, inadvertently but inevitably made Ukraine of much greater interest to the EU. "[N]o matter how frequently NATO and EU officials say that they do not intend to redivide Europe, and no matter how many 'partnership' agreements they offer to nonmembers, it is inevitable that admitting some countries to full membership of the two organisations and excluding others will produce 'insiders' and 'outsiders.'"[43] As a result, the EU's plans for its eastern borderlands overlapped with Russia's plans for its western border.[44] While Russia (and others) were much more stridently opposed to NATO expansion than to EU expansion, they had much the same effect in the

---

[41] After 2014, the island became part of the path for the bridge that Russia built to create a land link between Russia and Crimea.

[42] *Izvestiya*, quoted in Valerie Mason, "Ukrainian President Denounces Russian 'Imperialism' in Kerch Strait Row," *IHS Global Insight*, October 28, 1993.

[43] Margot Light, John Löwenhardt, and Stephen White, "Russia and the Dual Expansion of Europe," ESRC "One Europe or Several?" Policy Paper 02/00, 2000.

[44] This does not mean that EU expansion was a mistake. On the contrary, even with the recent "backsliding" in several of the states that joined the European Union in 2004, the process was widely regarded as having aided the causes of democracy, security, and prosperity in central Europe.

dilemmas they produced for Russia, for the "in-between" states, and for the organizations themselves. "More broadly, the historic enlargement of the European Union with the incorporation of ten new members on May 1, 2004, underscored the EU policy of constructing a Europe without any meaningful role for Russia."[45]

The European Union recognized that its expansion created "new impetus to the effort of drawing closer to the 385 million inhabitants of the countries who will find themselves on the external land and sea border, namely Russia, the Western NIS and the Southern Mediterranean," and stated its "determination to avoid drawing new dividing lines in Europe and to promote stability and prosperity within and beyond the new borders of the Union."[46] The result was the European Neighborhood Policy (ENP), which was designed to leverage the benefits of conditionality while making the conditions less stringent, both for the target countries and for the EU.[47] While those efforts were intended to include Russia, Russia clearly perceived a need to respond, not only due to its desire to control Ukraine, Belarus, and others politically, but also due to the need to avoid being cut off from them economically. Those efforts were in turn resisted in Ukraine. Andrei Zagorski worried at the time that "in the long run, the EU may become a revisionist power from Moscow's perspective, similar to the United States in Georgia and Ukraine."[48]

While Russian leaders were worried that the ENP might undermine Russia's goals in the region to its west, some recognized that pushing back might be counterproductive. There was also a sense that "the probability of the EU challenging the status quo in the 'shared neighborhood' at Russia's expense is so remote as to be unlikely to affect policy."[49] Moreover, many thought that EU and Russian goals could be squared if Russia merged its project of integrating its region with the project of integrating that region with the European Union. This would ensure that the other states did not integrate with the European Union more quickly than with Russia and would reinforce Russia's leadership in

---

[45] Andrei P. Tsygankov, "Putin and Foreign Policy," in Dale R. Herspring, ed., *Putin's Russia: Past Imperfect, Future Uncertain* (Lanham, MD: Rowman & Littlefield, 2007), p. 202.

[46] Commission of the European Communities, "Wider Europe – Neighbourhood: A New Framework for Relations with our Eastern and Southern Neighbours, COM(2003) 104 final, March 11, 2003, pp. 3–4.

[47] See Gwendolyn Sasse, "The European Neighbourhood Policy: Conditionality Revisited for the EU's Eastern Neighbours," *Europe-Asia Studies* 60, 2 (March 2008): 295–316.

[48] Zagorski, "Russia and the Shared Neighborhood," p. 77.   [49] Ibid., p. 75.

its immediate region and in Europe more broadly.[50] However, by the May 2003 EU-Russia summit, Russia had rejected that strategy, apparently because with Putin's power consolidated internally and rising energy prices giving Russia more power internationally, it felt that it could pursue its plans for integration in its region in competition with the European Union rather than in partnership with it.[51] Russia opposed the EU's project in the region in part because it was premised upon the "normative hegemony" of the European Union.[52] Thus, not only did the ENP and Russia's reaction constitute an economic security dilemma, it invoked the geopolitical consequences of democratization.

The geopolitics of democratization became as much about the EU, whose influence reached, through a series of partnerships, beyond its borders, as about NATO.[53] In June 1999, the European Union had advanced a "Common Strategy of the European Union" on Russia. The document began: "A stable, democratic and prosperous Russia, firmly anchored in a united Europe free of new dividing lines, is essential to lasting peace on the continent. The issues which the whole continent faces can be resolved only through ever closer cooperation between Russia and the European Union."[54] The document went into considerable detail on the importance of liberal norms and institutions: "The establishment of efficient, transparent public institutions is one of the prerequisites for confidence and wider adherence to democratic guidelines and the operation of the rule of law ... The emergence of civil society in all areas is indispensable for the consolidation of democracy in Russia."[55] The European Union was concerned with Russia's behavior in Chechnya as well as the perception that Russia had not fulfilled commitments made at the 1999 Istanbul OSCE summit regarding withdrawal of its troops from Moldova and Georgia.[56] As an analyst at the

[50] L. Karabeshkin, "Vostochnoye izmerenie politiki ES i Rossia," in Filip Kazin and Vladimir Kuznetzov, eds., *Vostochnoye izmerenie Evropeiskogo Soyuza i Rossia. Mezhdunarodnaya konferentsia. Sbornik dokladov. Veliky Novgorod, November 14, 2003* (St. Petersburg: BITS, 2004), pp. 34–45, cited in Igor Gretskiy, Evgeny Treshchenkov, and Konstantin Golubev, "Russia's Perceptions and Misperceptions of the EU Eastern Partnership," *Communist and Post-Communist Studies* 47 (2014): 376.

[51] Gretskiy et al., "Russia's Perceptions and Misperceptions," p. 376.

[52] Hiski Haukkala, "Russian Reactions to the European Neighborhood Policy," *Problems of Post-Communism* 55, 5 (September/October 2008): 40–48.

[53] As Haukkala (ibid., p. 41) points out, this process has its roots in the EU's 1993 Copenhagen criteria for potential new members.

[54] Common Strategy of the European Union of 4 June 1999 on Russia (1999/414/CFSP), p. 1.

[55] Ibid., p. 2.

[56] Dov Lynch, "Misperceptions and Divergences," in Dov Lynch, ed., *What Russia Sees*, Chaillott Paper No. 74 (Paris: Institute for Security Studies, 2005), p. 16. As well as

time put it: "The success of enlargement has strengthened the EU's claim that it has developed a unique capacity to promote the internal transformations of state, which is driven less by a realist calculus of military power than by the civilian tools of economic integration and moral persuasion."[57]

Increasingly, the EU project and the Russian project seemed incompatible. In September 2003, just before Kuchma signed the CES agreement, EU Commissioner Günter Verheugen acknowledged the incompatibility between the integration projects, telling Kuchma that "in case of establishing a customs union as part of the CES, the European integration process for Ukraine could be stepped down or even cease completely."[58] A central dynamic of the conflict that was to emerge in 2013 was already underway in 2003. A group of Russian scholars captured this dynamic:

Shying away from participating in the European Neighborhood Policy and having revitalized its policy in the post-Soviet territory, Russia, like no one else, has influenced the [Eastern Partnership] to take the very form that causes its own most fierce criticism … Russia's actions, aimed to consolidate the post-Soviet area, often against the will of individual states in that region, provoked retaliatory measures by Brussels and vice versa. As a result, the air of mutual distrust between the European Union and Russia was growing worse.[59]

Russia's Deputy Foreign Minister Vladimir Chizhov pointed out in 2004 that while Russia acknowledged "the EU's desire to create a friendly environment around its new borders," it did not want to see the region become an EU "near abroad … mostly oriented to EU standards."[60] By 2004, the European Union recognized that despite many common interests, notably in energy, the relationship had deteriorated. An uncommonly frank document identified a range of concerns, including "a more assertive Russian stance towards a number of acceding countries and the NIS."[61]

---

continuing to support the breakaway regions of Abkhazia and South Ossetia, Russia had accused Georgia of harboring Chechen fighters, and in 2002 had bombed Georgia's Pankisi Gorge region, claiming the need to attack Chechen rebels there.

[57] Roland Dannreuther, "Developing the Alternative to Enlargement: The European Neighborhood Policy," *European Foreign Affairs Review* 11 (2006): 183.

[58] Cited in Gretskiy et al., "Russia's Perceptions and Misperceptions," p. 377.

[59] Ibid., p. 376.

[60] Chizhov is quoted in Dmitry Danilov, "Russia and European Security," in Lynch, ed., *What Russia Sees*, p. 89.

[61] Commission of the European Communities, Communication from the Commission to the Council and to the European Parliament, on Relations with Russia, COM(2004) 106 final, February 2, 2004.

In practice, the ENP did not have much impact in Ukraine. As the British EU official Chris Patten wrote, "Europe's most effective instrument of soft power is the offer of membership in the European Union," and that was not on offer for Ukraine.[62] The problem with the ENP, from Ukraine's perspective, was that it required far-reaching and non-negotiable domestic changes without any commitment to membership. While the ENP was modeled on the enlargement process, the fact that enlargement was not on the table made it entirely different.[63]

The Evolution of Energy Politics

Ukraine's energy dependence on Russia continued to be a main avenue for conflict during this period, but the relationship evolved in two significant ways. First, in Ukraine, control of the gas trade increasingly became the focus of politics, both as the object of political machinations and as the source of power to prevail. Second, increases in global energy prices heightened Ukraine's and Europe's dependence on Russia and drove growth in Russia's economy, which both legitimized Putin's rule and increased Russia's power. By 2005, Ukraine's gas debt to Russia had grown to $23.9 billion.[64]

These developments were linked, as corruption in Ukraine facilitated Russia's tactics of gaining political leverage from the energy trade. Margarita Balmaceda has documented in detail how "domestic processes have been central in facilitating Russia's use of energy for foreign policy purposes through the maintenance of old dependencies and the development of new ones."[65]

In 2000–2001, Yushchenko and his deputy Yuliya Tymoshenko introduced reforms to the energy sector that outlawed barter, increased price transparency, and reduced the scope for rent-seeking.[66] Powerful oligarchs resisted, and this helps explain the coalition that developed to force Yushchenko from office in 2001 (Tymoshenko had been fired in January). As Balmaceda details, two competing trends were underway: Russian capital was gaining control of assets in Ukraine and Ukrainian

---

[62] Chris Patten, *Cousins and Strangers: America, Britain, and Europe in a New Century* (New York: Henry Holt, 2006), p. 158.

[63] Judith Kelley, "New Wine in Old Wineskins: Promoting Political Reforms through the New European Neighbourhood Policy," *Journal of Common Market Studies* 44, 1 (2006): 29–55.

[64] Margareta M. Balmaceda, *Energy Dependency, Politics and Corruption in the Former Soviet Union: Russia's Power, Oligarchs' Profits and Ukraine's Missing Energy Policy, 1995–2006* (Abingdon, Oxon: Routledge, 2009), p. 33.

[65] Ibid., pp. 1–2.   [66] Ibid., pp. 54–55.

"clans" were seeking greater control. Ukrainian groups found the money and political clout of Russian firms valuable in their battles with one another. The trick was to gain this help without losing control to Russian oligarchs. For none of these actors was the interest of the Ukrainian state vis-à-vis Russia of much concern.[67]

In keeping with Kuchma's tactical reorientation toward Russia, Ukraine signed a series of energy agreements in 2000–2004, including significant Russian investments in several Ukrainian refineries.[68] In July 2000, Kuchma agreed that the state would take over energy debts, undermining the Yushchenko/Tymoshenko reforms, and giving Russia a new lever. In February 2001, the two states agreed to link their electrical grids to facilitate supply management. In October 2002, Russia and Ukraine signed a deal creating a consortium on gas transport that would have eroded Ukraine's trump card in energy relations with Russia, its control of pipelines delivering Russian gas westward to the rest of Europe. Gaining control of these pipelines had been a goal of Russian policy since the early 1990s, so this appeared to be a major victory, but the agreement, like so many others, was never implemented.

The energy relationship stabilized, because it served most of the powerful actors' interests: Ukrainian oligarchs reaped massive rents. Kuchma used his ability to shape access to those rents to garner political support; Ukrainian consumers avoided the pain of reform; Russian elites also benefited from rent-seeking. The Russian government, which controlled Gazprom, was willing to tolerate payment arrears because the arrangement augmented Russia's power in the long term in two ways. As the debt grew, the likelihood that Ukraine would need to make major concessions in lieu of being able to pay it also grew. And by not forcing a crisis, Russia helped ensure that measures to reduce Ukraine's dependence were never taken. Europe's gas supply at this point remained uninterrupted, so it had no reason to intervene.

The West, Russia, and Ukraine

The new US President, George W. Bush, and the new Russian President, Vladimir Putin, had a famously positive first meeting, with Bush saying afterwards that "I looked the man in the eye. I found him to be very straightforward and trustworthy. We had a very good dialogue. I was able to get a sense of his soul; a man deeply committed to his country and the best interests of his country. And I appreciated so very much the

---

[67] Ibid., pp. 60–61.   [68] These are discussed in ibid., pp. 29–32.

frank dialogue." Bush went on to point out that the two states shared some common problems, such as terrorism, and stated that "The basis for my discussion began with this simple premise: that Russia and the United States must establish a new relationship beyond that of the old Cold War mentality."[69]

Putin echoed Bush's words:

I want to return now to what the President said very recently – that Russia and the United States are not enemies, they do not threaten each other, and they could be fully good allies. And taking into account the fact that the United States and the Russian Federation ... have accumulated huge amounts of nuclear weapons ... we bear a special responsibility for maintaining the common peace and security in the world, for building a new architecture of security in the world.

While Bush and Putin spoke with confidence about common interests, problems remained. Bush mentioned Chechnya and press freedom; Putin mentioned "some very difficult regional issues – the Near East and Afghanistan and the Balkans."[70]

NATO expansion continued to be a sore spot. In the spring of 2000, while campaigning for the presidency, Putin surprised many when, asked by David Frost of the BBC whether Russia could become a member of NATO, he responded: "Why not?"[71] In that interview, however, he also voiced his opposition to NATO expansion, and in that context twice stressed that Russia must be "an equal partner." In 2001, Putin laid out his thinking on NATO and Russia: "the simplest [solution] is to dissolve NATO, but this is not on the agenda. The second possible option is to include Russia in NATO. This also creates a single defense and security space. The third option is the creation of a different new organization which would set itself these tasks and which would incorporate the Russian Federation."[72] His advisor Sergei Markov pointed out the underlying problem: "Of course, the Europeans are afraid of Russia. ... If you just take a look at the map, you will see a crazy quilt kind of blanket on the left side, a lot of very small countries. And on the right looms a huge red or rosy colored part and of course they are afraid of us."[73]

---

[69] Both quotations are from Press Conference by President Bush and Russian Federation President Putin Brdo Castle, Brdo Pri Kranju, Slovenia, June 16, 2001, www.georgewbush-whitehouse.archives.gov/news/releases/2001/06/20010618.html.

[70] Ibid.

[71] "BBC Breakfast with Frost Interview: Vladimir Putin," March 5, 2000. In the same interview, Putin said "it is hard for me to visualise NATO as an enemy."

[72] Peter Baker, "Putin Offers West Reassurances and Ideas on NATO," *Washington Post*, July 18, 2001.

[73] "Press Conference with Political Studies Institute Director Sergei Markov," Official Kremlin International News Broadcast, June 26, 2001.

The problem of designing a post-Cold War security architecture for Europe remained unsolved. Russia sought a unified security system in which it played a leading role and held a veto. That would require dissolving, transforming, or superseding NATO. The West, including the EU, NATO, and their members, whose fear of Russia was growing, opposed dissolving NATO institutions or giving Russia a veto in it. Their implicit solution was for NATO to expand and for disagreements to be managed bilaterally between NATO and Russia. Underpinning this belief was the view that if Russia became a liberal democracy and accepted its role, problems would be minimal.

Ukraine was increasingly important in relations between Russia and the West. In 2002, responding to a question at a press conference with Kuchma, Putin said:

I am absolutely convinced that Ukraine will not shy away from the processes of expanding interaction with NATO and the Western allies as a whole. Ukraine has its own relations with NATO; there is the Ukraine-NATO Council. At the end of the day the decision is to be taken by NATO and Ukraine. It is a matter for those two partners.

He further said categorically that "Russia does not intend to join NATO."[74] Putin's diplomatic efforts may have had unintended consequences, for while Russia's opposition to NATO expansion was real and intensifying, western leaders could cite comments such as these as indicating that it was not an issue of fundamental concern for Russia.[75]

The attacks of September 11, 2001, had an immediate and far-reaching impact on US-Russia relations. US foreign policy, and by extension its relations with Europe and Russia, became increasingly dominated by the "Global War on Terror" and in particular the war in Iraq that was launched in March 2003. Russia saw its problem in Chechnya as one of combating Islamic extremism, and perceived a new common cause with the United States. In May 2002 Secretary of State Colin Powell said

---

[74] Vladimir Putin, "Press Statement and Answers to Questions at a Joint News Conference with Ukrainian President Leonid Kuchma," May 17, 2002, at Kremlin website, http://en.kremlin.ru/events/president/transcripts/21598. Putin later said that in his final meeting with President Bill Clinton he broached the idea of Russian NATO membership. According to Putin, "Clinton answered, 'I have no objection.' But the entire U.S. delegation got very nervous." See Radio Free Europe Radio Liberty, "Putin Says He Discussed Russia's Possible NATO Membership with Bill Clinton," June 3, 2017. It appears that Clinton has not denied Putin's account.

[75] James Golgeier and Michael McFaul speculated that "Putin had long realized that blustering about something he could not stop (as Yeltsin did) only made Russia look weaker." James M. Goldgeier and Michael McFaul, *Power and Purpose: U.S. Policy toward Russia after the Cold War* (Washington, DC: Brookings Institution Press, 2003), p. 323.

that "Russia is fighting terrorists in Chechnya, there is no question about that and we understand that," and in October 2002 the Bush administration designated three Chechen groups "terrorist organizations" and froze their assets in the United States.[76] Similarly, Russia's extensive experience in Afghanistan was potentially very helpful as the United States went to war and then tried to help build a stable government there.[77] The fact that Russia welcomed US forces into Central Asia was a remarkable turnabout which Putin directed despite likely opposition within the government. That potential for improvement, however, went largely unrealized, for several reasons.

First, the United States increasingly disapproved of domestic developments in Russia. While the Bush administration had come to power speaking of a more pragmatic foreign policy, after 9/11 it focused increasingly on democratization and human rights. Neoconservatives eclipsed realist pragmatists linked with Bush's father. Speaking at West Point in 2002, Bush said: "The 20th century ended with a single surviving model of human progress, based on non-negotiable demands of human dignity, the rule of law, limits on the power of the state, respect for women and private property and free speech and equal justice and religious tolerance."[78]

From this perspective, Putin's efforts to control Russia's media and to sideline political competitors appeared increasingly problematic, and while sympathy concerning Chechnya grew, there was still widespread opposition to the level of violence the Russian government was applying there. Speaking in November 2003, US ambassador to Russia Alexander Vershbow worried that a perceived "values gap" would injure the relationship, pointing in particular to the pressure on the Yukos oil company and its leader, Mikhail Khodorkovsky.[79] Sergei Karaganov captured the issue this way:

> The political classes in Russia and the EU have a noticeable difference in basic values. ... The Russian elite ... seeks to join the Old World of fifty or a hundred years ago. Meanwhile, contemporary Western Europe ... is developing a new,

---

[76] Ibid., pp. 316–317.

[77] See John O'Loughlin, Gearóid Ó Tuathail, and Vladimir Kolossov, "A 'Risky Westward Turn'? Putin's 9-11 Script and Ordinary Russians," *Europe-Asia Studies* 56, 1 (January 2004): 3–34.

[78] President Bush Delivers Graduation Speech at West Point, United States Military Academy, West Point, New York, June 1, 2002, www.georgewbush-whitehouse.archives.gov/news/releases/2002/06/20020601-3.html.

[79] US State Department, "Nov. 5: U.S. Ambassador to Moscow at World Affairs Council of Philadelphia," Press Release, November 10, 2003.

"post-European" system of values, which differs from its traditional one in renouncing the supremacy of the nation-state, [and] rejecting violence.[80]

While many in the West admired Putin's discipline and pragmatism, and hoped that despite his consolidation of power, he would prove a reliable partner in international affairs, others feared that Putin sought to rebuild an authoritarian and imperial Russia. In September 2004, 115 European and American officials, including former heads of state and US senators from both major parties, released a letter stridently criticizing Putin and the West's response to him. The letter stated that "President Putin's foreign policy is increasingly marked by a threatening attitude towards Russia's neighbors and Europe's energy security, the return of rhetoric of militarism and empire, and by a refusal to comply with Russia's international treaty obligations." "The leaders of the West must recognize that our current strategy toward Russia is failing." The correct course, they contended, was to "put ourselves unambiguously on the side of democratic forces."[81]

Many Russian elites had completely different interpretations of Putin's rule thus far, seeing it as "getting Russia back on its feet," and having prevented the country from fragmenting and stabilizing it after the chaos of the 1990s.[82] Similarly, Karaganov criticized what he called the notion of "democracy as a panacea for all social and economic problems," and worried that "[t]he international system, based on the primacy of sovereign states and the central role of the United Nations in governing international relations, is weakening."[83] More broadly, Andrei Tsygankov details how Russians across the political spectrum rejected Francis Fukuyama's "end of history" thesis and the liberal normative

[80] Sergei Karaganov, "Russia and the International Order," in Lynch, ed., *What Russia Sees*, p. 33. Karaganov goes on (p. 40) to point out that "this difference is greater with Europe ... and somewhat smaller with the United States."

[81] See "The Truth on Russia," *The Washington Post*, October 2, 2004, p. A20. The text of the letter is at www.aei.org/publication/an-open-letter/. Signatories included former Czech President Vaclav Havel, former Secretary of State Madeleine Albright, Senator John McCain, as well as former Italian Prime Ministers Giuliano Amato and Massimo D'Alema, former Swedish Prime Minister Carl Bildt, and Chair of the German Green Party Reinhard Bütikofer.

[82] Alexei Pushkov, "Putin at the Helm," in Lynch, ed., *What Russia Sees*, p. 46. Pushkov's essay, representative of moderate Russian thinking at the time, clearly lays out the case for Putin's changes.

[83] Karaganov, "Russia and the International Order," p. 24. It is notable that Russian leaders often spoke of the importance of the UN in governing the international system, when most observers around the world found the role of the UN in managing world affairs to be much more of a hope than a reality.

hegemony it assumed.[84] Tsygankov asserts that this thinking "denied Russia the legitimacy of its search for a post-Cold War identity of its own," contributing to the rise of "radically anti-western forces" in Russia.[85]

Second, in December 2001, just when US-Russian cooperation in Afghanistan was ramping up, the Bush administration announced that the United States was withdrawing from the 1972 Anti-Ballistic Missile (ABM) Treaty. While building a ballistic missile defense (BMD) system had been a goal of US conservatives and defense contractors since Ronald Reagan's 1983 "Star Wars" speech, Russia had steadily opposed such a deployment for several reasons. The ABM Treaty itself was seen by Russia as "the cornerstone of global strategic stability,"[86] and abrogating it was seen as a dangerous effort to gain a unilateral advantage. The fact that deployment of the system would require basing components in the new NATO members in central Europe further underscored the strategic impact of NATO enlargement.

Putin was frustrated that efforts to renegotiate the treaty rather than have the United States withdraw were rejected. Yet he refrained from the kind of rhetoric that became common later, saying "In the course of our contacts with President Bush, on no occasion did he deceive me or mislead me ... He always does what he says, and in that respect he is a reliable partner. ... Of course we have differences of opinion on some issues. ... If we treat each other as partners, solutions can be found."[87] Putin was apparently more focused on strengthening Russia's role in NATO, and did not want to undermine that effort. "If we intend to change the nature of our relationship between Russia and the West, Russia and the U.S., and if we take the road suggested by British Prime Minister Tony Blair concerning changing the relationship between Russia and NATO, then this overall question of confrontation will lose its relevance."[88] In the short term, this mild response won Putin considerable praise in the West.[89] However, in the longer term, Russia's perception was that "[W]hile widely acclaimed in the United States and Europe, this policy produced few practical gains for Russia."[90]

---

[84] See Andrei Tsygankov, "Rediscovering National Interests after the 'End of History': Fukuyama, Russian Intellectuals, and a Post-Cold War Order," *International Politics* 39 (December 2002): 423–446.

[85] Ibid., p. 325.   [86] Pushkov, "Putin at the Helm," p. 56.

[87] Megan Twohey, "Putin Says Russia Was Ready to Alter ABM," *Moscow Times*, December 18, 2001.

[88] Ibid.

[89] See, for example, Jim Heintz, "Two Years after Putin's Rise, Russia has Veered to Unexpected Western-oriented Course," Associated Press, December 30, 2001.

[90] Pushkov, "Putin at the Helm," p. 56.

The disappointment over the US decision on the ABM treaty did not prevent the establishment of the NATO-Russia Council in May 2002, replacing the Permanent Joint Council from the 1997 NATO-Russia Founding Act. The goal was to "provide a mechanism for consultation, consensus-building, cooperation, joint decision, and joint action for the member states of NATO and Russia on a wide spectrum of security issues in the Euro-Atlantic region" and to "serve as the principal structure and venue for advancing the relationship between NATO and Russia."[91] A new provision moved in exactly the direction Russia sought: On some topics, the states would meet as a single group of states ("at 20" in the jargon), rather than in NATO-plus-Russia ("19+1") format. Moreover, this group would "operate on the principle of consensus," giving each member, including Russia, a veto. While these arrangements applied only to those issues which the states agreed to address in this format, it appeared to be a step toward the kind of NATO that Russia would see as an asset rather than a threat. It would become more like a collective security organization with a Russian veto. "The new Council represented a first attempt to transform traditional Russia-West cooperation into a partnership of equals."[92] The process kicked off a debate within Russia concerning whether Russia should aim to join NATO.[93] While Russia was opposed to the NATO's decision in November 2002 to admit more new members, including the Baltic States, its response was muted.

The deepening relationship between Russia and NATO ignored a serious contradiction: The formation of the NATO-Russia Council was meant to assuage Russia's concern about expansion by giving it a larger voice. But to the extent that Russia had real influence in NATO decision making, it would seek to block expansion. Thus, Russia's influence in NATO was predicated upon Russia acquiescing to what it most objected to. As long as Europe's relations with Russia were improving, that might work, but as Europe and the United States increasingly objected to Putin's policies, it became untenable. In the short term, however, it was acrimony over Iraq that halted the warming in NATO-Russia relations.

A third factor undermining relations between the West and Russia was the US decision to invade Iraq. The Bush administration advanced two

---

[91] "NATO-Russia Relations: A New Quality. Declaration by Heads of State and Government of NATO Member States and the Russian Federation," Rome, May 28, 2002.

[92] Dmitry Danilov, "Russia and European Security," in Lynch, ed., *What Russia Sees*, p. 80.

[93] Ibid., p. 81.

primary reasons to attack: self-defense against a potential attack with weapons of mass destruction (WMD) and enforcement of earlier UN Security Council resolutions concerning Iraq's WMD program. Russia objected to the attack, insisting that there was no imminent threat that invoked self-defense and that the resolutions in question (some of which dated to 1991–1992) did not in fact authorize the use of force in 2003.[94] The invasion raised many of the same resentments that intervention in Yugoslavia had. Russia had extensive economic interests in Iraq that it wanted to protect, both in energy and in a large debt owed by the Saddam Hussein regime for weapons purchases. It also sought to resist further US pretensions to global hegemony.

Russia had resisted US blandishments to gain its support for a resolution authorizing force in Iraq, with Putin saying "we are not going to bargain, as if we were in an oriental market, selling our position in exchange for some economic benefits."[95] Just after the invasion began in March 2003, Putin warned that it was "in danger of rocking the foundations of global stability and international law," and said that the "only correct solution to the Iraqi problem is the immediate end to military activity in Iraq and resumption of a political settlement in the UN Security Council."[96] Maintaining a positive spin on relations with the United States was becoming harder. Sergei Karaganov argued that Russia's management of the disagreement over Iraq was "skillfully 'stage-managed,'" and that as a result, "real friction over the military operation in Iraq arose between the United States and its traditional partners in NATO and not with Russia."[97]

Russia hoped to take advantage of western disagreements about Iraq to pursue its goal of bringing Russia into Europe and reducing the US role. Both Germany and France strongly opposed the US decision to attack Iraq, and France joined Russia in threatening to veto a resolution authorizing the invasion. Many Europeans shared Russia's qualms about US claims to global hegemony and willingness to use military power. This opportunity was lost, in the view of a Russia commentator,

---

[94] The validity of the Bush administration's arguments for going to war in Iraq was contested far beyond Russia. For a discussion of different perspectives, see Brian C. Schmidt and Michael C. Williams, "The Bush Doctrine and the Iraq War: Neoconservatives versus Realists," *Security Studies* 17 (2008): 191–220.

[95] Quoted in Goldgeier and McFaul, *Power and Purpose*, p. 327.

[96] Carolynne Wheeler, "Weight of War Strains U.S.-Russia Relations: Putin and Bush Exchange Accusations on Iraq, Antitank Missiles and Spy Planes," *Toronto Globe and Mail*, March 29, 2003, p. A8.

[97] Karaganov, "Russia and the International Order," p. 31.

because "European criticism of the war in Chechnya poisoned the relationship."[98]

It is hard to overestimate the impact of the invasion of Iraq. Proceeding as it did without the approval of the UN Security Council, it was seen by Russia and by several US allies in Europe as an illegal use of force. The impression created was that the United States obeyed the "rules of the road" only when it suited their interests. The invasion eroded the norm against using force to resolve disputes, and it badly divided the western alliance. While those who blame the West for the events of 2014 tend to focus on the effects of NATO expansion, the invasion of Iraq might have had a larger impact in undermining the order the West was trying to build in Europe.

The period from 1999 to late 2004 was, despite many difficulties, one in which Russia and the United States perceived a renewed potential to work together. Although Putin was consolidating power at home and continuing to assert Russia's interests in the near abroad, he clearly sought positive relations with both the United States and Europe. That hope was reciprocated, but it was not clear that that the sides could agree on the basic terms on which cooperation would be built. The Orange Revolution dramatically reshaped Putin's assessment of relations with the West. For all of its international consequences, however, the Orange Revolution was above all about Ukrainian domestic politics.

The Orange Revolution: Prelude

The tensions that emerged on the streets in November 2004 reflected long-term institutional, regional, and oligarchic conflicts in Ukraine.[99] Institutionally, there was a conflict between president, prime minister, and parliament that had festered since the early independence period. Regionally, Ukrainian leaders had failed to build parties that stretched across Ukraine's east and west, and increasingly were using regional identities to mobilize voters, accentuating rather than bridging the regional divide. This was especially true of Yanukovych, who, with advice from Russia, painted the opposition as fascist supporters of the controversial World War II-era figure Stepan Bandera. The oligarchs were in a constant struggle for power, in which each tried to gain at the others'

---

[98] Pushkov, "Putin at the Helm," p. 57.

[99] The long-term roots of the Orange Revolution are stressed by Serhiy Kudelia, who dates the beginning of the crisis to 2000–2001. See Serhiy Kudelia, "Revolutionary Bargain: The Unmaking of Ukraine's Autocracy through Pacting," *Journal of Communist Studies and Transition Politics* 23, 1 (2007): 77–100.

expense and all of them feared that one of the others might become dominant.

It was widely anticipated that the 2004 election would be pivotal for Ukraine, because one of two things had to happen. If the election were free and fair, many believed, Kuchma (or his designated successor) would be defeated, reversing Ukraine's slide toward authoritarianism. Kuchma and his supporters were expected to try to rig the election through tactics including controlling the media, patronage, and fraud. That would consolidate autocracy and likely move Ukraine away from the West and toward Russia. Therefore, well before the election, opposition groups were preparing to run a parallel vote count and to challenge fraud through protest.

The United States and European Union preferred Yushchenko to Yanukovych, and they believed that if the election were free and fair, he would prevail. There was, however, no international plot to instigate a revolution. The international environment apart from Russia was important in four respects. First, the examples of the "Bulldozer Revolution" in Serbia and the "Rose Revolution" in Georgia provided examples of how fraudulent elections could help mobilize a critical mass of protesters, tactics that were central particularly to the Pora student movement.[100] Second, those two examples yielded a group of young, committed protest leaders who were willing to share their tactics and experience with Ukrainians, who already had extensive experience of their own, reaching back to the "Revolution on the Granite" of the late Soviet era. Because fraud was anticipated so far in advance, there was plenty of time to prepare protests. Third, western organizations, with a mix of NGO and governmental funding, provided training on how to conduct exit polling and alternative vote counts.[101] The fact that the elections were still being carried out under relatively open procedures facilitated vote checking. Fourth, once protests started, western leaders put considerable pressure on Kuchma not to forcibly repress the protests, and instead helped broker the talks that led to the resolution of the crisis.

The key developments were internal. There was speculation in Ukraine that Kuchma himself would run for a third term. While the

---

[100] On Pora, see Oleksandr Sushko and Olena Prystayko, "Pora – 'It's Time' for Democracy in Ukraine," in Anders Åslund and Michael McFaul, eds., *Revolution in Orange: The Origins of Ukraine's Democratic Breakthrough* (Washington, DC: Carnegie Endowment for International Peace, 2006), pp. 85–102.

[101] For a detailed accounting of the amounts involved, see Andrew Wilson, *Ukraine's Orange Revolution* (New Haven, CT: Yale, 2005), pp. 184–186. Wilson points out that due to anger over the Kolchuga missile affair, US support for democratization in Ukraine actually decreased in 2003.

Ukrainian constitution specified a two-term limit, many believed that Kuchma could get a court to rule that since the constitution wasn't adopted until after his first election, his first term did not count under the rule. It is not clear why Kuchma did not choose this option. His unpopularity may have convinced him he could not win; the increasingly powerful Donetsk clan may have insisted that its turn had arrived; Kuchma may not have wanted to undermine his own self-image as a democratic ruler.

It seemed like a "major mistake" to nominate Yanukovych to carry the torch for Kuchma and the Party of Regions.[102] Yanukovych was a convicted criminal, lacked charisma, and was widely unpopular outside the Donbas. Even so, and even after fraud in the second round had been exposed, he won 44 percent of the vote in the rerun of the second round. This implies that a more compelling establishment candidate would have been able to win fairly. However, that was not how the Party of Regions or Kuchma approached the election. The Party of Regions had won the "right," or at least had the power, to choose the candidate of the establishment, and its leader was Yanukovych.

Equally important was the ability of the opposition to unify. From the moment of independence in 1991, Ukraine's "pro-western" forces were notorious for their tendency for infighting (which would return after the Orange Revolution; see Chapter 5). Recognizing Yushchenko's popularity, Yuliya Tymoshenko agreed to withdraw her candidacy to support him. Yushchenko and Tymoshenko made a formidable team, with her charisma and confrontational approach complementing his image as a competent and honest technocrat. A wide variety of interests, ranging from idealistic student groups to self-interested oligarchs, grouped around this duo. The pro-Yushchenko forces were motivated in large part by the belief that a Yanukovych victory meant an end to democracy and to Ukraine's European aspirations.

In the weeks and months before the election, both sides prepared for a contest in the streets. The opposition honed tactics of decentralized organization. The government fortified key buildings. A few weeks before the election, when opposition leaders held a demonstration at the Central Electoral Commission, the authorities deployed water cannon. This was a practice run for both sides.

---

[102] Van Zon, "Political Culture and Neo-Patrimonialism under Leonid Kuchma," p. 21; see also Taras Kuzio, "From Kuchma to Yushchenko: Ukraine's 2004 Presidential Elections and the Orange Revolution," *Problems of Post-Communism* 52, 2 (March/April 2005): 33–35.

Into this situation, Vladimir Putin stepped boldly.[103] Putin sent one team of advisors, led by Gleb Pavlovskii, to Kyiv and another, led by Vyacheslav Nikonov, to Yanukvych's headquarters in Donetsk to help manage Yanukovych's campaign.[104] Russia's strategy was based on two assumptions. First, it assumed that if the choice were framed as one between the West and Russia, voters would choose Russia. Second, it assumed that the same tactics that worked in Russia (media blitz, coercion of state employees, voting fraud, and falsification of results), would work in Ukraine.[105] The week before the first round of the election, Putin traveled to Kyiv, appearing with Kuchma, Yanukovych, and Belarusian leader Alyaksandr Lukashenka at a huge military parade on Khreshchatyk. While in Kyiv, he gave a television interview, holding out the hope that visa restrictions between the two countries would be reduced.[106] Russian media praised Yanukovych widely and ran negative stories on Yushchenko. After Yushchenko ran surprisingly strongly in the first round (the official results put Yushchenko in front with 39.9 percent of the vote to 39.3 percent, but a delay in announcing them stoked the belief that the numbers had been manipulated and that Yushchenko's lead was much greater), Putin returned to Kyiv a second time before the second round. In contrast, the Bush administration kept a lower profile, perhaps, as *Novosti* put it, "because his advisers realize that his blessing for Yushchenko would send voters running the other way."[107]

The Orange Revolution: Crisis and Aftermath

The general story of the Orange Revolution is well known. After the second round, held on November 21, Yanukovych was announced as the winner, but exit polls indicated that Yushchenko had won and falsification of the vote was revealed. Protesters occupied the Maidan Nezalezhnosti. Eventually, a "pact" was reached that combined a rerun of the second round of the election with constitutional changes to reduce the

---

[103] Russia's involvement in the campaign is detailed in Nikolai Petrov and Andrei Ryabov, "Russia's Role in the Orange Revolution," in Åslund and McFaul, eds., *Revolution in Orange*, pp. 145–164.

[104] Ibid., p. 153.   [105] Ibid., pp. 148–149.

[106] For a contemporary description of the event, see Nick Paton Walsh, "Putin's Kiev Visit 'Timed to Influence Ukraine Poll': President's Remarks Helpful to Pro-Moscow Candidate, but Aides Deny any Attempt to Help Ally," *The Guardian*, October 27, 2004, p. 14.

[107] "Putin's Intense Interest in Elections," *RIA Novosti*, November 17, 2004.

power of the presidency.[108] The second round of the election was rerun on December 26, with Yushchenko winning.

In addition to the protesters in the streets, Ukraine's oligarchs played a large role in the revolution, probably out of fear of what a Yanukovych presidency might mean for them. A prominent example of oligarchic cooperation with the protests was that Channel 5, the television channel owned by Petro Poroshenko, defied Kuchma and broadcast positive news about the protests.[109] A second example was that in contrast to the "Ukraine without Kuchma" protests a few years earlier, when the Maidan was shut down and transport into Kyiv disrupted, transport to Kyiv and within it remained unchecked, and the Maidan was wide open. Kyiv Mayor Omelchenko and the Kyiv City Council, who had helped foil protests in 2001, denounced the results of the election. Finally, and in contrast to 2014, the security services signaled clearly that they would not violently repress the protesters. C. J. Chivers of the *New York Times* reported that the Security Service of Ukraine (SBU; successor to the Soviet KGB) signaled that it would defend the protesters if they were attacked by Interior Ministry forces.[110]

The oligarchs were intent on preserving their autonomy, and hence would oppose anyone becoming so powerful that he could control them, as Putin had done in Russia. They also feared too much Russian influence. "Ukrainian oligarchic groups ... do not desire to come under Moscow's control again as they are unable to compete directly against Russia's more powerful oligarchs."[111] Therefore, while on many matters the interests of the oligarchs coincided with those of Russia, in this case the interests of at least some of them did not. This does not mean that they were "pro-Yushchenko" or "pro-western" in any meaningful sense. It simply means that they preferred a leader who supported pluralism, and couldn't undo it even if he wanted to, to a leader with both the means and inclination to end Ukraine's political pluralism.

As in 2014, the tipping point occurred in parliament, where Kuchma's and Yanukovych's support crumbled as the scale of fraud became clear and as it looked more like Yushchenko would triumph. On November

---

[108] On the Orange Revolution as an example of "pacting," see Serhiy Kudelia, "Revolutionary Bargain: The Unmaking of Ukraine's Autocracy through Pacting," *Journal of Communist Studies and Transition Politics* 23, 1 (2007): 77–100.

[109] In addition to Poroshenko, Wilson (*Ukraine's Orange Revolution*, p. xi) lists David Zhvaniia and Yevhen Chervonenko as important business supporters of Yushchenko.

[110] C. J. Chivers, "How Top Spies in Ukraine Changed the Nation's Path," *The New York Times*, January 17, 2005. See also Wilson, *Ukraine's Orange Revolution*, pp. 137–138, who points to some doubts about the extent of SBU collaboration with the protesters.

[111] Haran and Pavlenko, "The Paradoxes of Kuchma's Russian Policy," p. 2.

27, five days after the vote, the parliament held a non-binding vote declaring the election invalid. Yanukovych's support was collapsing as elites strived to shift to the winning side.

The dispute predictably put the West and Russia on different sides and reinforced mutual perceptions of bad faith. Putin and EU leaders discussed the matter face to face at a previously scheduled EU-Russia summit on November 25 in The Hague. The summit had been postponed due to a lack of agreement on how to proceed on EU-Russia cooperation. The events in Ukraine, therefore, came at a time when the European Union and Russia were already struggling to find common ground, and it was precisely about democracy and Russia's role abroad that they disagreed. The dispute in Ukraine dramatically reinforced existing EU-Russia tensions, despite considerable desire on both sides to bridge the gaps.

When the European Union announced that it rejected the second round of the vote, the Russian Foreign Ministry reacted angrily:

The ministry cannot welcome the recent statement by the EU Office chairman qualifying the second round of the polls in Ukraine as counter to world standards and to the will of the Ukrainian people. Though the statement expresses hopes that the authorities and the sides concerned will not resort to violence, the plea itself indicates that Brussels, on the one hand, ignores the fundamental democratic principle – respect for the people's will [–] and on the [other] hand, is overtly pushing the opposition toward infringement [of the] law and use of force ... Since the outset, that is already during the first round, the only position favoured by the EU was that of either Victor Yushchenko will win, or the elections will be found anti-democratic, falsified and counter to world standards. He has lost and the EU reaction is quite predictable. But what has it to do with democracy and impartiality?[112]

According to Wilson, the harshness of this response (which came early in the crisis, on November 25) increased the EU's resolve to get involved in the crisis, and prompted Javier Solana, the high representative for foreign policy, to join Polish President Kwasniewski in traveling to Kyiv.[113]

This statement captured much of what was to become an orthodox Russian position on the Orange Revolution, having three key pillars. First, the West made up its mind ahead of time that the only acceptable

---

[112] "'The European Union's actual appeals to revise the results of the presidential elections in Ukraine are somewhat embarrassing,' the Russian Foreign Ministry has thus commented on Dutch Foreign Minister Bernard Bot's statement," *RIA Novosti*, November 23, 2004.

[113] Wilson, *Ukraine's Orange Revolution*, p. 138. Wilson points out that Kwasniewski's and Solana's presence in Kyiv brought credibility to the protests and bought time, by delaying any moves by the authorities.

outcome was a Yushchenko win. Second, the West, rather than internal Ukrainian opposition, was primarily responsible for the protests and overturning of the second-round result. Third, the process of overturning the result showed that the West's support for democracy and the rule of law was hypocritical and rife with double standards. For many in the West, Russia's credibility was undermined by its strident denial of such obvious fraud.

Despite this disagreement, the European Union and Russia jointly mediated the dispute, with a group consisting of Polish President Alexander Kwasniewski, Lithuanian President Valdas Adamkus, EU High Representative for Common Foreign and Security Policy Javier Solana, OSCE Secretary General Jan Kubish; and Speaker of the Russian Duma Boris Gryzlov.[114] This mediation may have prevented escalation by one side or the other, but did not itself lead to a resolution.[115]

The resolution came through a domestic bargaining process, in which the main Ukrainian participants were Yushchenko, Yanukovych, President Kuchma, and Speaker of the Parliament Volodymyr Lytvyn. The deal that was eventually hammered out traded rerunning of the second round of the election (which Yushchenko and the protesters demanded) for constitutional revisions reducing the president's powers.

Kuchma and his supporters, understanding they would likely lose any rerun of the election, wanted a less powerful presidency if they were not going to control it. Many others in Ukraine had long argued that the presidency was too powerful. Implementing the deal within the law and constitution took some gymnastics. While the Supreme Court had ordered the second round of the election rerun, a new election could not be implemented without changes to the election law. This gave parliament considerable weight, and gave Yushchenko incentive to compromise on the presidential powers. Yanukovych objected to the deal, but many of his allies were willing to bow to what appeared to be inevitable, accepting a rerun of the election in return for a weakening of the presidency. The election was rerun on December 26, with Yushchenko winning by 52 to 44 percent. This time, the OSCE declared the vote to be free and fair, while the CIS Election Monitoring Organization determined it to be fraudulent.

In the midst of this dispute, a group of Yanukovych supporters sought to organize an autonomy movement in the Donbas. On November 28, an

---

[114] Kudelia, "Revolutionary Bargain," pp. 94–97, provides a detailed discussion of the negotiations.

[115] Anders Åslund and Michael McFaul, "Introduction: Perspectives on the Orange Revolution," in Åslund and McFaul, eds., *Revolution in Orange*, p. 3.

"all-Ukrainian Congress" was held at an ice rink in Severodonetsk, in Luhansk oblast. Beneath a Russian flag, and joined by Moscow Mayor Yuri Luzhkov, who called the opposition a "sabbath of witches," delegates from eastern Ukraine and Crimea voted to hold a referendum on regional autonomy (federalism, not secession) if Yanukovych were not confirmed as the president.[116] The group declared: "In the worst-case scenario of the political situation in the country, we will be united and decisive in defending the will of the Ukrainian people, including holding a referendum on a possible change in the administrative and territorial status of Ukraine."[117] Odesa Mayor Ruslan Bodelan discussed forming a "Novorossiya," another prelude of what was to come in 2014.[118] These initiatives went no further, apparently because they failed to draw support from other elites or from much of the public. On December 2, Kuchma traveled to Moscow to consult with Putin, and on December 3 Putin, recognizing defeat, announced his support for rerunning the second round of the election.

Consequences of the Orange Revolution

"This was our 9/11," said Gleb Pavlovskii.[119] Russia was vulnerable in a way that it had not realized, it had been humiliated, and it was determined to act. If many Russians had assumed that sooner or later Ukraine would return to the fold, the Orange Revolution raised the prospect that it might be lost permanently, and western interference was seen as being to blame.[120] In some respects, the rest of this book is about the consequences of the Orange Revolution. The Russian press agreed that the events were a disaster. *Pravda* said that "Russia no longer exists as a world-class power," blaming the United States and worrying that Russia would be cut off from gas markets in the West. *Kommersant* predicted that "the Orange Revolution virus will now

---

[116] C. J. Chivers and Steven Lee Myers, "Premier's Camp Signals a Threat to Ukraine Unity," *New York Times*, November 29, 2004, p. 1.

[117] "Pro-Russia Ukraine Regions Threaten Split after Disputed Vote," Agence France Presse, November 28, 2004.

[118] "Ukrainian President Should Have Acted Differently, Says Kuchma Spokesman," BBC Summary of World Broadcasts, December 24, 2004.

[119] Quoted in Ben Judah, *Fragile Empire: How Russia Fell In and Out of Love with Vladimir Putin* (New Haven, CT: Yale University Press, 2013), p. 85.

[120] Tor Bukkvoll, "Why Putin Went to War: Ideology, Interests, and Decision-making in the Russian Use of Force in Crimea and the Donbas," *Contemporary Politics* 22, 3 (2016): 268.

spread to Russia" and that "It will not take long to dismantle the new Russian totalitarianism."[121]

The Orange Revolution was not exactly a turning point, because the various actors were already on a trajectory of increasing mistrust and conflict. But it dramatically heightened mutual mistrust and hostility. It led to domestic changes in both Russia and Ukraine that undermined their relations with each other and Russia's relations with the West. For all of the difficulties of the relationship from 1999 to late 2004, all of the actors sought ways to reconcile their competing goals and interests. After the Orange Revolution, this was much less true.

Russia's anger was directed primarily at the United States and NATO, rather than the EU. Speaking to reporters in Moscow on December 10, Putin said:

> If Ukraine wants to enter the EU and is welcomed there, then we can only be pleased. The issues of EU enlargement to include Ukraine does not concern us. We have a special relationship with Ukraine, economies that are closely interlinked, a very high degree of industrial cooperation. So the inclusion of that part of our economy in the European structure would, I hope, have a positive effect on Russia as well.[122]

In Ukraine, the change in pathway was dramatic, but ultimately less dramatic than it seemed. It is unlikely that Viktor Yanukovych would simply have delivered Ukraine into Russia's hands (he did not do so when he became president in 2010). Instead, his election would likely have led to consolidation of late Kuchma-era politics of autocratization. Whether he would have been able to consolidate hegemonic power (to form a "single-pyramid" system, in Hale's terms) is not certain. Nevertheless, his election would likely have played to Russia's advantage, which is why Russia worked so hard to promote it. Similarly, while it looked at the time as if Yushchenko was going to decisively turn the country westward, that happened in style more than in substance. In early December, at the height of the crisis, Yushchenko stressed that "We aren't going to choose only one side – Europe or Russia."[123]

Most dangerous for Russia was the merger of democratization and geopolitics represented by the Orange Revolution. The Orange

---

[121] *Pravda* and *Kommersant* are quoted in: Steven Eke, "Russians Rush to Rethink Ukraine," BBC, December 27, 2004.

[122] "Putin Says Russia Has no Objection to Ukraine's Joining European Union," Associated Press International, December 10, 2004. It may have been the case that Putin thought that EU membership for Ukraine was so unlikely that there was no reason to oppose it.

[123] Anna Melnichuk, "Ukraine President Asks Opposition to Stop Blockades; Scheduled Meeting of Rivals not Held," Associated Press, November 28, 2004.

Revolution appeared to consolidate the methodology of what Mark Beissinger called "modular revolutions." This tactic had been used to bring about an enormous geopolitical reverse for Russia, and it seemed to be aimed at other Russian neighbors. It had already been applied in Georgia, Kyrgyzstan was next, and there was even hope in the West for Belarus's 2006 election. Most worrying was the idea that such protests might threaten the Putin regime itself. Putin's representative to the EU, Sergei Yastrzhembsky, said at the height of the crisis:

In general, one gets the impression, unfortunately, that certain forces in the West have concluded that the post-Soviet space can be tested for strength by using the technologies of the so-called street anarchy and street democracy, call it what you like. These methods were tested in their time in Poland, I mean in the era of Solidarity; and more recently they were tested in Belgrade.[124]

The Orange Revolution changed Russian thinking in three ways. First, Russia viewed the colored revolutions as a tactic in substitute of war, and concluded that Russia had to learn what Pavlovskii called "the new revolutionary technologies of the globalization era."[125] The result was what later came to called the "Gerasimov doctrine" of hybrid war.[126] Similarly, Russian analysts wrote about Joseph Nye's concept of "soft power," which they tended to see as an instrument for coercion or subversion, not as a force of attraction.[127] "If we had had the power to consult our Ukrainian partners on preventative counter-revolution, and not just elections, then this misfortune wouldn't have occurred," Pavlovskii said.[128] These efforts led to the tactics deployed in 2014.

---

[124] TV Interview with Presidential Special Representative for European Union Sergei Yastrzhembsky Zerkalo RTR Saturday Program with Nikolai Svanidze, *20:20*, November 27, 2004, Official Kremlin International News Broadcast, November 29, 2004.

[125] Quoted in Wilson, *Ukraine's Orange Revolution*, p. 175.

[126] See Valerii Gerasimov, "Tsennost' Nauki v Predvidennii," *Boenno-Promyshlennyi Kur'er*, No. 8, February 27–March 5, 2013, pp. 1–2. Mark Galeotti, who coined the term "Gerasimov Doctrine," stressed that Gerasimov's article does not really express a "doctrine," but rather the prevailing understanding in Russia of what had happened in the colored revolutions and the Arab Spring. See Mark Galeotti, "The Mythical 'Gerasimov Doctrine' and the Language of Threat," *Critical Studies on Security* (2018): 1–5, https://doi.org/10.1080/21624887.2018.1441623. Gerasimov had written: "The experience of military conflicts including the so-called color revolutions in the North Africa and the Middle East confirms that a fully thriving state in a matter of months and even days can be transformed into an arena of intense armed struggle, become a victim of foreign intervention, and plunge into the depths of chaos, humanitarian catastrophe and civil war."

[127] See "Alexander Sergunin and Leonid Karabeshkin, "Understanding Russia's Soft Power Strategy," *Politics* 35, 3–5 (2015): 347–363.

[128] Quoted in Wilson, *Ukraine's Orange Revolution*, p. 175.

Second, the Russian leadership sought to preempt any such revolution in Russia by adopting a range of measures that included the formation of the youth group Nashi and restrictions on foreign NGOs. This additional suppression of democracy widened the perceived normative gap between Russia and the West. Third, Russia began pushing back against the international spread of democracy. Emphasis on the doctrine of "non-interference" increased, in spite of Russia's claims to a role in the "near abroad." Moreover, Russian leaders and theorists openly attacked the notion that values such as democracy are universally valid. Having invoked Nye on soft power, they also invoked Samuel Huntington on "civilizational pluralism."[129] Along with China and the Central Asian states, they started the Shanghai Cooperation Organization (SCO) as a bulwark against democracy promotion in the region. Overall, the response to democracy promotion was autocracy promotion.

As well as making Russia less trustful and more resentful of the West, the Orange Revolution dramatically reshaped western attitudes toward Russia. Both among the media and among policymakers, the near-unanimous opinion was that Russian behavior in Ukraine was both cynical and aggressive. The peaceful protests in Kyiv and Yushchenko's persistence after his poisoning inspired admiration, while the obvious election fraud and Putin's support for it were viewed as signs of bad faith. A few western commentators railed against what they saw as double standards, but they were in a decided minority.[130]

The Orange Revolution was especially corrosive to Russia's relations with the European Union. The episode consolidated the views that Putin was part of the problem, that Russia was using illegitimate tactics in Ukraine, and that Russia's goals were not compatible with those of the EU. The transformation of EU policy was dramatic. "The EU was ambivalent and hesitant to begin with because although the new EU member states favored promoting democracy in Ukraine, the old EU members began from a Russia-first position. However, as violations of democratic practice became rampant, the EU united around a pro-democracy position."[131] In January 2005, the European Parliament voted overwhelmingly for Ukraine to be given "a clear European

---

[129] See, for example, Boris Nezhuyev, "'Island Russia' and Russia's Identity Politics," *Russia in Global Affairs*, June 6, 2017; Andrei P. Tsygankov, "Pluralism or Isolation of Civilizations? Russia's Foreign Policy Discourse and the Reception of Huntington's Paradigm of the Post-Cold War World," *Geopolitics* 4, 3 (December 1999): 47–72.

[130] See, for example, Stephen F. Cohen, "The Media's New Cold War," *The Nation*, January 31, 2005.

[131] Åslund and McFaul, "Introduction," pp. 6–7.

perspective, possibly leading to EU membership."[132] This led eventually to the draft Association Agreement that kicked off the crisis in 2013.

Conclusion

While the Orange Revolution was driven mostly by factors internal to Ukraine, the international consequences were dramatic. Most important, the Orange Revolution tightened the links between the Ukraine-Russia relationship and the Russia-West relationship, making both harder to solve. Prior to the Orange Revolution, Russia and the West assumed that their underlying interests coincided, and that they could work through any problems. After the Orange Revolution, they increasingly saw each other as adversaries, and saw Ukraine as a critical area of disagreement. Similarly, it became clear that despite the 1997 Friendship Treaty, Russia and Ukraine continued to disagree fundamentally on Ukraine's independence. As leaders in both Russia and the West saw the power of protest to disrupt Russia's plans, democratization became almost inseparable from geopolitics.

By the end of the Orange Revolution in January 2005, it looked as though Ukraine had made a decisive turn westward. Adrian Karatnycky wrote at the time that it "set a major new landmark in the postcommunist history of eastern Europe, a seismic shift Westward in the geopolitics of the region."[133] Inside Ukraine, however, the "revolution" was more about continuity than change. The oligarchs who supported it were trying to defend, not overthrow, the political status quo in Ukraine. Similarly, the elites who brokered the compromise that ended the crisis were interested in tweaking the system, not overturning it. Many of the people who came to power were less interested in rooting out corruption than in getting their share of the benefits from it. Ukraine continued to be economically dependent on Russia, which limited its options, and it continued to be regionally divided, which further limited the likelihood of a dramatic foreign policy reorientation. While the European Union was inspired to get more involved, it maintained its standards and waited for prospective partners to meet them.

Ukraine's conflict with Russia and the West's conflict with Russia were now tightly bound together. The fact that the security dilemma had intensified with no change in Ukraine's (or any other actor's) military capabilities was due to the role that democratization had come to play in

---

[132] Adrian Karatnycky, "Ukraine's Orange Revolution," *Foreign Affairs* 84, 2 (March–April 2005): 50.
[133] Ibid., p. 35.

the region's geopolitics. The more Ukraine was viewed as having to choose either Russia or the West, the more intractable its regional divisions would become, and the more the West-Russia relationship would be a zero-sum game. For the West, and for pro-western Ukrainians, there was a new status quo, and efforts to undermine it would be seen as a threat. For Russia, and for pro-Russian Ukrainians, the status quo had been unfairly disrupted, and needed to be restored. Both sides' fear of losing something vital was increased. Rather than increasing a sense of urgency about reducing tensions, the Orange Revolution convinced both sides of the rightness of their views and the malign intentions of the other.

5   Reform and Reversal, 2004–2010

On December 27, 2004, Viktor Yushchenko, in a victory speech, said
"We are free. The old era is over. We are a new country now."[1] Nearly
everyone – in Ukraine, in the West, and in Russia – agreed. The Orange
Revolution appeared to have changed everything. Soon, it became apparent that a great deal, especially within Ukraine, had not changed. As time
went on, moreover, it seemed as if time were moving in reverse, as Viktor
Yanukovych, who had seemed to be politically dead in 2004, was again
appointed prime minister in 2006. Having failed to steal the presidency
in 2004, he won it fairly in 2010. Yushchenko, the hero of 2004, was by
2010 seen as a failure. The turnabout was hard to imagine.

Internationally, things did not go much better. After the Orange
Revolution, the European Union committed more fully to engaging
Ukraine. First the European Neighborhood Policy and then the proposed Association Agreement showed great potential for Ukraine's integration with the EU. The European Union also got involved in helping
Ukraine resolve its energy conflict with Russia, because the quarrel was
directly affecting customers in the EU. Increasingly, however, these
initiatives were hampered by Ukraine's domestic turmoil and were seen
as threatening by Russia.

The relationship between the West and Russia, in which Ukraine's
relations with both were embedded, lurched from one crisis to another,
despite repeated efforts to rescue it. The Orange Revolution soured EU-
Russian relations, but European leaders sought to rebuild them. The new
nadir in the West's relations with Russia was captured by the bitter
speech Vladimir Putin gave to the Munich Security Conference in
2007, expressing his resentment over how Russia had been treated by
the United States: "One state and, of course, first and foremost the
United States, has overstepped its national borders in every way. This
is visible in the economic, political, cultural and educational policies it

---

[1] Quoted in Adrian Karatnycky, "Ukraine's Orange Revolution," *Foreign Affairs* 84, 2
(March–April 2005): 47.

imposes on other nations. Well, who likes this? Who is happy about this?"[2]

The year 2008 saw two pivotal events: the Bucharest NATO summit and Russia's invasion of Georgia. At the Bucharest summit, NATO declined to offer Ukraine and Georgia Membership Action Plans, but said that they could eventually join. Depending on one's view, the decision not to offer a MAP was a concession to Russia's concerns, or an aggressive move to which it felt compelled to respond. Similarly, whether Georgia's actions justified it being invaded by Russia was highly debatable. While both the United States and European Union were appalled by Russia's actions, both made concrete efforts to put the episode behind them. In pursuing a "reset," the new Obama administration was accused of appeasement and naivete, and the strategy brought few results.

The themes highlighted in Chapter 1 were all dramatically on view between 2005 and 2010. The security dilemma in central Europe was exemplified by the Bucharest summit: Ukraine and Georgia, fearing Russia, sought a formal alliance with NATO; NATO worried about both those states but also about Russia's reaction, tried to have it both ways – acceding to Russia's opposition while reassuring Ukraine and Georgia – but even this was insufficient to assuage Russia's fears of an intolerable loss.

Mutually incompatible notions of the status quo exacerbated the security dilemma. For Russia, the perception after 2004 that Ukraine had been lost stoked resentment and determination to redress the problem. For the Yushchenko government and those who supported it, the Orange Revolution finally put Ukraine in its proper place, on the road to the West.

Normative disagreements continued to drive the West and Russia apart. The appointment of Dmitri Medvedev as Russian president in 2008 led to hope, both in Russia and the West, of a political liberalization and warming of relations, but there was little progress. Internationally, Russia now explicitly advanced an ideology counter to the West's universalist liberalism, stressing instead "civilizational pluralism," and creating institutions to further that agenda.

This nexus between geopolitics and democratization increasingly dominated the relationship. It was central in Russia's mind and in the mind of the West after the Orange Revolution. Failed protest movements in Uzbekistan and Belarus upped the stakes. While the European Union strongly believed that Ukraine must be free to determine its membership

---

[2] Vladimir Putin, "Speech and the Following Discussion at the Munich Conference on Security Policy," February 10, 2007, Kremlin website, http://en.kremlin.ru/events/president/transcripts/24034.

in international organizations, Russia saw the EU's promotion of democracy in Ukraine as a hostile geopolitical move.

For all these reasons, by the time of Yanukovych's election as president in 2010, tensions within Ukraine and over Ukraine had ratcheted up dramatically. Within Ukraine, regional divides had been reinforced, largely by Yanukovych's campaign tactics. The collapse of the "Orange Coalition" reopened the door to Yanukovych and to Russian influence and squandered the opportunity to integrate with Europe that the Orange Revolution had opened. This set the stage for Yanukovych's post-2010 assault on Ukraine's constitution, laws, and oligarchic pluralism, which increased domestic instability. Internationally, it became increasingly widely accepted that Russia and the West were adversaries and that Ukraine was at the heart of their contest. Even as determined European leaders sought to find common ground with Russia, their policies of broadening democratic integration inevitably threatened Russia's control over Ukraine.

The Collapse of the Orange Coalition and the Resurrection of Viktor Yanukovych

Almost immediately after it came to power, the alliance of forces that had prevailed in the Orange Revolution began to come apart. At the heart of the alliance were Yushchenko, leader of the "Nasha Ukraina" (Our Ukraine) bloc, who became president; and Yuliya Tymoshenko, leader of the Batkivshchyna (Fatherland) party, who became prime minister. The two had worked together under Kuchma when Yushchenko was PM and Tymoshenko was deputy PM, but then had been on opposite sides when Tymoshenko went into opposition and led the "Ukraine without Kuchma" movement, while Yushchenko crucially stood by Kuchma. Only in 2004 did they forge an alliance, recognizing that if they both ran for president, Kuchma and Yanukovych could apply divide and conquer tactics to defeat them. Two other actors were also important to the coalition: Oleksandr Moroz, leader of the Socialist Party, broadened the regional and ideological appeal of the anti-Kuchma group, and controlled a large bloc of votes in parliament. The chocolate magnate Petro Poroshenko provided financial support for the Orange Revolution and his Channel 5 was one of very few television networks to support the revolution.

With the election won, however, their rivalry emerged stronger than ever, based on at least three factors. First, the inherent tension in Ukraine's system, in which the president and prime minister shared control over the executive branch, had been exacerbated by the constitutional compromise of 2004. Under the new rules, some ministers were appointed by the president and others by the prime minister. Typical of the new era was when Tymoshenko accused Yushchenko's close ally Poroshenko, who headed the National Security and Defense Council, of usurping her power, in particular when he went to Moscow to try to reach a deal on gas supplies and pricing with Russia.[3]

Second, linked to these institutional prerogatives was control over the redistribution of economic assets. The ejection of the Kuchma group after ten years in power was going to lead to a redistribution of economic assets, and everyone wanted their share. Many people around Yushchenko and Tymoshenko sought the financial benefits of their new positions. By many accounts, the demand for bribes did not decrease, and may have increased. In September 2005, Yushchenko's chief of staff, Oleksandr Zinchenko, resigned saying that "corruption is now even worse than before," pointing specifically to Poroshenko.[4]

Third, the personal relationship between Yushchenko and Tymoshenko deteriorated rapidly. Yushchenko appeared to develop an intense hatred for his former ally, such that he chose to allow Yanukovych to return as PM in 2006 rather than allow her to do so, and then campaigned against her in 2010. Yushchenko's inability to rein in the corruption all around him and his inability to get along with Tymoshenko help explain how the advantages gained in 2004 were squandered, setting the stage for later conflict.

At the same time, Yanukovych was working to rehabilitate himself. He hired the American political consultant Paul Manafort, who advised him on strategy relating to Ukraine and also began a sophisticated campaign to burnish Yanukovych's image internationally. Part of that strategy was to stress Yanukovych's support for European integration.

With Yushchenko and Tymoshenko (and their teams) at barely disguised war with one another, Zinchenko's corruption accusations prompted Yushchenko to dismiss Tymoshenko as PM in September 2005, after less than nine months in office. Competition then shifted to parliamentary elections held in March 2006. The pro-reform forces that united in 2004 retained separate parties in 2006, competing with each other for centrist votes rather than competing with the Party of Regions in the east. The major results are shown in Table 5.1.

---

[3] Roman Kupchinsky, "Ukraine: Corruption Allegations Abound," *RFE/RL*, September 8, 2005. Tymoshenko and Poroshenko appear to have been rivals for influence within the Orange Coalition from the very beginning. Andrew Wilson shows that they were at odds even before Yushchenko was inaugurated. See Andrew Wilson, *Ukraine's Orange Revolution* (New Haven, CT: Yale University Press, 2006), pp. 159–161.

[4] "Ukraine Leader's Team 'Corrupt,'" BBC, September 5, 2005.

Table 5.1 *2006 parliamentary election results*

Party	Vote percentage	Seats (total 450)
Party of Regions	32.1	186
Batkivshchyna	22.3	129
Nasha Ukraina	14.0	81
Socialist Party	5.7	33
Communist Party	3.7	21
Others not winning 3%	24.6	0

These elections, held under a fully proportional system, with a 3 percent threshold, showed the resilience of the Party of Regions. Having supported Kuchma's Za Yedinu Ukrainu bloc in 2002, the Party of Regions now ran on its own, and finished first, with 32 percent of the vote, winning 186 of 450 seats. The Communist Party was a significant casualty of Regions' dominance, falling to 3.7 percent, just enough to clear the bar to enter parliament. Yushchenko's Nasha Ukraina received a strong rebuke, falling to third place behind Tymoshenko's Batkivshchyna, after having earned three times the percentage of proportional representation vote (and five times as many seats) in 2002.

While the Orange Coalition (Batkivshchyna, Nasha Ukraina, and the Socialists) had enough seats (243) to form a majority, their problem was that Poroshenko and Moroz both wanted to be speaker of the parliament. When a deal appeared imminent that would have made Poroshenko speaker, Moroz defected and struck a deal instead with his erstwhile enemy, the Party of Regions (as well as the Communist Party).[5] In return for their support for him becoming speaker, Moroz and the Socialist Party supported Yanukovych becoming prime minister. Yushchenko and the leaders of all the parliamentary parties except Tymoshenko's Batkivshchyna signed a "Universal of National Unity," a sort of grand coalition agreement stating an agreed program, and Yushchenko appointed Yanukovych prime minister. Among the most debated items was that on NATO, on which the parties agreed to "resolution of the issue of joining NATO according to the results of a referendum to be held after Ukraine has implemented all required procedures."[6] The Orange Coalition had been in power, and Yanukovych out of the prime minister's chair, for roughly seventeen months.

[5] Wilson, Ukraine's Orange Revolution, p. 171, reports that Tymoshenko was also trying to strike a deal with the Party of Regions.
[6] "Universal Natsional'noyi Yednosti: Tekst, pidpycanyi na kruglomu stoli," *Ukrayins'ka Pravda*, August 3, 2006, www.pravda.com.ua/articles/2006/08/3/3139284/.

Table 5.2 *2007 parliamentary election results*

Party	Vote percentage	Seats (total 450)
Party of Regions	34.4	175
Batkivshchyna	30.7	156
Nasha Ukraina/People's Self-Defense	14.2	72
Communist Party	5.4	27
Lytvyn Bloc	4.0	20
Others not winning 3%	11.2	0

"National unity" did not last long. A larger crisis ensued in 2007, after months of fighting between the parliamentary majority joined by the PM and cabinet against the parliamentary minority joined by the president. Once the opposition took over parliament, deputies began defecting from pro-Yushchenko parties to the parliamentary majority. This followed a pattern in which deputies bandwagoned to the majority, often enticed by substantial side-payments.[7] Under post-2004 legislation, deputies were bound to the parties on whose lists they were elected. Known as the "imperative mandate," the measure was designed to prevent this defection. Batkivshchyna and Nasha Ukraina leaders argued that under this rule, when the deputies left their parties, they surrendered their seats, and that by not expelling them, the parliamentary majority was violating the law.

As the Regions-led coalition neared 300 votes, which would have allowed it to change the constitution to erode further Yushchenko's power, Yushchenko acted. On April 2, Yushchenko declared the dissolution of the parliament and the holding of new parliamentary elections. This move kicked off an institutional crisis. The government, controlled by Yanukovych, refused to allocate funds for new elections, and the opposition contested the constitutionality of Yushchenko's acts. Yushchenko then dismissed three constitutional court judges. With the constitutional court delaying a ruling, the two sides reached a compromise that included new elections. This was another example where an elite bargain trumped strict constitutional procedure.

While the Party of Regions' and Nasha Ukraina's performance barely changed, Batkivshchyna improved dramatically, largely at the expense of the Socialist Party and the small parties (see Table 5.2). Moroz's Socialist Party failed to cross the threshold, as voters punished it for having gone into coalition with Regions. The big winner was Tymoshenko and

---

[7] In 2007, knowledgeable insiders in Kyiv told me that the going price to switch parties was $300,000.

Batkivshchyna, which gained almost 8 percent of the vote and twenty-seven seats. As a result, Batkivshchyna and Nasha Ukraina were able to forge a coalition and Tymoshenko was able to reclaim the prime minister's position. Even then, however, Yushchenko was toying with a "grand coalition" with the Party of Regions. A shadow of this coalition was established in the National Security and Defense Council, where several Party of Regions leaders were appointed.[8]

The new coalition lasted only until September 2008: Ukraine had yet another political crisis when the parliament, with Batkivshchyna joining with the Party of Regions and Communists, passed a package of laws tweaking the balance of power between the president and prime minister in favor of the PM. Yushchenko's party responded by withdrawing from the coalition. It appeared that yet another parliamentary election would be held, as Yushchenko could have called fresh elections if a new coalition were not agreed, but in December a new coalition was formed, with the Lytvyn Bloc joining Batkivshchyna and Nasha Ukraina. Tymoshenko remained prime minister and Volodymyr Lytvyn became speaker of parliament, replacing Nasha Ukraina's Arseniy Yatsenyuk.

In this third crisis, Ukraine's relations with Russia were directly involved. Yushchenko traveled to Tbilisi to support Georgia, while Tymoshenko criticized Yushchenko for taking sides. Yushchenko's advisor Andriy Kyslinskyi accused Tymoshenko of seeking Russia's support in the presidential election, and cited "signs of high treason and political corruption." It appeared that looking toward the 2010 presidential election, Russia saw Tymoshenko as a good alternative to Yushchenko, while Tymoshenko saw Russian support as potentially valuable. She traveled to Moscow in September 2008 and had cordial and widely publicized meetings with Medvedev, who had replaced Putin as president, and with Putin, who had become prime minister.[9]

This domestic conflict is crucial to understanding this period for two reasons. First, it shows that contrary to much of the narrative in the West at the time, the Orange Revolution did not decisively defeat Yanukovych and the Party of Regions. They actually tightened their grip over the electorate in eastern Ukraine and always had the largest bloc in parliament. This set the stage for the presidential election of 2010. Second,

---

[8] Taras Kuzio, "The Tymoshenko Government's Domestic and Foreign Policies: The First 100 Days," Institute for European, Russian and Eurasian Studies, George Washington University, April 17, 2008, p. 2.

[9] Christian Lowe, "Russia Finds Unlikely Ally in Ukraine's Tymoshenko," Reuters, October 5, 2008. For a more detailed discussion of Ukrainian leaders' and parties' responses to the Georgia war, see Dominique Arel, "Ukraine since the War in Georgia," *Survival* 50, 6 (2008): 15–25.

during a period in which the West was most favorably inclined to increasing integration with Ukraine, Ukraine itself was in chaos. Among other things, this helps explain why many NATO members were unenthusiastic about a Membership Action Plan in 2008.

Foreign Policy under Yushchenko

Yushchenko was seen in the West as the hero of the Orange Revolution, and in his first weeks in office he traveled extensively and was received very positively. But he ran into the same problem as Kuchma, namely that integrating with the West required not just good intentions, but the execution of far-reaching domestic reform. And the chaos and infighting of Yushchenko's time in office prevented such reform.

Moreover, it is not clear how hard Yushchenko tried to achieve it. If Kuchma had seen his role as brokering deals among different clans, Yushchenko stepped back from the fray, with the result that the role of the clans actually increased. With Ukraine apparently moving toward parliamentary democracy, the oligarchs put more money and effort into building political parties and they were in a strong position to resist reform. Toward the end of Yushchenko's term, European Commission President Jose Manuel Barrosso said: "I will speak honestly with you, Mr. President. It often seems to us that commitments on reform are only partly implemented and words are not always accompanied by action. Reforms are the only way to establish stability, and build closer ties with the EU."[10]

Nor was Russia any happier with Yushchenko's policies. Among other things, Yushchenko insisted that Russia withdraw FSB personnel from its forces in Sevastopol and he made it clear that he had no intention of extending Russia's lease on the base there.[11] In August 2009, President Medvedev sent a letter to Yushchenko summarizing Russia's complaints about Ukrainian policy, including support for Georgia in the 2008 war, the gas disputes of 2006 and 2009, interference in the Russian Black Sea Fleet, the status of the Russian language in Ukraine, and honoring Nazi collaborators. This letter formed the agenda for Russia's relationship with Ukraine's next president, and was widely seen as signaling to the Ukrainian population that a change in direction would be needed for

[10] Quoted in Taras Kuzio, "Viktor Yushchenko's Foreign Policy Agenda," *Eurasia Daily Monitor* 6, 230, December 16, 2009.
[11] Elizabeth A. Wood, "Introduction," in Elizabeth A. Wood, William E. Pomeranz, E. Wayne Merry, and Maxim Trudolyubov, *Roots of Russia's War in Ukraine* (Washington, DC: Woodrow Wilson Center Press, 2016), pp. 11–12.

relations with Russia to improve.[12] While Medvedev was widely seen as comparatively liberal among Russian leaders, the letter adopted many of the policies of Russian conservatives, complaining, for example, that "Russian-Ukrainian relations are tested by your administration's review of our general historical framework, glorification of Nazi collaborators, the exaltation of the role of radical nationalists, and attempts to press the international community in supporting nationalist interpretations of the 1932–1933 famine in the USSR as a 'genocide against the Ukrainian people.'" Referring to those in Ukraine who supported joining NATO, Medvedev said: "The 'argument' they use alludes to a 'Russian threat' to the security of Ukraine, which as you well know does not and cannot exist," and he reiterated the view that "[f]or centuries Russians and Ukrainians have been and remain not just neighbors but brothers who will always hold the best feelings; who share a common history, culture, and religion; and who are united by close economic cooperation, strong kinship, and human relations." It is notable that Medvedev presented these assertions not as hopes or aspirations but as facts. "I would like to inform you that because of anti-Russian Ukrainian government policies we have decided to postpone the appointment of our new ambassador. The specific date [of his appointment] will be determined later when there are genuine improvements in Russian-Ukrainian relations." The letter concluded with a reference to the upcoming elections: "Russia hopes that the new political leadership of Ukraine will be ready to build a relationship between our countries that will actually meet the genuine aspirations of our peoples and that this will be in the interests of strengthening European security."[13]

While Yushchenko was widely seen as a pro-western candidate (and compared to Yanukovych, he was), he was also a pragmatist, and sought to build a constructive relationship with Russia. At the same time, Russia, having bungled its attempt to help get Yanukovych elected, sought to gradually rebuild its position in Ukraine. With the Party of Regions controlling the Donbas and a large bloc in parliament, and with various Ukrainian oligarchs having interests that overlapped with Russia, its position in Ukraine was far from hopeless.

---

[12] Eugene B. Rumer and David J. Kramer, "Medvedev's Message," *New York Times*, August 20, 2009. Rumer and Kramer wondered whether "Russia is preparing to take drastic action – to reclaim the Crimean peninsula for example, with its ethnic Russian majority?"

[13] The text of Medvedev's letter is printed in English in Taras Kuzio, *Ukraine: Democratization, Corruption and the New Russian Imperialism* (Santa Barbara, CA: Praeger, 2015), pp. 438–439. The Russian original is at Poslaniye Prezidentu Ukrainy Viktoru Yushchenko," August 11, 2009, Kremlin website.

Russia Responds to the Orange Revolution

Immediately following the Orange Revolution, in early 2005, Putin was confronted by street protests of his own. The immediate cause was a reform of social payments that replaced Soviet-era pension benefits such as free public transportation and subsidized utilities with cash payments that many considered insufficient. While the protests did not aim to oust Putin, they criticized him directly.[14] He responded by increasing the cash payments dramatically. The protests seemed to some to bear out predictions in *Kommersant* that "the Orange Revolution virus will now spread to Russia ... It will not take long to dismantle the new Russian totalitarianism."[15] The "Tulip Revolution" that deposed Askar Akayev, the long-time ruler of Kyrgyzstan in March 2005, highlighted the threat, as did protests in Andijan, Uzbekistan, that were violently suppressed in May 2005.

The Russian government adopted a set of strategies intended to ensure that such a revolution could not happen in Russia or in other states in the region.[16] In February 2005, Defense Minister Sergei Ivanov criticized "exports of revolutions to the CIS states, no matter what color – pink, blue, you name it," continuing the Russian notions that these protests were exports rather than indigenous.[17] The following year, he argued that the military "should also be prepared for the possibility of coup d'états in some post-Soviet states and destabilization on the borders that may stem from these attempts."[18] Similarly, Vladislav Surkov, the deputy head of the presidential administration, listing the threats to Russian sovereignty, included "a gentle absorption using the modern 'orange technologies' in conditions of a weakened national immunity to outside influence." "We know how this is done: values are undermined, the state

---

[14] Claire Bigg, "Protests across Russia Force Putin to Double Increase in Pension Payments," *The Guardian*, January 19, 2005.

[15] Quoted in Steven Eke, "Russians Rush to Rethink Ukraine," *BBC News*, December 27, 2004.

[16] See Thomas Ambrosio, "Insulating Russia from a Colour Revolution: How the Kremlin Resists Regional Democratic Trends," *Democratization* 14, 2 (April 2007): 232–252; Vitali Silitski, "Contagion Deterred: Preemptive Authoritarianism in the Former Soviet Union (the Case of Belarus)," in Valerie J. Bunce, Michael McFaul, and Kathryn Stoner-Weiss, eds., *Democracy and Authoritarianism in the Post-Communist World* (New York: Cambridge University Press, 2010), pp. 274–299; and Jeanne L. Wilson, "The Legacy of the Color Revolutions for Russian Politics and Foreign Policy," *Problems of Post-Communism* 57, 2 (March/April 2010): 21–36.

[17] Council on Foreign Relations, "The World in the 21st Century: Addressing New Threats and Challenges," January 13, 2005, www.cfr.org/event/world-21st-century-addressing-new-threats-and-challenges.

[18] Sergei Ivanov, "Russia Must Be Strong," *Defense and Security*, January 13, 2006.

is declared inefficient and domestic conflicts are provoked ... if they succeed in four countries why not to do the same in a fifth."[19]

Surkov advocated "the formation of a nationally orientated stratum of society," and the formation of the youth group Nashi (Ours) was one way to do this. In May 2005, Nashi deployed 50,000 people to a demonstration in support of Putin in Moscow, and Gleb Pavlovskii, at a Nashi gathering later that year, was explicit about its role: "A revolution is a coup. They [the United States] have tried it before, and soon they will try it here, perhaps as early as the Moscow Duma elections this autumn. Your job is to defend the constitutional order if and when the coup comes."[20] "If there is an attempt to topple Putin, Nashi should go into the streets and prevent a coup."[21] The creation of Nashi was intended to counter the role of youth groups such as Pora in the Orange Revolution and Otpor in Serbia.

A related tactic to prevent political unrest was to undermine the NGOs that were implicated in organizing it. A 2006 law made it legal to deny registration to any group whose "goals and objectives ... create a threat to the sovereignty, political independence, territorial integrity, national unity, unique character, cultural heritage, and national interests of the Russian Federation," and prohibited foreign NGOs from transferring funds to their Russian branches.[22] The first requirement gave the government latitude to shutter NGOs it considered oppositional; the second undermined the financial basis for many NGOs.

The Russian government also came to reject the western practice of providing election monitors to assess the fairness of voting in new democracies. While the discovery of fraud in Ukraine's 2004 election was primarily the work of domestic Ukrainian actors, the role of external monitors in declaring the second round unfair, and the rerun fair, fit into the Russian narrative of western interference. Sergei Lavrov said "Election monitoring is not only ceasing to make sense, but is also becoming an instrument of political manipulation and a destabilizing factor."[23] In Russia's own parliamentary elections, in 2007, the

---

[19] "Putin's Aide on Main Threats to Russia's Sovereignty," BBC Monitoring Former Soviet Union, March 4, 2006.

[20] Julia Evans, "How Putin Youth is Indoctrinated to Foil Revolution," *The Times*, July 18, 2005.

[21] "Counter-Revolution and Fun at Pro-Putin Youth Summer Camp," Agence France Presse, July 19, 2005.

[22] Freedom House, "Factsheet: Russia's NGO Laws" (no date). The 2006 laws were relaxed under Medvedev in 2009, and a stricter version was implemented under Putin in 2012.

[23] Quoted in C. J. Chivers, "Russia Proposes Steps to Weaken Election Watchdogs," *The New York Times*, October 25, 2007, p. A14.

government sharply constrained the number of OSCE observers and their latitude, and as a result the OSCE's Office for Democratic Institutions and Human Rights declined to participate.

A fourth tactic to head off the transnational spread of democracy was to counter it with transnational promotion of autocracy. Russia pursued this both bilaterally, in support for various leaders in the region against democratic opposition, and also multilaterally, in the formation of the Shanghai Cooperation Organization along with China and several of the Central Asian states. Originally focused on border security, the organization increasingly came to focus on preventing domestic political turmoil, and promoting the norm of respect for different systems of government.[24]

In the short term, these events did not have a direct bearing on Russia's relations with the West or with Ukraine, but they had important implications for the future. They demonstrated how vulnerable Russian leaders felt to such a revolution and how clearly they attributed events in Ukraine to external manipulation. This meant that Russia could foment protests and counterprotests just as easily. The NGO laws furthered fear of the West as a means of consolidating autocratic rule in Russia. That further contributed to the view that Russia's prickliness on various issues was intended for domestic consumption, and need not be seen as truly representing Russia's foreign policy views.

Ukraine and the EU

Membership in the European Union was Ukraine's stated goal under Kuchma, and many perceived the potential to make dramatic progress with the change in leadership. In January 2005, speaking to the Council of Europe in Strasbourg, Yushchenko stressed the goal of membership and promised that his government would be "reorganized to add a real, rather than rhetorical, dimension and content to the process of integration into the European Union."[25] He created a new position, a deputy prime minister for European integration, and put his close ally Oleh Rybachuk in the position. But while the EU foreign policy head Javier Solana said that Yushchenko's administration "opens up new possibilities," and that "we must find the right actions to support this choice," the European Union demurred, as some members were hesitant.[26]

---

[24] The role of the SCO in combating the spread of democracy and in providing international organizations with a distinct narrative about domestic governance is discussed in Paul D'Anieri, "Autocratic Diffusion and the Pluralization of Democracy," in Bruce Jentleson and Louis Pauly, eds., *Power in a Complex Global System* (London: Routledge, 2014), pp. 80–96.

[25] BBC, January 25, 2005.   [26] Ibid.

The EU/Ukraine Action Plan of 2005 stated that "The European Union and Ukraine are determined to enhance their relations and to promote stability, security and well-being. The approach is founded on shared values, joint ownership and differentiation. It will contribute to the further stepping up of our strategic partnership."[27] But it made no mention of membership. Among the potential complications was that, while EU policy said that any European state was eligible for membership, it had not been determined whether Ukraine was a "European state."[28]

Thus the European Union and Ukraine were again caught in a familiar vicious circle: Ukraine said that it could not generate the sacrifices needed for far-reaching reform if membership were not promised in return, and the European Union could not make a membership commitment to a country that needed so much reform. On top of that dynamic, both sides had their own internal limits on the relationship: in Ukraine there were powerful interests that did not want EU-style reform, and it was not clear voters would support the actions needed even if membership were on offer. For the EU, "enlargement fatigue," Ukraine's very large size, and the Russian concerns also promoted hesitation in some states.

Yushchenko's team expected that it would fare much better than Kuchma had, and in 2005 he requested that the European Union begin negotiations on an Association Agreement and a "membership perspective."[29] The European Union was divided, however. While new members in central Europe, led by Poland, sought to move quickly on Ukraine (as they did with NATO), others were more cautious, reflecting both the traditional incremental methods of the European Union and the concerns noted above. While the European Union as a whole could not agree on a policy change, the bureaucrats could, and so a February 2005 "Action Plan" under the European Neighborhood Policy envisioned a new "enhanced" agreement, once the "Action Plan" was complete.[30]

Progress was very slow, however, in part due to Ukraine's domestic chaos, and in part because Ukraine was focused on completing accession to the World Trade Organization (WTO). After several years of negotiations, Ukraine finally joined the WTO in January 2008. In addition to providing Ukraine increased access to world markets and making Ukraine's markets more open, the accession was significant because

[27] "EU/Ukraine Action Plan," 2005, EU Neighbours Library, https://library.euneighbours.eu//content/eu-ukraine-action-plan-0.
[28] RFE/RL, "EU: Updated 'Action Plan' for Ukraine Wards off Talk of Membership," January 24, 2005.
[29] Rilka Dragneva-Lewers and Kataryna Wolczuk, *Ukraine between the EU and Russia: The Integration Challenge* (Basingstoke, Hampshire: Palgrave MacMillan, 2015), p. 41.
[30] Ibid., p. 42.

Ukraine joined before Russia. Russia opposed Ukraine joining first and, as a member, Ukraine would, at least in principle, be in a position to veto Russia's membership.[31] While that was unlikely, it might provide Ukraine a bit of leverage, and the symbolism of Ukraine joining first was significant. Yushchenko promised to "fully support" Russia's accession.[32]

Yanukovych's return to the role of prime minister in 2006 diminished the government's focus on EU integration. Speaking ahead of a visit to Brussels in September 2006, Yanukovych advocated more balance in relations with Europe and Russia, criticizing what he called "Euro-romanticism," and saying that "[w]e must not allow the imbalances that arose in the past year-and-a-half to continue."[33] He said that while he supported integration with the EU, "we are closer to Euro-pragmatism."[34]

In early 2007, the European Council adopted "negotiating directives for a new enhanced agreement between the European Union and Ukraine." The document stated that "through this [as yet not negotiated] agreement, the European Union aims to build an increasingly close relationship with Ukraine, aimed at gradual economic integration and deepening of political cooperation," but also that "a new enhanced agreement shall not prejudge any possible future developments in EU-Ukraine relations."[35] An Association Agreement, let alone membership, was not on the agenda.

It was not until the European Union established the Eastern Partnership in 2009 that progress on Ukraine-EU integration began to pick up speed again. The Eastern Partnership was proposed by Poland with support from Sweden.

The Eastern Partnership will bring about a significant strengthening of EU policy with regard to its Eastern partners by seeking to create the necessary conditions for political association and further economic integration between the European Union and its Eastern partners through the development of a specific Eastern dimension of the European Neighborhood Policy. To achieve this, the Eastern

---

[31] "Ukraine, Georgia May Put Forward New Demands to Russia in WTO Accession Process – Shokhin," *Ukraine Business Weekly*, February 6, 2008.

[32] "Ukraine to Give Full Support to Russia's Accession to WTO, Yushchenko Says," *Ukraine Business Weekly*, February 11, 2008.

[33] "Ukraine's PM Speaks against 'Euro-romanticism' ahead of Visit to Brussels," BBC Monitoring Kiev Unit, September 13, 2006.

[34] "PM: Ukraine to Stay on European Course," Interfax Russia & CIS General Newswire, September 6, 2006.

[35] Council of the European Union, Press Release 5463/07, 2776th Council Meeting, General Affairs and External Relations, External Relations, Brussels, January 22, 2007.

Partnership seeks to support political and socio-economic reforms, facilitating approximation and convergence towards the European Union.[36]

The documents stressed that "[s]hared values including democracy, the rule of law, and respect for human rights will be at its core, as well as the principles of market economy, sustainable development and good governance."[37] Crucially for Ukraine, the policy envisioned that "cooperation under the Eastern Partnership should provide the foundation for new Association Agreements between the European Union and those partners who have made sufficient progress."[38] At the same time, Ukraine was not thrilled to be included in the same category as the Caucasian states, which clearly would not be candidates for EU membership in the foreseeable future.

At the time, there was speculation that the goals were geopolitical as well as normative. The European Council said at the time that "Promoting stability, good governance and economic development in its Eastern neighborhood is of strategic importance for the European Union."[39] Moreover, the inclusion of Belarus, which under Lukashenka had done little to earn a deeper relationship with the EU, led to speculation that the European Union was seeking to provide a long-term alternative to Russia for Belarus.[40] Belarus's decision to participate in the Eastern Partnership sparked a quarrel with Russia, and it appeared that Russia was much more concerned about Belarus's participation than Ukraine's, because its economic integration and political domination of Belarus were much greater.

Russia perceived that the Eastern Partnership would likely injure its interests, and thought that it may have been designed to do so. President Dmitri Medvedev said that "Any partnership is better than conflict, but it is confusing for us that some states attempt to use the structure as a partnership against Russia."[41] Andrei Zagorski wrote that "The upgraded ambition of the EaP [Eastern Partnership] to offer Eastern neighbors an association with the EU, instead of an enhanced partnership and cooperation framework, is seen as aiming at and eventually

[36] Council of the European Union, "Declaration by the European Council on the Eastern Partnership," Annex 2, Press Release 5463/07, 2776th Council Meeting, General Affairs and External Relations, External Relations, Brussels, January 22, 2009, p. 19.
[37] Ibid., p. 19.   [38] Ibid., p. 20.
[39] Council of the European Union, "Presidency Conclusions – Brussels, 19/20 March 2009," 7880/1/09, April 29, 2009, p. 11.
[40] Andrew Rettman, "Values to Form Core of EU 'Eastern Partnership,'" *EU Observer*, March 18, 2009.
[41] Sergey Tumanov, Alexander Gasparishvili, and Ekaterina Romanova, "Russia-EU Relations, or How the Russians Really View the EU," *Journal of Communist Studies and Transition Politics* 27, 1 (March 2011): 131.

leading towards a progressive disassociation of those countries from the Russian Federation."[42] A group of Russian scholars evaluated the situation similarly: "While there is little discrimination in the political discourse of Russian elites in relation to the European Neighborhood Policy (ENP), in reality, as popular opinion indicates, those neighbors who openly show their allegiances to the European Union – Ukraine, Georgia and Moldova – have been increasingly categorized as hostile and unfriendly towards Russia."[43] Deeper integration between the European Union and the "neighbors" was expected to create new barriers to trade between the neighbors and Russia, and some noted that the adoption of the *acquis communautaire* had compelled the members added in 2004 to annul existing agreements with Russia, damaging several sectors of Russia's economy.[44] However, there was a basic obstacle to the deeper EU-Russia economic integration that Russia wanted: The European Union had no intention of modifying the *acquis* to suit Russia, and Russia had no intention of adopting European legal and economic norms.

Zagorski said Russia was concerned that the trade elements of the deal would interfere with Russia's own aspirations for trade with the states involved. He was particularly worried that integration of Ukraine's energy sector into the EU's would interfere with Russia's plans, and perceived (correctly, it seems) that any liberalization of mobility between the Partnership states and the European Union would complicate efforts to increase freedom of movement between those states and Russia. The consolation, Zagorski said, was that those potential consequences were far down the road, and it did not seem likely that the plan's aspirations would be achieved.[45] Medvedev himself said: "I see nothing miraculous about this Eastern Partnership and, frankly speaking, I do not see any advantage of it at all, and this is confirmed by all the participants of this project that I have spoken to. But I see nothing about it that is aimed directly against Russia."[46] The fact that only one major EU head of state – Germany's Angela Merkel – attended the kickoff in May 2009 was seen as a sign that the policy was not an EU focus.[47] At the same time, Russia

[42] Andrei Zagorski, "Eastern Partnership from the Russian Perspective," *International Politics and Society* 3 (2011): 41.

[43] Tumanov et al., "Russia-EU Relations."   [44] Ibid.

[45] Zagorski, "Eastern Partnership from the Russian Perspective," pp. 41–44.

[46] "Kremlin website transcript of Medvedev interview with Belarusian media," BBC Monitoring Former Soviet Union, November 27, 2009.

[47] Nico Popescu and Andrew Wilson, "The Limits of Enlargement-Lite: European and Russian Power in the Troubled Neighborhood" (London: European Council on Foreign Relations, 2009), p. 2.

held open the possibility that it would participate in at least some of the Partnership's projects.[48]

Nor was Russia standing still: "[W]hile Europe has largely been content to sit back and rely on the 'magnetism' of its model, Russia has been quietly working to boost its own attractiveness in the neighborhood, and in particular has learned the power of incentives. While the EU frustrates neighbourhood governments with its bureaucracy, Russia offers straightforward benefits such as visa-free travel and cheap energy."[49] Moreover, Russia had managed to maintain a military presence in each of the six "Partnership" participants.[50]

Energy Politics

Energy relations, long an avenue for Russian influence over Ukraine, evolved dramatically, as the shaky truce that existed prior to the Orange Revolution was shattered. With Ukraine having apparently turned its back on Russia, Russia was no longer willing to underprice gas or to tolerate non-payment.[51] Fearing potential for contagion of "colored revolutions," Russia wanted to send a signal to others that the price for bucking Russia would be high. Moreover, with world prices rising, the cost of subsidies to favored consumers was increasing, so Russia aimed to move all pricing to European levels by 2011.[52] Ultimately, Russia's change in policy helped draw the European Union further into Russia-Ukraine relations, because the 2006 and 2009 Russia-Ukraine "gas wars" led to cuts in gas deliveries to the EU. This prompted the European Union to get directly involved, which it had generally not done previously.

With the sector in flux, Russia sought both to reduce or end its subsidies and to ensure that the reorganization served its interests.[53] Almost immediately after Yushchenko came to power, in January 2005,

---

[48] "Russia Could Join EU Eastern Partnership: Lavrov," Agence France Presse, November 25, 2009.

[49] Popescu and Wilson, "The Limits of Enlargement-Lite," p. 3.   [50] Ibid., p. 4.

[51] As Robert Orttung and Indra Overland point out, the period after the Orange Revolution was a rare instance when Russia's strategic and economic interests overlapped, see "A Limited Toolbox: Explaining the Constraints on Russia's Foreign Energy Policy," *Journal of Eurasian Studies* 2 (2011): 75, 82.

[52] Ibid., pp. 78–79; Rawi Abdelal, "The Profits of Power: Commerce and Realpolitik in Eurasia," *Review of International Political Economy* 20, 3 (2013): 433. Abdelal stresses that this was a major revision in Russian policy: rather than ordering Gazprom to offer subsidies for political purposes, the government was now telling it to make as much money as possible.

[53] Simon Pirani, "Ukraine's Gas Sector," Oxford Institute for Energy Studies, June 2007, p. 23.

Russia complained that Ukraine was once again not paying for its gas supplies, and that it was diverting gas from the pipelines supplying western Europe. It then announced that it would begin charging Ukraine the market price, or $230 per thousand cubic meters.[54] Yushchenko agreed to pay the increased price but insisted that the increase take place gradually, and he increased the price for transporting Russian gas to Europe and shifted it from barter to a cash basis. As before, Russia sought control of the pipelines as a way of paying for its supply of gas to Ukraine. Meanwhile, Tymoshenko sought to eliminate the use of the intermediary firm RosUkrEnergo, and the Security Service of Ukraine (SBU), led by Tymoshenko ally Oleksandr Turchynov, began investigating the firm. "By July 2005, virtually all elements of the Russian-Ukrainian gas relationship – most of which had seemed to be settled a year earlier – had been reopened with little sign of resolution."[55] The two sides traded accusations throughout 2005 until, on January 1, 2006, Russia reduced shipments to Ukraine, providing only the amount that it had agreed to sell onwards to western Europe.

The immediate effect was a reduction of supplies to Europe. While Ukraine could have continued shipping gas westward while depriving its own customers, it reduced both the domestic supply and transshipment. By January 2, Hungary's supply was down by 40 percent, France's, Austria's, and Slovakia's by 30 percent, and Italy's by 24 percent.[56] The biggest impact was on Slovakia, which got all of its gas from Russia and saw its supply drop 30 percent. The perception was that the cutoff was intended to undermine Ukraine's new government, and so blame for the crisis was placed on Russia.[57] The French newspaper *Le Monde* stated that "Russia has just pressed the energy button," and that "the first war of the 21st Century has been declared," and much of the European press responded similarly.[58] Both EU Foreign Policy Chief Javier Solana and German Economics Minister Michael Glos urged

---

[54] It is impossible to know exactly how much Russia was subsidizing gas shipments to Ukraine, because these deals were wrapped up in larger barter deals involving Ukraine's transportation and storage of gas heading west. The absence of price transparency was clearly a feature rather than a bug, because it facilitated rent-seeking. See ibid., p. 24.

[55] Jonathan Stern, "The Russian-Ukrainian Gas Crisis of January 2006," Oxford Institute for Energy Studies, January 2006, www.oxfordenergy.org/wpcms/wp-content/uploads/2011/01/Jan2006-RussiaUkraineGasCrisis-JonathanStern.pdf, p. 6.

[56] Abdelal, "The Profits of Power," p. 432.

[57] Orttung and Overland, "A Limited Toolbox," p. 83. Even if Russia were not supplying Ukraine, Ukraine should have been able to ship Russian gas through pipelines to customers in the west. Ukraine's claims that it had the contractual right to take some of the gas were not convincing.

[58] *Le Monde* and other European papers are quoted in "Press Shivers from Gas Woes," BBC, January 3, 2006. See also Abdelal, "The Profits of Power," p. 432.

Russia to resume supplies to Ukraine, rather than focusing on Ukraine's role.[59] On January 4, the relevant Ukrainian and Russian firms, Naftohaz Ukrainy and Gazprom, announced a new deal, and the supply of gas resumed. The complicated new agreement raised prices both for Russian gas and for transit through Ukraine, but still not to market levels. After another supply disruption later the same month (blamed on very cold weather in Russia) Hungary sponsored a meeting of seven central European countries to discuss how to reduce dependence on Russian gas.[60]

This was clearly not what Russia had intended. While Russia had immense leverage over Ukraine and Europe, the dependence was mutual: Gazprom accounted for 12–13 percent of the Russian government's revenue and 8 percent of Russia's GDP,[61] and almost all of this came from payments from Europe rather than the former Soviet Union. Therefore, for economic as well as political reasons, Russia did not want to alienate its customers in western Europe or push them to seek alternate supplies, which would reduce both its bargaining power and its revenues.

The result of this episode was a new resolve in the European Union to find ways to stabilize their supply of gas. As Rawi Abdelal has shown, there were two kinds of tensions within the European Union over policy toward gas supplies from Russia. At the core was a tension between the distinct goals of large energy firms, including Germany's E.ON, France's EDF, and Italy's Eni, which focused on buying gas as cheaply as possible, and the goals of states, which were, at least to some extent, willing to incur higher costs in order to reduce dependence on Russia.[62] This disagreement was connected to the broader difference on Russia policy between the older, larger EU members further to the west, and the newer members closer to Russia, who sought greater unity in facing what they saw as a significant threat. Commercial interests and geopolitical interests overlapped, and in Abdelal's view, "a handful of French, German, and Italian corporations somehow [have] taken responsibility for formulating the energy strategy – and thus the Russia policy – for essentially all of Europe."[63]

The 2006 crisis increased the will of the states to take more control of the policy. One way to do this was to get more deeply involved in

---

[59] Andrew E. Kramer, "Russia Restores Most of Gas Cut to Ukraine Line," *New York Times*, January 3, 2006, p. A1. Gazprom's contracts with customers to the west of Ukraine were priced in terms of supply to the Ukraine-EU border, obligating Russia to get it there. This gave Ukraine a lot of power.

[60] Neil Buckley, "Europe Seeks to Cut Reliance on Russia Gas Supply," *Financial Times*, January 20, 2006, p. 10.

[61] Abdelal, "The Profits of Power," p. 434.   [62] Ibid.   [63] Ibid., p. 422.

Russian-Ukrainian relations to prevent further such crises. A second was to diversify supplies. A third was to diversify transit routes to take Ukraine out of the equation. This third goal served Russia's interest as well, as it would then allow Russia to cut off supplies from Ukraine without cutting off Europe, removing much of Ukraine's leverage. The means to do this was the Nord Stream project. Nord Stream succeeded in large part because it suited the interests of Europe's large energy firms, which had deep relationships with Gazprom and its predecessor in the Soviet era.[64]

Nord Stream was also, however, an early example of Russia's ability to gain influence among leading western politicians. Germany's chancellor from 1998 to 2005, Gerhard Schroeder, was a strong advocate of Nord Stream. Two weeks before leaving office, he signed the deal with Russia to build the pipeline, which, by going under the Baltic Sea, would avoid any transit countries between Russia and Germany. The deal was seen as undermining the positions of Ukraine, Poland, and the Baltics, all of which objected. Just after leaving the chancellor's office, Schroeder took a lucrative position with the Nord Stream consortium, and in 2017 he became a director of the Russian government-controlled oil firm Ros-Neft, which was under US sanctions.[65]

In the West, there was a debate among those who saw Gazprom as a "normal" company, pursuing profits and insisting that bills be paid, that just happened to be controlled by the Russian government, versus those who saw it as an arm of the Russian government, pursuing the foreign policy aims of the state. Put differently, there was a clash between the commercial logic of firms, for which eliminating Ukraine from the equation was highly valuable, and the political logic of states, which saw cutting Ukraine out as deeply damaging to its independence. In April 2006, Radoslaw Sikorski, the Polish Minister of Defense, called Nord Stream the "Molotov-Ribbentrop pipeline."[66] South Stream, an analogous project to circumvent Ukraine by piping gas under the Black Sea and through the Balkans to Italy, moved more slowly and was finally abandoned after the adoption of economic sanctions in 2014. Ultimately, the European Union pursued a mixed strategy. In the short term,

---

[64] Ibid., p. 437.

[65] Rick Loack, "He Used to Rule Germany: Now, He Oversees Russian Energy Companies and Lashes Out at the U.S.," *Washington Post*, August 12, 2017. On Schroeder and Nord Stream (and Nord Stream 2), see Judy Dempsey, "The (German) Politics of Nord Stream 2," Carnegie Europe, November 3, 2016; and Andrey Gurkov and Markian Ostaptschuk, "Nord Stream: A Commercial Project with a Political Vision," *Deutsche Welle*, July 7, 2011.

[66] Quoted in Abdelal, "The Profits of Power," p. 441.

recognizing that Russia would be an important source of supply, individual EU states and firms pursued strategies to secure their supplies and the European Union as a whole sought to use diplomacy to broker a truce between Russia and Ukraine that would secure European supplies without forcing Ukraine under Russia's thumb. In the longer term, moves were made both to diversify supplies from Russia and to find transit routes around Ukraine, such as Nord Stream. The fundamental problem for Ukraine, and for European strategy, is that the cheapest source of gas is Russia, and the most reliable way to get it would be to eliminate Ukraine as a transit country.

In 2007, Ukraine passed a law prohibiting the sale of Ukraine's gas transport system, which Russia had repeatedly sought in return for below-market gas prices.[67] But Ukraine continued to struggle to pay for the gas it received, and several times fell behind on payments. In 2008, a new agreement between prime ministers Tymoshenko and Putin raised prices further (though still well below the price western countries paid) and set prices through 2010.[68]

A second gas crisis emerged in 2009, and this one was more bitter and had more far-reaching consequences. The crisis emerged in part because rising energy prices increased everyone's incentives to control the trade, and in part because Ukraine's domestic political turmoil undermined the ability to forge a durable deal among competing oligarchs and politicians. As previously, the immediate cause of the shutoff was Ukraine's failure to pay for the gas it had received. On January 1, Russia again reduced the supply of gas to the Ukrainian pipeline to the level of what was to be shipped onward to the West. Again the supply of gas to customers in the European Union dropped, and again Russia and Ukraine blamed each other. On January 7, Russia went further, completely stopping the flow of gas into Ukraine.

The dispute was finally ended in late January by a deal Tymoshenko made with Russian leaders under which Ukraine would move toward European prices for gas. Among the perceived benefits of the deal for Ukraine was that it did away with intermediaries such as RosUkrEnergo, which were largely vehicles for stealing money from the state budget.[69] Narrowing the gap between the Ukrainian and European prices was intended to reduce the scope for corruption. Tymoshenko's rivals (Yushchenko and Yanukovych) sharply criticized the deal, and Yanukovych

---

[67] Dominic Fean, "A Return to Multi-Vectoral Balancing? Viktor Yanukovych's Government and Ukrainian Foreign Policy," *Politique étrangère* 2 (Summer 2010): 5.
[68] Abdelal, "The Profits of Power," p. 434.
[69] Fean, "A Return to Multi-Vectoral Balancing?" p. 4.

later used the deal as a pretext to imprison Tymoshenko on abuse-of-power charges (though he did not cancel the agreement). The deal included three provisions that were seen as highly unfavorable to Ukraine: a pricing formula that would actually have Ukraine pay more than other countries, a "take or pay clause" that required Ukraine to pay for certain levels (more than it needed) whether it consumed the gas or not, and a ban on reexporting gas to other countries. All three of these provisions were eventually thrown out by an international arbitration court in 2017.[70]

Later in 2009, Ukraine and the European Union reached an agreement to modernize the Ukrainian gas-transit system. The agreement "recognize[d] the importance of the further expansion and modernization of Ukraine's gas transit system as an indispensable pillar of the common European energy infrastructure, and the fact that Ukraine is a strategic partner for the EU gas sector."[71] Russia was not included in the agreement, and this was seen in Russia as undermining Russian-Ukrainian collaboration.[72] From the EU perspective, this was necessary to achieve better security of the supply to Europe, but Russia saw it as injuring Gazprom[73] and Russia's influence over Ukraine. While Ukraine had survived another crisis, it had also burned a lot of political capital in the EU. Frederick Reinfeldt of Sweden, the EU president in late 2009, said that "patience was lost" in this latest gas dispute.[74]

The West, Russia, and Ukraine

Under Kuchma, the long-stated goal of joining NATO had been abandoned in mid-2004. Yushchenko reinstated the goal of NATO membership in April 2005, and sought a "Membership Action Plan" (MAP) from NATO. In the coming months and years, extensive attention was given, both rhetorically and institutionally, to preparing Ukraine for possible membership. Under a 2007 Defense "White Book," Ukraine's armed forces stated a priority of gearing their modernization toward "European and NATO armed forces standards."[75]

---

[70] Anders Åslund, "Ukraine Beats Russia in Epic Gas Battle," Atlantic Council, June 1, 2017.
[71] "Joint Declaration Signed on Modernization of Ukrainian Gas," *Russia & CIS Business & Investment Weekly*, March 27, 2009.
[72] Tumanov et al., "Russia-EU Relations," p. 126.   [73] Ibid., p. 126.
[74] Volodymyr Yermolenko, "Mutual Distrust Blurs EU-Summit," euobserver.com, December 7, 2009.
[75] Marten Malek, "The 'Western Vector' of the Foreign and Security Policy of Ukraine," *Journal of Slavic Military Studies* 22, 4 (2009): 528.

In pursuing a NATO Membership Action Plan, Yushchenko was not only ahead of most NATO members. He was also ahead of the Ukrainian electorate. Support for NATO membership consistently received minority support in public opinion polls, even after a 2008 public relations campaign in favor of it.[76] When Prime Minister Yanukovych, visiting Brussels in 2006, said that "the Ukrainian people are not ready to consider possible membership" in NATO, he was probably closer to the truth than was Yushchenko.[77] Yushchenko himself was in no doubt about NATO, saying later, even after a MAP was denied, that Ukraine "has to move towards the NATO alliance. [...] It is the only way for our country to protect our national security and sovereignty. [...] I want to remind all political forces in our country that shout about the possible neutral status of Ukraine that neutrality can come at a very high price."[78] The Party of Regions insisted that Ukraine not join NATO without a referendum on the issue, and Yushchenko agreed to this in signing the "Universal of National Unity" sealing the coalition agreement that brought Yanukovych back to the prime minister's job in 2006.[79] A referendum was part of Tymoshenko's platform in 2008, and was required by a law passed by parliament that year.[80] While Yushchenko and other supporters of NATO membership believed they could build the needed support over time, polling data showed that they had a long way to go, and opponents would never have insisted on the referendum if they were not confident that it would not succeed. In that respect, the hesitation of the existing alliance members was only one major obstacle to membership; Ukraine's inability to achieve the required reforms was a second, and political opposition within Ukraine was a third.

The Bucharest Summit

In January 2008, Yushchenko, along with PM Tymoshenko and parliament head Arseniy Yatsenyuk, sent a letter to NATO Secretary General Jaap de Hoop Scheffer formally requesting that Ukraine be given a Membership Action Plan at the summit scheduled for April in Budapest. In contrast to other cases where the West or Russia seemed to force Ukraine to make a choice it did not want to make, in this case Ukraine was forcing NATO members to make a choice they did not want to make: many were not ready to seriously contemplate Ukraine's membership, but they also wanted to support Yushchenko and signal NATO's

---

[76] Ibid., p. 520.   [77] Quoted in ibid., pp. 530–531.
[78] August 23, 2008, quoted in ibid., p. 521.   [79] Ibid., p. 533.
[80] Ibid., pp. 534–535.

support for Ukraine's and Georgia's independence. The immediate response from US Defense Secretary Robert Gates was that Ukraine's membership in the alliance was not on the agenda, but there was disagreement within the Bush administration, with Vice President Dick Cheney an especially strong supporter of Ukraine. By March, the United States was supporting a MAP for Ukraine and Georgia. Just before the summit, Bush said: "NATO membership must remain open to all of Europe's democracies that seek it and are ready to share in the responsibilities of NATO membership."[81] Unusually, the issue was actually resolved at the summit, because the members could not agree in advance.[82]

Russia's position was clearly stated in its "Foreign Policy Concept," published in January 2008: "Russia maintains its negative attitude towards the expansion of NATO, notably to the plans of admitting Ukraine and Georgia to the membership in the alliance, as well as to bringing the NATO military infrastructure closer to the Russian borders on the whole, which violates the principle of equal security [and] leads to new dividing lines in Europe."[83] Putin received considerable attention in the western press that month when, at a press conference with Yushchenko, he said: "It is horrible to say and terrifying to think that Russia could target its missile systems at Ukraine, in response to deployment of such installations on Ukrainian territory. Imagine this for a moment. This is what worries us." It is important to note that, read closely, Putin appears to be threatening to target Ukraine not just for joining NATO, but if NATO missiles were deployed in Ukraine. In the same statement, he said that Russia has "no right to interfere" with Ukraine's foreign policy and that "if Ukraine wants its sovereignty restricted, that is its own business."[84] Alongside measured statements such as that one were the remarks of Foreign Minister Lavrov: "Russia will do everything it can to prevent the admission of Ukraine and Georgia into NATO."[85] Similarly, Putin advisor Sergei Markov stated that "Ukraine's accession to NATO would be perceived by many Russians as occupation of a part of their

---

[81] Paul Ames, "Bush Support Unlikely to Win NATO Membership Track for Georgia, Ukraine," Associated Press International, April 3, 2008.

[82] Samuel Charap and Timothy Colton, *Everyone Loses: The Ukraine Crisis and the Ruinous Contest for Post-Soviet Eurasia* (London: Routledge, 2017), p. 88.

[83] "Foreign Policy Concept of the Russian Federation," January 12, 2008, http://en.kremlin.ru/supplement/4116.

[84] Vladimir Socor, "Putin Warns Ukraine against Seeking NATO Membership," *Eurasia Daily Monitor* 5, 29, February 14, 2008.

[85] Quoted in Mark Kramer, "Russian Policy toward the Commonwealth of Independent States: Recent Trends and Future Prospects," *Problems of Post-Communism* 55, 6 (2008): 9.

homeland. Ukrainians are Russians anyway."[86] The contradictory statements among Russian leaders at the time allowed western leaders to hear
whichever message they preferred, and allowed later analysts to claim
either that Russia had clearly stated that it regarded membership for
Ukraine as a mortal danger, or that it had given no such indication.

For his part, Yushchenko tried to reassure Russia, saying: "Can one
imagine that there will be a NATO base in Sevastopol? Of course not,
and there never will be ... [we] are not going to take any steps that would
create threats to Russia."[87] After the misunderstandings around what
commitments were made during the German unification discussions in
1990, Russian leaders would not have been reassured.

That same day, Foreign Minister Lavrov, in Geneva, warned the West
against recognizing the independence of Kosovo. "Many of them [west-
ern countries], frankly, do not understand the risks and dangers and
threats associated with a unilateral declaration of Kosovo independence.
They do not understand that it would inevitably result in a chain reaction
in many parts of the world, including Europe and elsewhere."[88] This was
an issue that had continued to annoy Russia since 1999, and was later
used to justify supporting separatism in Georgia and the annexation of
Ukraine. At the moment in 2008, it was another case where Russia felt
that its interests were being ignored, and another way in which the
Yugoslav wars continued to corrode the West's relations with Russia.

It is not clear how hard the United States pushed for a MAP, but
France and Germany strongly resisted, and they carried the day, getting
the United Kingdom to back them. The discussion was animated, with a
Polish delegate accusing Germany of being "more worried for Moscow
than for your allies."[89] A MAP was rejected, but the two aspirants were
encouraged in the Declaration released at the end of the summit:
"NATO welcomes Ukraine's and Georgia's Euro-Atlantic aspirations
for membership in NATO. We agreed today that these countries will
become members of NATO."[90] Merkel, who had opposed a MAP, said
"It is their destiny and vocation to be partners in NATO," but "criteria
need to be met and we need another phase of intense commitment."[91]
The German deputy foreign minister, Gernot Erler, said: "There has

---

[86] Malek, "The 'Western Vector,'" p. 536.
[87] Quoted in Socor, "Putin Warns Ukraine."
[88] Rosalind Ryan, "'Join Nato and We'll Target Missiles at Kiev,' Putin Warns Ukraine,"
    The Guardian, February 12, 2008.
[89] Cited in Charap and Colton, *Everyone Loses*, p. 88.
[90] "Bucharest Summit Declaration," April 3, 2008, NATO Press Release (2008) 049.
[91] Quoted in Paul Ames, "Under Pressure from Russia, NATO Delays Membership Offers
    to Ukraine, Georgia," Associated Press International, April 4, 2008.

already been enough tension with Moscow regarding missile defense, for example."[92]

While the position taken at Bucharest reflected the need for compromise in the alliance, and also a compromise between Ukraine and Georgia's interests and those of Russia, Charap and Colton called it "the worst of all worlds: while providing no increased security to Ukraine and Georgia, the Bucharest Declaration reinforced the view in Moscow that NATO was determined to incorporate them at any cost."[93]

Aleksandr Torshin, first deputy chairman of Russia's Federation Council sounded satisfied with the outcome: "NATO made a sensible decision not to grant Membership Action Plans to Ukraine and Georgia, and this decision was influenced by Russia's firm and measured position."[94] Similarly, some in the West saw the decision as a "major diplomatic coup for Russia" and Putin, and some criticized NATO for letting Russia have too much influence and for seeming to abandon its principle that any European democracy was eligible for membership.[95] Others were more negative. Foreign Minister Lavrov said: "We will do all we can to prevent Ukraine's and Georgia's accession into NATO and to avoid an inevitable serious exacerbation of our relations with both the alliance and our neighbors."[96]

Putin, speaking in Bucharest at Russia's meeting with NATO the day after the NATO summit closed, said: "The emergence of a powerful military bloc at our borders will be seen as a direct threat to Russian security."[97] Putin was reported to have said to President Bush at the summit: "You realize, George, that Ukraine is not even a state! What is Ukraine? A part of its territory belongs to Eastern Europe, while another part, a significant one, was given over by us!"[98] In June, the Duma passed a measure urging Putin to withdraw from the 1997 Friendship Treaty if Ukraine was given a Membership Action Plan, confirming what many had suspected: that Russia's acceptance of Ukraine's territorial integrity was not unconditional. *Rossiiskaya Gazeta* urged a response:

[92] Paul Ames, "NATO Summit Set to Reject Bush Drive for Early Membership for Ukraine, Georgia, Macedonia," Associated Press International, April 3, 2008.

[93] Charap and Colton, *Everyone Loses*, p. 88.

[94] Quoted in Malek, "The 'Western Vector,'" p. 532.

[95] Andrew Blomfield, "Not Yet, NATO Tells Ukraine, Georgia; Denial of Membership Seen as Major Diplomatic Coup for Russia, Putin," *Ottawa Citizen*, April 4, 2008, p. A8.

[96] "Russia FM: Moscow Will Do All It Can to Prevent NATO Membership for Ukraine, Georgia," Associated Press, April 8, 2008.

[97] Quoted in Adrian Blomfield and James Kirkup, "Stay Away, Vladimir Putin Tells NATO," *The Telegraph*, April 5, 2008.

[98] Quoted in Malek, "The 'Western Vector,'" p. 539.

Russia must render comprehensive aid to all anti-NATO Ukrainian politicians and social forces, not sparing resources for that, including financial resources ... It is time to stop fearing the cries about 'the interference in the internal affairs of Ukraine' ... The nationalists in Kiev must receive an unambiguous warning that Russia does not have the slightest motivation and obligation to support the territorial integrity of Ukraine as a candidate for membership in NATO.[99]

The Bucharest commitment, while seen at the time as a step back from an immediate Membership Action Plan, was widely cited later by those arguing that western policy was the cause of the war in Ukraine. Whether that is true is impossible to say. The fact that a move intended as a concession to Russia may have deeply antagonized it points to how incompatible aims were and how intense the security dilemma had become. When Zbigniew Brzezinski said that the result of the summit was a "strategic victory and only a tactical defeat" for Ukraine, it is likely that in Russia this was seen as a tactical victory and a strategic defeat. Russians may have felt similarly about Georgian President Mikhail Saakashvili's statement that "This is a geopolitical coup."[100] In 2011, Sergei Karaganov spelled out the Russian position stridently "NATO expansion into Ukraine is something Russia would view as absolutely unacceptable because it then becomes a vital threat. In political jargon, this kind of threat means war."[101]

Russia Invades Georgia

The war in Georgia in 2008 marks an important turning point in Russia's policy.[102] While this was far from the first time that Russia had intervened in Georgia or another of the former Soviet states, earlier interventions were accompanied by claims that Russian forces were peacekeepers. In the 2008 invasion, Russian tanks crossed the border into Georgia and Russian aircraft bombed Georgian cities. Russia laid the groundwork for the conflict by issuing passports to residents of the breakaway regions of Georgia and, in the weeks before the war, there was a series of violent provocations by the separatist regimes in Abkhazia and

---

[99] Quoted in ibid., p. 540.   [100] Quoted in Ames, "Under Pressure from Russia."

[101] Sergei Karaganov, "An Iron Fist to Keep NATO at Bay," *Russia in Global Affairs*, March 4, 2011. Karaganov went on to state that NATO expansion to Ukraine and Georgia had been forestalled only by the "iron fist," Russia's invasion of Georgia.

[102] For a discussion of the war and its consequences, see Ronald Asmus, *A Little War that Shook the World: Georgia, Russia, and the Future of the West* (New York: St. Martin's, 2010); and Gerard Toal, *Near Abroad: Putin, the West and the Contest over Ukraine and the Caucasus* (New York: Oxford University Press, 2017), which stresses the similarities between Russia's intervention in Georgia and Ukraine.

South Ossetia that Russia supported. At the time, the invasion was seen as motivated by a desire to undermine Georgian President Mikhail Saakashvili, to demonstrate Russia's power (and the West's impotence in this region), and to clarify Russia's objections to NATO expansion. It was also seen as a "tit-for-tat" for western support for Kosovo's independence. A member of Russia's Duma said: "Today, it is quite obvious who the parties in the conflict are. They are the US, UK, Israel who participated in training the Georgian army, Ukraine who supplied it with weapons. We are facing a situation where there is a NATO aggression against us."[103] While Georgia has received much of the blame for igniting military conflict, Russia's response was clearly intended to do more than just stop the conflict or restore the status quo. In March 2008, the Russian Duma had passed a resolution urging the government to consider recognizing the independence of Abkhazia and South Ossetia, and Georgia complained of the "creeping annexation of a sovereign state."[104] This may have led the Georgian government to believe that drastic measures were needed to defend the status quo, but resorting to military force against territories backed by Russia was bound to turn out badly.

The damage caused to Russia's relations with the West was both profound and limited. On one hand, despite the widespread view that Georgian President Saakashvili was partly to blame for responding to provocations and giving Russia the excuse it sought to invade, the war increased the perception that Russia was actively seeking to overturn the post-Cold War order, and that it was now willing to use force to do so. In terms of concrete measures, however, very little was done. As at Bucharest, the traditional European powers, including France, Germany, and Italy, did not want to alienate Russia for the benefit of a small neighbor. They prevailed over the desire of the United States and the postcommunist EU members to respond more resolutely. There was a recognition that there was not much they could do to challenge Russia militarily in the Caucasus, and there was not much appetite for sanctions. Despite the outrage over the invasion, there were important joint interests that most leaders wanted to continue pursuing. Russia continued to facilitate transit to Afghanistan, and contributed a contingent to an EU peacekeeping mission in Chad in 2009.[105]

---

[103] "A Scripted War," *The Economist*, August 14, 2008.
[104] "Russia FM: Moscow Will Do All It Can to Prevent NATO Membership for Ukraine, Georgia," Associated Press, April 8, 2008.
[105] Tumanov et al., "Russia-EU Relations," p. 128.

Reset and Overload

In June 2008, Russia's new president, Dmitry Medvedev, speaking in Berlin, took a significant initiative to put Russia's relations with the West on a better footing. Medvedev proposed a new "European Security Treaty" that would create and codify a new security architecture for Europe, which many believed had been missing since the end of the Cold War.[106] Expressed in a "fourteen points" format that recalled Woodrow Wilson's post-World War I proposals, Medvedev sought to move past the emerging division of Europe into NATO members and non-NATO members. Having recognized that Russian NATO membership was no longer a real possibility, Russia now sought an arrangement that would surpass NATO as the most important institution for European security. That Russia must be a part of whatever organization was to be most important in governing European security was self-evident to Russians and to many in the West as well. The proposal was intended to create a new architecture for European security that included Russia, a task that had been unfulfilled since 1989.

Medvedev proposed as an underlying principle the "indivisibility of security." The draft treaty that emerged contained sweeping and vague commitments such as: "Any security measures taken by a Party to the Treaty individually or together with other Parties, including in the framework of any international organization, military alliance or coalition, shall be implemented with due regard to security interests of all other Parties" (Article 1), and "A Party to the Treaty shall not undertake, participate in or support any actions or activities affecting significantly security of any other Party or Parties to the Treaty" (Article 2, Paragraph 1).[107] On questions of armed conflict, the draft treaty combined a recapitulation of Article 51 of the UN Charter and Article V of the NATO charter. The key point was that "[E]very Party shall be entitled to consider an armed attack against any other Party an armed attack against itself" (Article 7, Paragraph 2). This would, in effect, bring Russia inside the NATO Article V commitment and give it considerable latitude to intervene abroad.

Medvedev's proposal did not get far for three reasons. First, it was seen as lacking substance. The language in the treaty all sounded good, but it

---

[106] The proposal is discussed in Nikita Lomagin, "Medvedev's 'Fourteen Points': Russia's Proposal for a New European Security Architecture," in Roger E. Kanet, ed., *Russian Foreign Policy in the 21st Century* (Basingstoke: Palgrave Macmillan, 2011), pp. 181–203; and Richard Weitz, "The Rise and Fall of Medvedev's European Security Treaty," German Marshall Fund of the United States, "On Wider Europe," May 2012.

[107] "The Draft of the European Security Treaty," Kremlin website.

was hard to imagine how it could be used practically to resolve the disagreements that the region faced, let alone a conflict like Yugoslavia. Like other collective security proposals, it seemed likely to work only when it was not needed. Referring in his Berlin speech to the League of Nations and Kellogg-Briand pact, which most regarded having failed spectacularly to preserve peace, Medvedev said that: "In today's world, when no one wants war in Europe and we have all been made wiser by the lessons of the twentieth century, such an agreement has a better hope of success."[108] Second, it was seen as a tactic to weaken NATO. While it made sense that Russia wanted to reduce the role of an organization from which it was excluded, NATO leaders continued to believe that, for all its faults, NATO was the best available instrument for managing post-Cold War security challenges in Europe. Third, shortly after Medvedev proposed the treaty, Russia went to war in Georgia. This reinforced the sense among many that the main problem of European security was Russia, and that limiting Russia's assertiveness was the best way to increase security. The failure of Medvedev's proposal to gain significant traction appears to have ended Russia's effort to forge a European-Russian "pole" in world affairs distinct from the United States. For all of western Europe's resentment over US behavior, most did not want to replace its role in Europe with Russia.

Even after the Georgia war, the West too sought to find ways to reduce tensions, and this desire drove the "reset" policy of the incoming Obama administration in 2009. Obama was undeterred by either the war in Georgia or Russia's announcement the day after his election that it would deploy Iskander missiles to Kaliningrad, the Russian exclave situated on the Baltic Sea between Lithuania and Poland. Not to be sidetracked, the Obama administration included Russia in its intention to revise US policy in a less assertive, less interventionist, and more pragmatic direction. For the first time in the post-Cold War era, the United States seemed willing to temper its support for democratization with a new realism.

In one of the more symbolic (but not truly substantive) episodes of the post-Cold War era, Secretary of State Hillary Clinton presented her Russian counterpart Sergei Lavrov with a large red "reset button" at a meeting in Geneva in March 2009. Unfortunately, the button prepared by the US side for the photo opportunity used the Russian word *peregruzka* (overload) rather than *perezagruzka* (reset or reboot).[109] The

---

[108] Medvedev, "Speech at Meeting with German Political, Parliamentary and Civic Leaders," June 5, 2008, http://en.kremlin.ru/events/president/transcripts/320.

[109] Mikhail Zygar, "The Russian Reset That Never Was," ForeignPolicy.com, December 9, 2016.

desire for a "reboot" was real, and the Obama administration made substantial moves to pursue it. The Obama team sought Russian help on a range of issues, such as preserving the "northern corridor" supply route into Afghanistan and containing Iran's nuclear program. In cutting funding for the deployment of missile defense systems in Europe, which were aimed at Iran but which Russia saw as threatening, Obama acceded to an important Russian wish in the field of security, and he was roundly criticized for it domestically. This represents one of those cases where a leader faced a significant domestic cost for trying to reduce tensions in this relationship.[110]

At the same time, the two sides retained vastly different perspectives on important issues. The underlying premises of US policy did not change, and the view of Russia as a country that had cynically invaded a small neighbor persisted. That Russia now had a sham president – everyone understood that important decisions were still being made by Putin – undermined respect for both Putin and Medvedev. For his part, Medvedev reasserted the Russian right to intervene in the near abroad. Speaking on Russian television at the end of August 2008, he asserted five principles for Russian foreign policy:

1 "the primacy of the principles of international law";
2 "the world should be multipolar";
3 "develop friendly relations with Europe, the United States and other countries, as much as possible";
4 "protecting the lives and dignity of our citizens, wherever they may be is an unquestionable priority…";
5 "there are regions in which Russia has privileged interests."[111]

These principles were essentially the same that had guided Russian foreign policy since 1992, and the fourth and fifth in particular were likely to lead to fear among Russia's neighbors and to the broader view that Russia was seeking to intervene abroad.

The Road to Ukraine's 2010 Presidential Election

As the year 2009 progressed, Ukraine became increasingly focused on the presidential election due to take place in two rounds in January and

---

[110] Senator John McCain called the decision "seriously misguided" and John Bolton, the former ambassador to the UN, said that "Russia and Iran are the big winners." See "Obama Scraps Bush-era Europe Missile Shield," nbcnews.com, September 17, 2009.
[111] Dmitry Medvedev, "Interview Given by Dmitry Medvedev to Television Channels Channel One, Rossia, NTV," August 31, 2008, Kremlin website.

February 2010.[112] In addition to all of the other problems facing Ukraine during the Yushchenko years, the country was hit hard by the global financial crisis that began in 2007. In 2009, Ukraine's GDP declined 15 percent, which by itself was probably sufficient to doom the reelection chances of an incumbent leader. President Yushchenko's popularity had plummeted. His tactical alliance with Yanukovych had alienated many of his core supporters, and the continuation of corruption in the country alienated many others. In polling in 2009, support for Yushchenko consistently registered in the single digits.

The frontrunners were two familiar faces, Yuliya Tymoshenko and Viktor Yanukovych. Both had served as PM in recent years, and they had been on opposite sides of the Orange Revolution. The economic decline, however, provided a political advantage to Yanukovych. Having lost the position of prime minister in 2007, he could run as an outsider who was not responsible for the current economic problems. Tymoshenko, as the sitting PM, was seen as largely responsible.

Tymoshenko's challenge was exacerbated by IMF policy, which continued (as it had for many years) to push Ukraine's government to reduce the government subsidy for gas. Tymoshenko resisted, knowing how unpopular it would be and, in part as a result, in October 2009 the IMF withheld a $3.8 billion tranche of a loan negotiated the year before. When Yushchenko then signed a law, supported by the Party of Regions, which increased pensions and salaries for state employees, the IMF withdrew altogether.[113] There was a basic contradiction between what Ukraine's elites saw as necessary to win the election and what was needed to maintain the support of western-led financial institutions. Meanwhile, Yanukovych had refashioned himself, with the help of American consultant Paul Manafort, as the competent manager that Ukraine needed.

Observers noted that the campaign was left without a viable candidate who was a strong booster of European integration. Arseniy Yatsenyuk was one of the last to abandon that policy, in favor of a vague notion of Ukraine remaining outside of trade blocs. The term "Euro-romanticism" that Yanukovych had aimed at Yushchenko in 2006 appeared to have stuck, and the failure of Yushchenko and the various prime ministers to deliver any real reform meant that the talk of European integration after 2004 had delivered little to voters.[114]

[112] On the 2010 election, see Nathaniel Copsey and Natalia Shapovalova, "The Ukrainian Presidential Election of 2010," *Representation* 46, 2 (2010): 211–225.

[113] Fean, "A Return to Multi-Vectoral Balancing?" p. 7.

[114] See Elena Gnedina, "EU Running on Empty in Ukraine," euobserver.com, November 16, 2009; and Volodymyr Yermolenko, "Mutual Distrust Blurs EU-Ukraine Summit," euobserver.com, December 7, 2009.

In the first round of the election, Yanukovych finished first with 35.3 percent and Tymoshenko second with 25.1 percent of the vote. Others were far behind (Yushchenko received a meager 5.5 percent). While Yanukovych looked to be the frontrunner going into the second round, it was expected that many of those voters whose candidates were eliminated would vote for Tymoshenko. In the second round, alliances from 2004 were turned on their head. Yushchenko supported his old enemy Yanukovych over his old ally Tymoshenko. The final result was close, with Yanukovych winning by 49.0 percent to 45.5 percent.

Despite widespread fears of a repeat of the 2004 electoral fraud, the 2010 election was widely regarded as "free and fair." The OSCE's Final Report on the election stated that: "The presidential election met most OSCE commitments and other international standards for democratic elections and consolidated progress achieved since 2004. The process was transparent and offered voters a genuine choice between candidates representing diverse political views. However, unsubstantiated allegations of large-scale electoral fraud negatively affected the election atmosphere and voter confidence in the process."[115]

As in previous elections, the vote was regionally polarized, with Yanukovych winning over 80 percent of the vote in much of eastern and southern Ukraine and Crimea, and Tymoshenko winning over 80 percent in much of the west. Across all of Ukraine's oblasts, the voting pattern of 2010 closely resembled that of 2004.[116] Tymoshenko also won a plurality in much of central Ukraine, but Yanukovych's huge margin in the heavily populated east was crucial. Equally important was low voter turnout: Yanukovych won the election in 2010 with 12.5 million votes, 360,000 fewer than he had garnered in finishing second in 2004. Tymoshenko, however, received only 11.6 million, 3.5 million fewer than Yushchenko had in 2004. The Party of Regions' ability to mobilize in the east was crucial.

Among Yushchenko's last acts as president was to bestow the title "Hero of Ukraine" on the World War II-era figure Stepan Bandera, who had been a leader of the Organization of Ukrainian Nationalists. It would be hard to think of a more divisive step. Among Ukrainian nationalists,

---

[115] OSCE Office for Democratic Institutions and Human Rights, "Ukraine Presidential Election 17 January and 7 February 2010: OSCE/ODIHR Election Observation Mission Final Report," April 28, 2010.

[116] Timothy J. Colton, "An Aligning Election and the Ukrainian Political Community," *East European Politics and Societies* 25, 1 (February 2011): 12.

Bandera symbolized the Ukrainians who had fought tenaciously for Ukraine's independence against the overwhelming might of the Soviet Union. But his collaboration with Nazi forces and his association with the murder of Jews and Poles made him, in the eyes of many, simply a fascist and a murderer. To many, it was inconceivable that he could be praised, let alone made a "Hero of Ukraine."[117] The historiography of Bandera and the Ukrainian Insurgent Army is among the most bitterly contested issues in Ukraine, and feeds the notion in Russia and the West that those most committed to Ukraine's independence are fascists or are tolerant of fascists. Yushchenko's decision was a godsend for those, like Yanukovych and the Russian government, who wanted to paint pro-western politicians as extremists.

Conclusion

Five years after being disgraced by transparent voter fraud and losing the rerun of the 2004 election, Viktor Yanukovych won the presidency freely and fairly. Ironically, Yanukovych achieved democratically what he could not achieve through fraud. Between 2004 and 2010, Ukraine had become a much more consolidated democracy, as the election showed, and partly due to that had become more integrated with Europe. Many in Ukraine and in the West believed that Yanukovych had accepted Ukraine's democratic transition and would now govern as a "normal" democratic leader. There was hope that in contrast to the inefficacy of the Orange Coalition, Yanukovych would be able to take the concrete steps needed to push integration forward, while also soothing Ukraine's regional divisions.[118]

The intervening five years had seen three broad developments that shaped the transition from the crisis of 2004 to that of 2014. First, within Ukraine, the record of progress was uneven. On the one hand, the

---

[117] Bandera's legacy is so divisive that it is almost impossible to characterize it in a way that will not be seen by one side or another as a dangerous distortion. For a valiant attempt to provide a balanced assessment of Bandera and his legacy by someone who has deeply researched the extreme violence that Ukraine experienced in that era, see Timothy Snyder, "A Fascist Hero in Democratic Kiev," *New York Review of Books*, February 24, 2010. Snyder concludes: "In embracing Bandera as he leaves office, Yushchenko has cast a shadow over his own political legacy."

[118] For one such optimistic assessment, see Samuel Charap, "Seeing Orange," Foreignpolicy.com, January 8, 2010. For a detailed discussion of those, including in the US State Department, who expressed optimistic views about Yanukovych, see Taras Kuzio, "Viktor Yanukovych Two Years On: Why Many Got Him Wrong," *Eurasia Daily Monitor* 9, 39, February 24, 2012.

creeping authoritarianism of the Kuchma era had been reversed, and
pluralism and political competition were thriving. On the other hand, this
increasing democracy did little to reduce the corruption that irritated
many Ukrainians or to advance economic reform. Many seemed to
believe, to the contrary, that the divisiveness of the Orange movement
had undermined reform, and that a stronger, or at least more unified,
leadership was needed. The hopes raised by many in 2004 that Ukraine
would move rapidly toward the West were not borne out, and the
squandering of this opportunity had immense consequences. After
2010, Ukraine was due to refight many of the battles that had led to the
Orange Revolution.

Second, Ukraine's position between Russia and the West continued
to create tension within Ukraine, between Ukraine and Russia, and
between Russia and the West. The Orange Revolution had not moved
Ukraine into the West, but it had increased the belief in the West that
this was Ukraine's natural place, as demonstrated by the vague commitment to eventual NATO membership. Russia, however, had not
abandoned its own claim to Ukraine, and expressed with increasing
stridence its opposition to Ukraine's westward trajectory. While invading Georgia may have been intended to signal Russia's seriousness, the
effect in the West was not to increase respect for Russia, but to reaffirm
to many the need to stand up to it. The West and Russia were more at
odds than ever about what constituted the status quo, and therefore
which changes were legitimate and which were signs of aggression.
A major change in this period was that after 2008 the European
Union's European Neighborhood Policy began to eclipse NATO
membership as the main vector of Ukraine's integration into the western institutions.

Finally, the question of democracy continued to challenge understandings of the status quo even further. Russia's "castling" move, which made
Putin prime minister and Medvedev president, was a transparent
manipulation, contrastingly sharply with Ukraine's competitive presidential election. In both Ukraine and Georgia, governments that came to
power through street protests were also seeking to join the West politically, a correlation that Russia saw as ominous. The promotion of autocracy was a clear part of Russia's strategy to maintain its declared sphere of
influence.

By 2010, Russia and the West were in a more conflictual position than
they had been in since the Cold War. The Orange Revolution, the war in
Georgia, autocracy in Russia, and disagreement over Kosovo all served
to drive the sides apart. Moreover, there was now no doubt that Ukraine
was a battleground between Russia and the West. The failure of NATO's

compromise at Bucharest showed how hard it was to avoid that conflict. There was, perhaps, one potential piece of good news. The election of Yanukovych made Russia feel more secure about Ukraine, and led many in the West to believe that Ukraine would have leadership of increased pragmatism and competence. Instead, Viktor Yanukovych was to be a new force of instability and conflict.

6 Viktor Yanukovych and the Path to Confrontation, 2010–2013

On February 25, 2010, Viktor Yanukovych was inaugurated as Ukraine's fourth president. In his address to parliament he stressed moderation and balance, both domestically and internationally. To his domestic opponents, he stressed the importance of working with the parliamentary opposition. "Says the Bible: 'Make your peace with your adversary quickly, while you are still on the road with him...' Life has confirmed this simple and obvious truth: people don't like being shown bare fists. They are more likely to trust those who stretch out their hands as a sign of peace."[1]

In foreign policy, his speech reasserted the "multivector" foreign policy of Leonid Kuchma, after the pro-western policy of Yushchenko:

As president, I have a clear understanding of what kind of foreign policy corresponds today with the national interests of Ukraine. Being a bridge between East and West, an integral part of Europe and the former Soviet Union at the same time, Ukraine will select the kind of foreign policy that would allow our state to receive the maximum benefit from the development of equal and mutually beneficial relations with the Russian Federation, the European Union and the United States and other countries that influence the situation in the world.

These two pronouncements played to two different sorts of wishful thinking. The first was the hope that the Yanukovych of 2010, who had campaigned as a moderate, reform-oriented pragmatist, had replaced the Yanukovych of 2004, who had tried to seize power via a rigged election. The second was Yanukovych's own hope that he could have it both ways in foreign policy, integrating to some extent with both the European Union and Russia while playing them off against one another. Both hopes turned out to be false, and the result in 2013 was confrontation in the streets over the two linked issues: would Ukraine be democratic, or

---

[1] "President Viktor Yanukovych's Feb. 25 Inaugural Speech in Parliament," *Kyiv Post*, February 25, 2010.

would Yanukovych eliminate opposition? And would Ukraine join Russia or the West?

Yanukovych Consolidates Power

While Yanukovych spoke in his inaugural address about respecting the opposition, he also asserted the need for a working parliamentary majority, and he proceeded to build one. However, he accomplished this using illegal means, and then used this majority to undertake further consolidation that many saw as undermining the country's de facto pluralism and democratic aspirations. He had been elected on a slim majority, and the country remained divided. This campaign to concentrate power and eliminate political competition, more than any other domestic or international force, set the stage for the Euromaidan, because it eventually created, for those in Ukraine opposed to Yanukovych or supportive of democracy, the same dilemma as that of 2004: was there any way to restore pluralism besides street protests?

Yanukovych's multi-pronged approach to concentrating power built upon the tactics that Kuchma had used earlier. To control formal institutions, such as the parliament, he relied largely on informal means, such as bribing deputies. He then used control of the parliament both to change laws that constrained him, and to ensure that parliament did not respond to various unconstitutional steps. The ability to win control of the Constitutional Court was essential in this process. Crucially, the amassing of political power was matched by an effort to concentrate economic power, which was both a goal by itself as well as providing the means to further political power.[2]

Three key moves by Yanukovych dramatically bolstered his power. The first was the formation of a majority in parliament that he controlled. As Henry Hale has shown, in "patronal" systems, there is an incentive for actors – even members of the opposition – to "bandwagon" with whomever is in power, in order to share the gains from patronage and to avoid being punished by selective law enforcement.[3] Fairly quickly after Yanukovych's inauguration, therefore, he was able to entice several members of opposition parties in parliament to switch sides, helping him form a majority. According to the law, however, members of parliament were elected as members of parties, and had to give up their seats if they left

---

[2] On Yanukovych's amassing of power, see Serhiy Kudelia, "The House That Yanukovych Built," *Journal of Democracy* 25, 3 (July 2014): 19–34.
[3] Henry E. Hale, *Patronal Politics: Eurasian Regime Dynamics in Comparative Perspective* (New York: Cambridge University Press, 2014).

their parties.[4] By retaining their seats while switching parties, the deputies were in violation of the law, but although the opposition howled, the majority ignored their protests. The Constitutional Court ruled that this was legal, showing that it was already in Yanukovych's camp.

With the parliament in his control, Yanukovych was able to have his preferred candidate for prime minister, Nikolai Azarov, selected. Azarov had overseen tax collection under Kuchma, and had helped Kuchma use tax collection to punish his adversaries. Yanukovych managed to accomplish what none of his predecessors had been able to do: to form a unified government in which parliament, prime minister, and president were united by a single political force. In the abstract, this would help overcome the divisiveness that had so often paralyzed Ukrainian politics. In practice, Yanukovych used this unification of power to pursue still greater power.

The next step was a revision of the constitution, which Yanukovych achieved not through the amendment process, but by getting the Constitutional Court to invalidate the amendments that were made as part of the pact that ended the Orange Revolution. Those amendments sought to limit the power of the presidency, which Kuchma had abused, by giving parliament the power to select the prime minister and giving the prime minister control over key ministries, such as Interior, which were prominent in law enforcement and, therefore, central to the use of selective law enforcement for political and economic purposes. In 2004, the Party of Regions had supported those changes, to ensure that if Yushchenko prevailed in the rerun of the election, he would not be too powerful. In 2010, with Yanukovych in office, the party reversed course, and an important element of balance was lost. Lacking the 300 votes in the parliament needed to amend the constitution, Yanukovych got the Constitutional Court to declare the 2004 changes themselves unconstitutional, on procedural grounds. Exactly how Yanukovych got the Constitutional Court to issue its decision (it had not objected to the measures previously) is unknown, though the general assumption is that bribery was involved.

This change gave Yanukovych unfettered control over appointments in the executive branch, which had both direct and indirect effects. The direct effect was that he could now appoint loyalists to key positions in all the ministries, including, crucially, those involved in law enforcement. In the Orange Revolution, Ukraine's security forces – including the military

---

[4] This "imperative mandate" had been the subject of intense criticism at the time it was adopted, but was intended to prevent this kind of poaching of deputies that occurred under both Kuchma and Yanukovych.

and the Interior Ministry – had not used force against protesters, and Yanukovych was intent on ensuring that the security forces would be loyal to him in any future showdown.[5] Indirectly, it meant that everyone in Ukraine knew that they could now be subject to politically motivated law enforcement. It also meant that everyone hoping to do business with any aspect of the government knew that it had to do business with Yanukovych.[6] As a result of these changes, by the end of 2010 Yanukovych had obtained the kind of strong presidential constitutional arrangement that was present in Russia, and had a tightly run patronage machine, based in the Party of Regions, that could reward friends, punish enemies, and raise money. The reversion to the 1996 constitution also allowed Yanukovych to appoint the oblast governors, and he took advantage of this to replace leaders around the country with Party of Regions loyalists.[7]

Having concentrated political power, Yanukovych also moved to consolidate control over economic resources, and this was perhaps equally important in strengthening the eventual opposition to him. With law enforcement under his control, Yanukovych was able to put the kind of pressure on Ukrainian businesses that Putin had done in Russia. Whereas Putin's implicit deal seemed be "stay out of politics and you can keep your assets," Yanukovych was more avaricious, and an increasing array of economic assets was collected into the hands of a group of close allies known as the "family."[8] Yanukovych's son Oleksandr, a dentist, became head of a holding company that quickly became Ukraine's fastest growing business.[9]

This model had the obvious benefits to Yanukovych of enriching his family and building a deeply committed circle around him. But as wealth was concentrated, the circle of those dedicated to supporting to Yanukovych narrowed, and the circle of those opposed to him – privately if not publicly – grew. "By shrinking the set of those enriched by rent-seeking, Yanukovych had strengthened the loyalty of his inner circle but had left many more feeling shut out and angry – an outcome that made the capacity to coerce businesspeople a higher regime priority."[10] According

[5] See Taras Kuzio, "Russianization of Ukrainian National Security Policy under Viktor Yanukovych," *Journal of Slavic Military Studies* 25, 4 (2012): 558–581.
[6] In interviews with former Ukrainian officials, I was told that kickbacks on government contracts had become nearly universal, down to "every pencil," in the words of one interviewee.
[7] Kudelia, "The House That Yanukovych Built," p. 22.
[8] See for example, Anders Åslund, *Ukraine: What Went Wrong and How to Fix It* (Washington, DC: Peterson Institute for International Economics, 2015), p. 91. Åslund called the Yanukovych regime "the ultimate predation."
[9] Kudelia, "The House That Yanukovych Built," p. 22.   [10] Ibid., p. 22.

to Anders Åslund, Yanukovych initially had nine different business groups represented in his cabinet, but by 2013 the number was reduced to two.[11] In this respect, even if his tactics were similar to Kuchma's, his goals were much more aggressive. Eventually, many of Ukraine's oligarchs went from seeing Yanukovych as an ally to seeing him as a threat. A good example was Petro Poroshenko, who was named minister of trade and economic development in February 2012. The very same day, his businesses were raided by the tax police, apparently as a warning to him.[12] Poroshenko then ran for a seat in parliament, left the government, and later supported the Euromaidan protests.

In forming his government, Yanukovych turned to figures linked to the energy industry, most notably appointing Yuriy Boyko as energy and fuel minister. Boyko had run one of the gas intermediaries that had been abolished, and was linked to Dmytro Firtash, a major owner of RosUkrEnergo. Serhiy Lyovochkin, another of Firtash's associates, was made head of the Presidential Administration.[13] Rinat Akhmetov also had his associates in the Yanukovych cabinet, most notably Deputy Prime Minister Boris Kolesnikov. Andriy Klyuyev was put in charge of the nuclear power industry. The appointment of Dmytro Tabachnyk as minister of science and education seemed calculated to alienate national-minded Ukrainians, as Tabachnyk had questioned Ukraine's independence and supported enhanced status for the Russian language.

A final means of consolidating power was the prosecution of his most prominent rival, Yuliya Tymoshenko. Tymoshenko had fought against Yanukovych both during the Orange Revolution and during Yushchenko's presidency (see Chapter 5), and had nearly defeated him in the 2010 presidential election. She clearly intended to continue challenging him. One way in which Yanukovych had applied his control of the parliament was to pass laws weakening the power of the Supreme Court to review appeals of lower court decisions and changing the appointment of judges so that he had indirect control over it.[14] Combined with his control over law enforcement this made it relatively easy to persecute his

---

[11] Anders Åslund, "Ukraine Crisis: Yanukovych and the Tycoons," *BBC News*, December 13, 2013.

[12] "The Chocolate King Rises," *Spiegel* Online, May 22, 2014. Poroshenko's opportunism is noteworthy even in Ukraine: in 1998 he joined the pro-Kuchma Social Democratic Party. He subsequently formed his own party, Solidarnist'. He supported the Orange Revolution and took a position in Yushchenko's government. He then joined Yanukovych's government, left to run for parliament, and finally supported the revolution that ousted Yanukovych.

[13] Dominic Fean, "A Return to Multi-Vectoral Balancing? Viktor Yanukovych's Government and Ukrainian Foreign Policy," *Politique étrangère*, 2 (Summer 2010): 12.

[14] Kudelia, "The House That Yanukovych Built," p. 23.

enemies. Whereas Kuchma had failed in a political prosecution of Tymoshenko a decade earlier, Yanukovych rapidly succeeded. She and her close associate Yuriy Lutsenko were found guilty of abuse of power in connection with the 2009 gas deal with Russia (which Yanukovych did not repudiate and continued to abide by). The judges in the case received promotions and financial benefits.[15]

2012 Parliamentary Elections

The 2012 parliamentary elections were a significant test of Yanukovych's new authoritarianism. Would he be able to sideline or coopt the opposition parties, as Putin had done in Russia? The answer, clearly, was no. The election results turned out mixed for Yanukovych: while the Party of Regions and its allies won a majority of seats, parties deeply opposed to him continued to do well.

In the runup to the 2012 elections, the election law was changed yet again, returning to the formula in which half the seats were elected via proportional representation (party lists) and half in single-member districts. The single-member districts were highly subject to the influence of "administrative resources," since, with multiple candidates dividing the vote, a relatively small swing could have a decisive difference in each district. This meant that the ability to coerce the employees of a single factory, hospital, or school could tip the district. The patronage power of the government and economic resources that Yanukovych had amassed provided a huge advantage, as it had for the pro-Kuchma forces in 2002. In the proportional representation vote, however, Yanukovych could not make inroads in the vast swathes of Ukraine that were either completely opposed to him or simply unsupportive.

New opposition parties emerged to compete in the election. Most notable among these was the Ukrainian Democratic Alliance for Reform, whose acronym UDAR conveniently spelled the Ukrainian word for "punch," which was appropriate as the bloc was led by the former world boxing champion Vitaliy Klitschko. This party allied itself with Tymoshenko's Batkivshchyna (which itself was allied with several other parties), along with the nationalist party Svoboda, in an anti-Yanukovych front.

The 2012 election was a step away from the free, fair presidential election of 2010. People inside and outside Ukraine complained of a wide variety of measures taken to skew the vote. Within Ukraine, the

---

[15] Ibid., p. 23.

opposition parties (Batkivshchyna, UDAR, and Svoboda) announced that they did not recognize the results, and said that they would work toward the impeachment of Yanukovych (which they clearly would not have the votes to do).

The OSCE final report on the election summarized:

while voters had a choice between distinct parties and election day was calm and peaceful overall, certain aspects of the preelection period constituted a step backwards compared with recent national elections. In particular, these elections were characterized by the lack of a level playing field, caused primarily by the abuse of administrative resources, lack of transparency of campaign and party financing, and the lack of balanced media coverage. While the voting and counting processes on election day were assessed positively overall, the tabulation of results was negatively assessed in nearly half of the electoral districts observed. Post election day, the integrity of the results in some districts appeared to be compromised by instances of manipulation of the results and other irregularities, which were not remedied by the Central Election Commission (CEC) or the courts.[16]

While the Party of Regions managed to form a majority coalition in the parliament, the election was seen as a rebuke. Despite controlling the presidency, changing the election law, and applying considerable "administrative resources," the party increased its number of seats by only 10, to 185, still falling far short of an outright majority. The party's vote count in the proportional representation part of the ballot decreased dramatically compared to 2007, indicating the limits of its popularity. Tymoshenko's Batkivshchyna Party continued to perform well, despite (or perhaps because of) her imprisonment (Table 6.1).

Table 6.1 *2012 parliamentary election results*

Party	Percentage PR vote	PR seats	SMD seats	Total seats
Party of Regions	30.0	72	113	185
Batkivshchyna	25.6	62	32	101
UDAR	14.0	34	6	40
Communist Party	13.2	32	0	32
Svoboda	10.5	25	12	37
Others	6.7 combined	0	7	7
Independents	n/a	0	43	43

[16] OSCE Office for Democratic Institutions and Human Rights, "Ukraine Parliamentary Elections 28 October 2012 OSCE/ODIHR Election Observation Mission Final Report," January 3, 2013, p. 1.

The performance of the nationalist party Svoboda, winning 10.5 percent of the PR vote, drew a great deal of notice. The party's growth seemed to show the polarizing effect that Yanukovych was having, but many speculated that the party benefited from covert support from pro-Yanukovych oligarchs seeking to divide the opposition and tar it with charges of extremism. The party had taken steps to moderate its image and had struck a deal with Batkivshchyna not to compete with each other in SMD constituencies.

The modest performance of the Party of Regions prompted Yanukovych to reorganize his cabinet in a way that further narrowed the circle of represented interests and strengthened the role of the "family." In 2013, Oleksandr Yanukovych's firms received 70 percent of all the contracts from the state railway company, totaling $875 million – and depriving other oligarchs of their "share" of these spoils.[17] People were already thinking about the 2015 presidential election, and the signs – both in the government and in how the 2012 election had been conducted – seemed to show that Yanukovych was not planning on competing fairly. This impression was furthered by the fact that his popularity was plummeting, and preliminary polls showed him losing a head-to-head election with Klitschko.[18] This created the sense of a door closing on democracy in Ukraine that provided the context for 2013.

A New Pivot to Russia

Given his domestic problems, Yanukovych had to look to foreign affairs to increase his popularity. Initially, it looked like the strategy was focused entirely on Russia. Having consolidated control over the parliament in early 2010, Yanukovych quickly moved to grant Russia some of the concessions it had been seeking.

The clearest way in which foreign policy could address domestic problems was in the area of energy prices. At a time when the global recession was depressing gas prices, Ukraine was stuck with the deal Tymoshenko had negotiated in 2009. Absent some new deal, Ukraine's gas bills were going to increase dramatically (from $170 per thousand cubic meters in 2007, Ukraine had paid $305 in the first quarter of 2010 and was paying $330 in the second quarter).[19] In April 2010, Ukrainian Prime Minister Azarov and Russian Prime Minister Putin met in Moscow to negotiate on a series of issues, resulting in an

---

[17] Kudelia, "The House That Yanukovych Built," pp. 25–26.   [18] Ibid., p. 26.
[19] Fean, "A Return to Multi-Vectoral Balancing?," p. 5; "Russia, Ukraine Voice Optimism at New Gas Deal," *Kyiv Post*, April 20, 2010.

agreement signed in Kharkiv by Presidents Yanukovych and Medvedev on April 21. The Kharkiv agreement, as it came to be known, essentially traded lower gas prices in return for concessions on the Black Sea Fleet and Crimea.[20]

Russia's apparent preference for moving to market prices in the gas sector, and for getting Gazprom to focus on profits over geopolitics, had been reversed, or perhaps simply trumped by a more important goal. Gas subsidies were again being used to induce Ukraine to move closer to Russia. Naturally, the increased subsidies would be popular with Ukrainian consumers, and naturally they would provide ample opportunity for rent-seeking by Ukrainian elites.

Yanukovych was able to negotiate a 30 percent discount on Russian gas through 2019. This represented both good and bad news. It was estimated to save Ukraine $4 billion per year,[21] but Ukraine would still be paying more than western European countries.[22] Moreover, onerous provisions such as "take or pay" remained in place. In return, the new agreement updated the 1997 Friendship Treaty, extending Russia's lease on the Sevastopol naval base for twenty-five years, to 2042.[23]

For Russia, the extension of the Sevastopol lease was important both symbolically and substantively. Symbolically, it maintained a Russian presence in Crimea, and gained Ukraine's acknowledgement that this was to be a long-term, rather than transitory, arrangement. Substantively, rather than beginning to transition operations away from Sevastopol in anticipation of the existing lease's expiration, Russia could now expand its footprint there. Following the agreement, Russia embarked on a major program of upgrading the base and deploying more modern weapons there.[24]

For Yanukovych, the agreement won the support of the Russian government, which had been lukewarm about his election, and provided some relief on one of the hardest issues in Ukrainian politics, the rising cost of gas. He gushed about it: saying that Ukraine's relations with

---

[20] Rawi Abdelal, "The Profits of Power: Commerce and Realpolitik in Eurasia," *Review of International Political Economy* 20, 3 (2013): 434.

[21] Sergey Tumanov, Alexander Gasparishvili, and Ekaterina Romanova, "Russia-EU Relations, or How the Russians, Really View the EU," *Journal of Communist Studies and Transition Politics* 27, 1 (March 2011): 126.

[22] Robert Orttung and Indra Overland, "A Limited Toolbox: Explaining the Constraints on Russia's Foreign Energy Policy," *Journal of Eurasian Studies* 2 (2011): 81.

[23] The agreement further stipulated that the lease would be automatically extended by five years if neither side objected. Following the Russian annexation of Crimea in 2014, Russia annulled the lease.

[24] Taras Kuzio, *The Crimea: Europe's Next Flashpoint?* (Washington, DC: Jamestown Foundation, 2010), p. 15.

Russia had shifted from "confrontation and anti-Russian rhetoric" to "equality and good neighborliness." "The whole civilized world has welcomed the results of my talks with President Medvedev. In Washington, Brussels and all the European capitals they are regarded as Ukraine's undeniable success."[25] For his voting base in eastern Ukraine, who supported closer relations with Russia, this was a positive move.

In contrast to the 1997 treaty, this one was quickly ratified by both parliaments, but in Ukraine, the ratification was tumultuous. Opposition to the agreement was intense, but Yanukovych had the votes, so opposition deputies resorted to throwing eggs and smoke bombs to disrupt the proceedings. Critics raised a large number of procedural problems with the ratification process.[26] For those committed to Ukraine's independence, the Kharkiv agreement seemed to confirm the worst fears about Yanukovych. The opposition online newspaper *Ukrains'ka Pravda* headlined "The Rada Gave Ukraine Away."[27] The *Guardian* judged that: "The deal is the most concrete sign yet that Ukraine is now back under Russia's influence following Yanukovych's victory in February's presidential elections. It appears to mark the final nail in the coffin of the Orange Revolution of 2004."[28] In May, with Russian President Medvedev at his side, Yanukovych stated that Ukraine was returning to the non-bloc status mentioned in its 1990 Declaration of Sovereignty, a move seen as stressing that Ukraine would not join NATO.[29]

However, Yanukovych resisted, as his predecessors had, Russian efforts to promote supranational integration and to gain control of gas infrastructure. His coalition of oligarchic support in the Party of Regions supported both better ties with Russia and the EU Association Agreement (AA). Yanukovych's team insisted that the deal with Russia would not impede progress on EU integration, and a Foreign Ministry spokesman said that "We want to move towards the west. But the best way of doing this is to get gas from the east."[30] Other steps, though, such as trying to dismantle the bureau of Euro-Atlantic and European Integration under the Cabinet of Ministers, called that claim into question. As became more obvious in negotiations over economic integration with

---

[25] Quoted in ibid., p. 14. Kuzio was one of very few who foresaw a Russian move to seize Crimea. He pointed out that even after the Kharkiv agreement, Moscow Mayor Yurii Luzhkov continued to insist that Sevastopol was a Russian city.

[26] See ibid., pp. 19–20.   [27] "Rada Zdala Ukrainu," *Ukrains'ka Pravda*, April 27, 2010.

[28] Luke Harding, "Ukraine Extends Lease for Russia's Black Sea Fleet," *The Guardian*, April 21, 2010.

[29] Vladimir Socor, "Non-Bloc Status Covers Ukraine's Shift to Russian-Vector Orientation," *Eurasia Daily Monitor*, May 21, 2010.

[30] Quoted in Harding, "Ukraine Extends Lease."

the European Union and the CIS Customs Union, Yanukovych was playing a cynical and perhaps impossible balancing game, trying to get cheap gas without joining a Russia-led bloc or undermining integration with the EU.

The Kharkiv agreement did not actually lead to cheaper gas for Ukraine, and Yanukovych likely felt duped. Just five days after it was signed, Medvedev advanced yet another proposal for Russia to take control over much Ukraine's gas production and transit systems.[31] In 2011, Yanukovych said that "we cannot agree with it," because it left Ukraine paying $200 more per thousand cubic meters than Germany. He asserted that the price should be the German price minus transit fees from Russia to Germany, which he put at $70 per thousand cubic meters. He complained about Russia's negotiating tactics, saying "Conditions are dictated as they would be to an enemy."[32]

The Kharkiv agreement, intentionally or not, tied Viktor Yanukovych personally to Russia's priority of retaining its naval base in Sevastopol. In 2014, therefore, Yanukovych's ouster likely appeared threatening to that goal in particular.

The 2012 Language Law

A separate move by Yanukovych that Russia had long sought was a revision of Ukraine's language law to allow regions to give Russian the status of an official language, along with Ukrainian. The question of whether Ukrainian should be the lone state language in Ukraine, or whether Russian (and perhaps other minority languages) should also have that status, had been discussed at the time of independence and again when the 1996 constitution was adopted.[33] Practically, the policy was of little consequence, as Russian-language media dominated much of Ukraine, Russian was widely used, especially outside of western Ukraine, and education was available in Russian in much of the country. Among politicians, the issue had been easily finessed, as Russophone politicians such as Leonid Kuchma and Yuliya Tymoshenko learned to speak passable Ukrainian in official roles, even if they used Russian in private.

---

[31] Rilka Dragneva-Lewers and Kataryna Wolczuk, *Ukraine between the EU and Russia: The Integration Challenge* (Houndmills, Basingstoke: Palgrave MacMillan, 2015), p. 64.

[32] "'Usloviya vypisany kak budto dlya vraga," Kommersant.ru, June 9, 2011.

[33] The literature on language politics in Ukraine is immense. A wide-ranging recent collection of essays is Michael S. Flier and Andrea Graziosi, eds., *The Battle for Ukrainian: A Comparative Perspective* (Cambridge, MA: Harvard University Press/ Harvard Ukrainian Research Institute, 2017).

Symbolically, however, the issue was of immense importance, because it was seen as establishing the identity of the Ukrainian state. Was Ukraine a *Ukrainian* state, as many nationalists asserted, or was it also a *Russian* state, as asserted by some in Ukraine and by the Russian government? For Russia, asserting the Russianness of Ukraine was part of the broader view that the two countries were not fully distinct. While the content of the bill was seen by many as not being particularly harmful, "the Party of Regions used this as a tool to mobilize a pro-Russian electorate, deflecting attention away from social and economic issues to a kind of culture war with western Ukraine. The nationalists were almost euphoric – these were their issues, they were fighting for their native language."[34] This polarization was part of Yanukvoych's strategy, and it contributed directly to his downfall.

It was one of those symbolic issues which Yanukovych had used to motivate his "base," and he had promised in the 2010 campaign to change the law. While he initially neglected this promise, his popularity, and that of the Party of Regions, was sagging prior to the 2012 parliamentary elections, and so passing the language law was a way to motivate his voters.[35] It also addressed one of the complaints Medvedev had raised in his 2009 letter to the Ukrainian leadership.[36]

While Yanukovych and the Party of Regions had the votes to pass the measure, opposition deputies bitterly opposed it. They surrounded the speaker of the parliament when the bill was brought up to prevent further progress on it, spurring one of the parliamentary fistfights that periodically earned Ukraine a spot on newscasts around the world. After the initial passage of the measure, a small riot broke out outside the parliament. For those who supported the status quo, the new measure represented a major reverse that itself needed to be undone. Tymoshenko, from prison, called the measure "a crime against Ukraine, the nation, its history and the people."[37] The attempted reversal of this law after Yanukovych's downfall in 2014 was seen as an aggressive nationalist move that helped justify

---

[34] Volodymyr Ishchenko, "Ukraine's Fractures," *New Left Review* 87 (May/June 2014): 27.

[35] See Steven Pifer and Hannah Thoburn, "What Ukraine's New Language Law Means for National Unity," Brookings Institution, August 21, 2012, www.brookings.edu/blog/up-front/2012/08/21/what-ukraines-new-language-law-means-for-national-unity/.

[36] Medvedev had complained of "continued repression of the Russian language in public life, science, education, culture, media, and judicial proceedings." The text of Medvedev's letter is printed in English in Taras Kuzio, *Ukraine: Democratization, Corruption and the New Russian Imperialism* (Santa Barbara, CA: Praeger, 2015), pp. 438–439. The Russian original is at "Poslaniye Presidentu Ukrainy Viktoru Yushchenko," August 11, 2009, Kremlin website.

[37] Howard Amos, "Ukraine Language Bill Prompts Clashes between Police and Protesters," *The Guardian*, June 5, 2012.

Russia's intervention. A new language law was passed in 2017, to further outrage. The issue is a vivid example of how competing versions of the status quo can lead both sides to see the other as being aggressive.

Russia, the United States, and Europe

Events between 2010 and 2013 further undermined trust between Russia and the West, building the conditions for complete breakdown in 2014. By 2010, Russia and the West had a lengthy list of disagreements and few issues that served to bring them together. After 2010, the Arab Spring and its consequences drove them further apart, while ongoing western support for democratization further threatened Putin. Those two factors combined to make democratic revolutions look more dangerous in Moscow than ever.

In June 2010, sandwiched between a Medvedev-Obama meeting in Washington and another in Ottawa, the United States arrested ten Russia "sleeper" agents who had been posing as Americans for years. The story spurred extensive news coverage in the United States (and a popular television series). The United States traded the spies for four Russians who had been arrested for spying, and there were no diplomatic expulsions or further repercussions at the time.[38] If this episode did not have the negative effect of the Ames case of 1993, it was because the relationship had deteriorated so far in the meantime.

The Arab Spring drove the sides further apart. Western governments were broadly supportive of the wave of revolutions that began in Tunisia in December 2010. By 2012, authoritarian regimes had been toppled in Libya, Egypt, and Yemen. Syria was descending into civil war, and several other states had experienced sustained street protests. These events ratcheted up Russia's fears of democratization by revolution, and the civil war in Syria put the two sides again on opposite sides of a conflict that combined democratization and geopolitics.

Regarding Libya, Russia and the West initially agreed on the need to protect civilian populations from attacks by the Libyan military. On February 26, 2011, the UN Security Council unanimously approved Resolution 1970 freezing Muammar Gaddafi's assets and referring his actions to the International Criminal Court. When Gaddafi's forces threatened to overrun the opposition in Benghazi, the UN Security Council passed, with Russia abstaining this time, a new resolution

---

[38] The case generated further rancor in 2018 when one of the western spies exchanged for the Russian agents, Sergei Skripal, was poisoned with the nerve agent Novichok in England.

creating a "no fly" zone over Libya and authorizing members to use "all necessary measures" to protect civilians.

This second resolution authorized NATO to begin a bombing campaign, which Russia initially approved of. Medvedev reportedly overruled the Foreign Ministry's recommendation to veto the resolution, hoping to establish his credentials as a supporter of democracy.[39] Putin chimed in critically soon after: "What concerns me most is not the armed intervention itself – armed conflicts are nothing new and will likely continue for a long time, unfortunately. My main concern is the light-mindedness with which decisions to use force are taken in international affairs these days."[40]

However, as the conflict dragged on, NATO's bombing campaign experienced "mission creep," from protecting civilians to backing the rebels' campaign to dislodge Gaddafi from power. The result was Gaddafi's summary execution in October 2011. This enraged Russia and Putin, and probably undermined Medvedev. Not only did Russia oppose such campaigns to overturn leaders, but Russian leaders felt deceived by what to them seemed like a "bait and switch." Russia also suffered significant economic losses due to Gadaffi's fall, including a $3 billion railroad deal, $3.5 billion in energy deals, and $4 billion in arms sales.[41] That the aftermath included the descent of Libya into civil war and the rise of ISIS there only confirmed the Russian view that the United States and the West were sowing chaos in the pursuit of geopolitical gain.

Speaking in December 2011, after announcing that he would return to the presidency in 2012, Putin was scathing about Gadaffi's fate and the US role in it: "Who did this? Drones, including American ones. They attacked his column. Then – through the special forces, who should not have been there – they brought in the so-called opposition and fighters, and killed him without court or investigation." "Sometimes it seems to

---

[39] Mikhail Zygar, "The Russian Reset That Never Was," ForeignPolicy.com, December 9, 2016.

[40] Quoted in ibid. Zygar points out that Putin's remarks spurred Medvedev to rebut him directly and publicly, focusing particularly on Putin's use of the word "crusade." "It is entirely unacceptable to use expressions that effectively point the way to a clash of civilizations. The word 'crusade,' for instance. We must all remember that such language could make the situation even worse."

[41] Lincoln Pigman and Kyle Orton, "Inside Putin's Libyan Power Play," Foreignpolicy .com, September 14, 2017. As Pigman and Ortion detail, Russia eventually came to support the Libyan National Army and its leader Khalifa Haftar, who were trying to overthrow the UN-recognized government of Libya.

me that America does not need allies, it needs vassals. People are tired of the dictates of one country."[42]

By late 2011, the danger to Putin and the Russian government from street protests seemed to be growing. Parliamentary elections held on December 4 were widely regarded as rigged, but rather than take it in their stride, thousands protested in the streets of Moscow on December 10 and again two weeks later. The movement's leader, Alexei Navalny, made a veiled threat: "I see enough people here to take the Kremlin and [Government House] right now but we are peaceful people and won't do that just yet."[43]

Putin blamed the protests directly on the United States, saying that opposition leaders "heard the signal and with the support of the US state department began active work. We are all grownups here. We all understand the organizers are acting according to a well-known scenario and in their own mercenary political interests."[44] It is unclear whether Putin actually believed that the United States was responsible for the protests, but the accusation was valuable domestically, and the open encouragement of protests by the United States seemed to infuriate him.

If the danger of the precedent to Putin were not clear, it was made so by Senator John McCain, who told the BBC in the fall of 2011 after Gadaffi's fall that "I think dictators all over the world, including Russia ... Maybe even Mr. Putin ... are maybe a little bit more nervous" and then, after the first December protest in Moscow, tweeted "Dear Vlad, the Arab Spring is coming to a neighborhood near you."[45]

The Russian government was further irritated when Michael McFaul was appointed US ambassador to Moscow in January 2012. Duma Deputy Andrei Isayev complained that "McFaul, who specializes in 'orange revolutions,' has been appointed as US ambassador to Russia."[46] McFaul's meetings with opposition groups and frequent presence on social media irked the Russian government, which repeatedly criticized McFaul and even harassed him.[47] This was another case where

---

[42] Quoted in Andrew Osborn, "Vladimir Putin Lashes Out at America for Killing Gaddafi and Backing Protests," *The Telegraph*, December 15, 2011.

[43] Quoted by BBC News, "Moscow Protest: Thousands Rally against Vladimir Putin," December 25, 2011.

[44] Quoted in Miriam Elder, "Vladimir Putin Accuses Hillary Clinton of Encouraging Russian Protests," *The Guardian*, December 8, 2011.

[45] "McCain Warns Putin of 'Arab Spring,'" *Moscow News*, December 6, 2011.

[46] Quoted in Fred Weir, "Moscow Ambassador McFaul's 'Reset' with Kremlin Stumbles," *Christian Science Monitor*, April 4, 2012.

[47] For a detailed recollection of Russia's harassment of McFaul, see Michael McFaul, "Putin Hazed Me: How I Was Stalked, Harassed and Surveilled by Kremlin Stooges," *Politico*, May 19, 2018.

perceptions clashed. In the United States, McFaul was seen as "a principal architect of the administration's efforts to repair ties with Russia after years of strain," and his appointment – which broke with tradition because he was not a career diplomat – was seen as a sign of Obama's seriousness about rebuilding the relationship with Russia.[48] Some Russians agreed. Alexander Konovalov, of Russia's Institute of Strategic Studies and Analysis, said that "McFaul is a young man, very close to Obama and a devoted supporter of his policy. Moreover, he is specializing on Russian issues. Since McFaul is a person from presidential staff, his appointment would show that Washington pays serious attention to the Russian politics."[49] But the more widespread view in Russia was that the United States had sent a promoter of "colored revolutions" to ply his trade as ambassador.[50] By 2013, US-Russia relations had reached what at that time was a post-Cold War low.

Integration: The European Union and Russia Compete for Ukraine

For the entire post-Soviet era, there had been a fundamental imbalance between Ukraine's relations with Russia and those with the European Union. Ukraine sought to trade with both and choose neither, and while Russia consistently wanted far more than Ukraine was willing to give, the European Union consistently offered much less than Ukraine wanted. This began to change after 2010, and by 2013 it looked as if the European Union, with some reservations, was more actively seeking to foster integration with Ukraine. Ukraine's discussions with the European Union and with Russia were proceeding simultaneously and were interacting with one another.[51]

Ever since 1991, Ukraine had sought to manage its interdependence with Russia in a way that maximized economic benefits while avoiding any kind of formal integration that limited its sovereignty. Russia had repeatedly sought to shift the management of interdependence to supranational bodies that it could control, beginning in the 1990s with the

---

[48] Joby Warrick, "Obama to Pick Non-Diplomat as Next Ambassador to Russia," *Washington Post*, May 30, 2011, p. A4.
[49] "McFaul's Appointment May Boost Trust between U.S., Russia – Expert," *RIA Novosti*, May 29, 2011.
[50] McFaul recalls his time as ambassador in Michael McFaul, *From Cold War to Hot Peace: An American Ambassador in Putin's Russia* (New York: Houghton Mifflin Harcourt, 2018).
[51] For a very detailed account of Ukraine-EU and Ukraine-Russia negotiations on integration in this period, see Dragneva-Lewers and Wolczuk, *Ukraine between the EU and Russia*, to which I referred in developing this chronology.

CIS. After 2010, while Yanukovych and Ukraine sought to reestablish "multivector" foreign policy, Russia was once again seeking deeper integration, and providing both carrots and sticks to achieve it. Russia's reassertion was likely driven by the broader assertiveness underway in its foreign policy, by the opportunity that Yanukovych appeared to present, and by the perception that Yanukovych's discussions with the European Union threatened to pull Ukraine out of Russia's orbit permanently.

While Yanukovych had rebalanced Ukraine's policy toward Russia, he had not abandoned the western "vector." As prime minister under Yushchenko, he had supported the development of the Association Agreement, as had the Party of Regions. Several of the party's most important oligarchs, including Rinat Akhmetov and Serhiy Lyovochkin, were seen as supporting it due to their business interests, and Yanukovych put his close associate, Secretary of the National Security and Defense Council Andriy Klyuyev, in charge of negotiating the agreement.

The European Union, in striving to build closer ties with its eastern neighbors, did not see itself playing geopolitics or "geo-economics." Rather it saw participation in European institutions as an obvious good that other countries wanted to join in on. For this reason, it did not take a "realist" approach to the negotiations (and was later criticized for this), and therefore did not take seriously the idea that Russia was threatened by EU integration with Ukraine.[52] Whether intended or even understood, what emerged was an economic version of the security dilemma: the actions that the European Union and Russia took as defensive and benign convinced each that there was a threat that needed to be countered.

In 2010, Russia, along with Belarus and Kazakhstan, formed the Eurasian Customs Union, with the goal of developing a fully fledged customs union by 2015.[53] While it started slowly, it became a priority for Putin after he returned as president in 2012. In April 2013, Putin stated that "In the event that Ukraine joins, the economic benefits to Ukraine will be … according to our estimates $9–10 billion a year."[54]

---

[52] Cornelius Adebahr, "Reconciling European Values and Western Interests in Ukraine," European Leadership Network, July 4, 2014.

[53] Belarus and Kazakhstan also resisted this plan, because it forced them to adopt Russia's obligations as a WTO member without the benefits of membership. On the mix of political and economic reasons for Russia's pursuit of a regional trade bloc, see Chris Miller, *Putinomics: Power and Money in Resurgent Russia* (Chapel Hill: University of North Carolina Press, 2018) pp. 140–144.

[54] "Putin sulit Ukrainye $10 mlrd ot Vstupleniya v TC," LB.ua, April 25, 2013. While saying that "We will respect the choice of our partners," he also pointed out that the other three members would suffer economically if Ukraine did not join.

The crucial change in Russia's position in 2010–2011 was that in creating a customs union analogous to that of the EU, it too was building an organization with a clear distinction between being inside and being outside. Ukraine's policy of picking and choosing which components of an agreement to adhere to would no longer be accepted. In 2011, Sergei Glazyev, the head of the Customs Union Commission, said: "The only option is Ukraine's full participation in all the Work of the Customs Union. All other forms are groundless and we have informed Kyiv about it." He continued that Ukraine's practice of conditioning agreement on the limits imposed by the Ukrainian constitution would no longer be acceptable.[55] In 2012, Yanukovych was still resisting a Russian invitation to join the Customs Union, and said it would be "necessary to change the constitution, which today prohibits us from creating supranational organs."[56]

Members of a customs union share both an internal free trade area and common barriers (tariffs and other measures) with external states. The rules of the internal free trade area and the common external policy need to be agreed upon. In the case of the European Union and of the Eurasian Customs Union, governance of many issues is delegated to a supranational decision-making body. Because of Russia's size and power (its GDP in 2010 was four and a half times that of Belarus, Kazakhstan and Ukraine combined[57]), it would dominate such decision making in the Eurasian Customs Union, so a decision to join the union would effectively be a decision to turn much of one's trade policy over to Russia. In the EU, by contrast, the largest member, Germany, accounts for less than a fifth of the vote on the issues that are not subject to unanimity.

Russia made three main arguments about why Ukraine should join the Customs Union. The first was that Ukraine would gain from improved access to the markets in Russia and the other members. The second was that, while energy was not included in the Customs Union, Russia would negotiate a better deal on gas. The third was that Ukraine would be at a disadvantage in the European Union. In fact, standard economics models applied to the two proposed deals showed that in the long term the EU Deep and Comprehensive Free Trade Agreement (DCFTA) would add 11.8 percent to Ukraine's GDP, while the Eurasian Customs Union would decrease it by 3.7 percent).[58] Slightly in contradiction,

---

[55] Quoted in Dragneva-Lewers and Wolczuk, *Ukraine between the EU and Russia*, p. 67.
[56] "Usloviya Vypisany kak budto dlya vraga," *Kommersant*, June 9, 2011.
[57] GDP figures from the World Bank; author's calculations.
[58] Veronika Movchan and Ricardo Giucci, "Quantitative Assessment of Ukraine's Regional Integration Options: DCFTA with European Union vs. Customs Union with

Putin argued that "accession to the Eurasian Union will also help countries integrate into Europe sooner and from a stronger position."[59] Russia also threatened retaliation if Ukraine joined the DCFTA with the EU, which would decrease Russia's access to the Ukrainian market.

Putin, speaking at the Valdai conference in 2013, showed why he placed such emphasis on the project: "The Eurasian Union is a project for maintaining the identity of nations in the historical Eurasian space in a new century and in a new world. Eurasian integration is a chance for the entire post-Soviet space to become an independent center for global development, rather than remaining on the outskirts of Europe and Asia."[60] Integrating Ukraine would serve both Russia's conception of its national identity and its economic and political interests. Richard Sakwa, while acknowledging the "hegemonic impulses" behind the plan, asserts that Russia saw a potential Eurasian Union as a second pillar, along with the EU, on which the "Common European Home" envisioned by Gorbachev would be built. He sees the Eurasian Union as a part of a broader policy of finding an alternative to what Russia saw as the hegemony of US- and western-led institutions.[61] Anders Åslund wrote that "the only way to make sense of the Kremlin's trade policy is to see it as politics mixed with old Soviet economic thinking."[62]

Putin deployed a completely separate argument: the unity of Russians and Ukrainians. In July 2013, he traveled to Kyiv to mark the 1025th anniversary of the adoption of Christianity in Kyivan Rus'. After taking part in a religious service led by the Russian Patriarch Kirill, he met briefly with Yanukovych and then attended a conference organized by the pro-Russian oligarch Viktor Medvedchuk, entitled "Orthodox Slavic Values: The Basis of Civilizational Choice in Ukraine." The point, apparently, was to argue that traditional Orthodox values were superior to the new liberal ideas taking hold in Europe. Putin said

[Y]ou are here to discuss the significance of Ukraine's civilizational choice. This is not just Ukraine's civilizational choice ... The Baptism of Rus was a great event

Russia, Belarus and Kazakhstan," German Advisory Group, Institute for Economic Research and Policy Consulting, Policy Paper PP/05/2011, November 2011, p. 11. The reasons for the decrease under the Customs Union were tariff increases in Ukraine and trade diversion, whereas the DCFTA would actually boost trade with the EU.

[59] Quoted in Dragneva-Lewers and Wolczuk, *Ukraine between the EU and Russia*, p. 69.

[60] Quoted in ibid., p. 80.

[61] Richard Sakwa, "How the Eurasian Elites Envisage the Role of the EEU in Global Perspective," *European Politics and Society* 17 (2016): 4–22.

[62] Anders Åslund, "Ukraine's Choice: European Association Agreement or Eurasian Union?" Peterson Institute for International Economics Policy Brief, September 2013, p. 6.

that defined Russia's and Ukraine's spiritual and cultural development for the centuries to come. We must remember this brotherhood and preserve our ancestors' traditions ... Let me say again that we will respect whatever choice our Ukrainian partners, friends and brothers make. The question is only one of how we go about agreeing on working together under absolutely equal, transparent and clear conditions.[63]

At the same time, Russia considered creating a free trade area with those CIS members that did not join the Customs Union, which would be analogous to Ukraine being in an FTA with the European Union while not fully joining its economic union. While Ukraine favored such an arrangement, Russia dropped the idea, apparently because it would not prevent Ukraine from signing the EU Association Agreement. Russia instead insisted that Ukraine join the Customs Union. This policy highlighted the fundamental disagreement between Russia and Ukraine, even with Yanukovych's more conciliatory approach. Russia sought a deal with Ukraine that would prevent Ukraine from signing the Association Agreement or joining the DCFTA with the EU. Ukraine was willing to integrate with Russia only to the extent that doing so did not rule out integration with the EU.

At that point, Russia and Ukraine were at an impasse, and a series of trade restrictions by Russia in 2011 put pressure on Ukraine to join the Customs Union. However, the situation was defused when the European Union refused to sign the AA while Tymoshenko was imprisoned. With the Agreement shelved for the time being, Russia relented, and the CIS Free Trade Area agreement was signed in October 2011. The agreement included a provision that would allow members to raise tariffs to previous levels if another member joined an organization that diverted trade elsewhere. While Ukraine was able to sign a deal with Russia that did not rule out signing the Association Agreement with the EU, the agreement created a mechanism for Russia to impose penalties on Ukraine should it do so.[64]

While the European Union would not sign the AA as long as Tymoshenko was in prison, it continued negotiating it, and an important preliminary agreement was reached just days after the CIS FTA was signed. In June 2012, the EU Parliament appointed European Parliament President Pat Cox and former Polish President Alexander Kwaśniewski to a "special mission" to Ukraine, charged with resolving

---

[63] Vladimir Putin, "Orthodox-Slavic Values: The Foundation of Ukraine's Civilisational Choice Conference," President of Russia website, Kremlin website, http://en.kremlin.ru/events/president/news/18961. See also David R. Marples, *Ukraine in Conflict: An Analytical Chronicle* (Bristol: E-International Relations, 2017), pp. 9–11.

[64] Dragneva-Lewers and Wolczuk, *Ukraine between the EU and Russia*, p. 76.

the Tymoshenko issue and getting the Association Agreement back on track. They shuttled back and forth between Brussels and Kyiv repeatedly over the next eighteen months.[65] Within the EU, leaders debated whether the European Union should isolate the Yanukovych government or engage with it. Kwaśniewski advocated engagement, arguing that isolating Ukraine would create another Belarus, and this position won out.[66]

When the European Union and Ukraine held a summit in February 2013, delayed from the previous December, EU President Herman Van Rompuy set a deadline in May for "determined action and tangible process" on criminal justice, which was seen as a requirement for Tymoshenko's release. He reasserted the EU's desire to sign the AA, but pointed out that this "implies a commitment to shared values," that some, including Germany, still doubted.[67] Yanukovych responded favorably, saying: "Ukrainian law says that EU integration is the most important direction for Ukraine to move toward and this cannot be changed today."[68]

Yanukovych's strategy, which was to try to gain the economic and political benefits of both EU and CIS integration, appeared to be working, but the respite was brief. With the European Union continuing to negotiate the AA, and Russia seeing the CIS FTA as a first step to deeper integration, the pressure continued for Yanukovych to choose one over the other. Yanukovych's team was itself divided, with some seeing Ukraine's – and their own – future better served in Europe and others favoring Russia.[69]

On May 31, 2013, Ukrainian PM Azarov signed a Memorandum of Understanding (MOU) on obtaining "observer" status in the Eurasian Economic Commission, the executive body of the Eurasian Customs Union (analogous to the EU Commission). This would create a Ukrainian seat on the Commission with the ability to make proposals but not to vote. While Russia saw this as the logical first step to becoming a full member, President Yanukovych assured European Commission President Jose Manuel Barroso that "this new model of cooperation

---

[65] The Cox-Kwaśniewski mission is described in extensive detail in Maciej Olchawa, *Mission Ukraine: The 2012–2013 Diplomatic Effort to Secure Ties with Europe* (Jefferson, NC: McFarland & Co., 2017). It was later disclosed that Kwaśniewski was employed by the European Centre for a Modern Ukraine, which was formed by Yanukovych supporters at the advice of Yanukovych's American advisor Paul Manafort to promote Ukraine's EU integration and Yanukovych's reputation in the West. See Shawn Donnan, Neil Buckley, and James Polity, "Manafort Charges Entangle Former European Leaders," *Financial Times*, February 25, 2018.
[66] Olchawa, *Mission Ukraine*, p. 50.   [67] Agence France Presse, February 25, 2013.
[68] EUObserver.com, February 25, 2013.   [69] Olchawa, *Mission Ukraine*, p. 44.

between Ukraine and the Eurasian Economic Union does not contradict membership of Ukraine in the WTO and the strategic course toward Eurointegration along the path of completing the Association Agreement and creation of a deep and comprehensive free trade area with the EU."[70] Russia's Prime Minister Medvedev reasserted that Ukraine could not receive the full benefits of the Customs Union without full membership. "They will be for us an external country."[71] When the agreement on observer status was signed at the end of May, Medvedev cautioned that "This is the first step, an important step, a necessary step, and we are very happy about it, but it could be the last step, if nothing more is done." Expressing his concern about Ukraine's dealing with the EU, he went on to say:

> But we understand that if our partners really want to take part in our newly created integration association – the Eurasian Economic Union – then they must take a whole series of very complicated, sometimes unpopular decisions. Moreover, all decisions, and not only their part, of course, *must not assume obligations that exclude participation in the Eurasian economic space and union.* This should be plain as day to everyone.[72]

The European Union, through its Eastern Partnership, had decided to consider signing an Association Agreement with Ukraine which would include a DCFTA. Yanukovych's election did not initially undermine this process, but his accretion of power, and in particular his jailing of Tymoshenko, became major concerns for the European Union. While the European Union never officially required Tymoshenko's release, referring instead to the issue of "selective justice," it was clear that resolving her situation was a prerequisite to signing a final deal.[73] The two sides continued to negotiate, and in part because of Yanukovych's control over the government and parliament, progress was steady on a range of issues.

The negotiations were handled by the most closely trusted of Yanukovych's advisors, including Andriy Klyuyev. Negotiations on the Association Agreement were completed in October 2011 and a draft initialed in March 2012; a draft DCFTA was initialed in July 2012. Together, the

---

[70] Yanukovych's press service, quoted in "Yanukovych Zaveril Glavu Evrokomissii v priverzhennosti evrointegratsii," LB.ua, June 1, 2013.
[71] "Medvedev: Ukraina budyet 'nyukhat' vozdukh' v TC," LB.ua, March 21 2013.
[72] "Medvedev: Ukraina sdelal shag k integratsii v TC," LB.ua, May 31, 2013, emphasis added.
[73] Speaking in Yalta in September 2013, Dalia Grybauskaite of Lithuania, which held the EU presidency at the time, said: "The request from the European Union on Tymoshenko's case is still on the table and, without a solution, I do not see a possibility for the signature." Daniel McLaughlin, "EU Warns Ukraine that Key Deals Depend on Tymoshenko's Release from Prison," *The Irish Times*, September 21, 2013.

documents ran to 1,200 pages.[74] The EU, however, deferred actually signing the agreements until progress was made on the rule of law, which came to be symbolized by the fate of Tymoshenko. EU leaders showed their displeasure by boycotting the final of the Euro 2012 soccer tournament, turning a public relations coup for Ukraine into an embarrassment.[75] In 2012 irregularities in the parliamentary elections made the European Union even more wary of completing the deal.

For his part, Yanukovych seemed uninterested in moving forward quickly, feeding the notion that he was realigning the country toward Russia. In particular, the offices in the executive branch responsible for making Ukraine's legislation compatible with that of the European Union were cut back or eliminated entirely.[76] While some oligarchs, including Yanukovych's ally Rinat Akhmetov, had much to gain from access to the European market, they also had much to lose from laws that undermined their control of the Ukrainian economy. As with other leaders before him, Yanukovych was more interested in the symbolism of integration than the substance, and when the substance clashed with his interests or those of the powerful oligarchs, it lost out. This was an old problem for the European Union, but it became more urgent as the EU became more interested in integration with Ukraine. It was getting harder for Ukraine's leaders to attribute the failure to integrate with the European Union to the EU's disinterest.

In December 2012, the EU Council published "Conclusions" on Ukraine that made clear its dissatisfaction with the lack of progress in Ukraine, and with the regression on some issues. "The Council notes with concern that the conduct of the 28 October parliamentary elections ... constituted a deterioration in several areas." It went on to criticize the "politically motivated convictions of members of the former Government after trials which did not respect international standards" and to stress the need for effective implementation of the new Criminal Procedure Code and other judicial reforms. "Enacting these conditions in a meaningful, sustainable way even by the most ardent, reform-oriented government would have been a formidable challenge."[77] Yanukovych's government was not so ardent. The European Union held out one important carrot, reaffirming "commitment to the shared objective of visa-free travel in due course."[78]

---

[74] Åslund, "Ukraine's Choice," p. 1.

[75] Svitlana Dorosh, "Ukraine Fights Euro 2012 Boycott," BBC.com, May 9, 2012.

[76] Dragneva-Lewers and Wolczuk, *Ukraine between the EU and Russia*, p. 56.

[77] Ibid., p. 60.

[78] Council of the European Union, "Council Conclusions on Ukraine," 3209th Foreign Affairs Council Meeting, Brussels, December 10, 2012.

This same "conclusions" document also mentioned continuing preparations for the AA to be signed at the Vilnius summit scheduled for November 2013. While setting a tentative date was necessary from a bureaucratic perspective, it may also have been intended to provide some urgency to Yanukovych to resolve the outstanding issues. The effect, however, was to light the fuse on a slowly developing crisis by appearing to set a deadline for Ukraine to make a choice between Russia and the EU. The approach of the Vilnius summit strongly conditioned the rise in intensity of negotiations and threats over the next eleven months. In that final runup to the crisis – which at this point no one foresaw – Russia increased pressure on Ukraine to join the Eurasian Economic Union and renounce the AA, the European Union sought to counteract Russia's pressure. Yanukovych struggled to find a way forward that did not involve rejecting either Russia or the EU, either of which might be disastrous to him politically. If he rejected Russia, Russia would punish him. If he rejected the EU, Ukrainian voters would punish him.

The insistence that Tymoshenko be released remained an obstacle to signing the AA. Yanukovych felt he could not release Tymoshenko, for at least two reasons. First, he was concerned about her as a political competitor. Either as an opponent in the 2015 election or as someone who could bring thousands of people onto the streets, she threatened his rule. He feared not only that she may lead a pro-western "colored revolution," but that she might conspire with Putin, with whom Yanukovych's relationship was strained.[79] Equally important, his willingness to imprison her against the EU's wishes sent a powerful message to other elites. In this respect, the EU's coercion did more harm than good: the higher the price Yanukovych paid to keep her behind bars, the more powerful a signal was sent to other elites about how intent he was on punishing those who threatened him.[80]

In April 2013, Yanukovych sought to make a concession to the EU's concerns without releasing Tymoshenko by pardoning Tymoshenko's ally Yuriy Lutsenko and several other political prisoners. The ploy failed, because the European Union was focused almost entirely on Tymoshenko. When Vitaliy Klitschko announced that he intended to run for president, Yanukovych pushed through parliament a law banning anyone who had lived in and paid taxes in a foreign country, effectively excluding Klitschko. Outsiders seem to have agreed with Yanukovych

---

[79] See Mikhail Zygar, *All the Kremlin's Men: Inside the Court of Vladimir Putin* (New York: Public Affairs, 2016), p. 259.

[80] See Serhiy Kudelia, "When External Leverage Fails: The Case of Yulia Tymoshenko's Trial," *Problems of Post-Communism* 60, 1 (January–February 2013): 29–42.

that Tymoshenko, not any of the lesser figures, was the likely challenger to Yanukovych, and that the preservation of political competition rested in large part on her fate. The European Union insisted on her release for exactly the same reason that Yanukovych resisted it. Most Ukrainians, however, were puzzled that the European Union would put so much emphasis on Tymoshenko, who was seen by many as just another oligarch.

By mid-2013, the European Union and Yanukovych had both become constrained by the web they had spun. As the Vilnius summit and the planned signing of the AA approached, the two were engaged in a game of chicken. Neither wanted to back down, but neither wanted to experience a collision. Yanukovych, knowing that deeper integration with the European Union was popular, continuously raised Ukrainians' expectations about what could be achieved. As long as the European Union resisted, Yanukovych did not have to deliver. In that respect, the EU's refusal to move forward while Tymoshenko was in jail solved a problem for Yanukovych. Not only would the Association Agreement anger Russia, it would likely eat into the rent-seeking opportunities he and his allies were exploiting. The EU's ultimatum on Tymoshenko allowed Yanukovych to blame the European Union for the impasse while avoiding problems with Russia and some of the oligarchs.

The European Union was also trapped by its commitment to Tymoshenko's release, because as long as that prerequisite remained in place, the Association Agreement could not go forward. In earlier years, the European Union would have been sanguine about this, not really needing Ukraine. But the perception that Yanukovych was both making a pluralist country autocratic and taking a potentially European country into Russia's orbit raised the EU's interest in getting the deal done. Some were beginning to argue that the European Union should sign the AA regardless of Tymoshenko's release, because the chances for democracy and reform in Ukraine were much higher as an associate of the European Union than completely outside it.

The two sides looked for a compromise, and in June a proposal was floated in which Tymoshenko would be allowed to travel to Germany for treatment for her bad back. In the short term, this would get her out of jail, but as Germany would not limit her movement, the likelihood that she would return to challenge Yanukovych remained. In October, as German Foreign Minister Guido Westerwelle was preparing to travel to Kyiv, Ukrainian Vice Prime Minister Olexandr Vilkul said that he was "confident some resolution will be found." But it did not happen, and Prime Minister Nikolai Azarov seemed genuinely angered by the EU's position, telling a London newspaper in October 2013 that "If all our efforts to reform are in vain because of one person it means total political irresponsibility."[81]

In August 2013, Russia began slowing the movement of goods across the Ukraine-Russia border, in what was seen as a warning to Ukraine not to sign the Association Agreement. The move appeared intended to show Ukraine what could happen if it signed the AA, and Putin advisor Sergei Glazyev said: "We are preparing to tighten customs procedures if Ukraine makes the suicidal step to sign the association agreement with the EU."[82] He said that Ukrainian businesses had not yet been influential in discussions of the AA, and apparently hoped that the border slowdown would encourage them to oppose it. In October, he was more explicit, saying that if joining the AA increased Ukrainian exports to Russia, Russia would raise tariff barriers. "[T]o the extent that Ukraine eliminates import tariffs with Europe, we will introduce import tariffs with Ukraine."[83] While the pressure was soon relaxed, the President of the EU Commission responded by saying: "We cannot accept any attempt to limit these countries' own sovereign choices. We cannot turn our back on them."[84]

In Ukraine, Russia's heavy-handed measures backfired by reinforcing the notion that integration with Russia meant being ruled by Russia.[85] In September, Yanukovych complained that "'Hoping for a relationship based on partnership and trust with the northern neighbor of Ukraine is futile."[86] Later that month, the Ukrainian government approved the final draft of the AA, and only the Tymoshenko issue remained outstanding. Paradoxically, Yanukovych may now have had an even stronger incentive not to release Tymoshenko: if he did so, the AA would go forward, and Russia would retaliate.

Yanukovych was constrained economically as well as politically. The absence of reform continued to hamper the economy, and the avarice of the "family" further undermined the government's finances. There were fears that without a new international loan, Ukraine would default on its debts, and by August 2013 Ukraine's foreign reserves had dropped to the

[81] Matthew Day, "Ukraine Warns EU that Tymoshenko's Fate Should Not Block Historic Trade Deal," *The Telegraph*, October 10, 2013.
[82] Filipp Sterkin, Maksim Tovkailo, and Maksim Glikin, "Prichina tomozhennoi voiny s Ukrainoi – bol'shaya politika," *Vedomosti*, August 19, 2013, quoted in Åslund, "Ukraine's Choice," p. 1.
[83] Sergei Glazyev, "Ukraina vo vlasti samoobmana," Izborskii Klub website, https://izborsk-club.ru/1901, October 3, 2013.
[84] Dan McLaughlin, "Russia Riled as EU Woos Ex-Soviet States," *Irish Times*, September 17, 2013.
[85] Dragneva-Lewers and Wolczuk, *Ukraine between the EU and Russia*, p. 80.
[86] Quoted in ibid., p. 81.

point where they could cover less than three months of imports.[87] Yanukovych was trying to negotiate a new loan agreement with the IMF, but its conditionality required reforms that he did not want to entertain. With the presidential election scheduled for February 2015, less than two years away, it was imperative that he avoid a cut in social spending (required by the IMF) as well as a default on loan payments and the collapse of the economy (which might happen without an IMF package). Thus the long-term question of Ukraine's economic integration with Europe versus Russia was squeezed aside by the short-term need to gain economic aid in time to win reelection in 2015. In October 2013, Glazyev explained why he thought economic reality made joining the Customs Union necessary, with only "politics" holding it back:

If Ukraine enters the Customs Union with us, she will receive an improvement in the terms of trade in excess of 10 billion dollars … This is what is needed to balance Ukraine's finances. Ukraine has a balance of payments deficit, chronic and large … If Ukraine does not balance its financial system now, then a default is not far off. It could happen in two to three months; maybe in half a year. It is critically dependent on the balance of trade and on the terms of trade.[88]

In an interview in November, Glazyev repeated the same economic argument in more detail and then turned to refuting the notion that Ukraine sought to make a "civilizational choice" in favor of Europe. Glazyev argued that

in Russian and in Ukrainian historiography no one disputes the elementary fact that contemporary Russia is, in fact, the continuation of Kievan Rus. The civilizational choice was made more than a thousand years ago … Thanks to this choice, our country became a superpower and became the largest and most powerful country in the world … If we analyze this seriously, we must understand that the main distinction between the European civilizational choice and ours is the departure from Christian values, the de-Christianization of Europe, the celebration of open signs of Sodom, the celebration of vice … [T]his is the choice not of God, but of the devil; that is, they are pulling Ukraine, to speak in a spiritual language, into the kingdom of the antichrist … [E]verything we are told today by Ukrainian eurointegrators is a complete lie.[89]

How different Russians weighed the economic, geopolitical, civilizational, and theological threats from the Association is difficult to weigh.

---

[87] Åslund, "Ukraine's Choice," p. 7.

[88] Sergei Glazyev, "Ukraina vo vlasti samoobmana," Izborskii Klub website, October 3, 2013.

[89] Sergei Glazyev, "Iskusstvenno Sozdannoe Navzhdenie," Izborskii Klub website, November 7, 2013.

The danger of default was real for Ukraine. Yanukovych sought economic aid from both the European Union and Russia, and Russia offered much more. For Russia, supporting Yanukovych financially might kill two birds with one stone, getting Ukraine to choose Russia over the European Union and solidifying in Ukraine a politician whom Russia could work with. Yanukovych sought a significant financial aid package from the EU, ostensibly to help offset the costs of joining the Association Agreement, but the figure of $160 billion that he sought was not seen as credible (it apparently came from Russian sources) and struck the European Union as a request for a gigantic bribe. Ukrainian leaders in turn expressed outrage, with PM Azarov saying, referring to EU bailouts of Greece and others "the EU ... spent €400 billion to save those countries from default ... and we are told $160 billion is an exorbitant figure for Ukraine, Europe's largest country by area and one of the biggest by population."[90]

Some, even in Yanukovych's camp, believed the best solution was a new agreement with the IMF. Tyhypko, a Party of Regions MP and former Governor of the National Bank of Ukraine, said "The IMF is much needed even now. I'm sure that we have our own reserves, but I think that without IMF we'll have a very hard period of time."[91] Sergei Glazyev, the Putin advisor in charge of integration, asserted repeatedly in September and October that a default, which might cause Yanukovych's overthrow, could be prevented only by rejection of the AA: "I say again: the Association Agreement will lead to default in Ukraine because Russia stops [providing] loans. Today Ukraine's balance of payment is based on Russian loans and investments ... Default is inevitable and this can lead to changing power."[92] This, more than anything, was what Yanukovych feared, and Russia was threatening that it would strive to ensure it if Yanukovych signed the Association Agreement. Speaking in December, after the decision to opt out of the AA, but before the worst of the protests, PM Azarov specifically said that the need for a loan of $10 billion was essential in the decision to reject the AA, as the EU was only offering €610 million.[93]

Speaking at a conference in Yalta in September, Glazyev openly threatened dire consequences if Ukraine signed the AA. "We don't want

[90] Quoted in Dragneva-Lewers and Wolczuk, *Ukraine between the EU and Russia*, p. 86.
[91] "New IMF Program to Remove Ukraine Default Issue from Agenda, Say Experts," Ukraine General Newswire, September 24, 2013.
[92] "Ukraine Can Face Default in 2014 after Signing AA with EU – Presidential Adviser," *ITAR-TASS*, October 4, 2013.
[93] "Ukraine Needs $10 bln to Avoid Default – Deputy PM," Interfax Ukraine General Newswire, December 7, 2013.

to use any kind of blackmail. But legally, signing this agreement about association with the EU, the Ukrainian government violates the treaty on strategic partnership and friendship with Russia." That, he said, would mean that Russia would no longer guarantee Ukraine's statehood and might intervene if pro-Russian regions sought help from Russia.[94] He continued: "Who will pay for Ukraine's default, which will become inevitable? Would Europe take responsibility for that?"[95] Saying that Ukraine's default would be inevitable was saying that Russia would make sure it happened. "Signing this treaty will lead to political and social unrest. The living standard will decline dramatically … there will be chaos." The audience, which included diplomats and elites from around the world, responded with jeers, and European leaders present strongly rejected his tactics. Lithuanian President Dalia Grybauskaite responded that "Ukraine is too big, too strong and too important to allow others to decide its fate. It is the decision of Ukraine to be with the European Union or not," and Polish Foreign Minister Radoslaw Sikorski rejected Russia's "19th-century mode of operating towards neighbors." Even one of Ukraine's more pro-Russian oligarchs, Viktor Pinchuk, called Russia's tactics "totally stupid."[96] This may have been Russia's clearest signal that it would go beyond the existing "rules of the game" to prevent Ukraine from joining Europe, but the threat was considered unacceptable, and it was rejected rather than taken seriously.

As the fall wore on, it increasingly looked as if Yanukovych was simply seeing who would offer the biggest aid package. A slightly different interpretation is that Yanukovych never intended to release Tymoshenko from prison, but used this possibility to keep the EU discussion going and drive up the size of the package he would eventually get from Russia. However, the shock expressed by his closest colleagues about the abandonment of the AA project indicates that he had planned to sign the agreement and then changed his mind. In discussions recounted later in interviews by the Ukrainian journalist Sonya Koshkina, several Yanukovych associates said that his explanation for the turnabout focused on economic factors.[97]

---

[94] Shaun Walker, "Ukraine's EU Trade Deal Will Be Catastrophic, Says Russia," *The Guardian*, September 22, 2013.

[95] "Ukraine and EU Ridicule Russian Threats," euobserver.com, September 23, 2013. As Glazyev made clear elsewhere, his claim that signing the AA would violate the 1997 Friendship Treaty rested on the assertion that it would violate article 13, which pledged the two states to avoid "from any actions which could incur economic damages to each other." See "Ukraine's Signing EU Deal Violates Friendship Accord with Russia – Putin's Aide," BBC Monitoring, September 6, 2013.

[96] "Ukraine and EU Ridicule Russian Threats," euobserver.com, September 23, 2013.

[97] Sonya Koshkina, *Maidan: Nerasskazannaya istoriya* (Kyiv: Brait Star, 2015), pp. 51–54.

As cynical as Yanukovych was, he confronted a real dilemma. His mismanagement of the economy meant that he needed to get an aid package from someone, and only Russia was willing to provide a substantial bailout without requiring extensive reforms. Yet by raising expectations that a deal would be signed with the EU, he made it politically dangerous to abandon it. As Yanukovych was aware, membership in the Customs Union was not popular among Ukrainians. A May 2013 poll by the Razumkov Centre put support for joining the European Union (which was not on the table) at 42 percent and for joining the Eurasian Economic Union at 31 percent. Yanukovych's advisors told him that his chances for reelection in 2015 depended on closing the deal on the Association Agreement,[98] but Russia was signaling that if he did sign it, Russia would take steps to undermine his reelection chances.

The incompatibility between integrating with the European Union and with Russia had several aspects to it. The most important was that it was practically impossible for Ukraine to be a member of both the DCFTA with the European Union and an FTA with the Eurasian Economic Union. As Stefan Fule explained:

It is true that the Customs Union membership is not compatible with the DCFTAs which we have negotiated with Ukraine, the Republic of Moldova, Georgia, and Armenia. This is not because of ideological differences; this is not about a clash of economic blocs, or a zero-sum game. This is due to legal impossibilities: for instance, you cannot at the same time lower your customs tariffs as per the DCFTA and increase them as a result of the Customs Union membership.[99]

The European Union could not, according to its rules, have a preferential trade agreement with countries not in the WTO, which ruled out Kazakhstan and Belarus. Moreover, there was no sign that Russia wanted to grant EU firms greater access to its market, or to adopt the EU's other rules.

As November and the Vilnius summit approached, the pace of negotiations quickened further. Kwaśniewski and Cox shuttled back and forth between Brussels and Kyiv trying to broker an agreement. They needed the matter of Tymoshenko resolved by 13 November, so that the European Commission, which would meet on November 18, could formally approve the AA in time for the Vilnius summit, scheduled for November 28–29. In talks during the first week of November, Yanukovych told them that he would support legislation that would allow Tymoshenko to

---

[98] Åslund, "Ukraine's Choice," p. 10; Marples, *Ukraine in Conflict*, p. 19.
[99] "Stefan Fule: We Have Seen Enormous Pressure Being Brought to Bear upon Some of Our Partners," ARMINFO, September 12, 1993.

leave Ukraine for medical treatment in Germany. It appeared that the impasse had been broken and that Yanukovych, for all of his pro-Russian policies, had decided to take Ukraine into the Association Agreement.

However, having told the European Union team that he approved the deal, Yanukovych appears to have then ensured that the Party of Regions parliamentary leadership, which he controlled, rejected it. Yefremov, the leader of the Party of Regions parliamentary group, told Cox and Kwaś-niewski that he had no control over his members' votes and expressed indignation that he had not been consulted previously.[100] When legislation reached the floor of the parliament on November 13, a vote was postponed until the next week, when Party of Regions deputies voted down six different drafts presented by opposition parties and presented none of their own.[101] By this time, the government had announced it was halting work on the AA. It was unclear whether Yanukovych was still hoping to sign the agreement without releasing Tymoshenko, or whether he had decided not to sign it after all, in order to get financial support from Russia.[102]

In between Yanukovych's apparent decision to release Tymoshenko and his reversal, discussions between Yanukovych and Putin appear to have been sustained and intense. They met secretly during the third week in November, and then their prime ministers met the following week. The meetings were "secret" (unannounced but reported in the press), so we do not know exactly what was said, but an aide to the Lithuanian President Dalia Grybauskaite said that Yanuvovych had told her, just before announcing his rejection of the AA, that Moscow had put immense pressure on him, presumably along the lines Glazyev had repeatedly threatened.[103] At the Vilnius summit, Yanukovych said to Grybauskaite and Angela Merkel: "I'd like you to listen to me. For three and a half years I've been alone. I've been face-to-face with a very strong Russia on a very unlevel playing field."[104] On November 19, Russian PM Medvedev said that he had told Ukraine that the Customs Union might raise barriers to trade with Ukraine if it signed the AA. He specifically

---

[100] On the conversations between Cox and Kwasniewski, on one hand, and Yanukovych, parliamentary speaker Volodymyr Rybak, and Party of Regions leader Oleksandr Yefremov, see Mustafa Nayem, "Partiya Rehioniv hotuye zryv Samitu u Vil'nyusi," *Ukrayinska Pravda*, November 8, 2013; and Olchawa, *Mission Ukraine*, pp. 65–66.

[101] "Ukraine Suspends Preparations for EU Trade Agreement," *BBC News*, November 21, 2013.

[102] Nayem, "Partiya Rehioniv."

[103] Ian Traynor, "Russia 'Blackmailed' Ukraine to Ditch EU Pact," *The Guardian*, November 22, 2013.

[104] Yanukovych's remarks can be seen on video at www.youtube.com/watch?v= 1QNFDPcPm3U and are translated in Zygar, *All the Kremlin's Men*, p. 260.

referred to "supplement 6" of the 2011 CIS free trade agreement, which stipulated that such measures could be taken if one of the members joins another trading bloc.[105]

Yanukovych found himself between a rock and a hard place, largely due to his own actions. He had repeatedly promised EU integration, so those who protested the suspension of the negotiations were actually supporting Yanukovych's earlier policy, even though they did not support him personally.[106] Signing the Association Agreement would have allowed him to run for reelection in 2015 having delivered on the promise of promoting EU integration.[107] But if he did so, Moscow would retaliate severely, causing genuine harm to Ukraine, and undermining his reelection chances. Not signing it would alienate those in Ukraine who had been assured that the country was on the path to European integration. It would also deprive Yanukovych of his best bargaining chip vis-à-vis Russia.

Russia had the ability to make Yanukovych's immediate problems much worse, or to make them better (by providing the money to avoid default). The European Union appeared to be offering only long-term benefits, along with potentially fatal short-term costs, and no clear way out of the default problem. "Yanukovych's brazen looting of the state and assault on democracy meant that he maneuvered himself into a corner where the solution to his problems lay in the Kremlin; and the Russia leadership did not hesitate to exploit his dependence in pursuit of its regional objectives."[108]

Once Yanukovych walked away from the European Union deal, he became even more important to Russia. In signing the Kharkiv agreement and not signing the EU Association Agreement, Yanukovych was personally responsible for accomplishing two of Russia's primary objectives in Ukraine. Even as he became more dependent on Russia, Russia became more dependent on him remaining in power.

One of the many interesting counterfactuals is what might have happened if the European Union had offered the kind of aid package that Yanukovych was desperate for and that Russia provided. It should be recognized that that this is a very ambitious counterfactual: this was

---

[105] "Medvedev Reminds Ukraine that Customs Union May Take Protective Measures if Ukraine-EU Association Agreement Is Signed," Ukrainian News Agency, November 20, 2013.

[106] Volodymyr Ishchenko, "Ukraine's Fractures," New Left Review 87 (May/June 2014): 7–33.

[107] Andrew Wilson, Ukraine Crisis: What It Means for the West (New Haven, CT: Yale University Press, 2014), p. 63.

[108] Dragneva-Lewers and Wolczuk, Ukraine between the EU and Russia, p. 98.

simply not the kind of thing that the European Union did with aspiring members. In this respect, it was still not playing geopolitics.

On November 21, the Ukrainian government announced that it was halting preparations to sign the Association Agreement at the Vilnius summit in order to "ensure the national security of Ukraine," an apparent reference to Russian threats.

The European Union responded with both disappointment and anger, placing the blame squarely on Russian coercion. Alexander Kwaśniewski, the former Polish president who had served as an envoy to try to broker a compromise, said: "Our mission is over." Carl Bildt, the foreign minister of Sweden tweeted: "Ukraine government suddenly bows deeply to the Kremlin. Politics of brutal pressure evidently works."[109] Stefan Fule, the EU commissioner for enlargement, who had invested much time in the Association Agreement, said it was "hard to overlook in [the] reasoning for today's decision [the] impact of Russia's unjustified economic & trade measures."[110] Putin returned the charge of blackmail: "We have heard threats from our European partners towards Ukraine, up to and including promoting the holding of mass protests. This is pressure and this is blackmail."[111]

In Kyiv, *Deutsche Welle* reported, "On the Maidan, a few thousand people are out protesting against Yanukovych and calling for the 'victory of revolution.' Meanwhile, all around them, millions of people in Kyiv go about their daily business."[112] That was soon to change.

Yanukovych, Autocracy, and Revolution

It was surprising to many that after Viktor Yanukovych sought to steal an election in 2004, he was able to win fairly in 2010. It was equally surprising that having won that election, he proceeded to govern in a way that led directly back to street protests reminiscent of those of 2004, but with even worse consequences for him. That he did so, even when many respected analysts expected that he would govern more moderately, says a great deal about Yanukovych and about Ukraine.

It was quite clear by mid-2010 that Yanukovych had not in fact become a "normal" democratic leader. He was intent on eliminating any major sources of competition. This followed the model that prevailed

---

[109] Quoted in "EU Trade Deal Deadlocked over Tymoshenko Release," *France 24*, November 24, 2013.
[110] "Ukraine Suspends Preparations for EU Trade Agreement," *BBC News*, November 21, 2013.
[111] Quoted in Traynor, "Russia 'Blackmailed' Ukraine to Ditch EU Pact."
[112] "'Putin's Presents' Split Opinion in Kyiv," *Deutsche Welle* World, December 18, 2013.

further to the east, in Russia and in Central Asia, in which hegemonic leaders tolerated opposition only to the extent that their rule was not threatened. In the Russian model, the role of the opposition was to allow the government to claim to be democratic, not to actually challenge it. What Yanukovych learned from 2004 was not that such a model was inappropriate, but rather that he had been unfairly deprived of his place, and that more determination was needed to succeed the next time. This determination was focused on two areas: the security services and the economy. Yanukovych focused on staffing the upper levels of the security forces with people loyal to him. The goal was that in the event of some future protests, they could be counted on to repress protesters rather than standing aside as they had done (apparently against his urging) in 2004. He also sought to forge a single dominant group in the economy, as he had in politics, by concentrating economic assets in a small group of highly loyal associates known as the family. In sum, the model was to concentrate power.

Leonid Kuchma famously said that "Ukraine is not Russia," and Yanukovych's reign demonstrated this as well. Ukraine had at least three significant characteristics that not only made it harder to concentrate power there, but promised a backlash against those who tried to do so. The first was its regional diversity. While Ukraine's regional diversity is a liability in many respects, it makes building a single nationwide political force extremely difficult. This was as true for Yushchenko as for Yanukovych. In the period between 2010 and 2013, Ukraine's regional diversity demonstrated itself both in the tension over whether to join the Association Agreement, which many in central and western Ukraine wanted, or the Eurasian Economic Community, which many in eastern and southern Ukraine wanted. Either choice was dangerous, underscoring the societal basis for Kuchma's multivector approach. Second was the strong normative basis for democracy in Ukraine. The number of people willing to protest against concentration of power proved to be large, and the sense that many shared after the failure of the Orange Revolution that Ukrainians had become cynical and would not join street protests again turned out to be false.

Third, and perhaps most important, is that the pluralism of oligarchic groups in Ukraine was self-reinforcing, in the way that a balance of power in international politics is often self-reinforcing. Oligarchs are not democrats, and they were eager to do corrupt business with Yanukovych's government. But Ukraine's oligarchs jealously guarded their self-interest, which meant preventing anyone from becoming powerful enough to dispossess them, as Putin had dispossessed oligarchs like Mikhail Khodorkovsky in Russia. The more powerful Yanukovych became, the more his power threatened other oligarchs, and the more they sought to clip his wings. Moreover, his greed threatened their interests directly. As in 2004, the fear of Yanukovych united the interests of Ukraine's pro-European prodemocracy activists with those of its oligarchs. Both groups, for their own motives, strove to avoid Ukraine becoming a Russia-style autocracy. This accidental alliance of idealistic, prodemocracy street protesters with cynical and powerful oligarchs was as powerful in 2013–2014 as it had been in 2004.

In this way, by the time that the crisis over the rejection of the Association Agreement began in November 2013, the preconditions for the Orange Revolution had been reproduced in Ukraine. Yanukovych's rule was popular in parts of the country but bitterly opposed elsewhere. His power, corruption, and flouting of the law increased the sense that he was a threat to democracy. In particular, there was a widely shared view that if something did not change, it was highly unlikely that Ukraine would have another free and fair election in 2015. Similarly, oligarchs had already been put in a position where they would be better off without Yanukovych. However, without some event to spark protest it would have been very hard for the disparate forces opposing Yanukovych to coordinate a movement. And had Yanukovych responded differently, the protests likely would have ended with Yanukovych still in power. That had been the case with the "Ukraine without Kuchma" protests in 2001. Why the 2013 protests led to a second overthrowing of the government, rather than to something less dramatic, is a question we take up in Chapter 7.

Conclusion

Viktor Yanukovych's presidency saw a sharpening of Ukraine's internal contradictions, as well as those between Ukraine and Russia and between Russia and the West. Yanukovych's approach to leadership had much to do with this, as he was determined to overturn the prevailing pluralism in Ukrainian politics and replace it with the dominance of a single elite group (his own "family" and the Party of Regions). Yanukovych's efforts to consolidate power domestically inevitably had international consequences, because democracy had become so closely connected to geopolitics in the region. The corruption and spending that were essential to Yanukovych's popularity forced him to secure external support, and that drove him toward Russia.

If Yanukovych's disruption of the status quo in Ukraine was deliberate, the international status quo, and Ukraine's balancing act, was becoming shaky for unintended reasons. The extension of the European Union to the Ukraine-Poland border created new barriers between Ukraine and its closest western partner. The European Union recognized Ukraine's potential isolation, and the planned Association Agreement was a response. That agreement, however, required domestic steps that completely contradicted Yanukovych's domestic agenda, as symbolized by the impasse over Yuliya Tymoshenko. "[T]he EU was basically asking Yanukovych to dismantle his system of power."[113]

Moreover, the Association Agreement was viewed by Russia as a major threat. This can be attributed both to the security dilemma and to Russia's insistence on retaining Ukraine within a Russian sphere of influence. The security dilemma in this instance was primarily of an economic nature, but it was real: while the AA was not aimed at Russia, the DCFTA would have had at least some negative impact on Russian firms' access to the Ukrainian market. But Russia seems to have been much more concerned with the belief that the Association Agreement would lead to Ukraine leaving the Russian sphere permanently. To the extent that Russia saw the loss of Ukraine as a fundamental threat to its interests, the Association Agreement was a threat whether Ukraine and the West intended it or not. Russia responded with an escalating set of threats both to Ukraine and to Yanukovych personally to head off this perceived loss. One important question of interpretation is whether trying to collaborate with both the European Union and Russia had become inherently impossible or whether Yanukovych might have pulled it off with a bit more skill – perhaps by signing the AA and then reaching some further agreement with Russia.

Russia's relations with the West were souring at the same time. In 2012 Vladimir Putin replaced Medvedev as president, confirming Russia's autocracy, and ratcheting up the rhetoric from Moscow. The ouster of Muammar Gaddafi was viewed by Putin as both a threat to the international order that he preferred and to him personally. The worsening Russia-West conflict no doubt strengthened Russia's determination not to suffer a strategic loss in Ukraine. This influenced policy leading up to the Vilnius summit as well as after Ukraine descended into crisis. This environment not only made the events of 2014 more likely, but also meant that they would lead to what many described as a new cold war.

---

[113] Wilson, *Ukraine Crisis*, p. 63.

On the evening of November 21, 2013, following the announcement that Ukraine was suspending discussions over the EU Association Agreement (AA), a few thousand protesters gathered on the Maidan Nezalezhnosti (Independence Square), the main site of protests going back to 1990. Calls went out over social media for a bigger protest the next Sunday, November 24; and an estimated 100,000 people turned out to protest. When a small group of protesters sought to break through a police cordon surrounding government buildings, police fired tear gas and arrested several of them.[1]

The situation calmed for a few days, and Prime Minister Nikolai Azarov insisted that negotiations with the European Union would continue. But the Vilnius summit ended on November 29 with no progress. That evening, about ten thousand protesters turned out in Kyiv. Most went home, but a few remained in place overnight. At 4:00 the next morning the Interior Ministry's elite Berkut forces attacked using batons and stun grenades, arresting several protesters. This attack began the escalation that turned an issue-specific protest into a contest over the future of the Yanukovych regime, ultimately leading Yanukovych to flee the country three months later, providing the opportunity and excuse for Russia's seizure of Crimea and intervention in eastern Ukraine.

Had Ukraine not come so close to signing the agreement, it is unlikely that its failure would have spurred such a reaction, but the long-running question of releasing Tymoshenko seemed to have been resolved and it appeared that the deal was set to be signed, so the subsequent step back from it was seen as a loss and, as we have stressed, people react very strongly to perceived losses. Moreover, there was a sense that Yanukovych's behavior, bad as it had been, had been moderated by the process of negotiating the AA, and that with the agreement now dead, he would feel unconstrained.[2] The harsh repressions of November 30 heightened

---

[1] BBC, "Huge Rally over EU Agreement Delay," November 24, 2013.
[2] Andrew Wilson, *Ukraine Crisis: What It Means for the West* (New Haven, CT: Yale University Press, 2014), p. 68.

the sense that Ukraine was undergoing an irreversible shift toward authoritarianism and away from Europe. Even so, the protests were initially very small

How did protests over the Association Agreement lead to the deposing of an elected government and then to war? There are two broad answers to this question. The first is that the context had, over the previous twenty-two years and especially since Yanukovych's inauguration, turned Ukrainian politics, Ukraine-Russian relations, and Russia's relations with the West into zero-sum games, with the room for mutually acceptable compromise narrowed. The Polish prime minister, Donald Tusk, stated at the height of the crisis that "the developments in Ukraine will decide the history and the future of the whole region."[3] The second is that Yanukovych's responses to the conflict – a mix of repression that enraged the protesters and forbearance that empowered them – could scarcely have been better designed to see protests endure and the demands of protesters escalate. Yanukovych had sought to learn the lessons of 2004, but ended up producing a manual on how to turn small protests into disaster.

The overthrow of Yanukovych created both threats and opportunities for Russia: the threat was to Russia's deep-seated commitment to controlling Ukraine, to its goal of keeping NATO from expanding further eastward, and to Putin's immunity to protests in Russia. But it also created the opportunity to kill four birds with one stone. Seizing Crimea and intervening in the Donbas regained territory that Russia had always wanted; it showed that Russia could defy the West with impunity; it boosted Vladimir Putin's domestic popularity; and it hamstrung Ukraine's new government.

This chapter chronicles and seeks to explain these two processes – from protests to "revolution" and from intervention to partly frozen conflict – with Putin's decision to seize Crimea as the pivotal event. For all the problems of the previous decades, almost no one in 2013 anticipated that something like this would happen. While it is tempting in retrospect to see the outcome as inevitable, it clearly was not.

The Emergence of Protest: November–December 2013

When the Berkut attacked protesters on the Maidan in the early morning of November 30, several dozen protesters retreated uphill to the St. Michael's Monastery.[4] By the evening of November 30, there

[3] Steven Lee Myers, "Violence in Ukraine Creates Deepening Clash between East and West," *New York Times*, February 19, 2014.
[4] Several book-length treatments of the "Revolution of Dignity" or "Euromaidan" are available. For a detailed chronology based on interviews with many key actors and a

were an estimated ten thousand protesters on St. Michael's Square and many more were on the way. The protesters began organizing the "self-defense" units that were to play a growing role in subsequent events.

The police violence of November 30 was crucial in spurring the protest movement. A movement against police brutality and authoritarianism drew much broader support than did one against the suspension of the AA negotiations. The scholar Volodymyr Ishchenko recalled:

At first, I was very skeptical, especially when it was so purely a "Euromaidan" – I couldn't be so uncritical of the EU ... But then, when the attempt at a crackdown took place in the early morning of 30 November, the character of the protests changed – this was now a movement against police brutality and against the government.[5]

The authorities' mix of coercion and accommodation served to enrage protesters and increase their numbers without either deterring them or preventing access to the main protest sites. Interior Minister Vitaly Zakharchenko first criticized the Berkut, saying that they had abused their power, but then said that "if there are calls for mass disturbances, then we will react to this harshly."[6] Having cleared the Maidan and forced protesters to relocate to St. Michael's square (see Map 7.1), the authorities then allowed them to reoccupy the Maidan. Access to the Maidan was subsequently controlled by the protesters, not the government, which focused on protecting government buildings nearby. The electricity remained on in the Maidan, supplies came in and waste out, cell phone networks operated, and the Kyiv metro continued to run, including at two stops inside the protest zone. The combination of repression and accommodation helped the protests grow.

There was disunity not only among the groups on the Maidan, but between the Maidan as a whole and the opposition political parties Batkivshchyna, UDAR, and Svoboda. Many protesters considered the opposition parties to be part of the corrupt system that they wanted to end. While extreme nationalists were a very small minority in the large demonstrations, their persistent presence, willingness to face violence from the security forces, and readiness to use direct action themselves,

---

useful list of the key personnel, see Sonya Koshkina, *Maidan: Nerasskazannaya Istoriya* (Kyiv: Bright Star Publishing, 2015). See also Marci Shore, *The Ukrainian Night: An Intimate History of Revolution* (New Haven, CT: Yale University Press, 2018); David Marples and Frederick V. Mills, eds., *Ukraine's Euromaidan: Analyses of a Civil Revolution* (Stuttgart: ibidem, 2015); and David R. Marples, *Ukraine in Conflict: An Analytical Chronicle* (Bristol: E-International Relations, 2017).

[5] Volodymyr Ischenko, "Ukraine's Fractures," *New Left Review* 87 (May/June 2014): 12.

[6] Marie-Louise Gumuchian and Victoria Butenko, "Ukraine Protests Grow as President Responds," CNN.com, December 3, 2013.

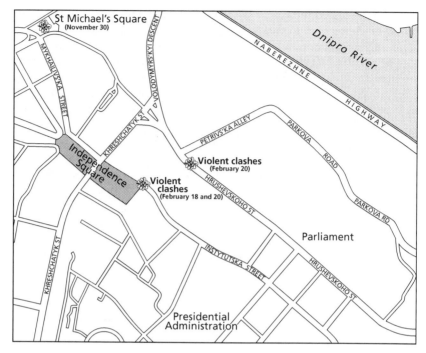

Map 7.1 Central Kyiv, November 2013–February 2014

gave them disproportionate influence. The mainstream protesters and parties could have denounced the extreme nationalist groups or refused to collaborate with them, but they could not exclude them from the Maidan or control them. One important victory for nationalists was that the traditional nationalist slogan "Glory to the Heroes!" [Heroyam Slava!], which had roots in the controversial World War II-era Organization of Ukrainian Nationalists and Ukrainian Insurgent Army, was adopted by the mainstream of the protest movement, becoming a routine response to the more traditional and less controversial Slava Ukrayini! (Glory to Ukraine).[7] This undoubtedly fed the perception that extreme nationalists dominated the Maidan.

The aims of the protesters varied, and they evolved over time, as shown by the competing labels for the upheaval well after it took place. Some

---

[7] Ishchenko provides one of the more nuanced discussions of the role of nationalists on the Maidan. See also Volodymyr Ishchenko, "Far Right Participation in the Ukrainian Maidan Protests: An Attempt of Systematic Estimation," *European Politics and Society* 17, 4 (2016): 453–472.

called it the "Euromaidan," emphasizing the EU Association Agreement. Others called it the "Revolution of Dignity," focusing on frustration with petty corruption and Yanukovych's repression of protesters. Until mid-January 2014, most protesters sought not to depose Yanukovych, but to get the AA signed, to protest corruption, to reassert Ukraine's democracy and to ensure that the 2015 presidential election would be fair. One concrete goal on which many agreed was the reinstatement of the 2004 constitution, which Yanukovych had illegally modified.[8]

Yanukovych Looks to Russia

Having shunned the EU, Yanukovych had no option but to take what Russia offered and claim victory. On December 17, 2013 he traveled to Moscow and received his reward for jettisoning the AA. He and Putin agreed on a nearly 50 percent discount on Russian gas and a $15 billion loan that would allow Ukraine to avoid default without a deal with the IMF and the reforms it would require. This was especially important because the unrest underway in Kyiv caused fears of a fall in the value of the hryvnya that would exacerbate Ukraine's payments problem.[9] Prime Minister Azarov stated that "The president reached agreement on exceptionally beneficial conditions for crediting Ukraine's economy, which allows us to carry out wide-ranging plans for economic modern-ization."[10] Putin, recognizing how sensitive the Customs Union was in Ukraine at that moment, reassured its opponents that the union had not been discussed in his meeting with Yanukovych.[11] Work on it must have continued, however, because in January Ukraine's Cabinet of Ministers adopted a "program of cooperation with the members of the Customs Union through 2020."[12]

From mid-December 2013 until mid-January 2014, the conflict ebbed, in part due to the holidays. It appeared that a waiting game would pit the patience of Yanukovych against the endurance of protesters camped outdoors in the Ukrainian winter. By mid-January, hundreds rather than thousands of protesters remained camped on the Maidan.

---

[8] Olga Onuch, "Who Were the Protesters?" *Journal of Democracy* 25, 3 (July 2014): 44–51.
[9] "Protests in Ukraine Deepen Economic Crisis," Agence France Presse, December 8, 2013.
[10] Shaun Walker, "Vladimir Putin Offers Ukraine Financial Incentives to Stick with Russia," *The Guardian*, December 18, 2013.
[11] Ibid.
[12] "Kabmin prinyal programmu sotrudnichestva s Tamozhennym soyuzom," LB.ua, January 15, 2014.

At this point general opinion was that "the protests do not appear to have threatened Yanukovich's grip on power."[13]

Again, however, the government took a step that provoked widespread anger and reenergized the protests. On January 16, the pro-Yanukovych majority in the Rada pushed through a series of laws outlawing particular protest tactics and curtailing the activities of foreign NGOs. The laws were voted on by a show of hands, in contravention of the parliament's rules, and votes were counted for deputies who were absent, leading some to call the act a "coup."[14] Interior Minister Zakharchenko, echoing language he had used at the beginning of the crisis, said that "every offense will be met on our side by a tough response within the framework of the current legislation."[15] The laws quickly became known collectively as "the dictatorship laws." Ukraine's democracy appeared to be at stake.

On January 19, thousands of protesters, outraged by the "dictatorship laws," confronted security forces protecting government buildings.[16] The ensuing violence further radicalized the protests. As a result of the "dictatorship laws" and the violence of January 19, opinion among the protesters began to solidify around a set of new demands. These included the release and amnesty of arrested protesters, the reversal of the January 16 laws, and reversion to the 2004 version of the constitution. Many now called for Yanukovych's resignation.

The following week, Yanukovych met with Batkivshchyna leader Arseniy Yatseniuk and offered to appoint Yatsenyuk prime minister and Vitaliy Klitschko deputy prime minister for humanitarian issues. He also offered to reconsider the "dictatorship laws." Yatseniuk insisted that he was willing to negotiate, but also said that signing the EU Association Agreement was a key demand. No agreement was reached at this time and, as became apparent later, it is not clear that Yatsenyuk had any mandate to negotiate on behalf of protestors. Yanukovych put the opposition parties in a difficult position. An agreement was necessary to end the crisis, but negotiating to join Yanukovych's government would undermine their credibility.

On January 28, Yanukovych fired Prime Minister Azarov and the parliament reversed several of the "dictatorship laws" While these concessions were cheered on the Maidan, they did little to defuse the

---

[13] "Ukrainian President Approves Strict Anti-protest Laws," *The Guardian*, January 17, 2014.

[14] "Ukraine's President Signs Anti-protest Bill into Law," BBC.com, January 17, 2014.

[15] "Zakharchenko obitsyaye zhorstko reahuvaty na kozhnoho, khto ne khoche 'myru i spokoyu,'" *Ukrayinska Pravda*, January 18, 2014.

[16] Ishchenko, "Far Right Participation," p. 18.

protests.[17] The protesters were seeking repeal of all the "dictatorship laws" as well as returning to the 2004 constitution and signing the AA. While protesters increasingly rejected compromise with Yanukovych, they had no way to put more pressure on him other than turning to violence, which most still rejected.

In late January and early February, two seemingly contradictory trends coexisted. On one hand, negotiations between the Yanukovych regime and opposition leaders appeared to be making progress. On the other, the likelihood of violence was increasing. The threat of violence may have spurred Yanukovych to seek a compromise, but it also empowered the more extremist protesters.[18] On January 21–22, three protesters were killed by police.[19] A protest on February 2 drew an estimated fifty thousand people to the Maidan, rather than the several hundred thousand that took part in December. That may have emboldened Yanukovych while concentrating the influence of the more militant among the protesters.

The Russian government advocated ending the protests forcibly. Putin's advisor on Ukraine issues, Sergei Glazyev, said in an interview that "In a situation when the authorities encounter a coup attempt, they simply have no choice [but to use force]. Otherwise the country will be plunged into chaos." Accusing the United States of arming Ukrainian protesters and training them at the US embassy in Kyiv, Glazyev went on to say that under the Budapest Memorandum of 1994, Russia was obliged to intervene to prevent such a threat to Ukraine's sovereignty.[20] Reuters reported that Russia was withholding a $2 billion loan until the protesters were cleared from the Maidan.[21]

In early February, Batkivshchyna party leader Arseniy Yatseniuk continued negotiating with Yanukovych, saying that he would agree to become prime minister, with Yanukovych remaining president, if the 2004 constitution were reinstated and if a government of opposition figures was appointed with assurances that they would not soon be fired. "We have a short- and a long-term plan. The long-term plan foresees the preparation of a new Constitution draft and its adoption by September. Our short-term prospective is to achieve the return to the Constitution

[17] "Ukraine Crisis: Parliament Abolishes Anti-protest Law," BBC.com, January 28, 2014.
[18] Serhiy Kudelia, "When Numbers Are Not Enough: The Strategic Use of Violence in Ukraine's 2014 Revolution," *Comparative Politics* 50, 4 (July 2018): 501–521.
[19] Oksana Grytsenko and Shaun Walker, "Kiev Becomes a Battle Zone as Ukraine Protests Turn Fatal," *The Guardian*, January 22, 2014.
[20] "Ukraine Crisis: Putin Adviser Accuses US of Meddling," BBC.com, February 6, 2014.
[21] Pavel Polityuk and Marcin Goettig, "Ukraine Police Charge Protesters after Nation's Bloodiest Day," Reuters, February 18, 2014.

of 2004 as a temporary decision until we adopt a new Constitution."[22] At this point, constitutional reform and a change of course, not the ouster of Yanukovych, were still the main goals of the mainstream opposition, but support for Yanukovych's resignation was growing.

Progress was also made on the protesters' demand for the release of arrested protesters. On February 14–16, a compromise was reached in which the government released 234 prisoners arrested since December, and protesters vacated city hall and other buildings, and some of the barricades around the Maidan were breached.

On February 18, however, progress toward a peaceful settlement collapsed. An estimated twenty thousand protesters marched on the parliament building to push for reinstitution of the 2004 Constitution. They were confronted by security forces using live ammunition, rubber bullets, tear gas, and flash grenades. Some of the protesters were also using firearms. At 4:00 pm, The Interior Ministry and SBU announced that "If by 6 p.m. the disturbances have not ended, we will be obliged to restore order by all means envisaged by law."[23] The ensuing attack by police pushed the protesters back onto the Maidan, where barricades finally held. By the day's end, at least eighteen people were dead, including several members of the security forces. The violence of February 18 caused both sides to harden their positions, even as government and opposition leaders frantically sought to avoid further bloodshed.

After this violence in Kyiv, the use of force also increased in other cities where demonstrations had been taking place. In several western Ukrainian cities, people occupied regional administration buildings, attacked police stations and seized weapons. Ukraine was approaching a situation in which both protesters and government forces would be wielding firearms. Equally important, the seizing of local police stations and administration buildings all over Ukraine initiated a tactic that was to be turned against the anti-Yanukovych movement very quickly after he fell.

On the evening of February 19, the foreign ministers of France (Laurent Fabius), Germany (Frank-Walter Steinmeier), and Poland (Radoslaw Sikorski negotiated with Yanukovych for several hours, trying to find a compromise that would avert more violence. However, Yanukovych would not accept the demand for early elections, which protesters saw as a compromise from their demand that he step down immediately. While scheduled elections were, by this time, only a year

---

[22] "Yatseniuk Ready to Head Cabinet of Ministers, but Only if It Consists of Opposition," Interfax-Ukraine, February 6, 2014.

[23] Polityuk and Goettig, "Ukraine Police Charge Protesters."

away, the opposition feared that Yanukovych would use any respite to clamp down further and to rig the election.

Early on February 20, protesters attacked a police line at the southeastern end of the Maidan. Interior Minister Zakharchenko announced that he had signed a decree authorizing security forces to use live ammunition against the protesters.[24] After protesters broke through a police line, the police opened fire, both from on the ground and from sniper positions. By day's end, another roughly seventy protesters had been killed and over five hundred wounded, and several more security forces had been killed.[25] The UN later reported a total of 108 protesters and 13 law enforcement officials in Kyiv from November to February.[26]

There is considerable speculation concerning who was shooting at whom on February 20. There have been allegations that a "third force" was shooting at both sides, trying to spur on the conflict, from high in the Hotel Ukraina, overlooking Instytutska Street and the Maidan. Some point to Georgians, some to Ukrainians, and some to Russians. The chaos of the day and the intense efforts at disinformation that have ensued have made it impossible to disconfirm these theories. The most sophisticated effort to address the issue, carried out at Carnegie Mellon University, found conclusively that at least some of the protestors on Instytutska Street were killed by Berkut forces on the ground.[27]

The violence of February 20 demolished the government's legitimacy in the eyes of many in Ukraine, and increased people's resolve that Yanukovych had to resign. It had the same effect in the West, which previously had sought to broker solutions that would have kept him in office. Even more important, as it became clear that Yanukovych might lose power, his supporters began hedging their bets or simply abandoning him. Beginning with Kyiv Mayor Volodymyr Makayenko, Party of Regions officials began announcing their defection from the party. They were likely appalled by the violence, and were also probably determined to retain their positions once power shifted. The fear that they might be confronted by protesters without the security forces to protect them would have underscored their decisions.

---

[24] "Ukrainian Police Authorized to Use Live Ammo as Battle Rages," *RIA Novosti*, February 20, 2014.

[25] Ian Traynor, "Ukraine's Bloodiest Day: Dozens Dead as Kiev Protesters Regain Territory from Police," *The Guardian*, February 21, 2014.

[26] Office of the United Nations High Commissioner for Human Rights, "Accountability for Killings in Ukraine from January 2014 to May 2016," July 2016.

[27] Mattathias Schwartz, "Who Killed the Kiev Protesters? A 3-D Model Holds the Clues," *New York Times*, May 30, 2018.

On the night of February 20–21, Yanukovych belatedly came to an agreement with the three main opposition party leaders. The deal was brokered by the foreign ministers of France, Germany, and Poland, along with Russia, which sent human rights ombudsman Vladimir Lukin, apparently at Yanukovych's request. The deal included a return to the 2004 constitution, formation of a "unity government" including opposition members, and early elections, in return for the protesters leaving occupied streets and buildings. A ceremony was held in which the opposition party leaders and Yanukovych, along with the three western foreign ministers, signed the agreement and shook hands. Though Putin was later to excoriate the West for the deal's abandonment, Russia decided not to sign it.

The terms negotiated may have garnered support from protesters a few days earlier (when Yanukovych rejected them) but after the violence of February 20, Yanukovych's resignation was now a nonnegotiable demand for many. In a meeting with the coordinating council of the Maidan, Polish Foreign Minister Radoslaw Sikorski urged the protest leaders to accept the deal. "If you don't support this deal you will have martial law, the army. You will all be dead."[28] The group reluctantly agreed to back the deal by a vote of 34–2.[29]

When Vitaliy Klitschko appeared on the stage at the Maidan to announce the deal the next evening, February 21, however, the crowd vocally opposed it. Volodymyr Parasiuk, a twenty-six-year-old leader of one of the "self-defense" groups that had been engaged in the bloody battle the day before, took the stage to denounce the deal and to issue an ultimatum: if Yanukovych did not resign by 10:00 am the next day, the protesters would start taking government buildings by force.[30] This met with the crowd's approval. The protesters on the Maidan thus rebuked the opposition party leaders, rejected the agreement that many hoped had resolved the crisis, and upped the ante. The violence of February 20 had not frightened the protesters, but rather enraged them and steeled their will to finish the job. While the security forces retreated, the protesters expanded the territory under their control and strengthened their barricades.

When the Ukrainian parliament met on the afternoon of February 21, many of the Party of Regions deputies and Communist Party deputies did not show up for the session, leaving parliament in control of the opposition and recent defectors. The parliament passed a measure

---

[28] Roland Oliphant and Shannon Strange, "Ukraine Protest Leaders Warned: 'Sign Deal or You Will All Die'," *The Telegraph*, February 21, 2013.
[29] Wilson, *Ukraine Crisis*, p. 93.   [30] Ibid., p. 93.

on returning to the 2004 constitution, decriminalized the acts under which Yuliya Tymoshenko had been imprisoned and amnestied those arrested during the protests. It also fired Interior Minister Zakharchenko and forbade the armed forces from attacking the protesters. While Yanukovych had agreed to some of these measures, the parliament had essentially turned on him, as Party of Regions members announced that they were leaving the party. It was reported that many of these deputies had abandoned Kyiv, along with other Party of Regions leaders. Yanukovych himself had left the city after signing the agreement with the opposition leaders.

Seeing Yanukovych's political support eroding, security forces abandoned their posts in large numbers. Several thousand were escorted out by protesters; many others simply left. Polish Foreign Minister Sikorski, who had warned the protesters of a violent crackdown, called this development "astonishing."[31] The Yanukovych government was collapsing, leaving a vacuum. Yanukovych left Kyiv, apparently for a previously scheduled meeting, strengthening the perception that he had been defeated. Late that night, Yanukovych left Kyiv for Kharkiv, and for a time it was not clear exactly where he was.

The next day, February 22, Speaker of the Parliament Rybak resigned, claiming to be ill. The parliament declared that Yanukovych had abandoned his office.[32] On those grounds it elected Oleksandr Turchynov of the Batkivshchyna party as acting president, and scheduled presidential elections for May 25. While Yanukovych was effectively ousted, he was removed without going through the constitutionally prescribed impeachment process, which would involve several steps, including a vote by three-quarters of the total membership of the parliament. The shortcuts taken led many to see the ouster as flawed or even illegitimate, and were grounds for the charge, made by Putin and by some western critics, that the events of February 21–22 constituted a "coup."[33]

In Kharkiv on February 22, Yanukovych recorded an address denouncing the steps taken to remove him and declared that he would not resign.[34] He apparently tried to travel from there to Russia by air, but

[31] "Poland's Crucial Role as Yanukovych's Rule Crumbled," BBC.com, February 25, 2014.

[32] The resolution, available on the Rada website, was entitled "On the Self-Removal of the President of Ukraine from the Exercise of Constitutional Powers and the Holding of Extraordinary Elections of the President of Ukraine," https://zakon1.rada.gov.ua/laws/show/757-VII.

[33] See Daisy Sindelar, "Was Yanukovych's Ouster Constitutional?" Radio Free Europe Radio Liberty, February 23, 2014.

[34] Shaun Walker, "Ukraine's Former PM Rallies Protesters after Yanukovych Flees Kiev," *The Guardian*, February 23, 2014.

was denied permission. Instead, he traveled by car to Donetsk and on to Crimea, where Russian forces took him to Russia in the evening of the same day.[35] As became clear later, he had begun preparations to leave Kyiv on February 19, *before* the worst day of violence, *before* he signed the deal with opposition leaders that would have kept him in power at least until new elections, and *before* the ultimatum from the Maidan.[36]

The way that the protests ended played an important role in the composition of the interim government. The most important spots in the new government, including that of prime minister, were held by Tymoshenko's Batkivshchyna party, but because the far-right groups had played a central role in forcing Yanukovych from power, they successfully demanded several spots in the new government. The willingness of the mainstream parties to ally with the far-right groups was cited by both Russian and western critics as evidence of the illegitimate nature of new government and of the threat to Russians in Ukraine.

Among the first measures passed by the post-Yanukovych parliament was a reversal of the 2012 language law. To head off controversy, Interim President Oleksandr Turchynov refused to sign the new law, leaving the 2012 law in place, but this was not widely reported. Instead, the attempt was reported as a sign that an aggressive nationalist agenda would be pushed. This view was spread widely by Russian media, and fit with the narrative that Ukraine had been taken over by right-wing extremists. While in substance the reversal of the law was not far-reaching, and symbolically it was very important to many of those who had supported the protests, it was a tactical blunder, feeding the narrative that Russia and Yanukovych (who was now in Russia) were promoting.[37]

Reaction in Russia and the West

Russia and the West took diametrically opposed positions on the crisis in Ukraine. Although the United States and European Union struggled to coordinate their actions, their approaches were largely compatible with each other. Both the United States and most EU members were much more sympathetic to the protesters than to Yanukovych, and they all strongly rejected the use of violence by either side. Both sought to broker a compromise that would stop the violence and trade an end to protests for concessions by Yanukovych. If there was a difference in approach, it

---

[35] See "Tropamy Yanukovycha. Poslednye dny eks-presydenta v Ukraine glazamy ego okhrannykov. Rekonstruktsyya," Strana.UA, January 18, 2018.

[36] Ishchenko, "Far Right Participation," p. 21.

[37] A new, highly controversial language law was passed in 2019.

was that some US politicians more clearly seemed to be supporting the overthrow of Yanukovych, and were less inclined to worry about what Russia thought.

From the early days of the demonstrations in December, western leaders supported the protests. The speaker of Lithuania's parliament Loreta Graužinienė and Polish parliamentarian Marcin Święcicki spoke to the crowd on November 26 and 27, and several EU ambassadors greeted the protesters who amassed in St. Michael's square on November 30. While Barack Obama remained silent until the Crimea operation began at the end of February, his administration clearly supported the protesters. On December 10, Secretary of State John Kerry spoke of the US government's "disgust with the decision of Ukrainian authorities to meet the peaceful protest ... with riot police, bulldozers, and batons, rather than with respect for democratic rights and human dignity." "The United States stands with the people of Ukraine. They deserve better."[38] The following day, Victoria Nuland, assistant secretary of state for European and Eurasian affairs, appeared on the Maidan and met with protesters, a visit seen as highly symbolic of US support. That was reinforced when two US senators, Republican John McCain and Democrat Chris Murphy, visited protesters on the Maidan the following weekend. McCain told the protesters: "We are here to support your just cause, the sovereign right of Ukraine to determine its own destiny freely and independently. And the destiny you seek lies in Europe."[39]

While the European Union was clearly frustrated with the Ukrainian government, it continued to try to complete negotiation of the Association Agreement, finally giving up only in mid-December. The *Guardian* quoted a "senior EU diplomat" as saying. "I don't think Yanukovych will sign the accords. It's blackmail actually. He's saying he will only sign if he gets a lot of money. He's trying to maneuver between [the EU and Russia], to get money or concessions. He's trying to avoid reforms, but the EU agreements are all about reforms."[40]

Most EU leaders were also supportive of the protesters' aims, and especially of their right to protest. The British foreign secretary, William Hague, said that "It is inspiring to see these people standing up for their vision of the future of Ukraine: a free, sovereign, democratic country with much closer ties to the European Union and a positive relationship of

---

[38] "Top U.S. Official Visits Protesters in Kiev as Obama Admin. Ups Pressure on Ukraine President Yanukovich," CBSNews.com, December 11, 2013.

[39] "John McCain Tells Ukraine Protesters: 'We Are Here to Support Your Just Cause,'" *The Guardian*, December 15, 2013.

[40] Ian Traynor, "Ukraine Integration Pact on Hold as Brussels Vents Frustration," *The Guardian*, December 15, 2013.

mutual respect with Russia. This is a vision I share." While saying that he recognized Russia's "strong and legitimate interests in stable relationships with its neighbors," he said that "Russia cannot dictate terms to them ... This is not a zero-sum game: the choice is not either Russia or the EU. It's about Ukraine finding its true, stable place in the politics of Europe."[41]

When Yanukovych, in January 2014, was seeking a compromise that would bring leaders of opposition parties into the parliament, the United States strove to get the opposition leaders to go along and was trying to bring in others, including the UN, to encourage this. The United States hoped that Arseniy Yatseniuk, rather than Vitaliy Klitschko, would become the new prime minister, apparently due to Yatseniuk's greater economic expertise. It also wanted to keep the far-right Svoboda leader Oleh Tyahnybok out of the government.[42] This was much the same deal that the EU foreign ministers sought to negotiate with Yanukovych after the February 18 violence. Despite Nuland's complaints about the EU, the European Union and United States were advancing very compatible positions. Later, western leaders were aligned again in blaming Yanukovych, not the protesters, for the violence of February 18–20. In the aftermath of the February 18 violence, both German Chancellor Angela Merkel and French President Francois Hollande blamed the violence on Yanukovych, for his unwillingness to support a compromise.[43] Both the European Union and United States enacted a visa ban and asset freeze on government officials in the "full chain of command" responsible for the February 18 crackdown.[44]

Russia took a very different approach, with Putin's spokesman saying: "In the president's view, all responsibility for what is happening in Ukraine rests with the extremists."[45] It said the protests were illegal and the protesters themselves fascists, warned of the dangers of destabilizing Ukraine, and blamed the West for the protests. Russia used its close relationship with Yanukovych to provide advice and it used its economic leverage – increased since the collapse of talks over the AA – to pressure

---

[41] Quoted in "Ukraine Protests Backed by William Hague," *The Guardian*, December 16, 2013.

[42] Details of the US position were captured (presumably by Russia) in a cell phone conversation between Assistant Secretary of State for European and Eurasian Affairs Victoria Nuland and Ambassador to Ukraine Geoffrey Pyatt. Amidst Nuland's expletive-laden criticism of the EU, and the tiff that her outburst provoked, US support for a deal that kept Yanukovych in power was largely overlooked. See "Ukraine Crisis: Transcript of Leaked Nuland-Pyatt Call," BBC.com, February 7, 2014.

[43] Myers, "Violence in Ukraine Creates Deepening Clash between East and West."

[44] Ibid.   [45] Ibid.

the Ukrainian government. There is some evidence that the Russian government pressured the Yanukovych government to forcibly repress the protests, but it is unclear how strong such pressure was or what impact it had. More generally, Russia's position was that Yanukovych and the Ukrainian parliament were legitimately elected, and that protesters should not be able to eject a duly elected government or overturn its policies. Russia was, of course, somewhat flexible in when it insisted on the rule of law in Ukraine and when it did not. It is worth stressing, however, that until Yanukovych fled on February 22, the European Union and United States agreed with Russia that the constitution should be followed. For that reason, western governments supported bringing the opposition into government and revising the constitution, not removing Yanukovych as president.

Yanukovych's departure drove Russia and the West even further apart. While Russia, which had not signed the February 20 agreement, accused the West of treachery for not enforcing it, western governments, which had signed the agreement, took Yanukovych's departure from the country as a *fait accompli* that made the February 20 agreement irrelevant. Prime Minister Medvedev said:

If you consider Kalashnikov-toting people in black masks who are roaming Kiev to be the government, then it will be hard for us to work with that government. Some of our foreign, western partners think otherwise, considering them to be legitimate authorities. I do not know which constitution, which laws they were reading, but it seems to me it is an aberration ... Something that is essentially the result of a mutiny is called legitimate.[46]

The US government, in contrast, issued a statement supporting the "constructive work" of the parliament and advocated "the prompt formation of a broad, technocratic government of national unity."[47]

Russia Seizes Crimea

On February 20, the worst day of violence in Kyiv, the speaker of the Crimean parliament, Vladimir Konstantinov, who was in Moscow, spoke of the possibility that Crimea could secede.[48] According to the medal later given by the Russian government to participants in the takeover of

---

[46] Ian Traynor, "Russia Denounces Ukraine 'Terrorists' and West over Yanukovich Ousting," *The Guardian*, February 24, 2014.

[47] William Booth, "Ukraine's Parliament Votes to Oust President; Former Prime Minister Is Freed from Prison," *Washington Post*, February 22, 2014.

[48] "Spiker VR ARK vvazshaye, shcho Krym mozhe vidokremytysya vid Ukrayiny," *Ukrayinska Pravda*, February 20, 2014.

Crimea, the operation began the same day. This was two days before Yanukovych fled. Daniel Treisman asserts, based on interviews with leaders in Moscow, that Russian troops in Novorossiysk, Russia and in Sevastopol were put on alert on February 18, and were given orders to begin "peacekeeping" operations on February 20.[49]

In various cities in Crimea, demonstrations were held both for and against the Maidan protests. After Yanukovych's departure on February 22, some protesters called for secession. On February 26, groups of pro-Russian and pro-Maidan demonstrators faced off in Sevastopol. Konstantinov declared that day that Crimea would remain part of Ukraine, and that statements to the contrary were "a provocation."[50]

In the early hours of February 27, sixty heavily armed men seized the buildings of the Crimean parliament and Council of Ministers, and raised Russian flags. A meeting of some parliament members was then held, and allegedly voted to replace the Crimean prime minister, Anatoly Mogilev, with the pro-Russian Sergei Aksyonov. Whether there was a quorum present and how the vote went are unknown, because the gunmen limited access to the building and confiscated lawmakers' cellphones. Mogilev himself was not allowed in, and at least one lawmaker reported that his vote was recorded even though he was not in Simferopol.[51] Aksyonov, also known as "Goblin," was associated with an organized crime group[52] and led the Russian Unity party in Crimea, which had never won more than a few percent in elections. This meeting also announced a referendum on May 25 on expanding Crimean autonomy.

That same morning, units of the Berkut, which had been dissolved by the Ukrainian parliament on February 25, seized strategic crossings on the Isthmus of Perekop that links Crimea to the rest of Ukraine. It is unclear who ordered or coordinated these movements, which included heavy equipment such as armed personnel carriers.

The operation to seize Crimea became much more visible on February 28, when soldiers in unmarked uniforms, later widely known as "little green men," seized the airports in Simferopol and Sevastopol. While the identity of these soldiers was obscured, there was no doubt

[49] Daniel Treisman, *The New Autocracy: Information, Politics, and Policy in Putin's Russia* (Washington, DC: Brookings Institution, 2018), pp. 287–288.
[50] Laura Smith-Spark, Phil Black, and Frederik Pleitgen, "Russia Flexes Military Muscle as Tensions Rise in Ukraine's Crimea Region," CNN.com, February 26, 2014.
[51] Alissa de Carbonnel, "How the Separatists Delivered Crimea to Moscow," Reuters, March 12, 2014.
[52] Paul Rexton Kan, *Drug Trafficking and International Security* (Lanham, MD: Rowman & Littlefield, 2016), pp. 125–126.

about the identity of the Russian navy ship that that blockaded the harbor at Balaklava, home to the Ukrainian coast guard.

On March 1, the significance of the installation of Aksyonov as prime minister became clear when he requested Russian intervention: "I call on the president of the Russian Federation, Vladimir Putin, to provide assistance in ensuring peace and tranquility on the territory."[53] This provided the pretext needed for Russia to intervene more openly, and Putin later cited this request in justifying Russian intervention. That same day, Putin formally asked the Federation Council permission for "using the armed forces of the Russian Federation on the territory of Ukraine until the normalization of the socio-political situation in that country,"[54] which the Federation Council approved unanimously hours later. The measure specified "the territory of Ukraine," not just Crimea, wording that implied a threat that Russia would invade other parts of Ukraine if Ukraine resisted the takeover of Crimea.

Over the next few days, the takeover of Crimea by Russian forces proceeded quickly.[55] The operation appeared to be well choreographed and Ukrainian defenses collapsed. Two factors made a military defense impossible. One was that the speed and surprise of the operation caught Ukrainian forces off guard, so that even those inclined to fight found themselves confronted by superior forces. The second was that most were not inclined to fight. Many Ukrainian military units in Crimea surrendered or switched sides en masse. Units in Crimea were staffed mainly by soldiers from Crimea. Many of the officers were veterans of the Soviet armed forces who had been skeptical about Ukrainian independence from the beginning.

Governmental chaos in Kyiv further improved the conditions for the takeover of Crimea. The change of government bolstered the claim, legally specious but politically effective, that the nonconstitutionality of Yanukovych's departure in Kyiv somehow justified invading and annexing Ukraine's territory. Equally important was that the Ukrainian government was in chaos, and therefore unable to respond effectively. While Turchynov had been appointed acting president on February 22, the entire top stratum of the government had been Yanukovych loyalists, and

---

[53] "Ukraine Crisis: Crimea Leader Appeals to Putin for Help," BBC.com, March 1, 2014.

[54] "Putin: Russian Citizens, Troops Threatened in Ukraine, Need Armed Forces' Protection," RT.com, March 1, 2014.

[55] The military aspects of the seizure of Crimea are discussed in detail in Roger N. McDermott, *Brothers Disunited: Russia's Use of Military Power in Ukraine* (Leavenworth, KS: Foreign Military Studies Office, 2015); and Michael Kofman, Katya Migacheva, Brian Nichiporuk, Andrew Radin, Olesya Tkacheva, and Jenny Oberholtzer, *Lessons from Russia's Operations in Crimea and Eastern Ukraine* (Santa Monica, CA: RAND, 2017).

they fled, were ousted, resigned, or supported Russia. On March 1, Acting President Turchynov appointed Denis Berezovsky as commander of the Ukrainian navy. The next day, Berezovsky pledged his allegiance to Crimea, and a few weeks later he was made deputy commander of the Russian Black Sea Fleet.[56]

On March 4, Putin gave a press conference at which he stated that the forces in Ukraine were not Russian, but were rather local Crimean forces.[57] He also said that Russia retained the right to use "all means" to address "anarchy" in its neighbor. On March 6, the Crimean parliament voted to seek accession to the Russian Federation and moved up the referendum date to March 16.

A stunned world watched and complained but could do very little. Representatives from the OSCE, United Nations, and European Union documented their inability to enter Crimea to conduct missions there. The G7 said it would not recognize the results of the referendum, and urged Russia to do whatever it could to stop it. Russia instead began a new series of previously unannounced military exercises near the Ukrainian border in the vicinity of Kharkiv. Ukrainian policy makers later indicated that one reason they did not resist the annexation is that they feared a broader invasion that they were in no position to repel.[58]

The referendum was held on March 16. Voters were offered two choices, neither of which was to maintain the existing situation:

1 Are you in favor of the reunification of Crimea with Russia as a part of the Russian Federation?
2 Are you in favor of restoring the 1992 Constitution and the status of Crimea as a part of Ukraine?[59]

While there were no international observers and few journalists on hand to document the conditions of the referendum, the turnout and vote figures that were released officially, 83 percent turnout with 95.5 percent in favor of annexation by Russia, were almost certainly false. Yevgeny Bobrov of the Russian President's Council on the Development of Civil Society and Human Rights wrote that the numbers were likely

---

[56] "New Head of Ukraine's Navy Defects in Crimea," BBC.com, March 2, 2014.

[57] Putin both denied that there were Russian forces in Crimea and explained why their deployment was justified. These positions were contradictory, but his approach seems to have been to cover all possible objections.

[58] This view was conveyed in several interviews with Ukrainian leaders in Kyiv in May 2018.

[59] Noah Sneider, "2 Choices in Crimea Referendum, but Neither Is 'No'," *New York Times*, March 14, 2014. The 1992 constitution had been adopted by the Crimean parliament but rejected by Kyiv. Implementing it would have made Crimea an independent part of Ukraine, likely facilitating further moves toward secession.

much lower: "In the opinion of practically all of the interviewed special-
ists and citizens: The overwhelming majority of the residents of
Sevastopol voted in the referendum for joining Russia (with a turnout
of 50–80%), and in Crimea [outside Sevastopol], according to various
data 50–60% of voters for joining Russia, with an overall turnout of 30–
50%."[60]

Given the widespread view that most Crimeans supported annexation
to Russia, it is not clear why Russia did not sponsor a more orderly
referendum and allow international observers and journalists to witness
it. Subsequent polling by international firms indicated that most
Crimeans said that they agreed with the outcome of the referendum.
However, polling conducted by the Kyiv International Institute of Sociology, shortly before the fall of Yanukovych and seizure of Crimea, put
support for joining Russia much lower: 41 percent in Crimea, 33 percent
in Donetsk, 24 percent in Luhansk and Odesa oblasts, and 13 percent
nationwide.[61] One interpretation is that after annexation people hesitated
to say they opposed it. Another is that the ouster of Yanukovych
increased Crimeans' support for annexation to Russia.

On March 17 the Crimean parliament requested annexation to the
Russian Federation, and on March 18 a treaty of accession was signed
which brought Crimea and Sevastopol into the Russian Federation as
two distinct subjects. On March 21, the Federal Assembly ratified the
treaty and Putin signed it into law. Crimea was annexed. All in all, the
process took just over three weeks from the appearance of the "little
green men" at Simferopol airport, and just under four weeks from
Yanukovych's departure from Kyiv.

The organization, speed, and efficiency with which the operation was
conducted leads to the conclusion that the operation was planned well in
advance. That observation, however, leaves many questions unanswered.
First, when was the decision to seize the territory actually taken? Were
the plans that were executed in February–March 2014 simply contingency plans, as many militaries have for many possible eventualities, or
had the decision to seize Crimea had been made much earlier, with only
the timing to be determined by the advent of a good opportunity?

Treisman points out that while the military part of the operation
seemed well prepared and ran very smoothly, the political arrangements,

[60] Yevgeny Bobrov, "Problemy Zhitelei Kryma," Blogi Chlenov Sovieta, Sovyet pri
Prezidente Rossiiskoi Federatsii po razvitiyu grazhdanskogo obshchestva I pravam
cheloveka, April 24, 2014, www.president-sovet.ru/members/blogs/bobrov_e_a/
problemy-zhiteley-kryma-/.
[61] Kyiv International Institute of Sociology, "How Relations between Ukraine and Russia
Should Look Like? Public Opinion Polls' Results," March 3, 2014.

including who would be in charge in Crimea and whether Crimea would seek autonomy or to join Russia, seemed chaotic and improvised. He infers from this that the invasion was primarily driven by the goal of preserving control over the naval base in Sevastopol.[62] In Kyiv, many attribute this mix of military efficiency and political improvisation to a Russian assumption that protests against Yanukovych would not take place until the 2015 presidential election; hence Russia was only partly prepared. This perspective fits with the even more improvised subsequent actions in eastern Ukraine.

The date on the medals given to participants in the annexation indicates that the operation started on February 20, at which time Yanukovych was still in power in Kyiv. Consistent with that, Putin said later in a documentary on the takeover that the decision was made by a tight circle of advisors in the closing days of the Sochi Olympic Games (which ended on February 23). If we take the date February 20 seriously, we must consider two different striking conclusions. One possibility is that Putin already knew on February 20 that Yanukovych would flee Ukraine. That fits with video recovered from Yanukovych's residence that showed his aides packing up at that time, but his packing could merely have been a precaution. Another possibility is that the decision to seize Crimea came before Yanukovych's downfall, and therefore was not caused by it. A third alternative, however, must also be considered: that the date on the medals was put there for some other reason that has nothing to do with when the decision to annex Crimea was taken. What is clear, however, is that the notion that the seizure of Crimea was simply a spontaneous reaction to Yanukovych's ouster is extremely difficult to square with the timing of the operation and the incredible smoothness with which it was pulled off. At a minimum, Russia had made plans for the military seizure of Crimea well in advance.

The West Responds on Crimea

Stunned western leaders unanimously criticized Russia's invasion. On March 1, Obama spoke directly with Putin. According to the White House statement on the call:

President Obama spoke for 90 minutes this afternoon with President Putin of Russia about the situation in Ukraine. President Obama expressed his deep concern over Russia's clear violation of Ukrainian sovereignty and territorial

---

[62] Treisman, *The New Autocracy: Information,* chapter 11.

integrity, which is a breach of international law, including Russia's obligations under the UN Charter, and of its 1997 military basing agreement with Ukraine, and which is inconsistent with the 1994 Budapest Memorandum and the Helsinki Final Act. The United States condemns Russia's military intervention into Ukrainian territory.[63]

Russia released its own version of the Obama-Putin call:

Vladimir Putin drew his attention to the provocative and criminal actions on the part of ultranationalists who are in fact being supported by the current authorities in Kyiv. The Russian President spoke of a real threat to the lives and health of Russian citizens and the many compatriots who are currently on Ukrainian territory. Vladimir Putin stressed that in case of any further spread of violence to Eastern Ukraine and Crimea, Russia retains the right to protect its interests and the Russian-speaking population of those areas.[64]

This threat was effective, and while western governments expressed outrage, they also urged Ukraine not to do anything that might provide a pretext for further invasion, as had happened with Georgia in 2008. US Secretary of State Kerry praised Ukraine's Interim President Turchynov for "showing the utmost restraint,"[65] though Ukraine was not in a position to do much. When acting Prime Minister Arseniy Yatsenyuk contacted Russian leaders on March 4, he was in the awkward position of not only protesting the intervention in Crimea, but asking whether Russia still intended to provide the $15 billion loan promised to Yanukovych, which Ukraine still needed. Putin, meanwhile, rejected the legitimacy of the interim government.[66]

The West focused on persuading Russia to change course. An initial step was to announce that they were suspending preparations for the G8 summit planned for Sochi in June. Discussion quickly focused on economic sanctions. On March 17, the day after Crimea's referendum on joining Russia, the European Union and United States announced sanctions against twenty-one Russian and Ukrainian officials deemed to have taken part in "actions threatening Ukraine's territorial integrity."[67] The list included the new prime minister of Crimea, Aksyonov, and the speaker of the Crimean parliament, Vladimir Konstantinov, as well as Putin's advisor on Ukraine Sergei Glazyev. Most observers recognized that sanctions would not compel Russia to relinquish Crimea, but many

---

[63] Steve Wilson, Peter Foster, and Katie Grant, "Ukraine as It Happened," *The Telegraph*, March 2, 2014.
[64] Ibid.   [65] Ibid.
[66] "Ukraine Makes First Contacts with Russia to Avert War," Agence France Presse, March 4, 2014.
[67] European Council, "Foreign Affairs Council, 17/03/2014."

argued that they were valuable anyhow as a means of demonstrating unity and resolve and demonstrating that there would be a cost for any future aggression.[68]

NATO's Response

On March 2, as the takeover of Crimea was unfolding, the North Atlantic Council convened in Brussels to consider a response. Secretary General Anders Fogh Rasmussen said that "What Russia is doing now in Ukraine violates the principles of the United Nations charter. It threatens peace and security in Europe. Russia must stop its military activities and its threats."[69] On March 5, the NATO-Russia Council met, after which Rasmussen announced the suspension of the first planned joint NATO-Russia mission, the suspension of all staff meetings between NATO and Russia, and a review of "the entire range of NATO-Russia cooperation." "At the same time, we do want to keep the door open for political dialogue. So we are ready to maintain meetings of ambassadors in the NATO-Russia Council, as we have done today."[70]

Over the next few months, NATO agreed on several new force deployments intended to address the threat exposed by Russia's invasion of Crimea. It had long been recognized that NATO could not repel an invasion of the new members that bordered Russia, but an invasion had been seen as unlikely, and preparing for it would have alienated Russia. Crimea altered that calculus, kicking the security dilemma into high gear. NATO and its members now feared not only an invasion, but the potential for this vulnerability to compel concessions to Russia.

At the 2014 Wales summit, therefore, NATO agreed on a set of "Assurance" and "Adaptive" measures to reassure allies and to give the alliance a better chance to back those assurances up. These measures included increasing rotations of troops through Estonia, Latvia, Lithuania, and Poland, increasing air patrols in the border regions, increasing the "Response Force" to 40,000 troops, and creating a new "Very High Readiness Force" of 5,000 troops that could be deployed within a few days.[71] Thus, one side effect of the conflict in Ukraine was a substantial

---

[68] See Daniel W. Drezner, "Bringing the Pain, Can Sanctions Hurt Putin Enough to Make Him Give Up Crimea," Foreignpolicy.com, March 7, 2014.

[69] CNN, March 2, 2014.

[70] "Remarks by the NATO Secretary General, Anders Fogh Rasmussen, at the Press Conference Held Following the Meeting of the NATO-Russia Council at NATO HQ, Brussels," States News Service, March 5, 2014.

[71] Louisa Brooke-Holland, "NATO's Military Response to Russia: November 2016 Update," House of Commons Briefing Paper Number 07276, November 2016.

increase in NATO activity near Russia's border, something that Russia had long opposed and NATO had long refrained from.

Intervention in Eastern Ukraine

Russia's success in Crimea was followed quickly by a more slow-moving operation in eastern Ukraine. It remains unclear to what extent the protests in the east were initiated by local dissatisfaction with the situation in Kyiv, and to what extent they were organized and supported from Russia, and whether the conflict that emerged was a "civil war" or an "invasion" has divided scholars and analysts along predictable lines. Clearly there were elements of both local separatism and Russian support, and the mix likely differed in different places. The dichotomy being argued over is at least in part a false one.[72] Many violent conflicts have elements of both international and civil wars. In Ukraine, the distinction between "internal" and "supported by Russia" has never been clear, because Russia consistently supported and encouraged those in Ukraine who sought closer ties with Russia. Those who supported greater autonomy for eastern regions, and closer relations with Russia, naturally looked to Russia for support, and Russia was eager to provide it.

As time went on, Russia's direct involvement became harder to deny, and played a growing role in sustaining the anti-Kyiv forces. In places where there was little internal support for separatism, Russian assistance was unable to generate a sustainable movement. But where there was more substantial internal support, Russia was able to provide the organization, intelligence, encouragement, money, and arms to enable relatively small groups to sustain serious challenges to the Ukrainian government. And when the Ukrainian state regrouped and threatened to defeat the separatist movements in August 2014, Russia's intervention with regular army units was decisive in defeating Ukrainian forces and maintaining the separatist governments of Donetsk and Luhansk oblasts.

On March 1, as the Crimea operation was progressing, pro-Russia activists occupied regional administration buildings in several eastern and southern Ukrainian regions, but pro-government forces quickly retook control. On April 7, forces occupying the state administration buildings in Donetsk and Kharkiv declared the establishment of the

---

[72] See, for example, David A. Lake, "International Relations Theory and Internal Conflict: Insights from the Interstices," *International Studies Review* 5, 4, December 1, 2003, pp. 81–89.

"Donetsk People's Republic," and the "Kharkov[73] People's Republic." (The "Luhansk People's Republic" appears to have first been declared by a crowd of separatists outside the Luhansk state administration building on April 27.) The Ukrainian government tried to respond with a hard line, with the new Interior Minister Arsen Avakov setting an April 11 deadline for separatists to evacuate government buildings. The deadline passed without incident because there was no one that the Ukrainian government could call on to eject the occupiers. The regional administration building in Kharkiv was surrendered quickly. In contrast, on April 12, gunmen seized government buildings around Donetsk, in a series of coordinated attacks. The police chief in Donetsk Oblast, Kostyantyn Pozhydayev, resigned at the demand of protesters.[74]

On April 13, the Ukrainian government declared an "Anti-Terrorist Operation" (ATO) in the eastern part of the country. This terminology was adopted to frame the action as a select targeting of "terrorists," rather than the population or territory of eastern Ukraine. Acting President Turchynov recognized the delicacy of the situation: the government sought to reverse the separatist seizures without alienating the broader population, most of whom, it was assumed, did not support the separatists but would be alienated by a heavy-handed military intervention. "The Donbass is in colossal danger. Besides the Russian special forces, besides terrorists, Donbass also has hundreds of people who have been deceived by Russian propaganda. And besides them are hundreds of thousands of completely innocent Ukrainians. That is why an anti-terrorist operation must be carried out responsibly."[75] Meanwhile the UN released a report saying that "Although there were some attacks against the ethnic Russian community, these were neither systematic nor widespread," and pointing to "misinformed reports" and "greatly exaggerated stories of harassment of ethnic Russians by Ukrainian nationalist extremists."[76]

The Ukrainian government was unprepared to address this challenge in the east for three reasons. First, the upper levels of the state security

---

[73] The "Kharkov" referred to here is the Ukrainian region/city of Kharkiv. The separatists used the region's Russian name.

[74] Mark Rachkevych, "Armed Pro-Russian Extremists Launch Coordinated Attacks in Donetsk Oblast, Seize Regional Policy Headquarters, Set Up Checkpoints (UPDATE)," *Kyiv Post*, April 12, 2014.

[75] Roland Oliphant, "Ukraine Launches 'Anti-Terrorist Operation' in the East; Ukrainian Forces Set Up Checkpoints as Acting President Announces Operation to Root Out 'Separatists' in Pro-Russian East," *The Telegraph*, April 15, 2014.

[76] Office of the United Nations High Commissioner for Human Rights, "Report on the Human Rights Situation in Ukraine, 15 April 2014," pp. 4, 21.

services had been hollowed out and were yet to be rebuilt. Second, the lower level security forces in the region were both unsympathetic to the new government in Kyiv and were likely disoriented by the rapidly shifting chain of command. Many supported the separatists or stood aside. Third, some eastern Ukrainian elites supported the separatist efforts, increasing the legitimacy of separatists, and raising the level of force that would be needed to retake seized buildings. Had the Kyiv government used violence against the occupiers, it would likely have escalated the conflict, just as had happened when Yanukovych used force against the protesters in Kyiv. Finally, the Ukrainian armed forces were utterly incapable of addressing the situation. At the time the conflict started, the Ukrainian military had no units stationed east of the Dnipro river that could be deployed to combat separatists before they became entrenched.[77]

Russia's Diplomatic Offensive

Accompanying events on the ground, the Russian government undertook a massive diplomatic and public relations campaign in support of its intervention in Ukraine. The main themes were four-fold.

First was a disinformation campaign aimed at denying the role of Russian forces in Crimea and eastern Ukraine. Second was an effort to delegitimize the new regime in Kyiv by questioning the way it came to power and by repeatedly exaggerating the role of what it called "fascists" in the Maidan movement and the new government. This was part of a broader campaign in Russia to link the war in Ukraine to World War II.[78] Third, arguments that Crimea and eastern Ukraine were "really" Russian, which Russian nationalists had argued for years, were now widely disseminated in the government-controlled press and by Russian leaders. Fourth, a series of charges of western hypocrisy were used to put the West on the defensive and to counteract the obvious violation of

---

[77] Interviews with Leonid Polyakov, and Viktor Hvozd, Kyiv, May 2018. Polyakov was the deputy defense minister in the interim government (March–May 2015), and Hvozd was a former chief of military intelligence who served as head of the Foreign Intelligence Service in the interim government. The incapacity of the Ukrainian armed forces, which began the post-Soviet era with 700,000 forces and an enormous arsenal, is a part of this story that has received insufficient attention.

[78] Jade McGlynn, "Historical Framing of the Ukraine Crisis through the Great Patriotic War: Performativity, Cultural Consciousness and Shared Remembering," *Memory Studies* (2018): 1–23, https://doi.org/10.1177%2F1750698018800740. See also Elizabeth A. Wood, "Performing Memory: Vladimir Putin and the Celebration of WWII in Russia," *The Soviet and Post-Soviet Review* 38 (2011): 172–200.

international law. Central to this strategy was the argument that Russia's seizure of Ukraine was no different than the West's support for Kosovo's independence.

All of these arguments were articulated by Putin in a marathon phone-in performance on April 18.[79] He called the events in Kyiv "an unconstitutional coup, an armed seizure of power." He then accused the new government of wanting "to invalidate some of the ethnic minorities' rights, including the rights of the Russian minority." Similarly, asked about his decision making on Crimea, he started by saying that "the Russian speaking population was threatened" and that "[t]his is what made Crimean residents, the people who live there, think about their future and ask Russia for help. This is what guided our decision." He insisted that "There are no Russian units in eastern Ukraine – no special services, no tactical advisers. All this is being done by the local residents." On Crimea, he stated that "Certainly, Sevastopol is a city of Russian naval glory, which every Russian citizen knows. We will be guided by this understanding." He stressed that the population of Crimea was essentially Russian, and that the results of the referendum there "gave us no other choice." He insisted that the souring of relations with the United States was not Russia's fault, but that of US "double-standards:"

We see a situation in which it's appropriate to act the way the United States did in Yugoslavia, Iraq, Afghanistan, Libya but it's inappropriate for Russia to defend its interests. I gave you the example of Kosovo, which is totally obvious and clear to the average person not involved in politics. Everything is being turned upside down. This position is devoid of any logic, any logic whatsoever.

The one exception to this overall line was Putin's acknowledgement that the "little green men" in Crimea were in fact Russian soldiers.

In a speech in March, Putin laid out in systematic detail his justification for seizing Crimea, making many of the same points.[80] He pointed to historical ties, Russian military battles, and the ethnic and linguistic makeup of the population. He also presented the transfer of Crimea and "large sections of historical the South of Russia" to Ukraine as illegitimate decisions which became more consequential when "[u]nfortunately, the impossible became a reality. The USSR fell apart." "It was only when Crimea ended up as part of a different country that Russia realized that it

[79] Quotations in this paragraph are from "Kremlin Text of Russian Leader Vladimir Putin's Phone-in," BBC Monitoring Former Soviet Union, April 18, 2014.
[80] Address by President of the Russian Federation, Moscow, March 18, 2014, Kremlin website.

was not simply robbed, it was plundered." He then turned to an attack on the protests and the ouster of Yanukovych, calling the new government the "ideological heirs of Bandera, Hitler's accomplice during World War II." With relish, he quoted a statement that the United States made regarding Kosovo in 2009: "'Declarations of independence may, and often do, violate domestic legislation. However, this does not make them violations of international law.' End of quote. They wrote this, disseminated it all over the world, had everyone agree and now they are outraged. Over what?" He then compared Crimea's joining Russia to the United States' independence from Britain and to the unification of Germany. None of these arguments contradicted the fact that the seizure of Crimea was a blatant violation of international law, but that was beside the point. This set of arguments was very influential, overlapping as it did arguments made by some western elites, many of whom had criticized NATO expansion, the US war in Iraq, and the bombing of Yugoslavia. Many analysts blamed the conflict on the West in terms similar to those used by Putin.

Attempts at Conflict Resolution

In April, the first international effort to resolve the crisis in eastern Ukraine took place when diplomats from Ukraine, Russia, the European Union, and the United States met in Geneva. The four sides released a "Joint Statement" specifying several steps to be taken to deescalate the conflict, including:

- "All sides must refrain from any violence, intimidation or provocative actions."
- "All illegal armed groups must be disarmed; all illegally seized buildings must be returned to legitimate owners; all illegally occupied streets, squares and other public places in Ukrainian cities and towns must be vacated."
- "Amnesty will be granted to protesters and to those who have left buildings and other public places and surrendered weapons, with the exception of those found guilty of capital crimes."
- "The announced constitutional process will be inclusive, transparent and accountable. It will include the immediate establishment of a broad national dialogue."
- "It was agreed that the OSCE Special Monitoring Mission should play a leading role in assisting Ukrainian authorities and local communities in the immediate implementation of these de-escalation measures wherever they are needed most, beginning in the coming days.

The U.S., E.U. and Russia commit to support this mission, including by providing monitors."[81]

For Russia, the Geneva agreement accomplished three important goals. First, in Russia's interpretation, it committed the Ukrainian government to refraining from the use of force against the separatists. Second, it intervened in Ukraine's constitutional process, where Russia strongly supported decentralization. Third, it dealt with the crisis as an internal Ukrainian conflict – Russia itself took on no obligations.[82] An additional benefit was that it made no mention of Crimea. Ukraine also saw some advantages. The signing of the agreement represented a de facto Russian recognition of the new Ukrainian government, and Ukraine was able to show that it was serious about resolving the conflict peacefully.

Ukraine's interim leadership quickly moved to promise a "comprehensive constitutional reform that will secure powers of the regions,"[83] and initiated a ceasefire to allow the Geneva agreement time to take effect. However, separatist leaders, who did not take part in the Geneva process, quickly rejected the deal. Separatist leader Denis Pushilin argued that the Geneva agreement's stipulation that occupied buildings be vacated applied also to the government buildings in Kyiv in which the new government was working. "They must free the seized administrative buildings [in Kiev] and disarm the illegal armed formations, the national guard and the Right Sector, and free political prisoners." This case demonstrated the flexibility in Russia's position: it could appear to play a constructive role in negotiations, only to have the forces it supported in Ukraine reject what it had agreed to. On April 21, Russian Foreign Minister Lavrov accused Ukraine of violating the Geneva agreement: "The Geneva accord is not only not being fulfilled, but steps are being taken, primarily by those who seized power in Kiev, that are grossly breaching the agreements reached in Geneva."[84] The different sides' positions appeared incompatible, and since the battle on the ground was increasingly being won by Russia's allies, they had little incentive

---

[81] "Joint Geneva Statement on Ukraine from April 17: The Full Text," *Washington Post*, April 17, 2014.
[82] Agata Wierzbowska-Miazga and Wojciech Kononczuk, "The Geneva (Dis)agreement on Ukraine," *Ośrodek Studiów Wschodnich*, April 24, 2014.
[83] Sergei L. Loiko and Carol J. Williams, "Pro-Russia Gunmen Defy Geneva Pact in Ukraine; Separatists Refuse to Disarm and Say the Accord Means the Interim Government and Army Must Retreat," *Los Angeles Times*, April 19, 2014, p. A3.
[84] "Ukraine Crisis: Russia Accuses Kiev of Violating Geneva Accord; Russian Foreign Minister Accuses the Ukrainian Authorities of Breaking Last Week's Geneva Accord on Resolving the Crisis," *The Telegraph*, April 21, 2014.

to make any concessions. The Ukrainian government, meanwhile, was struggling to mount a response from its security services.

Ukraine Holds Elections

Amidst this burgeoning war, Ukraine held presidential elections in May and parliamentary elections in October to replace the interim president appointed in February and the parliament that had been elected under Yanukovych in 2012. In Crimea, no voting was possible, and while the government tried to hold elections in as much of the Donbas as possible, voting was impossible in some areas and turnout dramatically depressed more broadly in the east.[85] The presidential vote was decisive: Petro Poroshenko, a chocolate magnate who had supported Yushchenko in 2004, then been a minister under Yanukovych, then became an early supporter of anti-Yanukovych protests, was elected decisively, winning 54.7 percent of the vote in the first round, the first time since 1991 a presidential election had been decided without a runoff. Poroshenko's victory was facilitated by the decision of another popular opposition figure, Vitaliy Klitschko, to run for mayor of Kyiv instead.

Poroshenko called early parliamentary elections for October to try to consolidate his political support. Poroshenko's bloc won the largest number of seats, with many wins in single-member districts compensating for a narrow defeat in the proportional representation ballot. Prime Minister Arseniy Yatseniuk's "People's Front" edged the Poroshenko bloc with just over 22 percent of the PR ballot, but ended up with far fewer seats. These results dramatically transformed Ukraine's parliament. The Party of Regions, which had dominated the previous parliament and been a major player since 2002, was gone, with its improvised replacement, the Opposition Bloc having won only 29 seats, compared with the Party of Regions' 185 in 2012. Poroshenko's power was reinforced, though his bloc's 132 seats left him needing to form a coalition to hold a majority (Table 7.1). The subsequent coalition included the Poroshenko Bloc, Narodnyi Front, Samopomich, Batkivshchyna, and the Radical Party, as well as some independents.

---

[85] On the difficult holding the elections and the results, see Erik S. Herron, Michael E. Thunberg, and Nazar Boyko, "Crisis Management and Adaptation in Wartime Elections: Ukraine's 2014 Snap Parliamentary and Presidential Elections," *Electoral Studies* 40 (2015): 419–429.

Table 7.1 *2014 parliamentary election results*

Party	Percentage PR vote	PR seats	SMD seats	Total seats
Poroshenko Bloc	21.8	63	69	132
Narodnyi Front	22.1	64	18	82
Samopomich	11.0	32	1	33
Opposition Bloc	9.4	27	2	29
Radical Party	7.4	22	0	22
Batkivshchyna	5.7	17	2	19
Others	22.52	0	n/a	0
Independents	n/a	0	96	96

While the coalition was never fully in Poroshenko's control, the new majority represented the victory of the pro-western forces that Russia feared. The coalition agreement included EU integration, revocation of "non-bloc" status, and membership in NATO.[86]

The Conflict Grows

Through April and May 2014, separatists supported by Russia fought battles against the Ukrainian government, which was supported by paramilitary groups, in towns and cities throughout eastern Ukraine. Separatist forces gradually expanded islands of control into contiguous areas and sought to expand the areas of control. In several cities, however, local opposition successfully contested them for power. In Mariupol, on the Black Sea Coast, separatists seized control but were then defeated by Ukrainian forces supported by paramilitaries. In Kharkiv, the people who seized the state administration building left within a few days, and while demonstrations for and against the government in Kyiv and separatism proceeded through the summer and fall of 2014, Kharkiv never came under the control of separatist forces. Apparently there was both less support for separatism and more support for the new government, both among elites and the populace.

There were some efforts taken to extend the secessionist movements beyond Crimea and the Donbas. Throughout the spring of 2014, Putin had used the term "Novorossiya," which in the nineteenth century referred to a wide swath of territory that in 2014 comprised much of eastern and southern Ukraine, including the large Black Sea port of

---

[86] Tadeusz A. Olszański, "The Ukrainian Coalition Agreement," *Ośrodek Studiów Wschodnich*, November 14, 2014.

Odesa, which like Crimea had been seized in the 1780s and had a large Russian-speaking population.[87]

On May 2, pro- and anti-Maidan protesters in Odesa clashed violently. Anti-Maidan protesters, outnumbered, retreated to the Trade Union Building, which caught fire and burned, killing forty-two anti-Maidan activists. Four other anti-Maidan activists, as well as two pro-Maidan activists, were killed in the related fighting.[88] Surprisingly, this event, one of the most violent so far in the crisis, did not lead to further escalation in Odesa. Instead, local leaders managed to deescalate the conflict, and stability returned.

On May 11, Donetsk People's Republic (DNR) and Luhansk People's Republic (LNR) leaders held a referendum on autonomy for the areas they controlled, the results of which were almost certainly falsified. The following day, the separatists declared the independence of the DNR, and the Supreme Council of the DNR appointed Alexander Borodai, a Russian citizen, as prime minister. Igor Girkin (also known as "Strelkov"), a Russian former army and FSB (Federal Security Service, successor to the KGB) officer, declared himself "Supreme Commander" of the DNR, vowed that any Ukrainian forces remaining in the region would be destroyed, and requested military support from Russia. Both Borodai and Girkin had participated in the separatist movement in Moldova in the 1990s, and both had been directly involved in the annexation of Crimea, Girkin by leading troops and Borodai as an advisor to Sergei Aksyonov. While the Russian government claimed that these individuals were acting on their own, the fact that movement's leaders came from Russia undermined the argument that this was an internal Ukrainian uprising, and Borodai was replaced with Alexander Zakharchenko in August 2014.

The DNR's declaration of independence kicked off a more militarized phase of the conflict, as the focus spread from occupying specific buildings to securing the entire territory of Donetsk and Luhansk. This led to a series of attacks by separatist forces on facilities of the Ukrainian state, including a violent battle for control of Donetsk International Airport in late May.

As the fighting escalated and the Ukrainian government recovered from its original disarray, the scale of operations and weaponry deployed

[87] See John O'Loughlin, Gerard Toal, and Vladimir Kolosov, "The Rise and Fall of 'Novorossiya': Examining Support for a Separatist Geopolitical Imaginary in Southeast Ukraine," *Post-Soviet Affairs* 33, 2 (2017): 124–144.
[88] Henry E. Hale, Oxana Shevel, and Olga Onuch, "Believing Facts in the Fog of War: Identity, Media and Hot Cognition in Ukraine's 2014 Odesa Tragedy," *Geopolitics* 23, 4 (2018): 852.

increased. At the same time, Russian involvement grew and became harder to hide. The separatists were increasingly armed with heavy weapons, including tanks, which came from Russia and in some cases originated in Crimea. In early June, Ukrainian attack aircraft were used against occupied state administration buildings in eastern Ukraine. The use of fighter aircraft, which the separatist forces did not have, had the potential to tip the military balance in favor of the Ukrainian government. The air war escalated when a Ukrainian troop transport was shot down on approach to Luhansk, killing forty-nine people.

In late June, Ukraine declared a ceasefire to accompany a peace plan advanced by Poroshenko. The ceasefire lasted until July 1, when the government restarted attacks on separatist positions around Kramatorsk and Sloviansk in Donetsk oblast. This began a series of victories by Ukrainian forces that threatened the overall position of the separatist forces in Donetsk. In the coming weeks, several other positions fell to government forces. When shells landed inside Russia on July 14, Russia blamed Ukraine and said that the incident might prompt Russia to deploy aircraft against Ukraine, while Ukraine called the incident a provocation.

The West's Response to the War in Eastern Ukraine

While the annexation of Crimea and Russian support for separatism in eastern Ukraine appalled and worried people across the western world, there was a wide range of opinion on how to respond. Many saw Russia's actions both as a moral affront and as an act of aggression that needed to be met with a resolute response. People in this school of thought tended to think of the events of 2014 in the context of 1938, with the lesson being that aggressive dictators are better confronted sooner than later. Many others, however, were inclined to come to a new accommodation with Russia. To those convinced that Russia's claim to Crimea had some merit, and that Russia was an important economic power and a great power whose claims could never be ignored, escalating the conflict seemed unlikely to accomplish much.

While Poland, the United Kingdom, and the United States preferred a resolute response, Germany was much more divided. Chancellor Angela Merkel, long a friend of Putin, had lost patience with him, but many other German elites were unwilling to forsake profitable trade relations, especially in energy, over Ukraine. In July, a lengthy analysis in *Der Spiegel* sought to explain why Germany seemed determined to maintain a "special relationship" with Russia. It pointed out that recent revelations of spying by the US National Security Agency on Merkel's mobile phone had soured opinion on the United States, feeding anti-Americanism that had already worsened under the George W. Bush administration.[89] Sanctions on Russia were expected to have dramatically different impacts on different states, depending on their trade relations with Russia. In May, a leaked report from the European Commission warned that sanctions could remove a full percentage point from Germany's GDP growth for 2014.[90]

In the US, opinion was much less divided. While several influential intellectuals blamed the West for the conflict and advocated a new accommodation with Russia, the vast majority of politicians from the two major parties joined to push for harsh sanctions.

Despite these differences, however, the European Union and United States repeatedly agreed to strengthen the sanctions regime in response to events in eastern Ukraine. On June 26, the European Commission signed the Association Agreement with Ukraine that had sparked the initial crisis the previous November. In early July, yet another set of sanctions was adopted by the European Union, and the United States cut off several Russian energy firms and banks from access to US financial markets. Eventually, most of the Russian energy, oil, and arms sectors were denied access to western capital markets. These sanctions went beyond the individuals targeted by the first round of sanctions to aim at key sectors and at leaders who were connected to the intervention in Ukraine.

Russia reacted to sanctions with defiance. Responding to the Obama administration's extension of sanctions in July, Prime Minister Medvedev said "Sanctions are evil," and warned that they would make matters worse, not better. Deputy Prime Minister Dmitry Rogozin tweeted that "The sanctions imposed by Washington on Russian defense sector majors are unlawful and demonstrate that the U.S. is engaged in unfair competition on the arms market. Anyway, the Americans cannot put a lid on the ongoing re-arming of the Russian armed forces or shatter the export potential of our defense sector." Putin himself said that sanctions "generally have a boomerang effect and, without a doubt, in this case, are driving the Russian-U.S. relations into a stalemate and seriously damaging them."[91] Analysts have debated how much sanctions have injured Putin and other targets, and whether they may even have

---

[89] Markus Feldenkirchen, Christiane Hoffmann, and René Pfister, "Will It Be America or Russia?" *Spiegel* Online, July 10, 2014.

[90] Justin Huggler and Bruno Waterfield, "Ukraine Crisis: Russia Sanctions Would Hurt Germany's Growth; Europe's Biggest Economy Could Be Severely Affected by Future Sanctions against Russia," *The Telegraph*, May 9, 2014.

[91] CNN, July 17, 2014.

backfired.[92] The sanctions that Russia enacted in response served to shield Russian producers from foreign competition, at the cost of higher prices to Russian consumers.

MH17: The Conflict Changes Course

On July 17, a Russian Buk surface-to-air missile shot down Malaysian Airlines flight 17 en route from Amsterdam to Kuala Lumpur.[93] Shooting down the airplane was almost certainly an accident, probably a case of mistaken identity in which the civilian aircraft was wrongly identified as a Ukrainian military plane, even though it was flying at over thirty thousand feet.

By spurring widespread outrage and undermining those who advocated conciliation, the downing of MH17 dramatically changed the course of the broader conflict between Russia and the West. In the West, people were angered not only at the killing of so many innocents, but by Russia's cynicism in denying responsibility and by the rebels' obstruction of the investigation. As a result, more people advocated sanctions against Russia, and fewer spoke openly against them. A week after the disaster, yet another new round of sanctions was announced.

The fighting continued to escalate throughout the summer. During the second half of July, as the diplomatic battle over responsibility for the tragedy raged, Ukrainian forces made progress in reducing the territory held by insurgents. The Ukrainian army had regrouped and, while it was still very flawed, it was augmented by paramilitary groups formed in part from the self-defense groups that had organized security on the Maidan. While these paramilitaries tended to be highly motivated and in some

[92] The impact of the sanctions is evaluated in Mikhail Alexseev and Henry Hale, "Crimea Come What May: Do Economic Sanctions Backfire Politically," unpublished paper, 2018.

[93] There has been, of course, extensive argumentation to the effect that Russia's responsibility has not been proven, but all the credible sources that have examined the matter in depth reach that conclusion. Only the Russian government, which advanced a range of theories, has stuck with the assertion that Ukraine was responsible. In May 2018, an international "joint investigative team" stated that they had "legal and convincing evidence that would stand up in a courtroom" that the BUK missile system that shot down the plane came from Russia's 53rd Anti-Aircraft Missile Brigade, stationed at Kursk. See Shaun Walker, "MH17 Downed by Russian Military Missile System, Say Investigators," *The Guardian*, May 24, 2018. The Joint Investigation Team update from May 2018, along with a video presentation, is at www.om.nl/onderwerpen/mh17-crash/@103196/update-criminal-0/. On competing views of responsibility for the downing of the airliner, see Gerard Toal and John O'Loughlin, "'Why Did MH17 Crash?' Blame Attribution, Television News and Public Opinion in Southeastern Ukraine, Crimea and the De Facto States of Abkhazia, South Ossetia and Transnistria," *Geopolitics* 23, 4 (2018): 882–916.

cases exhibited extraordinary bravery, they were neither well armed nor well trained, and command and control was weak. However, the separatists were also relatively poorly armed and trained, and the tide began to turn.

On August 20, Ukrainian government and paramilitary forces seized Ilovaisk, between the city of Donetsk and the Russian border, as part of an effort to separate Donetsk and Luhansk separatist forces and to disrupt supply lines. The Ukrainian government believed it was on the verge of a decisive victory, and apparently the Russian government agreed. An insurgent counterattack was bolstered by the entry into the conflict of regular Russian army forces crossing the nearby border. The Russian forces, well equipped and trained and with superior command, control, and intelligence, encircled a large group of Ukrainian forces. An attempt to relieve them was repulsed by Russian forces, and the Ukrainian forces were then routed, with many being taken prisoner.[94]

The Russian victory around Ilovaisk forced Russia to make a decision. With regular Russian army units now in Ukraine (though Russia still denied this) Russia could push further into Ukraine, with a variety of strategic goals possible. A maximalist goal would be to aim all the way across southern Ukraine, not only forging a land link with Crimea but also seizing the entire Ukrainian Black Sea coast (landlocking Ukraine), taking Odesa, another coveted city, and establishing contact with Russia's proxy republic in Transnistria. A more modest goal would have been to push through Mariupol, which had already seen a temporary takeover by separatist forces, to establish a land link with Crimea. The downside of such a strategy was that it would have turned a local proxy war into a general war between Russia and Ukraine, and destroyed the fiction that Russia was not involved.

Russia's restraint in this episode is worth noting, as it demonstrates some limit to Putin's appetite or his risk acceptance. To the extent that Putin's rhetoric about reestablishing "Novorossiya" was serious, the events of the spring and summer of 2014 may have disabused him of the notion that it would be easy to accomplish. In most of eastern and southern Ukraine, pro-Russian movements had failed to catch on, undermining the widely held belief that all Russophone Ukrainians identified with Russia and wanted to join it. Crimea, Donetsk, and Luhansk were exceptions, not the rule, and even in those places, separatism relied decisively on Russian military support. By September it had become clear that in most regions of Ukraine, small bands of pro-Russian activists

[94] The battle is described in Tim Judah, "Ukraine: A Catastrophic Defeat," *The New York Review of Books*, September 5, 2014.

supported by the Russian government could not spark a broader movement. If Russia wanted to create "Novorossiya," it would need to invade on a large scale, and it was not willing to do this at that time.

From Geneva to Normandy to Minsk

The downing of MH17, along with the escalation of fighting and the involvement of Russian army forces around Ilovaisk, seemed to increase the desire on all sides to rein in the conflict. For Ukraine, the rout of its forces made it clear that Russia could thwart any attempt to win the war on the ground. While Ukrainian forces could take on the Donbas separatists, they could not defeat the Russian army. For Russia, the easy victory in Crimea had become much more dangerous in Donbas, because the myth of Russian noninvolvement would have to be surrendered to help the separatists succeed. Moreover, the shooting down of MH17 had galvanized western cohesion against Russia. For the West, the prospect of a broader war, either between Russia and Ukraine or perhaps against NATO weak points in the Baltics, caused a great deal of fear. Everyone now had reason to want to see the conflict deescalate.

However, various peace efforts had already been made, and had been stymied by the same set of problems. Not only were the different sides' goals incompatible, but their understandings of who was at war, and therefore who should be negotiating, were equally incompatible.

On June 6, while leaders were gathered in Normandy to mark the seventieth anniversary of the D-Day landings, leaders from Ukraine, Russia, Germany, and France met to discuss the crisis. This meeting initiated what became known as the "Normandy format," which was to become the main international forum to address the conflict. The shift from the Geneva process to that of Normandy was significant in that the new format did not include the United States. It made the process a European one, but appeared to shift the weight in Russia's favor and to further the Russian goal of cleaving off the EU powers from the United States.

On June 20, Petro Poroshenko advanced a peace plan containing fifteen points. Putin offered general support for the plan, but insisted that the separatists be made party to the negotiations. This issue continued to divide the Russian and Ukrainian approaches. While Ukraine denied the legitimacy of the separatists and believed that Russia ought to negotiate because it was supporting them, Russia stuck by the notion that the separatists were an independent force and the Russia was not a party to the conflict.

By the end of August, having relieved pressure on its allies in the Donbas and sent a powerful signal that it would not allow Ukraine to achieve a military victory, Russia was willing to stabilize its gains. Ukraine, in contrast, was reeling, and sought to do what it could to prevent the military disaster from expanding. Western governments were afraid yet again that a more general conflict might break out. This constellation of interests formed the underpinning of the first Minsk agreement, reached in September 2014.

The "Protocol on the Results of the Consultations of the Trilateral Contact Group," known initially as the "Minsk Protocol" and later as "Minsk-1," was signed on September 8, 2014. The Normandy format was largely retained, though rather than German and French representatives, the OSCE was represented along with Russia and Ukraine (hence the group was called the "Trilateral contact group").

The agreement achieved its immediate aim, which was to consolidate a decrease in the violence. But as with the Geneva statement, profound differences were papered over with vague language, and the two sides interpreted the agreement completely differently. The agreement contained twelve points, the first of which was the "immediate bilateral cessation of the use of weapons." The third addressed decentralization of power in Ukraine, referring to "certain areas of the Donetsk and Luhansk regions." The ninth point required "the holding of early local elections in accordance with the Law of Ukraine 'With respect to the temporary status of local self-government in certain areas of the Donetsk and the Lugansk regions.'" Item 10 was "Remove unlawful military formations, military hardware, as well as militants and mercenaries from the territory of Ukraine." Significantly, the agreement was signed not only by representatives of Russia and Ukraine, but by representatives of the DNR (Aleksander Zakharchenko) and LNR (Igor Plotnitsky). This achieved another Russian goal, having Ukraine recognize the leaders of the separatist republics at the bargaining table.

This formula, which remained as the reference point for discussions of a resolution in the coming months and years, offered something for everyone, but reflected deep contradictions in the sides' positions rather than resolving them. The timing for "early" elections was obviously vague, but the bigger question was whether they would occur before or after other steps, such as "permanent monitoring of the Ukrainian-Russian state border ... by the OSCE" (item 4). In the coming years, Ukraine insisted that Russia follow provision 10 ("remove unlawful military formations") while Russia denied their existence. Russia insisted on implementing decentralization of power, to which many Ukrainians were resolutely opposed and others saw as a final step, not a first one.

The Battle for Debaltseve and Minsk-2

The signing of the Minsk agreement was a result, rather than a cause, of the slowdown in the fighting that both sides sought after the battle of Ilovaisk. By January 2015, however, strategic considerations led to a new escalation. The subject of renewed large-scale fighting was the town of Debaltseve, to the northeast of the city of Donetsk. The area comprised a government-controlled salient, largely surrounded by separatist-held territory, as well as the symbolically important Donetsk International Airport. It was significant as a junction of roads and railroads, and hence was important for the lines of communications of both sides. On January 22, separatists renewed a large-scale attack to seize the salient. The battle continued for several weeks, with artillery and rocket attacks razing the city and civilians struggling to escape the fighting. By February 10, the separatists had nearly cut off the government forces by seizing the main road out of the salient. They were determined to maximize the extent of their gains before the Minsk-2 agreement stabilized new lines of control. The separatists continued their assault even after a new ceasefire agreement was reached on February 12. Finally, on February 18, Ukrainian forces began to withdraw from their unsustainable position in the city. As in Ilovaisk the previous summer, the result was a disaster for Ukrainian forces, many of whom were killed or captured, despite the ceasefire.

The fighting around Debaltseve demonstrated that the Minsk Protocol of 2014 was a shambles. Despite that failure, the parties put the same process into effect in February 2015. On February 7, Germany's Angela Merkel and France's Francois Hollande developed a new plan after consulting with Poroshenko and Putin. The US government was discussing shipping arms to the Ukrainian government, which Hollande and Merkel feared would lead to an escalation of the conflict. As was the case before, Ukraine had an incentive to do anything that would limit the rout of its troops, while Russia was willing to see its latest gains recognized in an agreement. By avoiding the trickiest issues, such as demarcating control of Debaltseve, where lines of control were unclear as the agreement was being drafted, the process strengthened the incentive for both sides to fight more intensely, not less, as a ceasefire approached.

The agreement reached was technically called the "Package of Measures for the Implementation of the Minsk Agreements," but is generally known as Minsk-2. The plan established what its authors hoped was a set of steps that would resolve the conflict. Major provisions among the plan's thirteen points included withdrawal of "foreign armed formations," the holding of local elections, "decentralization" in Ukraine, and the reestablishment of Ukraine's control over its borders. There were numerous problems. Russia was still denying that it had "foreign armed formations" in Ukraine, so implementing that crucial measure would be difficult. Equally problematic was the timing of the proposed steps. If local elections were held before the territory was returned to Ukraine's control and in the absence of strong international oversight, Ukraine would regard them as rigged. Ukraine committed to "decentralization," but it was not clear exactly what this meant. Greater autonomy at the level of the oblast, which is what it seemed to mean, would require amending the constitution, and opposition to such a move in Ukraine was high.

As in the case of Minsk-1, Minsk-2 served the immediate needs of the various parties, but established a road map for the future which could not actually be followed. The proposal for greater regional autonomy was seen as a "poison pill" for Ukraine. It would make Ukraine responsible for rebuilding the devastated regions, while giving the regions (and by extension, it appears, Russia) a veto over Ukraine's future reform and international orientation. Russia and the separatists had little interest in the withdrawal of Russian forces or in reestablishing Ukraine's control over the border. Each side expected that the commitments it favored were nonnegotiable, while seeking to avoid the commitments that it found unacceptable. The result was an agreement that could not be implemented, but also could not be abandoned. The good news was that fighting again ebbed; the bad news was that there was no path to ending the violence altogether. Since Minsk-2, the conflict in Donbas continued, and while the territorial lines of control stabilized (see Map 7.2), a steady stream of casualties ensued. By 2018 total casualties had surpassed ten thousand and the threat of a reescalation to all-out fighting was constant.

Conclusion

While disagreement over Ukraine's status had been growing for years, within Ukraine, between Russia and Ukraine, and between Russia and the West, few foresaw, even in the fall of 2013, that Ukraine would experience a "revolution" over the matter in early 2014. Similarly, even as protests in Kyiv reached a peak in February 2014, very few anticipated that Russia would seize Crimea and intervene in eastern Ukraine in support of separatist movements. That these events were so shocking suggests that until the moment it broke out, conflict was not inevitable.

Both within Ukraine and internationally, matters that had festered for years came to a head. The possibility that one side might win the battle permanently prompted those on the other to raise the stakes. Within

Map 7.2 Line of control, Donetsk and Luhansk oblasts, July 2019

Ukraine, Viktor Yanukovych's efforts to irreversibly consolidate his power prompted protesters first to try to get him to change course, and then to try to eject him from power. Between Ukraine, Russia, and the West, the possibility that Yanukovych's ouster would permanently reorient Ukraine toward the West seems to have convinced Putin that there was little to lose, and perhaps much to gain, in seizing territory that Russia had long claimed.

The source of escalation within Ukraine after 2010 was Viktor Yanukovych's effort to concentrate power and introduce a more authoritarian model. Yanukovych had been elected fairly in 2010, but he sought to ensure that he would not face a fair election in 2015, and he had already done a great deal to eliminate political competition in the country and to control an increasing share of economic assets. Yanukovych's aggrandizement was bound to generate three different kinds of resentment: one from those who supported democracy over his autocracy; a second from those who supported a pro-European line against the pro-Russian line that seemed to follow naturally from autocracy; and a third from economic elites whose wealth was threatened by Yanukovych's greed. The decision not to sign the AA spurred protest, but it was only Yanukovych's response to the protests that moved the situation toward a potential revolution. Repression and violence was sufficient to anger protesters and broaden their support, but not to impede the protests' growth. This caused the cycle to escalate until Yanukovych's allies began deserting him and he fled.

A second conflict was between Ukraine and Russia. While Viktor Yanukovych sought Russia's help in establishing his domestic hegemony, he did not seek to become a vassal of Russia. Instead, he sought to gain both the domestic political and economic benefits of an Association Agreement with the European Union and the benefits, including less expensive energy, from a positive relationship with Russia. These goals were incompatible for both technical and political reasons. Technically, the Deep and Comprehensive Free Trade Area (DCFTA) envisioned with the European Union was incompatible with the Customs Union envisioned by Russia. Politically, Putin was not willing to countenance a closer relationship between Ukraine and the EU. As he made clear in the fall of 2013, Putin would seek to create an economic crisis for Ukraine, and a political crisis for Yanukovych, if the Association Agreement went ahead. Putin saw the AA as threatening the permanent loss of Ukraine, which Russia had, since 1991, seen as artificial and temporary. This compelled Yanukovych to take the steps that kicked off the protests. It also meant that Russia refused to accept the outcome of the protests, deploying military force against Ukraine rather than accepting a political defeat.

The third conflict was between the West and Russia. Both the European Union and Russia misunderstood how serious the other was about Ukraine. The European Union underestimated how determined Putin was to keep Ukraine in Russia's orbit, while Putin underestimated how determined the European Union was to defend the principle that no external state could have a veto on the EU's relations with a third country. The EU's principle that no one, not even Russia, could veto another state's relations with the European Union clashed directly with Russia's insistence that as a great power it had a veto over European security affairs and that it had a sphere of influence in its immediate neighborhood. While the European Union did not perceive its expanded relationship with Ukraine as aimed against Russia, it became less willing over time to sacrifice its relationship with Ukraine to placate Russia.

These three conflicts were distinct from each other in theory, but by the fall of 2013 they had become largely intertwined. Ukraine's domestic order was tightly connected to how it would relate to Russia – a more democratic Ukraine would also be a less pro-Russian one. And both questions became connected to the growing tension between the West and Russia. Well before 2013, some observers had pointed to a new cold war. Whether that rhetoric was warranted or not, the tension between an increasingly authoritarian Russia and a western Europe built around EU norms had grown dramatically, and Ukraine was seen as a territory that would likely soon land in one camp or the other. The status quo in Ukraine was increasingly shaky, and both Russia and the European Union sought to see that Ukraine ended up on its side of the line that was increasingly dividing Europe.

As we have shown in detail in this chapter, the period of the Euromaidan or "Revolution of Dignity," from late November 2013 until February 22, 2014, was one in which small decisions had magnified and often unpredictable effects. An initial decision to beat protesters on November 30 led to a huge escalation in the protest movement. The passage of "dictatorship laws" in mid-January revived an ebbing protest movement. Clashes between protesters and security forces on February 18 and 20 fractured Yanukovych's loyalists. The decision by protesters to reject a deal negotiated between EU and Russian diplomats, party leaders, and Yanukovych was predicted to lead to harsh repression. Instead, the regime collapsed within hours.

While the course of the protests was impossible to predict, the effect of the results seemed clear: Ukraine was going to turn toward Europe. Putin responded by invading and annexing Crimea and by fomenting a rebellion in eastern Ukraine. The alternative for Putin, it seemed, was to accept the loss of Ukraine. Clearly, he could have chosen to do that, and Russia had made treaty commitments to that effect. He chose instead to seize the unique opportunity that presented itself to seize Crimea and to make a bid for a much larger part of Ukraine. Whether in supporting separatists in eastern Ukraine he hoped to repeat the Crimea scenario, or whether he intended to create the ongoing instability that has resulted, we do not know.

8 Conclusion: Ukraine, Russia, and the West – from Cold War to Cold War

Greeting acting Prime Minister Arseniy Yatseniuk in Brussels in March 2014, as the annexation of Crimea was in progress, NATO Secretary General Anders Fogh Rasmussen said: "We clearly face the gravest threat to European security since the end of the Cold War." "And this is not just about Ukraine. This crisis has serious implications for the security and stability of the Euro-Atlantic area as a whole … And your sovereignty, your independence, and your territorial integrity are key factors for stability and security in the region."[1] Few disagreed with the view that the crisis in Ukraine was the most dangerous threat to broader security in many years. How did it happen that Ukraine came to be the pivot of what many called a new cold war?[2]

This book has stressed the underlying causes of the conflict. While the change in power in Kyiv in February 2014 was the immediate spark that prompted Russia to invade Crimea and to support separatism in eastern Ukraine, that event would not have occurred or have had the impact it did but for a much deeper set of conflicts that emerged with the end of the Cold War and the collapse of the Soviet Union, and that got progressively worse over the entire post-Soviet period. To explain the outbreak of violent conflict in 2014 without looking at its long-term sources is to take the events of 2013–2014 out of context and therefore to misinterpret them. The events that defined Russia's relations with Ukraine, the West's relations with Russia, and the contest between democracy and authoritarianism in both Russia and Ukraine all began in the 1990s. If we want to understand why the various actors did not manage to find the "exit ramps" on the path to conflict, we must look not only at events going

---

[1] "Joint press point with NATO Secretary General Anders Fogh Rasmussen and the Prime Minister of Ukraine, Arsenii Yatseniuk," March 6, 2014.

[2] The comparison of the current era to the Cold War is controversial. For a detailed argument that the characterization is apt, see Robert Legvold, *Return to Cold War* (Cambridge: Polity, 2016).

back to 1991, but to the dynamics of international interactions that constrained all the actors.

Disagreements from the Start

The events of 1989–1991 ended the Cold War, which was characterized both by profound discord and by an increasingly stable set of "rules of the road" meant to prevent accidents, if not to resolve all differences. After 1989, the new Europe was characterized by increasing perceptions of harmony, but not by any newly agreed rules of the road. As we showed in Chapter 2, even before the breaching of the Berlin Wall, Soviet and western leaders had very different ideas about what kind of post-Cold War world they were trying to create. The West envisioned a "Europe whole and free," characterized by liberal democracy, free markets, and international law. Mikhail Gorbachev envisioned "Europe as a common home," in which a reformed and more vibrant Soviet Union would continue to play the role of superpower globally and on the European continent. The defining event of this early relationship was the response to Iraq's invasion of Kuwait in 1990. The United States sought UN Security Council sanction to restore Kuwait's territorial integrity, and Russia voted for that resolution. When Boris Yeltsin took control of the Russia, shorn of the fourteen other Soviet republics, he endorsed a friendly relationship with the West while believing that Russia would continue to control the post-Soviet region and to wield a veto over European and global security affairs.

Feodor Lukyanov wrote in 2016 that "Russian leaders have all agreed on one thing: the "new world order" that emerged after 1991 was nothing like the one envisioned by Mikhail Gorbachev and other reform-minded Soviet leaders."[3] The different visions for post-Cold War Europe would likely have generated some tension in any event, but Russia's dissatisfaction over the loss of Ukraine created a problem that festered over time. Insistence that Ukraine remain closely tied to Russia helped prompt the coup attempt of August 1991, and while that attempt failed, it did so not because Russian elites supported the end of the Soviet Union, but because they supported the end of Soviet communist rule. Moscow's intent to retain some form of control over Ukraine remained. Those who opposed Ukraine's sovereignty (and especially Ukrainian control of Crimea) and rapid market reforms were called "hard liners," but they comprised a large part of the Russian elite and the populace.

---

[3] Fyodor Lukyanov, "Putin's Foreign Policy: The Quest to Restore Russia's Rightful Place," *Foreign Affairs* (May/June 2016): 32.

While Russia could not halt Ukraine's independence and rejected the use of force to reverse it, most Russians fully expected that some kind of "center" would remain in Moscow, and that over time Ukraine would, voluntarily or by necessity, return. It seemed sensible, to others, to assume that Russia would eventually come to accept Ukraine's independence, but the issue became a favorite theme of nationalists and communists in Russia, and they increasingly found common cause in seeking to reassert control over Ukraine.

The key event defining this early period was the meeting at Belavezha in December 1991, described in Chapter 2, at which the Soviet Union was formally dissolved and the Commonwealth of Independent States was formed. Boris Yeltsin did not want to accede to the demolition of the Soviet Union, but had to do so in order to unseat Gorbachev and to have the *Russian* government take over the functions of the *Soviet* government in Moscow. He believed that the Commonwealth of Independent States would keep Ukraine joined to Russia in defense and economic matters, and thus partially sovereign. Just before traveling to Belavezha, Yeltsin said "we must without fail work out a viewpoint that will prevent our three Slav states from splitting apart, no matter what happens."[4]

Thus, Russia and Ukraine disagreed fundamentally, already in December 1991, about where the relationship would head in the future. Russia saw the CIS as an institution that would serve to unite the post-Soviet states under Russian leadership, which would be strengthened in the future to that end. Ukraine saw it as a "bridge for us over the chaos," on the way to a fully independent Ukraine moving toward Europe.[5] With some differences, that is the disagreement that, recast as Ukraine's membership in the Eurasian Economic Community, drove the fight over the EU Association Agreement in 2013.

A third disagreement at the outset of the era arose within independent Ukraine about its relationship with Russia. The issue that sparked the demonstrations in 2013 was already on the agenda: how closely should Ukraine's economy be linked to that of Russia? Some saw Russia's economic involvement in Ukraine as inherently dangerous to Ukraine and sought to reduce it. Others also sought to redirect trade to western Europe, out of a desire to link to wealthy and admired countries rather

---

[4] "Yeltsin's Arrival Statement in Minsk," Radio Moscow, December 7, 1991, in FBIS, Soviet Union, December 9, 1991, p. 50, as quoted in Raymond L. Garthoff, *The Great Transition: American-Soviet Relations and the End of the Cold War* (Washington, DC: Brookings Institution, 1994), p. 483.

[5] Dmytro Pavlychko, chair of the Verkhovna Rada's Foreign Affairs Committee, quoted in Fred Hiatt, "Russia, Ukraine See Commonwealth Differently," *Washington Post*, December 13, 1991, p. A1.

than one that was in the throes of economic collapse. Still others, however, especially in eastern and southern Ukraine, saw Ukraine's close economic ties with Russia as essential and beneficial, and viewed efforts to turn away from Russia as self-destructive. This question continued to divide Ukrainian politics, driving all of its presidential elections as well as its two revolutions. The argument was not about whether Ukraine should be independent, should trade with Europe, or should be democratic; on all of those questions there was consensus in Ukraine. The question was how to deal with Russia while pursuing all those goals. Given Russia's goals and Ukraine's internal debate, the temptation for Russia to intervene in Ukraine's politics was irresistible.

From its emergence in 1991, democracy in Russia was undermined both by ideological opposition to it and by an institutional struggle between President Boris Yeltsin and the Russian Duma. Both claimed democratic legitimacy, but while Yeltsin sought rapid economic transformation, the Duma sought to slow it, and while Yeltsin prioritized good relations with the West, the Duma sought to assert Russian power. The battle over reform merged with the battle over institutional powers. In the fall of 1993, barely two years after the coup, and seven years before Putin became president, Russian democracy was grievously injured when armed forces loyal to Yeltsin forcibly disbanded the parliament. Yeltsin then wrote a constitution that gave the presidency the extensive powers that Putin later enjoyed.

Ukraine was an indirect cause of this conflict because one of the main arguments of the anti-Yeltsin faction in the parliament was that Yeltsin had let Ukraine go and was doing too little to bring it back. That faction, with evolving composition, saw its influence grow when, under new elections held in December 1993, Vladimir Zhirinovsky's Liberal Democratic Party of Russia finished first. The potent mix of nationalism and Soviet nostalgia that welcomed the annexation of Crimea in 2014 was already present in the "red-brown" (communist-fascist) coalition of 1993.

There was one major success in the early period of Ukraine-Russia-US relations: Ukraine's nuclear disarmament. Ukraine's surrender of its nuclear weapons was a high priority for both the United States and Russia, and they finally impelled Ukraine to agree to it in the 1994 Trilateral Agreement. That ended up being a source of great regret for Ukraine, as the security assurances it was given at that time turned out to be hollow. In the shorter term, however, the agreement paved the way to a closer relationship with the West, including NATO. Ukraine's enthusiastic participation in the Partnership for Peace helped Ukrainians feel safer from Russia, but also irritated Russia, the first in a long series of instances in which Ukraine's relations with NATO caused Russia to fear both that NATO might move closer and that Russia's goal of regaining Ukraine was in danger.

Events That Drove Wedges

By the time the post-Cold War world was consolidating in 1994, new problems were already emerging. We might divide these, for the sake of analysis, into three categories: those between Ukraine and Russia, those directly between Russia and the West in Europe, and those elsewhere in the world that increased distrust.

Between Ukraine and Russia, the same set of issues tended to come up over and over again. Russia made claims on Crimea and especially on Sevastopol, increasing Ukraine's fears, which prompted Ukraine to seek support from the West. Russia also insisted that Ukraine join a Russia-led economic bloc, which was rejected even by Ukraine's more pro-Russian leaders, Kuchma and Yanukovych. Ukraine's insistence on turning west irked Russia, as did its inability to pay for the Russian energy it consumed.

Between Russia and the West, an even longer list of disagreements emerged. How to deal with the collapse of Yugoslavia arose over Bosnia in 1994–1995, over Kosovo in 1999, and over the recognition of Kosovo's independence in 2007. Economic reform in Russia divided the sides in the 1990s, with the Russian financial crisis of 1998 convincing many in Russia that the western model was undermining Russia. From the beginning, the West was worried about the progress of democracy in Russia, and this worry increased dramatically after Vladimir Putin came to power in 2000. Restarting the war in Chechnya, quashing the independent media and selectively prosecuting political opponents all generated criticism in Europe, but those steps consolidated Putin's personal power and strengthened the Russian state. The expansion of NATO, beginning with the initial decisions in 1994 and continuing through the Bucharest summit in 2008, was a constant source of acrimony. Russia's invasion of Georgia in 2008 consolidated the perception in the West of Russia as an active security threat. Increasingly, Russia and the West disagreed directly about Ukraine.

Events beyond questions of European security and Ukraine-Russia relations further aggravated the relationships. The passing of the Cold War led to the fading of global competition between the United States and Russia, but new problems emerged. Russian support for Iran's nuclear program was an early disagreement that was managed. The biggest disagreement was over the US invasion of Iraq in 2003, whose impact on Russian foreign policy has probably been underestimated. The US deployment of ballistic missile defense and abrogation of the 1972 ABM treaty irked Russia particularly because of the unilateral nature of the decisions and because they dismantled Soviet-era agreements that played into Russia's claim to be a power of the same status that the Soviet Union had been. The Arab Spring, beginning in 2011, further increased Putin's fear that the West was fostering protest movements to overthrow governments that did not accede to US hegemony, and that Russia might be next.

There were, to be sure, many other developments that demonstrated efforts on all sides to improve relations, but what is striking is how these efforts tended to founder or to be swamped by more negative developments. Western aid to Russia was real, but it was much smaller than hoped, and engendered as much resentment as gratitude. Ukraine's agreement to surrender its nuclear weapons may have helped avoid deeper conflict with Russia and the US, but even at the time the weaknesses of the security guarantees Ukraine received left many there resentful, while the United States and Russia were irritated that Ukraine had bargained over the weapons. Similarly, the 1997 Friendship Treaty brought little in the way of friendship, opposed as it was by many Russian elites. The signing of the agreement, largely driven by NATO's intent to sign an agreement with Ukraine, had little impact on Ukraine-Russia relations.

Similarly, the opportunity provided by the changing of leaders in Russia and the United States in 2000–2001 had little impact. George Bush famously glimpsed Putin's soul, but that did not incline him to change course on ballistic missile defense. Even the attacks of September 2001, which had an impact on US politics and foreign policy that is hard to overestimate, had little impact on US relations with Russia. Much was made of Putin's ability to be the first on the phone to express condolences to Bush, and the two states collaborated against the Taliban in Afghanistan, but the relationship did not change dramatically. The United States attacked Iraq over strident objections from Russia and many US allies, and Russia attacked Georgia over objections from the United States and all of Europe.

The "reset" policy of Barack Obama, beginning in 2009, was indicative of the broader trend where sincere efforts to improve relations failed. Under Obama, the United States put the invasion of Georgia behind it, committed itself to a less unilateral foreign policy, and was much more reluctant to use force. The replacement of Putin with Dmitri Medvedev as Russian president seemed to open a door to a new relationship. But these changes had little impact on US-Russia relations. Even the decision to defer indefinitely a NATO Membership Action Plan for Ukraine accidentally provoked Russia. It had the further unintended consequence of prompting the European Union to increase its efforts to integrate economically with Ukraine, leading to the draft Association Agreement that spurred confrontation in 2013.

Events and Explanations

Why, given the seemingly huge benefit to peace created by the end of the Cold War and the recognition of problems in the following years, were Ukraine, Russia, and the West unable to manage those issues on which they disagreed? Why did small disagreements fester, while significant concessions, such as the Obama "reset," have so little impact? One reason stressed in this book is that the underlying disagreements were deep and fundamental. The second reason is that three underlying structural constraints – the security dilemma, democratization, and domestic politics – hampered efforts to manage those conflicts of interest and principles.

First is the security dilemma. States worried about their security naturally do things that make their neighbors less secure. Throughout the period in question Russia, Ukraine and the West all took actions that made others feel less secure, even as they tried to reassure the others about their intentions. The most prominent example was NATO expansion. It is hard to know how much conflict NATO expansion avoided by eliminating security dilemmas among the new members in eastern Europe, but it is clear that it made Russia feel less secure. Even if Russia did not seriously fear that NATO would invade Russia, enlargement brought more and more of Europe into an organization in which Russia had no voice. Another example was Russia's never-quite-ceasing claims on Ukraine. Russia considered a voice in Ukraine as essential, but the assertion of these interests inevitably seemed threatening to Ukraine and to states further west, such as Poland. Ukraine and NATO responded by drawing closer together, increasing Russia's sense of insecurity.

All of the actors showed some awareness of the security dilemma, and exerted some effort to reduce the threat perceived by their actions. Ukraine went the furthest, surrendering its nuclear weapons in return for security commitments from the United States, United Kingdom, and Russia. NATO, in expanding, took care to create the "NATO-Russia Council" and to avoid creating new NATO bases on the territories of the new members. Russia endured a series of reverses in the 1990s with measured responses. In the short term, these actions managed the security dilemma, but they did not change the underlying dynamic.

The security dilemma was exacerbated by unanticipated changes in the status quo that the states interpreted very differently. In this conflict, the status quo was repeatedly overturned by events that were not predicted. Initially, the collapse of the Soviet Union demolished the previous order, and the various actors never agreed on what the new status quo was or should be. Russia perceived a strong sense of loss in the post-Soviet situation, while Ukraine and the West saw potential loss in Russia's desire to redress its losses. Similarly, the protests that broke out in Kyiv in the fall of 2014 and the departure of President Yanukovych in February 2014 threatened to realign political power in Ukraine and to tip Ukraine toward the West. Russia saw this both as a loss and as an opportunity to undo the loss of Crimea, which it had resented for years. In general, Ukraine, Russia, and the West all believed that they were defending the status quo while others were trying to overturn it. These incompatible perceptions of the status quo made the security dilemma especially corrosive.

Second, democratization was a powerful disrupter in post-Cold War Europe. If there was a new status quo after the collapse of the Soviet Union, the consequences of democratization repeatedly undermined it. As the postcommunist states sought to build and consolidate democracy, they sought membership in western institutions to bolster their democracy, to confirm their identity as "European" states, and to provide security. Their security fears stemmed from decades of occupation, from potential border conflicts, and from the catastrophe that was unfolding in Yugoslavia. For the West, the spread of democracy was viewed as bolstering security in Europe, and membership in NATO and the European Union were important tools to promote it. This contributed to many in the West playing down Russia's objections to the eastward expansion of NATO. Moreover, events such as Vladimir Zhirinovsky's triumph in the 1993 parliamentary elections strengthened the case that hedging against Russian revanchism was prudent.

Russia saw the eastward expansion of NATO as a threat, and as a violation of an understanding at the time of German reunification that NATO would not move east. While Ukrainian membership in NATO was not seriously discussed until after the Orange Revolution, Russia was even more adamantly opposed. However, as with its neighbors to the west, Ukraine coveted the chance to be recognized as a member of Europe, and even though Viktor Yanukovych opposed NATO membership, he pursued an Association Agreement with the European Union. As with others, Ukraine saw collaboration with NATO as one way of protecting itself against Russian assertiveness. Eventually, Russia opposed not only Ukrainian membership in NATO, but Ukraine's participation in an EU Association Agreement, because it would have made joining a Russia-led economic bloc impossible.

While democracy consolidated in central Europe, Putin consolidated authoritarianism in Russia. Inevitably, there would be a line in Europe between the nondemocratic and democratic parts, and that line would have significance for international politics. Similarly, once western institutions began moving from west to east, the unavoidable question was where they would end, and what it would mean for those on the outside. While many in Ukraine sought close economic ties with Russia, very few wanted to be on the Russian side of a new divide in Europe. Russia, however, became increasingly insistent that Ukraine would remain with it.

Third, democracy was important not only to geopolitics, but also to foreign policy making. In all of the countries involved, leaders were repeatedly prevented by domestic politics from pursuing policies that would have mitigated the security dilemma. While in the big picture democracy was expected to increase international security, public opinion repeatedly constrained leaders from taking a more cooperative line.

In Ukraine, regional divisions (along with economics) tightly limited foreign policy options by fostering steady opposition to a decisive choice in the direction of either Russia or the West. Even as multi-vectorism became less viable internationally, it became more pragmatic domestically. Moreover, the weakness of public support in Ukraine for economic reform has been underemphasized. From independence onward, opposition to market reforms, especially in the energy sector, helped maintain Ukraine's vulnerability to Russian coercion and to Russia's penetration of the Ukrainian elite. While Russian leaders recognized that a strong state (*derzhava*) was a key element of national power, and strove to reconsolidate state power under Putin, Ukrainian divisions ensured that the state remained weak vis-à-vis society and penetrated by oligarchs, even as it became less democratic.

In the United States, electoral considerations prevented Presidents George H. W. Bush and Bill Clinton from contributing a significant amount of funding to cushion Russian economic reform in the 1990s. It is impossible to know whether more economic aid would have helped, or just how much it would have taken for economic reform to succeed, or whether the success of economic reform would have sustained democracy, or whether a democratic Russia would have behaved significantly differently. At the time, however, US leaders considered this chain of causes to exist, and yet found that pushing for significant aid put them in jeopardy of losing their next election. In contrast, there was bipartisan support for the idea that expanding NATO eastward was good for security in Europe, for the United States, and for the new members.

In Russia, domestic politics were even more important. From the very beginning of his presidency, Boris Yeltsin found himself under attack from communist and nationalist revanchists. One of their main criticisms was that he was losing battles with the West and that he had failed to regain Ukraine. In forging an amicable relationship with the United States and signing the 1997 Friendship Treaty with Ukraine, Yeltsin was overriding the objections of much of the Russian public. The point was made by Andrei Kozyrev in 1994: "Russian foreign policy inevitably has to be of an independent and assertive nature. If Russian democrats fail to achieve it, they will be swept away by a wave of aggressive nationalism, which is now exploiting the need for national and state self-assertion … Russia is predestined to be a great power."[6] Kozyrev's assertion that in order for democracy to survive in Russia, Russia had to have an assertive foreign policy turned the notion of the "democratic peace" on its head. Vladimir Putin gained more latitude, sidelining the media and oligarchs, winning control of the Duma, and building high popularity. But he did so in part by taking a harder line toward the West, by reasserting Russia's great power status, and then by regaining Crimea.

These three dynamics – the security dilemma worsened by an ambiguous status quo, the merger of democracy and geopolitics, and the constraints of domestic politics – are crucial to understanding the conflict for two reasons. First, they help explain why, despite the enormous improvement in perceived relations after the Cold War, the various countries did not manage to work their way through their disagreements. Put differently, if the security dilemma can sometimes be resolved, these factors explain why it was so hard to do in this case. Second, by showing that the leaders in the various countries often found themselves constrained – whether by others' actions or by their own electorates – there is an important distinction between explaining conflict and assigning blame. Individual leaders often found themselves buffeted by forces they could not control, and with a limited range of realistic options. Impersonal forces such as the security dilemma, democratization, and public opinion play a role as well. Given the deep disagreement about what post-Cold War Europe should look like and what rules should govern it, these three factors made it much harder to find some kind of compromise.

Was War Inevitable?

Given the underlying disagreement and the dynamics that undermined efforts to manage it, was war inevitable? Clearly it was not. One way to see this is by looking back at the Cold War itself, which was much more

---

[6] Andrei Kozyrev, "The Lagging Partnership," *Foreign Affairs* 73, 2 (May/June 1994): 60.

intense, and yet was managed for over four decades until the underlying conflict faded away. Similarly, the disagreements over post-Cold War Ukraine could have been managed until they became more tractable.

A different way to see that the conflict was not inevitable was to look at the decisions leading up to it. Somewhat obviously, Russia could have chosen to respond to the events in Kyiv in 2013–2014 without seizing Crimea and without interfering in the unrest in Ukraine's east. This would have meant swallowing a painful defeat, but as the aftermath of the Orange Revolution showed, Russia could refrain from war and maintain its influence in Ukraine.

Going back only a bit further in time, had Viktor Yanukovych accepted a deal that would have left him as president but reinstated the constitutional provisions that he had annulled, he probably could have remained in power. Had Russia pressured him to accept this deal, instead of counseling him to repress the protesters, he may have agreed to this measure. Similarly, had international leaders succeeded in convincing protesters to accept a similar deal after the violence of February 20, 2014, Yanukovych might not have fled. There is some evidence, of course, that the action to seize Crimea had already been launched at this point, but the broader point is that had protesters struck a deal that kept Yanukovych in power, the chain of events leading to war might have been broken. Had Yanukovych remained in power, he might have succeeded in consolidating his authoritarianism, but war may have been averted.

This possibility points to the difficulty in considering how the broader conflict might have been managed better. Nearly all the policies that would have made a dramatic difference would have required someone to give up something they deeply valued. Russia could have accepted the loss of Ukraine. Ukraine could have forgone its dreams of genuine independence. NATO could have rejected the pleas of potential new members. It is not hard to imagine why leaders sought to avoid these difficult sacrifices, and instead assumed that others would adjust.

This discussion of how the war might have been averted also points to why the question of blame cannot be resolved by looking at the facts of what happened. Someone would have to surrender something important to decrease the chances of war. Who should have made the necessary concessions – and is to blame for not making them – is a matter of opinion. In many respects, the problem of blame boils down to what one thinks of Russia's claim on Ukraine. To the extent the claim is not legitimate, Russia is to blame for pursuing it. To the extent that claim is legitimate, one can blame Ukraine for not acquiescing to it and the West for backing Ukraine. Similarly, whether the West should have recognized Russia's claim to great power privileges or deferred to Russia's local military superiority, or whether Russia should have acceded to the West's claims about democratic norms, is a matter of values.

These are normative questions whose answers depend on further assumptions about the rights of great powers, the inviolability of sovereignty and international law, the boundaries of *realpolitik*, and so on. How one answers those questions will determine whose claim one believes has greater weight, who should therefore have backed off, and who, in the final analysis, is guilty of not backing off and therefore to blame for the conflict. Even in February 2014, violence could have been avoided as long as each side refrained from shifting to violence. Whether that move to violence should be blamed on protesters in Kyiv, on Yanukovych, or on Russia also falls back on normative assumptions. Thus, rather than history or analysis resolving who is to blame, how one assigns blame tends to shape how one writes or reads the analysis.

Russia's Motives

Because Russia initiated military action, we need to focus on its decision to do so, and yet we know much less than we would like, and the signal-to-noise ratio is very low. The combination of the Russian government's secrecy and its (dis)information campaign means that we have a great amount of material on Russia's reasons for going to war, but we do not know which arguments reflect Russian leaders' thinking and which are intended for public consumption.

With those caveats, the material presented in the previous chapters shows that Russia was dissatisfied from 1991 onwards both with its relationship with Ukraine and with its role in Europe. It expected that, over time, Ukraine would accept a junior role in a Russia-led bloc, but this did not happen. Similarly, Russia believed that its power and history earned it a major voice and a veto in European security affairs, but the West rejected that view, and instead promoted a vision for a Europe governed by democracy, protection of human rights, and the sovereign equality of states. On Yugoslavia, Russia found that the West's emphasis on human rights clashed with its support for its ally. On Ukraine, Russia found that the West's support for the rights of smaller states clashed with its claims on Ukraine. More broadly still, the US war in Iraq prompted some in Russia and elsewhere to believe that the United States cynically cited or ignored these norms as its interests dictated.

The proposed EU-Ukraine Association agreement threatened to permanently end the chance for Ukraine to be drawn into Russia's orbit. To forestall this, Russia put immense pressure on Viktor Yanukovych not to sign the deal. It applied "carrots," such as a massive loan package and a new price for energy that would pave the way to Yanukovych's reelection, and "sticks," including the threat that it would induce chaos in Ukraine's economy that would doom Yanukovych. These tactics worked, and Yanukovych canceled the signing of the agreement. The street protests that followed not only threatened to undo this victory, but represented a renewal of a phenomenon that threatened Putin and the Russian leadership, who saw it as being orchestrated from abroad rather than driven from within Ukraine.

While Yanukovych was preparing to flee Ukraine, Putin was putting the Crimea plan into action. We still do not know much about when this plan was developed, though it seems to have predated the crisis in Kyiv. Nor do we know whether there was a preexisting determination to seize Crimea, or whether the events in Kyiv provided an opportunity that was too good to pass up. All we really know is that at this point in time Putin felt that the benefits of seizing Crimea outweighed the costs.

That decision was likely assisted by the fact that seizing Crimea served multiple goals. It retrieved a territory that Russia had always claimed. It secured the base at Sevastopol. It showed how costly deposing leaders via street demonstrations might be. It showed that Russia could defy the West. And it boosted Putin's popularity immensely. The social scientist wants to identify a single cause, but for the politician, a policy that promotes multiple goals is the most attractive.

Russia's intervention in eastern Ukraine appears to have been less thoroughly prepared. This leads to the conclusion that the decision to launch it was based in part on the fact that an opportunity arose. Intervening in eastern Ukraine also added a benefit that annexing Crimea did not: It put immense pressure on the Ukrainian economy and government and left Russia with the ability to increase or decrease the level of fighting as it desired.

Prospects for Peace

The analysis of underlying causes presented here forces us to be pessimistic about the chances of resolving either the Ukraine-Russia conflict or the broader conflict between Russia and the West any time soon. As we have noted, the two conflicts have become one, and each makes the other harder to solve. The deeper problem, however, is that all of the underlying causes of the conflict discussed in this book still exist, and now they have been exacerbated by the conflict itself, which has strengthened mutual perceptions of aggressiveness and bad faith.

The disagreement that Ukraine and Russia have today is not fundamentally changed from the disagreements the two sides had in December

1991. But while in 1991 there was a commitment to working on issues and a very high degree of economic interdependence, today the two countries are at war and interdependence has decreased. For example, in 1991 Ukraine was not seriously aiming to join NATO, but now that goal is widely (though far from unanimously) held among the country's elite. As then, economic interdependence is seen by Ukraine as a hazard to its independence, not as a mutually beneficial relationship. And as then, Russia has long-term ambitions for Ukraine that are at odds with Ukraine's desire for full sovereignty.

Similarly, from the very beginning of the post-Cold War period, Russia and the West have had very different notions of what a post-Cold War Europe should look like. That fundamental disagreement persisted to 2014, and has become much worse since. Russia is now seen not only as a hazard to its neighbors, but as threating to infiltrate and subvert western democracies, as was feared in the 1950s. Russia is more convinced than ever that the West seeks to isolate it internationally and to undermine its government domestically. The relationship now embodies both a conflict of values and a conflict of interest, making it harder to solve, because giving in on the principles would also require giving in on the presumed territorial division of Europe between the West and Russia.

The security dilemma and incompatible versions of the status quo have become worse, not better, since the outbreak of the war. The West and Russia are now engaged in a series of moves, each of which is justified as a response to something the other has done. For example, Russian military exercises in 2018 were widely seen as practice for an invasion of the Baltic States. The intensification of the security dilemma has dramatically increased the chances of an accidental war, a fear that had largely disappeared in the 1990s. On top of the preexisting conflict, there is now the issue of Crimea, which creates an impasse of its own. It seems unthinkable that Russia will give it back, but even if the international community wants to get past the issue, finding a way to legitimize Russia's ownership will be challenging.

Russia's goal of getting Ukraine to join a Russia-led bloc is further than ever from being realized. While many Ukrainians prefer to have good relations with both Europe and Russia, the events of 2014 have made that harder, and polling shows that, forced to choose, most would choose the EU.[7] The war has soured the Ukrainian public toward Russia, and the fact that much of the pre-2014 population that was most pro-Russian

---

[7] In a poll taken in March 2018, 52 percent preferred the European Union to 18 percent the Customs Union of Russia, Belarus and Kazakhstan. That has been a consistent pattern since 2014. See International Republican Institute, "Public Opinion Survey of Residents

resided in Crimea or the occupied Donbas, and cannot now vote, makes it harder still that a pro-Russian government will come to power in Kyiv.[8] So the tension between Ukrainian democracy and Russia's ambitions there is higher than ever.

Finally, domestic politics continues to constrain leaders from making concessions. Polling data shows Ukrainian citizens committed to regaining the lost territories in eastern Ukraine, and reaching some kind of settlement that surrenders the territories is seen to be so toxic in Kyiv that people do not want to talk about it, even as they acknowledge that it might be better for Ukraine to surrender the territory and move forward from there. In the United States, Donald Trump's statements indicating his desire to make a deal with Putin met with a bipartisan bill preventing him from lifting sanctions without congressional approval. A Congress that is bitterly divided on nearly every issue is unified in supporting sanctions against Russia.

In terms of domestic politics, more change is underway in Europe, where there was much less enthusiasm about confronting Russia and enacting sanctions in the first place. A series of developments in 2017 and 2018 made it more likely that governments would have more latitude to make a deal with Russia on terms that Russia might welcome. In Germany, Angela Merkel approved the Nordstream 2 pipeline, and weaknesses in her coalition raised the possibility that the Social Democratic Party, which supported a détente with Russia, would come to power. In 2017, Christian Lindner, the SPD leader, endorsed seeing Russia's control of Crimea as a "permanent provisional arrangement."[9] Similarly, the weakness of the Conservative Party in Britain opened the possibility that Labour would come to power, and Jeremy Corbin, who wrote that "[Nato's] attempt to encircle Russia is one of the big threats of our time,"[10] would become prime minister. In Italy, elections in 2018 brought to power an avowedly pro-Putin leadership. Interior Minister Matteo Salvini, who headed one of the two parties in Italy's ruling coalition, endorsed the annexation of Crimea and said the 2014 revolution was a "pseudo-revolution funded by foreign

of Ukraine March 15–31, 2018," p. 48, www.iri.org/sites/default/files/2018-5-21_ukraine_poll_presentation_0.pdf

[8] Paul D'Anieri, "Gerrymandering Ukraine? Electoral Consequences of Occupation," *East European Politics and Societies* 33, 1 (February 2019): 89–108.

[9] See Marco Siddi, "German Foreign Policy towards Russia in the Aftermath of the Ukraine Crisis: A New Ostpolitik?" *Europe-Asia Studies* 68, 4 (June 2016): 665–677; and Tuomas Forsberg, "From Ospolitik to 'Frostpolitik'? Merkel, Putin and German Foreign Policy toward Russia," *International Affairs* 92, 1 (January 2016): 21–42.

[10] Kiran Stacey, "Spotlight Falls on Corbyn's Foreign Policies," *Financial Times*, August 19, 2015.

powers."[11] To the extent that Europe continues in this direction, and to the extent that it, not the United States, drives the agenda, the possibility of a settlement would increase, and would likely accept at least a large part of the Russian position on the conflict.

While public opinion plays a different role in Russia than it does in democracies, it creates incentives for Putin to resist compromise on Ukraine. Even given the limitations of polling in Russia, it appears that the annexation of Crimea is hugely popular in Russia and has helped Putin boost his popularity despite other challenges, such as economic slowdown and a very unpopular plan to raise the pension age. The biggest danger to Putin from the conflict in Ukraine is that Russian public opposition to sending soldiers to Donbas increases, which would be likely only if the fighting were to escalate, leading to large numbers of Russian casualties. That factor might incline him to try to contain the conflict, but does not provide an incentive to end it. In sum, in Russia, the United States, and Ukraine, domestic politics continues to constrain leaders from the kinds of steps that would end the conflict.

Potential Ends to the Conflict

If the underlying disagreement and the dynamics that make it hard to compromise are still in place, what are the possible paths to an end to the war? And what are the policies that might bring it about? As in any war, an end can come through one side winning on the battlefield, through one side capitulating because the cost is too high, or through some compromise. In practice, the line between "victory" and compromise is often unclear. People who feel that too much has been surrendered to reach a compromise will call it a "capitulation," while those who are more worried about losing may call it a victory. As we have stressed, this perception rests heavily on what one believes the likely alternative status quo was.

The conflict in Ukraine resists resolution not only because the causes of it continue to be in force. Although the death toll and economic cost continue to mount, both Russia and Ukraine can sustain the post-Minsk level of conflict indefinitely. That fact may help prolong the war. Put differently, the cost of continuing the war seems relatively low compared to the costs of making the concessions needed to end it.

Whether that continues to be true depends a great deal on Russia's ambitions, which have been difficult to gauge. If Russia's goal was to take

---

[11] Lally Weymouth, "Italy Has Done a Lot – Maybe Too Much," Interview with Matteo Salvini, *Washington Post*, July 19, 2018.

over Crimea and parts of eastern Ukraine, to weaken Ukraine, and to send a message to the West, then it is in the enviable position of simply having to freeze the conflict in order to achieve its goals. From early 2015 until the Kerch Strait incident in November 2018, Russia focused not on changing facts on the ground, but rather on getting the West to accept them. The primary focus appeared to be on weakening the West's resolve to maintain sanctions, and it appeared to be succeeding. The renewed use of force to take control of the Kerch Strait and the Sea of Azov called into question whether Russia's strategy was simply to defend the new status quo.

Two aspects of Russian strategy remain unclear. First, does Russia seek further territorial gains in Ukraine? There were signs in 2014 that it hoped to seize more of "Novorossiya," a much bigger swath of territory spreading across southern Ukraine to Transnistria. Later speculation focused on the city of Mariupol, and the possibility of seizing a land corridor to Crimea to supplement the bridge that was hastily constructed. To the extent that Russia has further territorial aspirations in Ukraine, does it plan to play a long game, waiting for another opportunity to arise, or does it have more active plan to take more territory? In 2018, actions in the Sea of Azov looked like a Russian program to take full control of that body of water, a sign that Russian geographic expansion is not necessarily complete.

Second, what does it plan or hope to eventually do with the territories its proxies control in eastern Ukraine? While it is tempting to assume that sooner or later Russia will want to resolve their status – by annexing them, supporting their independence, or facilitating their reintegration into Ukraine – the experience of Transnistria indicates that a "grey" status might become somewhat permanent. As with Transnistria in Moldova, the ambiguous status of the Donetsk and Luhansk republics facilitates Russia's leverage over Ukraine and avoids the political and economic costs of integrating the territories into Russia or supporting their sovereignty. Because the current situation suits Russia well, it can resist any solution that it does not see as even better – such as one that brings the territories back into Ukraine with Russian influence.

The West is in a more difficult position, as it is now seeks to get Russia to alter the existing territorial status quo. It has few levers with which to do this. For this reason, many discussions in the West focus on postponing any resolution to the conflict until Putin passes from the scene in Moscow. Because Russia's actions in Ukraine are so closely associated with Putin, and because Putin is so powerful within Russia, one assumes that little will change until he passes from the scene. Speculation will increasingly focus on who might succeed him and when. As under the tsars and Soviets, Russian leadership succession appears once again to be a matter of biology.

However, the belief that Putin's passing will solve the problem likely relies on wishful thinking. Logically, assuming that change cannot come until Putin passes does not mean that change *will* come *when* he does. This book has presented a great deal of evidence showing that Putin's attitudes toward Ukraine in general and Crimea in particular have been widely shared in Russia since the Soviet collapse. Therefore, whether there is a contest to succeed Putin as autocrat, or a democratic election to choose a new leader, the candidates will face powerful pressures to show that they can maintain or extend Russia's gains in Ukraine. It is hard to see how giving back Crimea or returning the Donbas on Kyiv's terms would not be detrimental for any potential successor to Putin.[12] In sum, while democracy in Russia would be a very good thing, it is very unlikely to solve the Ukraine conflict, and might make it worse. Western strategy, however, seems heavily dependent on precisely such a solution.

Compromise?

Many compromises have been suggested by academics, analysts, and officials. It would seem that some kind of "grand bargain" ought to be reachable, in which each side gets some of what it wants, but not all. Most importantly, the "grand bargain" approach assumes that such a bargain would leave all sides satisfied with the status quo, removing the underlying cause for conflict that has persisted since the end of the Cold War.

Particularly in terms of territory, it is not hard to see the basis for such a grand compromise. It would combine the redrawing of boundaries in Russia's favor with Russian commitments to end the current fighting and to respect the new borders. Three major issues (and more minor ones) would have to be resolved.

First, where would the lines be drawn? Any territorial revision would begin with Ukraine and the West accepting Russian sovereignty over Crimea. But what would be done in eastern Ukraine? Russia seems unwilling to let Ukraine have full sovereignty over Donbas; while Ukraine rejects allowing the territory to return on Russian terms (such as those in

---

[12] In 2014, Alexei Navalny, one of Putin's strongest critics in Russia, asserted that even though it was seized illegally, "Crimea is now part of the Russian Federation." "So let's not kid ourselves. It will remain part of Russia and will never become part of Ukraine in the foreseeable future." Quoted in Robert Mackey, "Navalny's Comments on Crimea Ignite Russian Twittersphere," *New York Times*, October 16, 2014.

the Minsk agreements). Perhaps Russia would be willing to jettison these territories in return for recognition of its control over Crimea.

An alternative, which a few people in Ukraine have advocated, is that the occupied Donbas become part of Russia. Paradoxically, there are good reasons for pro-western Ukrainians not to want to reintegrate the regions into Ukraine, and good reasons for Russia and pro-Russian Ukrainians to want them in Ukraine. Without the populations of Crimea and the occupied Donbas, the Ukrainian electorate would be much less divided, and more pro-European, than it was before. Having Russia annex those territories as well as Crimea would solve some practical problems for Ukraine politically. But it would be extremely difficult for any Ukrainian leader to accept such a solution, let alone advocate for it. And, crucially, it would dramatically reduce Russia's scope for political interference in Ukraine in the future.[13]

Second, if Ukraine and the West agree to legitimizing the transfer of Crimea (and perhaps parts of eastern Ukraine), what then becomes of Ukraine? The whole range of possibilities has been suggested. Some would have it, in return for those concessions, become wholly independent and free to join western institutions. Others would have an agreement that ruled out joining NATO, but would allow it to join the EU. Others would have it be a neutral buffer, joining neither Russian-led nor western organizations.[14] Unfortunately, the war has had the effect in Ukraine of making neutrality much less attractive, not more, especially since neutrality of the sort that Austria had during the Cold War is dependent upon precisely the kind of agreements of noninterference contained in the failed Budapest Memorandum on Ukraine.

These possibilities raise problems of both practicality and principle. There remains a fundamental disagreement on the principles of European international relations. The European Union stresses the principle that "third parties" (in this case Russia) should not be able to veto the choices of other states. In this view, NATO or the European Union can choose not to invite a new member, but a third country (Russia) cannot veto it, and membership of a particular country cannot be definitively excluded. An agreement by which Russia and NATO or the European

---

[13] This option is discussed in D'Anieri, "Gerrymandering Ukraine."

[14] See, for example, Sergei Kudelia, "Posle Rozmezhivannia: Kak dostich' rossiisko-ukrainskogo soglasiia?" *Rossiya v Globalnoi Politike*, April 2018. The problems with neutrality are discussed in Mariana Budjeryn, "The Reality and Myth of Ukrainian Neutrality," *World Affairs Journal*, no date. Ukraine's "Declaration of State Sovereignty" of July 1990 declared the goal of "permanent neutrality," but that was when Ukrainian leaders (still mostly communists) imagined "sovereignty" within a looser Soviet confederation, not complete independence.

Union agreed over Ukraine's objections that it could not decide what it wanted would violate that principle. Russia, in contrast, has maintained precisely the opposite: that as a "great power" its veto on security arrangements beyond its borders, and especially in Ukraine, must be recognized. Despite that disagreement, it seems possible that NATO, Russia, and Ukraine could jointly agree that Ukraine would not become a member of NATO, or that it would not be considered for some period of time. Especially if Ukraine agreed to the provision, it might not seem too large a breach of the principle.

The much bigger problem is making Ukraine "neutral" economically. Although free trade is under fire around the world, it remains hugely advantageous. More specifically, one does not want to trade at a disadvantage relative to one's competitors. That is precisely the position Ukraine would be in if it remains outside both the European Union and the Eurasian Customs Union. As Britain is finding in its departure from the EU, the cost of being outside can be very high, and Ukraine is in a much weaker position than Britain. That is why it was assumed that if Ukraine did not join the EU Association Agreement it would have to join the Eurasian Customs Union.

So while Ukraine could conceivably agree to forgo NATO membership, it could not agree to forgo deep economic ties with the European Union. The question is whether Russia would be satisfied with such an arrangement. Essentially this would mean, in return for an agreement that Ukraine would not join NATO, Russia would surrender its claim to a sphere of influence in Ukraine.

A compromise even more favorable to Russia, which some in the West have apparently recommended, is that the West simply accede to Russia's demand for a sphere of influence in Ukraine. It is unclear exactly what that would mean, but presumably it would compel Ukraine to join a Russian-led trade bloc and give Russia a veto over Ukraine's foreign policy.

The big question, however, points to the third obstacle to any compromise: would Russia, after any of these compromises, actually be satisfied with the new status quo or would it continue exerting pressure for more? For example, if Russia agreed to respect Ukraine's sovereignty in return for more autonomy for Ukraine's eastern regions, would it really do so? The fact that Russia guaranteed Ukraine's security and borders in return for Ukraine surrendering its nuclear weapons and then behaved as it did in 2014 might make one skeptical.

Even if the West adopts the more "realist" solution of simply accepting a Russian sphere of influence over Ukraine, is there any reason to believe that would solve the problem as opposed to just moving it closer to

Poland and Germany? What precautions would Poland and Germany need to take if Russia controlled Ukraine, and what new spiral of insecurity might that ignite?

This problem points to the deeper problem with those arguments claiming to be based in realism that place blame for the conflict on the West and advocate in Russian control over Ukraine.[15] They are realist in their argument that the West should not particularly care what happens to Ukraine, and in their skepticism that organizations such as the European Union or institutions such as democracy can bring security to Europe. But they are decidedly unrealistic, and perhaps even idealistic, in their argument that if Russia is given the territory it demands, it will automatically be satisfied and will stop trying to expand its influence or undermine the US role in the world. This belief relies on two assumptions. First, it relies on the most optimistic version of realism ("defensive realism") being true. This version of realism holds that as long as states are satisfied with the status quo, the security dilemma can be managed. Second, it relies on Russia being satisfied with the status quo. Traditional ("offensive") realist theory has always argued that because the security dilemma is inescapable, states should seek to expand their power regardless of what others do. In this view, the West is bound to collide with Russia, and the only question is where that happens.

Leaving debates over realist theory aside, the crucial question for any policy of a "grand bargain" is whether it would actually solve the underlying problems pointed to in this book: would Russia be satisfied with the status quo? Would the West stop promoting the spread of democracy? Would a set of "rules of the road" be agreed upon? There is some reason for optimism: Russia has seemed transfixed with Ukraine in general and with Crimea in particular. Perhaps it will be satisfied with having gained Crimea and part of the Donbas. The West might decide simply to wait for change in Russia and the region's other authoritarian states, rather than trying to promote it. And a de facto creation of a Russian sphere might address the rules of the road by acknowledging that one part of Europe would be dominated by Russia, with its rules, while in the western part of Europe a different set of rules, defined by the European Union and NATO, would prevail.

Any "grand bargain" would depend crucially on what Russia can and cannot accept in Ukraine. A great deal of Russian rhetoric has focused not just on Crimea, but on the historic role of Kyiv itself in forming

---

[15] These problems are analyzed in greater detail in Paul D'Anieri, "Magical Realism: Assumptions, Evidence and Prescriptions in the Ukraine Conflict," *Eurasian Geography and Economics* 60:1 (2019) 97–117.

modern Russia. An arrangement in which Ukraine retains a high degree of independence in return for surrendering territory will fail if Russia does not give up the aspirations on Ukraine it has voiced fairly consistently since 1991.

The same is true of western policy. Any mutual acceptance of the status quo implies an acceptance of the regime in Moscow as legitimate. This would not require endorsing it, but it would require the West to refrain from supporting its overthrow, which currently is the fulcrum of the West's strategy. A decision to strike a "grand bargain" thus implies jettisoning the focus on spreading democracy that has been central to the West's approach since 1989. Because democratization tends to upend the international status quo, it is in tension with any bargain that presumes freezing alignments in time. This was recognized by Russia when it pursued the Holy Alliance in the nineteenth century, and it appears to be true still.

The New Conflict in Europe

Where does this leave Ukraine? Fighting a war that it cannot win and that it cannot end. Ukraine cannot recapture Crimea or the occupied Donbas, but neither can it let them go. The prospect is that Ukraine will be dealing with this conflict for many years. Russia's attack consolidated Ukraine as the axis of the conflict between Russia and the West, and so the opportunity to collaborate with the West rose dramatically again after 2015. The entry into force of the EU Association Agreement in 2017 was emblematic of that opportunity. As always, the question was whether Ukraine could seize the opportunity, and as always, the answer appears to be no. Russia appears to be betting that Ukraine cannot reform, especially with Russia interfering, and that the West will lose interest before Russia does. In this, it may well be right. Ukraine's inability to reform, rather than Russian policy, continues to be the biggest threat to its national security.

Where does this leave Russia? In one respect, Russia might be seen as having prevailed: it has established that Russia's wishes, and not just western rules, will shape what happens in eastern Europe. But in other respects, Russia is exactly where it did not want to be: politically isolated from the rest of Europe and decisively rejected by Ukraine. As has often been the case, Russia's efforts to enhance its security have left it less secure. Russia gained a western sphere of influence, but it is a pretty small sphere, including only Belarus, Crimea and part of the Donbas. Moreover, maintaining this sphere is costly. Russia may be able to keep Ukraine out of European institutions, but that is now the best it can do. Including Ukraine in a Moscow-centric integration project, which used to be the minimal goal, now seems to be out of reach short of military conquest.

Where does this leave Russia and the West? In a battle in which geopolitics and democracy continue to be merged. Russian rhetoric has pitted "civilizational pluralism" against democracy, with the change in vocabulary obscuring the fact that the disagreement is almost precisely what it was in 1989, when Bush promoted "a commonwealth of free nations" and Gorbachev a "common European home."

This battle is both global and European. On a global scale, the question is whether the world will be unipolar or multipolar. Here Russia has many allies, most important of which is China. But while US hegemony continues to erode, the attractiveness of the western model is likely to endure despite its current tribulations. Chinese influence is substantial, but it is almost entirely transactional – based on concrete material inducements rather than any shared values. Russia has shown its ability to make mischief and to make friends among outcast regimes, but whether these can be meaningful contributors to the kind of great power status it longs for remains to be seen.

On the European scale, the question is where the line between a Russian-dominated zone of autocracy and an EU-led region of democracies will be drawn. Here, Russia has few allies. Maintaining its small sphere of influence will be costly, and expanding it will be costlier still. While Russia has had some success sowing divisions within Europe's democracies, this practice takes it further from the institutionalized respect it demands.

Is there a vision of European order that is consistent both with western norms and with Russia's great power aspirations? This is the basic question about European security that was never worked out after 1989. As in 1989, the answer after 2014 appears to be "no." Security in western Europe is built on great power restraint in a way that many have failed to appreciate. For Russia to join Europe, it would have to model its role not on that of the United States (which for geographic and historical reasons is seen as less threatening), but on Germany, which after World War II and again after 1989 deliberately limited its military power and bound its economic power within EU institutions. Where Germany recognized that its power and history cause fear in others that stokes the security dilemma and undermines Germany's interests, Russia insists on retaining its historical role and relishes the fear it induces. One can speculate that the different approaches come out of the two societies' readings of World War II. The defeated Germany accepted that its power was inherently threatening to its neighbors, while the victorious Soviet Union decided that it had earned the right to rule its neighbors.

With no agreement on the architecture of European order, we are left with competition. In that competition, democracy remains central to the West's values and to its strategy. Now, as in the Cold War, the West's strategy is to wait for a friendlier regime to come to power in Russia and in particular to wait for the Russian people to demand a democratic government. However, as the past quarter century has shown, if adopting democracy means surrendering Russia's great power identity, many Russians will oppose it.

If the West's strategy is based on waiting for democracy to come to Moscow, Russia's strategy is based on helping autocracy and anti-EU/NATO sentiment to come to power in western capitals. Since 2015, Russia seems to be winning more battles in the West than the West is in Moscow. If Russia is to achieve the kind of Europe it seeks, this new policy will have to succeed, because the seizure of Crimea and the Donbas did not achieve it.

A Final Word

This book has stressed the deep and fundamental conflicts that underpin the war between Ukraine and Russia. The end of the Cold War ended the intense ideological conflict between liberal democracy and communism, and ended the sharp territorial division of Europe. The collapse of the Soviet Union went even further by bringing independence to fourteen new states and creating a democratic opening in Moscow. But by freeing Ukraine and challenging Russia's status as a great power, the collapse of the Soviet Union left Russia deeply dissatisfied with the status quo. By 2014, Russia's desire to control Ukraine remained, but any sense of needing to follow Europe's rules had receded. The overthrow of Viktor Yanukovych both outraged Russia and threatened its interests, but it also provided an opportunity to take at least some of what it had long claimed in Ukraine.

The overarching conclusion of this book is that the causes of the conflict were deep and remain persistent. Therefore, resolving it will be difficult. When Radoslaw Sikorski criticized "Russia's 19th century approach" to security in 2013,[16] he made an important point: Russia seeks an order based on the dominance of the great powers that was widely accepted in the era prior to World War I. The West rejects this idea, insisting instead on an order based on a combination of democracy and international institutions. That disagreement emerged from the

---

[16] Andrew Rettman, "Ukraine and EU Ridicule Russian Threats," euobserver.com, September 23, 2013.

moment that Mikhail Gorbachev was loosening the Soviet Union's control over central Europe in 1989. Russia's deployment of force in 2014 can be viewed as a determination to no longer accept the results of a set of rules it did not endorse. Ending the conflict will require, and will likely help shape, a new set of security arrangements in Europe. Until Russia accepts the West's vision for Europe or the West accepts Russia's, the conflict will endure, with Ukraine caught in the middle.

To return to the book's epigraph, "our idea is that the wolves should be fed and the sheep kept safe." We want Russia to be satisfied and Ukraine kept independent and whole. It is not clear that both goals can be accomplished.

Index